ENVIRONMENT AND DEVELOPMENT ECONOMICS

Environment and Development Economics

Essays in Honor of Sir Partha Dasgupta

EDITED BY SCOTT BARRETT,
KARL-GÖRAN MÄLER,
AND ERIC S. MASKIN

OXFORD
UNIVERSITY PRESS

OXFORD
UNIVERSITY PRESS

Great Clarendon Street, Oxford, OX2 6DP,
United Kingdom

Oxford University Press is a department of the University of Oxford.
It furthers the University's objective of excellence in research, scholarship,
and education by publishing worldwide. Oxford is a registered trade mark of
Oxford University Press in the UK and in certain other countries

First Edition published in 2014

Impression: 1

Published in the United States of America by Oxford University Press
198 Madison Avenue, New York, NY 10016, United States of America

British Library Cataloguing in Publication Data

Data available

Library of Congress Control Number: 2013954859

ISBN 978–0–19–967785–6

Printed and bound by
CPI Group (UK) Ltd, Croydon, CR0 4YY

Preface

This is an unusual Festschrift, but it would have to be, for it is honoring a singular economist. Partha Dasgupta has devoted himself to more than research and writing, seminars and lectures. Perhaps because he was born in India and later lived and worked in England and the United States, Partha has endeavored to bring academics from these two worlds (the "South" and the "North," we sometimes call them) into contact with each other. This book is a tribute to that enterprise.

The contributors to this book include Nobel laureates and young academics just starting out, professors privileged to work at the world's top universities and people making the best of the opportunities afforded by their home institutions in developing countries. Many of the authors are his closest friends. They include his former teachers and students and his current and former collaborators. Unusual for a Festschrift, some other authors barely know him personally (we'll explain why below).

Partha has long chastised development economists for neglecting the natural environment, despite its importance to the livelihoods of the rural poor. He has also leaned on environmental economists for thinking about the environment as an amenity, while overlooking its relevance to poverty. If the literature ignored the connections between poverty and the environment, he believed, then so would the lecturers and professors teaching these subjects in developing countries; and then so would *their* students neglect these issues. The economics they would learn would be divorced from the world in which they and so many of their fellow citizens lived. Together with one of us (Mäler), he launched an initiative with the Beijer Institute of Ecological Economics of the Royal Swedish Academy of Sciences to conduct teaching and research workshops in environmental economics for lecturers and professors living and working in developing countries. Partha's convening power was such that faculty on these workshops included some of the world's leading economists, many of them contributors to this volume. A better teaching and research program on this subject could not be found anywhere in the world.

The workshops were held "on location," in places like Elmina, Ghana; Kathmandu, Nepal; near Mount Kinabalu on the island of Borneo; and on the coast of Bahia, Brazil. The logistics of gathering everyone in these places were sometimes a headache, but the payoff was huge: by bringing together people from the same region—in most cases, for the first time—the Beijer workshops spawned a number of professional networks. These include the South Asian Network for Development and Environmental Economics (SANDEE), the Latin American and Caribbean Environmental Economics Program

(LACEEP), the Centre for Environmental Economics and Policy in Africa (CEPA), and the Economy and Environment Program for South East Asia (EEPSEA). We relied on these networks in organizing this Festschrift.

We knew that the Festschrift had to coincide with the honoree's retirement, and we knew some of the people who had to be involved. What we didn't know was how we could bring everyone together. How could we fund such a gathering? It was at this point that we approached colleagues in the World Bank. Shanta Devarajan was especially helpful, suggesting that we try to piggyback on the World Bank's flagship Annual Bank Conference on Development Effectiveness (ABCDE). He also had the wonderful idea that we invite contributors based in developing countries, including alumni of the Beijer workshops. He reckoned that the Bank and those of us involved in the Festschrift would both gain from this exchange, and the Bank's Chief Economist, Justin Lin, agreed. The Bank would help pay travel expenses, and we would attract an accomplished and diverse group of economists to the conference. As it turned out, our side of the bargain was easy: everyone we asked jumped at the chance to come. They all wanted to be there to honor Partha.

Our next move was to ask the leadership of the aforementioned networks (Priya Shyamsundar of SANDEE, Francisco Alpizar of LACEEP, Rashid Hassan of CEPA, and Herminia Francisco of EEPSEA) to invite their members to submit papers for both the Festschrift and ABCDE conference. Some of these contributors did not know Partha personally, but such is his influence that no one was more than one colleague removed from him. Once we received these abstracts, we assembled session proposals and submitted these to the ABCDE's organizing committee. Selection was highly competitive, but we were fortunate; two of our proposed sessions were accepted. All these papers are represented here along with a couple of other chapters submitted to us separately in a subsequent round of solicitations. The other chapters in this volume were either given as plenary lectures at the conference or were prepared specially for this Festschrift.

The conference had the feel if not the appearance of a Beijer research workshop, with leading economists, many of them Nobel laureates, not only giving lectures but also acting as discussants for less famous researchers based in developing countries. In contrast to the usual academic conference, the developing country researchers weren't always able to apply the most advanced methods (such as randomized trials). They sometimes had to make do with limited data. But their research invariably unearthed information of great importance to their home regions, and the more famous economists recognized the value in these efforts. (We remember with particular fondness Joe Stiglitz's animated commentary on the perilous economics of home fires and cookstoves in the Himalayan region!) Their commentaries are included in this volume.

Production of this book would not have been possible without the cooperation of all the chapter authors, the editorial assistance of Jackson Barrett, and the support and patience of Adam Swallow and Aimee Wright of Oxford University Press. To all these good people, we are most grateful.

It was fortuitous that the 2010 ABCDE conference was to be held in Stockholm, home of the Beijer Institute. At the invitation of the Beijer's current director, Carl Folke, an intimate dinner was held in Partha's honor at Klubvilla on the grounds of the Academy. As with all Beijer events, the dinner was adeptly and, in this instance, lovingly organized by Christina Leijenhuvud. In addition to Calle and Christina (and her husband, Ivar), the people gathered for the dinner included Partha's wife, Carol, and many of the contributors to this book: Paul Ehrlich, Peter Hammond, Geoff Heal, Simon Levin, Dilip Mookherjee, Lin Ostrom, Priya Shyamsundar, Bob Solow, David Starrett, Joe Stiglitz, and the three of us. Though unable to come to Stockholm, Ken Arrow phoned in from Palo Alto to extend his warm wishes. Other guests included Sara Aniyar, Anne-Sophie Crépin, Mia Horn af Rantzien, Justin Lin, Jim Mirrlees (who provided commentary at the conference), Gayle Sawtelle, Thomas Sterner, Joakim Stymne, and Jörgen Weibull (and his wife, Karolina).

That evening, after a number of us had shared reminiscences, Partha told us all that he had never been ambitious. What he meant was that he had never been *personally* ambitious. He said he welcomed the approval of others, but for him the work was its own reward, especially when it enabled him to collaborate with friends. Those of us who have been fortunate to work with (and, in the case of one of us, study under) Partha know that this is true. But we also know that Partha's work—its subject and content—couldn't be more ambitious. We hope that this Festschrift pays tribute to both of these aspects of Partha's character—the high aspiration and brilliance of his scholarship together with the warmth and magnetism of his fellowship.

Scott Barrett, Karl-Göran Mäler,
and Eric S. Maskin

Contents

List of Figures

List of Tables

List of Contributors

Krister Andersson, Associate Professor of Political Science, University of Colorado, Boulder

Manel Antelo, Associate Professor of Economics, University of Santiago de Compostela

Kenneth J. Arrow, Professor of Economics (Emeritus), Stanford University

Jean-Marie Baland, University of Namur

Scott Barrett, Lenfest-Earth Institute Professor of Natural Resource Economics, Columbia University

Kanchan Chopra, formerly Director and Professor, Institute of Economic Growth, Delhi

The Late **Sanghamitra Das**

Shantayanan Devarajan, Chief Economist, Africa Region, World Bank

Paul R. Ehrlich, Bing Professor of Population Studies, Stanford University

Clark Gibson, Professor of Political Science, University of California, San Diego

Peter J. Hammond, Professor of Economics, University of Warwick

A. K. Enamul Haque, Professor, United International University, Dhaka, Bangladesh

Rashid Hassan, Professor and Director, Centre for Environmental Economics and Policy in Africa, University of Pretoria

Geoffrey Heal, Donald C. Waite III Professor of Social Enterprise, Columbia Business School

Albert N. Honlonkou, Ecole Nationale d'Economie Appliquée et de Management of Université d'Abomey-Calavi, Republic of Benin

Zakir H. Khan, Transparency International, Bangladesh

Simon A. Levin, George M. Moffett Professor of Biology, Princeton University

Karl-Göran Mäler, Professor of Economics (Emeritus), the Stockholm School of Economics, and former Director of the Beijer Institute of Ecological Economics, the Royal Swedish Academy of Sciences

Eric Maskin, Adams University Professor, Harvard University

Dilip Mookherjee, Professor of Economics, Boston University

Mani Nepal, Environmental and Development Economist, South Asian Network for Development and Environmental Economics

The Late **Elinor Ostrom**

Rosalina Palanca-Tan, Associate Professor, Ateneo de Manila University

Krishna P. Pant, Visiting Faculty, Kathmandu University

Subhrendu K. Pattanayak, Professor of Public Policy, Environment, Economics, and Global Health, Sanford School of Public Policy, Duke University

Shubhayu Saha, US Centers for Disease Control

Barendra Sahoo, CTRAN Consulting

Karnjana Sanglimsuwan, Bangkok University

Amita Shah, Director and Professor, Gujarat Institute of Development Research

Sujai Shivakumar, Senior Program Officer, National Research Council, The National Academies

Priya Shyamsundar, South Asian Network for Development and Environmental Economics

Erin O. Sills, Professor, North Carolina State University

Ashok Singha, CTRAN Consulting

Robert Solow, Institute Professor, Emeritus; Professor of Economics, Emeritus, Massachusetts Institute of Technology

David Starrett, Professor of Economics (Emeritus), Stanford University

Joseph E. Stiglitz, University Professor, Columbia University

U. Rashid Sumaila, Professor and Director of the Fisheries Economics Research Unit, University of British Columbia

Min B. Malla Thakuri, Practical Action, Kathmandu, Nepal

Sebastián Villasante, Lecturer in Economics, University of Santiago de Compostela

Part I

Introduction and Overview

1

Partha Dasgupta's Contributions to Environment and Development Economics

Scott Barrett, Karl-Göran Mäler, and Eric Maskin

1.1 INTRODUCTION

Academics don't usually begin their working lives with a grand ambition. They start by writing a single paper—usually, the chapter of a PhD thesis. Then they write another. If they like the work, they keep at it. Sometimes the idea for a new paper comes from the last one. At other times it is inspired by another person's work or the suggestion of a possible collaborator. It may come from reading the newspapers or being eyewitness to an event. When academics collaborate, they combine their ideas and talents. Along the way, they accumulate new technical skills and knowledge. The field also moves forward, and each researcher moves with it, though not always in lockstep; the best move out ahead. Some work turns out to be a dead end. Some may be abandoned at an early stage. But some of it, if a researcher is lucky or unusually brilliant, opens up whole new areas for exploration. Most of the time, a researcher doesn't think about any of this. He just tries to finish the thing he's working on. But when a researcher gets to a certain age, he can look back and see what he has done.

Partha Dasgupta did this recently when compiling the two volumes of his *Selected Papers* (Dasgupta 2010a, 2010b). What he saw was not a collection of papers so much as an evolution in ideas. In the preface to the first volume, he describes his work as being constructed "brick by metaphorical brick," with some papers building on previous ones, resulting in "a growing realization" about his subjects, rather than "a blinding revelation." Recognizing that the best research occurs where conscious ignorance meets the frontiers of knowledge, he comments as much on the results that have eluded him as on what he has discovered. At the end of the introduction to the first volume he says, "There is a great deal left to be understood." At the close of second he writes, "There is much left to be done."

Indeed. And it really could not be otherwise, because Dasgupta has taken on some of the biggest questions in economics. This volume pushes a little deeper into his research territory, with both conceptual and empirical contributions. All these chapters add to our knowledge, even as they pay tribute to Dasgupta's body of work. In this introduction we map the area studied by Dasgupta and show where the chapters in this volume fit within his landscape.

Much of Dasgupta's work navigates within the wake created by Thomas Malthus's *An Essay on the Principle of Population*. Knowing there must be limits to population growth, what will these be? Malthus's prophecy was gloomy; he thought that the "power of population" would overwhelm "the power of the earth to produce subsistence for man." Dasgupta's perspective is more refined; he sees that nature's abundance has bounds, but that human institutions can both limit population (through, for example, an evolution of norms) and ease resource constraints (by means of substitution and especially technological advance—the subject of Joseph Stiglitz's main contribution to this book). At the same time, Dasgupta doesn't believe Nature's constraints are endlessly mutable or that effective institutions can be counted on to spring up from nowhere just when they are needed. He has been critical of the assumption underpinning many economic analyses that growth (specifically, total factor productivity) can continue without limit, noting that over the very long arc of human history the rate of growth in per capita income has only squeaked above zero. He doesn't fear that we will run out of resources; he fears we will undermine the ecological systems that support the human enterprise. (In this volume, Kenneth Arrow, Paul Ehrlich, and Simon Levin similarly emphasize "how deeply intertwined are the problems of improving the welfare of humanity, especially the half in need of 'development,'... and the problems of maintaining... crucial [ecosystem] services.") The neglect of nature in modern economic analysis, particularly in development economics, has long been a thorn in Dasgupta's side.[1]

Other work by Dasgupta is more in the tradition of Adam Smith's *An Inquiry into the Nature and Causes of the Wealth of Nations*. Indeed, the title of Dasgupta's own magnum opus, *An Inquiry into Well-Being and Destitution*, teasingly invites the comparison. But whereas Smith was interested in the "civilized and thriving nations," Dasgupta's focus has been on the societies Smith ignored—the people we now call "the bottom billion." Smith wanted to explain how the rich countries became rich. Dasgupta aimed to explain

[1] See especially Dasgupta (1982) and the introduction to Dasgupta and Mäler (1991).

"the circumstances in which people are born, and the manner in which they live and die in rural communities of poor countries" (Dasgupta 1993: viii). But if Dasgupta's concerns are different, his approach resembles Smith's own. Smith wrote on the *wealth*, not the income, of nations. Today's convention is to look at income as a measure of economic success and income growth as a metric for economic progress, but Dasgupta has restored wealth's place of importance in economic theory. In *Human Well-Being and the Natural Environment*, Dasgupta shows that wealth (specifically, *inclusive* wealth) is the correct indicator of "sustainable development," not Gross Domestic Product (GDP), or Net National Product, or even Green GDP. His conceptualization of sustainable development reflects the concerns that were uppermost in the minds of the Bruntland Commission when they popularized the term. It also reflects the concerns Dasgupta has long brooded over, including the loss of ecosystem services ("inclusive" means inclusive of natural capital assets that may be un-priced in the marketplace).

There aren't many economists whose contributions can be compared with giants like Malthus and Smith, but there is no economist in the modern era like Partha Dasgupta. In addition to the work already mentioned, Dasgupta has made seminal contributions to game theory, industrial organization, voting and social choice theory, science and research-and-development (R&D) policy, social capital, and project appraisal. In this Festschrift, however, we celebrate the subject that has been Dasgupta's consuming passion, the subject he has made his own: the poverty-population-environment nexus.

1.2 OVERVIEW

Partha Dasgupta's abiding interest has been with the human condition, something he calls *well-being*. His analyses embrace all of humanity, but his greatest concern has been with the poor, especially the abject poor—the illiterate, the undernourished, the landless, and the destitute. In his *Economics: A Very Short Introduction*, Dasgupta (2007a) compares the lives of two (fictional) 10-year-old girls, one born in the United States and the other in Ethiopia. As children, these girls are indistinguishable; they both like to play, to gossip, and to eat a good meal. Their parents are also alike; they love their daughters, and will do all they can to give them a good start in life. And yet the well-being that can be attained by these two girls differs dramatically, thanks to the contrasting circumstances of their births. One enjoys great opportunities; the other faces harsh constraints.

Neither girl can change this. The best each girl can do is to make use of the opportunities available to her, and to adapt to, and cope with, the constraints she must face. Some people are of the mind that, with effort, thrift, and determination, anyone can achieve success in life. These are admirable personal traits, for sure, but, as Dasgupta argues, what a person can make of her life depends on much more than her character.

From the perspective of the societies into which these girls are born, however, the circumstances of their births are not entirely fixed. The opportunities available to these girls can be widened. The constraints they face can be eased. The inheritance of the girl born in Ethiopia, in particular, can be improved. There is a role for government; public investments and policies can make a difference.

Some development specialists see poverty in its many expressions as requiring an overarching and simple remedy—"structural adjustment," meaning market-liberating reforms. Others are more inclined to prescribe concrete remedies for specific ills: to reduce population growth, make contraception available; to supply clean water, drill more boreholes, and so on. Dasgupta looks at both the macro condition (the extent of poverty, say, or the depth of the water table) and its micro-behavioral causes. He shows that liberalization won't help the destitute if they are caught in a poverty trap, and that improved access to contraception won't reduce population if couples are *choosing* to have more children.

It is a habit and convenience for economists to look at economic life as being lived at or near an optimum (thus, for example, the terms "first best" and "second best"). Dasgupta has always looked at its fuller spectrum. He has, in particular, shown how the lives of people can be improved even in the most dysfunctional of states. This was a key contribution of his earliest work on project evaluation (Dasgupta, Marglin, and Sen 1972). It remains a central feature of his latest work on measuring intergenerational well-being (Dasgupta 2001).

A defining aspect of Dasgupta's work is the respect he shows for the common man, woman, and child. The poor in his work are neither feckless nor irresolute. Nor are they saints. He sees them as people who have the same virtues and faults as the rest of us, only lacking the advantages many of us are lucky to have. He doesn't think the destitute can change their lot by self-help alone. But neither does he propose as a remedy for their plight that developing countries be given a hand out. More than anything, he sees the lives of the poor and destitute as being bombarded by externalities. He sees these people as facing relative prices that, because of institutional and policy failures, work against their collective interests. He sees that their lives can be improved (e.g., by correcting prices), even in the absence of aid. In fact, aid is rarely mentioned in his work on development. This is just as well for, as the late Elinor Ostrom and her coauthors Clark Gibson, Sujai Shivakumar, and Krister Andersson show in their chapter in this volume, the very provision of aid changes the incentives governments have to develop their economies. Countries can use aid to propel their development, or they can use it to mismanage their economies so as to obtain yet more aid.

Dasgupta often succeeds in ruling out perspectives rather than in identifying a single, pure truth. He knows that a theory can be disproved, when its predictions conflict with the facts, but he also knows that there may be different explanations for the same facts. It is often claimed that people disagree about policy because they have different values. Dasgupta sees things differently. In the introduction to his *An Inquiry into Well-Being and Destitution*, Dasgupta says that he thinks people have different opinions because they have different perceptions about "how the world 'works'"(Dasgupta 1993: 6). They agree destitution is lamentable; they disagree about cause and effect—about *how* the destitute can be helped. More than anything, Dasgupta's research has tried to illuminate these relationships.

Although Dasgupta gives names to the girls mentioned in the opening to his *Economics: A Very Short Introduction*, we can think of these girls not as particular individuals so much as representatives of their respective communities. At the same time, Dasgupta recognizes that communities are more than assemblages of autonomous individuals. People are connected to one another; they have bonds (some of which are mutually beneficial, and some of which are exploitative); they have identities (brother, sister, mother, father, son, daughter, neighbor, clansman, caste member, etc.). Communities have a character of their own. They can sustain different norms; they can display different characteristics of "social capital." These features of a community in turn shape the outcomes that can be attained by the individuals who make up the community—think of the difference a norm such as, "girls should be educated," can make. As well, these features of a society are the product of the behavior of the individuals that comprise a community. Norms and social capital are defined and sustained by *practice*. By combining the insights of an array of literatures, from psychology to sociology, anthropology to political science, and history to game theory, Dasgupta is able to demonstrate not only that communities matter, or that they vary, but that the characteristics (culture) they display are neither inevitable nor fixed. In a phrase, "Social systems have multiple equilbria" (Dasgupta 2005b: S5).

Policies and projects affect many individuals. When we ask if a policy or project is "good," we want to know if it is good *overall*. But to answer this question, we need a measure of society's well-being. What do people care about?

One thing people have come to care about is "sustainable development," meaning "development that meets the needs of the present without compromising the ability of future generations to meet their own needs" (World Commission on Environment and Development 1987). The current generation can't guarantee the well-being of future generations, but it can (and, according to this view, is obligated to) try to ensure that future generations have the *wherewithal* to meet their needs. This "wherewithal" consists of the stock of capital assets—knowledge, plants and machinery, an educated population, natural resources, and so on. It also consists of a country's institutions, including its "social capital."

When introduced in the 1980s, the concept of "sustainable development" was given a welcome reception. It seemed to tap into a concern many people had had for a long time. Dasgupta, however, had written about it years before—only he didn't give it a catchy name. His collaboration with Geoffrey Heal, especially their seminal book, *Economic Theory and Exhaustible Resources*, already laid the foundations for how to think about sustainable development. Previously, the economics of exhaustible resources had focused on the mine owner and the market for its ore (Hotelling 1931). Dasgupta and Heal (1979) looked on the extraction of resources as a societal matter loaded with ethical, especially intergenerational, implications. Their book includes an analysis of renewable resources as well, but Dasgupta (1982) subsequently developed this work in much greater detail in *The Control of Resources*, emphasizing the intimate connections between poverty and mismanagement of the environment. After the Bruntland Commission report was published, he developed a more comprehensive theory of the measurement of sustainable development. The theory is now pretty well developed, but Dasgupta continues to work on its implications and relevance for policy.

1.3 NUTRITION

Though Dasgupta starts from the perspective of the individual, he doesn't just take the individual as given; he observes that a person's genetic makeup can depend on events that preceded her birth.

An individual's genetic inheritance is expressed in the embryonic stage. It isn't only nature (DNA) that determines a person's future, but the nourishment a foetus obtains from his mother in the first weeks of pregnancy. A mother's nutritional health can thus cause epigenetic changes that determine the body size and cognitive development of her child—and thus his future prospects. As Dasgupta (2013: 115) explains, "the experiences that shape an adult start even before his birth and perhaps even before his mother's birth."

How might a child's mother have come to lack the nutrition necessary for him to have a good start in life? Famine and undernourishment are both possibilities. Famine more readily attracts our attention; it's an event. The slow grind of malnutrition is a more chronic and pervasive condition, perhaps more resistant to change.

Consider a person so deprived of nutrition that he is unable to exert great effort. As a consequence, his income is reduced. But, having less income, he can now afford less food, making him weaker still, and so lowering his income still further. Even if the circumstances of his birth and childhood were favorable, he is now caught in a downward spiral. Pretty soon he is trapped. To obtain more calories, he needs a higher income, but to acquire a higher income he must first be better fed.

Why do some people get trapped and not others? Is the reason indolence, bad luck, or something else? Dasgupta and Debraj Ray (1986, 1987) analyze this formally. In their model, different people hold different quantities of assets (land) from which they can earn a non-wage income. In the labor market, people are paid efficiency wages. That is, they are paid a wage rate (per hour of input) that minimizes the wage per unit of labor power (a measure of what a person can accomplish in an hour). Labor power is the real input, and it depends on an individual's consumption, especially his nutritional intake. Fitter people make better (more productive) workers. This is where the distribution of assets comes in. People with assets can afford to buy more food at a given wage than the assetless, and so are cheaper (per hour) to hire than the assetless. In a competitive equilibrium, not everyone willing to work at the going wage may find employment. Some people—some of the landless, perhaps, or all of the landless and some smallholders—may find themselves both unemployed and undernourished. "The market" has many virtues, but it cannot necessarily be relied upon to help the destitute.

How *can* the destitute be helped? The essential problem highlighted in this model is the distribution of assets. The obvious policy remedy is thus redistribution. Dasgupta and Ray show that land reform can be transformative, reducing the number of involuntarily unemployed and malnourished while at the same time increasing aggregate output. However, they caution that any old land reform won't do. This is because the people who are made more productive by the reform could displace other persons who were employed previously. Suggested reforms, if they are to be sure to improve matters, must be underpinned by careful empirical analysis.

Land reform isn't a policy advocated by the "Washington Consensus." But the prescription of remedies needs to be preceded by careful diagnosis. Orthodoxy won't do. As is typical of Dasgupta's approach, this model first explains why a situation emerges—why, for example, some people can be malnourished in a land of relative plenty. Only then is it used to explain how matters could be improved. The approach is crucial: unless we understand the mechanisms and pathways that lead to an undesirable outcome we won't make policy recommendations that are likely to make people better off. "Getting the prices right" won't help if the causes of human misery lie elsewhere.

1.4 POPULATION

As noted by Arrow, Ehrlich, and Levin in this volume, critical ecosystem services "are under unprecedented assault as a result of a still rapidly growing human population." Isn't a central problem that there are too many people?

Asking this only begs another question: what is the optimal population size?

One approach to answering this question, Average Utilitarianism, defines the optimum as the population size that maximizes *average* well-being per person. A different approach, called Classical Utilitarianism, defines the optimum in terms of *total* well-being. Which is better? Start with the population that maximizes average well-being. Now add a person to this population. By definition, average well-being must fall. But shouldn't the well-being of the person just added also be counted? If it should be counted, and if this person's well-being exceeds the loss experienced by all the others, then total well-being will have improved by the addition to population. Classical Utilitarianism would thus say that we should add this person. In fact, we should continue to add people until we reach the point at which the addition of one more person causes aggregate well-being to decline.

Average well-being could decline very, very slowly as numbers increase, making the Classical Utilitarian optimum very large indeed. How large? Conceivably, the product (average well-being times population) could continue to grow even as average well-being declined towards zero—a level Dasgupta (2005a) calls "carrying capacity." What does it mean for well-being to equal zero? Positive well-being implies a good life. Negative well-being implies a life that is not good. But a life that is not good may still be worth living. After all, Dasgupta observes, the wretched cling tenaciously to life, demonstrating that their lives are worth living even if we believe the conditions of their existence are deplorable and should not be wished on anyone.

There is clearly something wrong with both of these approaches. Dasgupta's great insight was to see that both perspectives err by presuming that we are *starting from a clean slate* (the so-called Genesis Problem). That is, they both presume that everyone is a potential person, and that no one is an actual person. Dasgupta saw that we needed to distinguish between these types of person, and that existing people have rights that do not extend to potential people. Existing people, however, may wish for others to exist in the future. This is how potential people enter into the calculus.

History matters. The current generation starts the process off. Its fertility choices affect the next generation; the next generation's choices affect the generation that follows; and so on indefinitely. In this intergenerational game, each generation chooses a fertility rate (and associated investment rate) that determines the optimal size of the next generation—where "optimal" is defined from the perspective of the generation that chooses how many children to have. In this formulation, optimal population isn't decided from behind a veil of ignorance. It is decided from the perspective of each generation. Appropriately enough, Dasgupta calls this *generation-relative utilitarianism.*

The earlier approaches looked at population as if it were to be chosen by a philosopher king. Dasgupta sees it as being determined by the people who are alive at any one time. These people also face ethical choices. For example, a couple contemplating having another child must think about the implications of this decision for the children they already have, especially if having more children means offering less to the children they currently have. The suggestion in his theory is that ethical considerations *by the family* will limit population size.

Dasgupta's framework is richer than that of Average or Classical Utilitarianism for thinking about population. Analytically, though, it is more difficult to work with. One interesting feature of the theory is that the optimum sequence of population levels (and capital stocks) may not be unique. However, for an analytically tractable specification of the problem, Dasgupta has shown that, in general, generation-relative utilitarianism will commend a smaller population than Classical Utilitarianism. The two would make the same recommendation only if the weight attached to potential persons were equal to the weight attached to actual (living) persons—a condition Dasgupta argues can't be ethically justified.

1.5 HOUSEHOLDS

Resource allocation decisions within the household are also important. They determine who gets fed, who gets educated, who receives health care, how much a person works, the nature of that work, and so on. These choices in turn affect "outputs" like fertility, child survival, life expectancy, and literacy. As might be imagined, there is strong evidence that household allocation can be very unequal, with boys being favored over girls, older children over their younger siblings, men over women, and the strong over the weak. In addition, the extent of discrimination appears to vary with the overall prosperity of the household. In situations of famine in the Indian sub-continent, for example, there is evidence of men deserting their families—an act that benefits the man (given the extreme nature of the situation) at the expense of his wife and children (Dasgupta 1993: 305–42).

In this volume, Krishna Prasad Pant, Subhrendu Pattanayak, and Min Bikram Malla Thakuri explain that women and children bear the largest cost within the household of using traditional cookstoves. They gather the fuel; they breathe in smoke from the fire. Pant, Pattanayak, and Thakuri calculate that switching to improved stoves would yield a substantial net benefit to the household—and yet they find that very few families switch. This, these authors say, is a puzzle. Years ago, however, Dasgupta (1993: 335) remarked on the problem:

> Wherever household demands for goods and services in the market reflect male concerns, the direction of technological change can be expected to follow suit.... Thus, cooking in South Asia is a central route to respiratory illnesses among women: women sit hunched over ovens fuelled by cowdung, or wood, or leaves. It is inconceivable that design improvements couldn't be realized at a

> slight cost. But entrepreneurs have no incentive to bring about such technological innovations. Household demand for them would be low.

According to Dasgupta, a reason for the puzzle may be that households don't decide as a unit. Choices reflect bargaining within the household. This suggests that the way to address the problem is by redistributing bargaining power within the household—perhaps by making it possible for women to buy on credit, or by educating girls so as to improve their outside options as adults.

Joseph Stiglitz, in his commentary on the Pant, Pattanayak, and Thakuri chapter, suggests a different remedy. As Pant, Pattanayak, and Thakuri show, there are global benefits to switching to improved stoves. Stiglitz, however, thinks their calculations underestimate the true global costs by an order of magnitude. The problem would be solved, he thinks, if donor countries financed the switch.[2] Everyone would gain.

Household decision-making also features in the chapter by A. K. E. Haque, Z. H. Khan, M. Nepal, and P. Shyamsundar in this volume. They found that families in Bangladesh were more likely to avoid public wells painted red to indicate high arsenic levels (wells with safe water were painted green) when more male members were affected by arsenic poisoning than female members—even though women are responsible for water collection. Clearly, what is best for the man may not be best for the woman and vice versa. In this situation, however, we can't necessarily rely on donor aid to solve the problem. Arsenic in the water is a natural condition, a purely local phenomenon.

Moreover, the observed failure may have a multiplicity of causes. David Starrett, in his commentary on the Haque, Khan, Nepal, and Shyamsundar chapter, suggests two others—high discounting of future benefits from switching wells, and scepticism about benefits (as in, people need to see the benefits with their own eyes). Both problems will be difficult to overcome. Arsenic poisoning is a slow process.

1.6 COMMUNITIES

Why do people wish to have children? One motivation is the desire for their own creations, including their values, to live on, "projects that justify life rather than merely serve it." (Dasgupta 2010b: 271). This is also a perspective Dasgupta has taken to discounting, discussed later in this chapter.

Another reason is social or cultural, with couples, for example, taking cues from their community about the appropriate family size. When fertility is high,

[2] Of course, this suggestion only puts the spotlight on another incentive problem—collective action at the international level.

it is expected that every couple will have many children, and every couple is inclined to conform to those expectations. When fertility in the community is low, the target family size is lower, and the tendency to conform just as strong. These influences are hard to measure. For example, in a world in which community fertility is high, the returns to investing in female education will be low, and if young women are less educated, the opportunity cost to them and their husbands of having children will be low. This means that norms of offering little education to girls and high fertility may be mutually reinforcing. More generally it means that the outcomes we observe could be otherwise. Societies could just as easily sustain norms of educating girls and having small family sizes.

Yet another motivation for having children is the work that they can perform, and here again there can be a link to the community. As Dasgupta has repeatedly emphasized, the majority of the poor in the poorest countries rely on environmental resources for their livelihoods, with children contributing to the production possibilities of the family. "From about the age of six years, children in poor households in the poorest countries mind their siblings and domestic animals, fetch water, and collect fuel-wood, dung (in the Indian sub-continent), and fodder. Mostly, they do not go to school" (Dasgupta 2000: 634). When the resources available are owned by the community, and are poorly managed, more children may be needed as these resources are depleted, with the resulting increase in population putting yet more pressure on the resource. As Chopra et al. (1990), Ostrom (1990), and Baland and Platteau (1996) have all documented, communities are often successful in managing their shared resources. But the norms supporting effective management can turn sour; and, when they do, additional children create an externality for the community—an example of what Dasgupta (2000: 634) calls the "demographic free-rider problem."

The implication is unsettling. Even if couples have complete control over their fertility, and contemplate deeply the ethics of their decision to have children, they may end up having "too many" children due to circumstances outside their control. And the appropriate policy response may be complex: "the most potent avenue open for bringing down fertility rates in the semi-arid regions of sub-Saharan Africa and the Indian sub-continent involves the simultaneous deployment of a number of policies, not a single panacea, [with] the relative importance of the various prongs [depending] on the community in question" (Dasgupta 2000: 636).

This is a very different conclusion from the suggestion that, to lower fertility, we only need to "get the prices right" (a favorite among economists) or make birth control available. When you read Dasgupta's great work, *An Inquiry into Well-Being and Destitution*, you don't come away with a simple story line. Indeed, that is the point. Anyone who thinks that the secret to development is as simple as free markets, private property rights, or more overseas assistance hasn't understood the reasons for poverty.

His sensitivity to local conditions also sets him apart. His remarkable book (Dasgupta 1982), *The Control of Resources*, is sprinkled with evidence gleaned from field studies of the lives of the poor and their dependence on and exploitation of their local ecosystems. It is a tribute to his enthusiasm for such work that the chapters in Part III—the biggest part of this volume—are all based on empirical analyses of local conditions.

1.7 THE COMMONS

Failure to manage common property resources affects more than population size. In some rural areas, families obtain a third or more of their income from shared resources. For many who lack private assets, this common capital is of supreme importance.

Garrett Hardin's (1968) famous essay, "The Tragedy of the Commons," tells a parable of how self-interest causes herders to add cattle to the shared grazing lands without limit. The inevitable consequence, he argues, is ruin.

Hardin's description is vivid and unforgettable. But in his book, *The Control of Resources*, Dasgupta (1982) shows how easy it is for Hardin's powerful metaphor and compelling narrative to mislead. Using a simple model, he shows that, yes, herders have incentives to ignore the wider consequences of putting more cattle on the grazing lands. But he also shows that they don't have incentives to add to their herds without limit. There comes a point where even the private cost of adding an animal to the commons exceeds the private benefit. This needn't be the point of ruin.

It has also been observed that open access is not the same thing as common property, and that the alternatives to open access are not limited to government regulation and privatization. Communities can manage their locally shared resources, sometimes with remarkable success (Ostrom 1990; Baland and Platteau 1996).

But there has perhaps been a tendency to emphasize the advantages of communal management, while ignoring the disadvantages. Noticing that the theory of repeated games explains why communities may be able to manage their shared resources effectively, Dasgupta (2008) has observed that this same theory also explains that cooperation is hardly inevitable. Social norms can sustain a great variety of outcomes, including ones characterized by extreme inequality and inefficiency. Moreover, equilibria can be fragile. In particular, they can be knocked off their perches by external forces, such as improved opportunities for private investment over communally held property. The advantages of communal management over the alternatives can also change over time. As shown in the chapter by Jean-Marie Baland, the late Sanghamitra Das, and Dilip Mookherjee, community management of forests in South Asia by the so-called Van Panchayats can be very effective. However, such organizations are hardly a cure-all. Worse, they can favor elites.

Baland, Das, and Mookherjee suspect that one reason for failure of local commons is the presence of non-local externalities. Many of the externalities in the countryside (landslides, siltation, and floods) are regional rather than local in nature. Indeed, by absorbing CO_2 in the process of photosynthesis, local forests have a global effect: on climate. Baland, Das, and Mookherjee find that pressures on the forests can be reduced by subsidizing heating gas in cylinders. They calculate that a subsidy of Rs. 200 per cylinder would reduce firewood consumption by 40 percent. In discussing their chapter, Geoffrey Heal argues that the value of forest conservation for carbon storage alone is substantial. Agreeing with Stiglitz, Heal supports a global subsidy.

1.8 INFORMATION PROBLEMS

Like community management, regulation of externalities can be imperfect. A central problem is information: the individuals and firms the regulator wishes to influence have private information. To regulate efficiently, the regulator needs that information. But the parties involved have incentives to keep their cards close to their chests. If pressed, they have incentives to lie. A central challenge is how to change these incentives—to get these parties to show their hands.

Common property management becomes more difficult as the number of users increases. Regulation can similarly become more difficult as the number of parties being regulated increases, so long as the marginal effect of the actions of each party depends on the actions of all the other parties—a common situation for environmental and natural resources. For example, the optimal pollution level will depend on abatement costs, which may be known to firms but not the regulator. Dasgupta, Hammond, and Maskin (1980) give conditions under which the optimum can be attained, despite the informational asymmetry, through a nonlinear tax scheme.

The analysis by Albert Honlonkou and Rashid Hassan in this volume is similarly concerned with incentives and information, but with a focus on forest management and imperfect information. Just as Dasgupta, Hammond, and Maskin (1980) rule out collusion among firms, so Honlonkou and Hassan assume that forest users act independently. However, Honlonkou and Hassan allow collusion between these users and their local supervisory agency. This opens the door to users paying the supervisor not to reveal evidence of illegal logging to the government—in a word, corruption. The government offers incentive contracts (akin to the tax schedules noted above) to both the supervisor and the forest users. It wants the users to comply with the law. But to be sure that the users comply with the law, the government needs the supervisor to monitor the users, and to report truthfully whether the users are indeed complying with the law. Applying their analysis to the management of Benin's forest reserves, Honlonkou and Hassan argue that the contract currently offered by the government of Benin misjudges the incentives. No wonder there has been excessive deforestation in the country.

In commenting on this chapter, one of us (Eric Maskin) agrees with the authors that rewards are as important as punishments. But the comment also notes that, under the scheme proposed by Honlonkou and Hassan, the "supervisor" of forest activities would be rewarded by the government only for providing evidence of wrongdoing—meaning that he would have been paid nothing if he had succeeded in stopping all illegal activity! Just as important, this comment argues, the "agent" should also be rewarded for *obeying* the law.

1.9 THE TRANSNATIONAL COMMONS

In the transnational commons, there isn't a single government able to tax or regulate so as to correct an externality; there are, instead, a multiple of governments. In this volume, Sebastián Villasante, Rashid Sumaila, and Manel Antelo investigate the exploitation of a fishery shared by two countries that also straddles the high seas.

The fishery in question is for the Argentine shortfin squid, and the two countries are Argentina and the Falklands (Malvinas) Islands. (The United Kingdom controls the Falklands, although Argentina also claims sovereignty; in 1982 the two countries went to war over the islands.)

Villasante, Sumaila, and Antelo point to an opportunity for both sides to gain from cooperative management of the fishery. Compared to the non-cooperative outcome, effort should be lower and the stock of fish higher, resulting in larger joint profits. However, the authors also show that, compared to the non-cooperative outcome, this improved situation benefits the Falklands at the expense of Argentina. Clearly, side payments from the United Kingdom to Argentina could help. However, introducing them might raise significant political questions.

In his extensive and fascinating commentary on the Villasante, Sumaila, and Antelo chapter, Peter Hammond recasts their model in the framework of Dasgupta, Hammond, and Maskin. Hammond retains the dynamic dimension of the former chapter, but adds asymmetric information as regards harvesting costs as in the latter. This set up yields a dynamic version of the nonlinear tax (license fee) schedule.

1.10 NON-RENEWABLE RESOURCES

We usually think of the resources of the commons as being renewable, at least potentially so. Examples studied in this book include forests, aquifers, and fisheries. Of course, non-renewable resources can just as easily be held in common. Indeed, unitization of oil fields (whereby each owner receives a fixed share of the combined production rate) is an early example of redress for the tragedy of the commons. However, the aspect of non-renewable resources that disturbs us most is not their over-exploitation. It is their finite nature. We fear running out of them.

For some resources, exhaustion wouldn't be of great consequence. For the resources that are essential to production, however, it could be calamitous. Oil is the resource that comes quickest to mind.

In a seminal paper (Dasgupta and Heal 1974) and their now classic book (Dasgupta and Heal 1979), Dasgupta and Heal explore the nature of this problem. As might be expected, the optimal rate of depletion is a cousin of the optimum population problem. Deriving answers to both problems requires that consideration be given to investment. In the case of non-renewable resources, special attention also needs to be paid to the possibility that reproducible capital (machinery and so on) can substitute for the non-renewable resources, and that technologies can render non-renewable resources inessential (allowing a positive level of consumption forever).

While their model is quite general, its implications come into sharper view when Dasgupta and Heal make assumptions that focus attention on key parameters—the pure rate of time preference (or utility discount rate), the elasticity of the marginal utility of consumption (which captures the shape of the utility function, or social aversion to consumption inequality), and the elasticity of substitution between reproducible capital and the non-renewable resource (a feature of the production function). As might be expected, the results are of particular interest as the resource nears exhaustion. For example, Dasgupta and Heal (1974) show that it would never pay to exhaust a resource so long as its marginal product grows large as use of the resource declines, whether or not the resource is essential. Rather obviously, exhaustion is also undesirable if production is impossible without the resource.

This still leaves many possibilities for extraction and (after taking into account investment) consumption. An intuitively compelling benchmark is to maintain a constant consumption stream across the generations. This would be equitable, but it would also make the future captive to today's capital stock; there would be no development. As an alternative, we might allow early generations to lower their consumption so as to allow future generations to consume more. (In later work, Dasgupta has noted that this is what people have done for millennia: parents sacrifice for their children.)

Instead of forcing the model to give a particular solution (as in the constant consumption case), Dasgupta and Heal (1979) investigate a welfare optimum from more primitive considerations. In a utilitarian framework, they show that, for positive time preference, the utilitarian optimal consumption path necessarily declines toward zero in the long run. This seems transparently unethical. Ruling out time discounting, they show that rising consumption is feasible (with the human-made capital stock substituting for resource extraction over time). More than that, they show that rising consumption can be *desirable*, with the optimal path for consumption depending on the social preference for a more egalitarian distribution of consumption. Intuitively, as this preference for equity increases, the consumption path becomes flatter. In the limit, if we insist on complete equality, we obtain the same result as before: a constant consumption stream. Backing off from this, saving by the current generation allows the future to consume even more—this being the central object of development.

One lesson of this analysis is that our judgment about ethical norms ought not to be contemplated solely in the abstract. As Dasgupta has repeatedly emphasized, the *implications* of an ethical stance should be considered before the stance is adopted. (We give a further example of the importance of this approach later in this chapter.)

In this volume, the chapter by Karnjana Sanglimsuwan, Erin Sills, Subhrendu Pattanayak, Shubhaya Saha, Ashok Singha, and Barendra Sahoo looks at another aspect of mining—its effects on the health of people working in and living near the mines. At first blush, it seems that mining would have to be harmful to health. After all, it is a dirty business. However, mining also brings employment; it raises incomes, and not only for workers and their families but also for the nearby community that serves them. To uncover the full effect of mine development on human health (let alone welfare) requires careful analysis. Using a survey of 600 households spread across twenty villages in Orissa, India, Sanglimsuwan, and coauthors are able to discern differential effects. Working in the mines increases the incidence of respiratory disease but reduces fever associated with malaria. By contrast, living near the mines increases the incidence of fever and waterborne disease. Unfortunately, the pathways that may be causing these effects are unclear. As Robert Solow remarks in his commentary, they bear closer examination. Solow also notes that the Orissa results may not generalize to other areas "because other causal chains and their interactions will be different." Dasgupta, as we have said before, has always put great stress on uncovering pathways and attuning policies to local conditions.

1.11 R&D, SCIENCE, AND TECHNOLOGICAL CHANGE

Dasgupta and Heal (1979) argue that the exhaustibility of a resource is of great concern only rarely because the resource is essential; usually, human-made capital can be substituted for the resource to some degree. The more serious problem is that the resource endowment may be so small that substitution doesn't allow a reasonable standard of living to be maintained indefinitely. Technological change is then of great importance. It can ease the constraint of scarcity.

Technological change can take different forms. It can be disembodied, acting on the whole of the production function. It can be resource-augmenting, acting only on the resource input to production. It can also take the form of the invention of a "backstop technology," which substitutes perfectly for the resource at a high but constant marginal cost. If the date of the backstop's appearance is endogenous, there can be interesting strategic interactions between the parties that shape technological readiness and the parties that control the resource. It can be optimal for the resource importing country to bring forward the date at which the backstop becomes available, or to delay its introduction. Either way, the purpose is strategic: to influence pricing of the resource (Dasgupta, Gilbert, and Stiglitz 1983).

The example of a backstop technology that Dasgupta and Heal mention in their book is controlled nuclear fusion. That was back in 1979. Even now, fusion energy is a long way from being available. Indeed, a sustained chain reaction has yet to be achieved, despite tremendous investment. Before a fusion energy technology can be invented and developed, a lot more basic knowledge is needed. This is the realm of science (indeed, "big" science).

Most of us think of science as being abstract, basic, and speculative, resulting in knowledge whose main value is as an input in the production of yet more knowledge, including knowledge that may be used to develop new technologies or improvements in technologies. Dasgupta and Paul David (1987) propose a different classification. To them, the difference between science and technology is the "social ethos" of research. The goal of science is the creation of knowledge. The goal of technology is profit. In the scientific community, knowledge is to be disseminated for free. In the technology community, it is to be privatized for profit. The motivation of the scientist is recognition. The motivation of the technologist is profit. As between the two endeavors, Dasgupta and David believe that progress in science, which depends on public financing and self-regulation by the scientific community, is the more fragile.

But there are also problems with technological change. Though patents reward innovation, they also create monopolies. Dasgupta and Stiglitz (1980a and b) showed that market structure and innovation need to be considered jointly. Their research showed that there could be too much R&D, or too little; that there could be too much risk-taking, or too little; that there could be duplication of R&D effort; and that the pace of R&D could be excessive. Dasgupta and Maskin (1980) demonstrated that different firms' R&D efforts are likely to be too highly correlated. Essentially, these three papers showed that markets involving innovation are rife with failures. In this volume, Stiglitz builds on this and related work to develop the theory of growth and development based on endogenous learning. His aim is to shift the discussion away from policies that move developing countries closer to their production possibilities frontier at any one time and towards policies that push the frontier out over time. The policies he advocates are industrial policies.

The intertwined problems of innovation and growth are particularly important as regards environmental resources. So long as externalities are unregulated and thus un-priced, not only will *current* allocations be inefficient, but the direction of technological change will also be systematically directed against the environment. This problem applies in spades for climate change, both because fundamental new technologies will be needed to reduce greenhouse gas emissions and because it is not within the power of any country to correct this externality on its own.

1.12 CLIMATE CHANGE

What to do about climate change? The optimization problem looks familiar. If we fixed the target steady-state concentration level (a stock), we could calculate the optimal path for emissions. This is the optimal depletion problem in reverse. Assuming that concern about climate change would make us want to leave some fossil fuels in the ground, the binding constraint would not be the resource reserve base but the target concentration level. Rather than optimize the exhaustion of a resource we should instead optimize the time-path for filling up of the atmospheric reservoir.

A more complete optimization analysis would involve choosing the steady-state concentration level. More particularly, it would involve solving *jointly* for the optimal extraction path and the optimal steady-state stock.

As might be expected, calculation of this optimum depends on the way in which the future is discounted. In a recent paper, Dasgupta (2012) provides a clear exposition of how previous researchers have approached this problem. He then shows that previous conceptualizations are wrong. More than that, he goes on to propose a completely novel conceptualization of the discounting problem.

Previous approaches all begin in the same way, by writing down an expression for human welfare. Intragenerational differences are averaged out. Population is also held to be constant over the generations. Each generation's utility is assumed to depend solely on its consumption level. Intergenerational well-being is assumed to depend on the time-discounted sum of these utilities.

Ramsey's (1928) enduring formulation of optimal growth, subsequently embraced by Cline (1992) and Stern (2007) for climate change, evaluates the ethics of choosing the time (or utility) discount rate directly. Should the utilities of future generations be given less weight than those of the current generation? There seems to be no justification for this: zero seems to be the only ethically defensible value. But this presupposes that future generations will exist. Suppose there is a small probability that humans will become extinct. Then discounting would be permitted, but for factual rather than ethical reasons.

Koopmans (1960) took a different approach. He observed that, by investing in reproducible capital, saving by the current generation makes the future materially better off. Rather than choose the discount rate in an ethical vacuum chamber, he reasoned that consideration should be given for what this choice *implies*. In this framework, values for the discount rate and other parameters can be tried out. The emphasis here is on evaluating the consequences of choosing parameter inputs, not on the inputs themselves. Dasgupta clearly sides with Koopmans.

There is yet another approach. This is to choose a discount rate based not on ethics but on the values reflected in the choices people make in the marketplace. This is how Nordhaus (1994) has tackled the problem.

Cost-benefit analysis measures gains and losses in consumption, not utility, units. So it is consumption, not utility, that needs to be the basis for discounting for cost-benefit purposes.[3] The consumption rate of discount has two components, the time discount rate and a second term, equal to the growth rate in consumption times the elasticity of the marginal utility of consumption. The second term discounts the future if and only if future generations are better off than the present (consumption is higher), with the weight attached to this increase in consumption determined by social preferences for a more egalitarian distribution. If intertemporal equity was of no concern, this second term would be zero. If, to the contrary, there was a very strong preference for egalitarian outcomes, the second term would be very large.

One important implication of this is that, if climate change was expected to be calamitous, consumption would be forecast to decline in a business-as-usual world. As Dasgupta notes, if the elasticity of the marginal utility of consumption was positive and large enough, the discount rate on consumption would be *negative*. Obeying this formula, the current generation, quite reasonably, would be called upon to sacrifice more for future generations as compared with a situation in which climate change was not calamitous (Dasgupta, Mäler, and Barrett 1999).

Of course, if the current generation made this sacrifice, business as usual would not be realized. We see, then, that we should think of future consumption

[3] This is also the approach taken in Dasgupta, Marglin, and Sen (1972) for project evaluation. Little and Mirrlees (1969) use investment as the numeraire. It shouldn't matter for decision-making which approach is used, so long as each is used correctly and consistently. If consumption is the numeraire, then costs and benefits must be discounted at the consumption rate of discount. If investment is the numeraire, costs and benefits must be discounted at the investment rate of discount.

not as a forecast but as something to be chosen. This is the problem of optimal growth with climate change.

As noted before, Nordhaus takes his values for the consumption discount rate from market observations—the rate of return on capital. This is a valid procedure for an optimal economy, but the real world is far from optimal, not least because it has failed to limit climate change! At the same time, Stern ignores the opportunity costs of investing in CO_2 abatement—the returns that could be used by investing that money elsewhere in the economy. As Dasgupta explains, the way to address opportunity cost is to revalue the price of investment for abatement, not to fiddle with the discount rate. So Nordhaus is wrong to force discount rates to equal their market values, while Stern is wrong to price abatement as if there were no opportunity cost.

Dasgupta clarifies how we ought to evaluate climate policy. But he then takes a bold and original move. He suggests that we need to rethink the welfare function. By assumption, the standard formulation discounts all utilities the same, the utilities of a single individual over his or her lifetime, and the lifetime welfare of future people. He notices, however, that intertemporal choices have both private and public consequences. As with his approach to population (recall the way he distinguishes actual from potential people), he respects the decisions people make about distributing lifetime consumption over their own lives, while at the same time recognizing that these same people may wish to discount the lifetime welfare of future people at a different (lower) rate. By this formulation if people live very, very short lives, only the discount rate on lifetime welfare matters, and we are back to the standard interpretation. If, however, people live forever, then only private rates of discount matter. For the average human lifespan, the discount rate suggested by this formulation lies between these extremes. By extension (and Dasgupta demonstrates this), it lies between the discount factors employed by Nordhaus and Cline/Stern.

Overall, then, Dasgupta's new formulation embraces the ethical challenge of climate change, but not from the lofty perspective of the philosopher king. It respects market values as these determine opportunity costs, without letting these values be the sole determinant of one of the biggest ethical problems in human history. As with his work on population, his perspective is decidedly democratic. It also has empirical content, being sensitive to the choices people make and would like to see being made.

1.13 SUSTAINABLE DEVELOPMENT

The concept of sustainable development, which burst onto the scene in the 1980s, shows no sign of disappearing. One reason for its appeal is that the alternative, "unsustainable development," is repugnant to anyone who thinks the continued existence of *Homo sapiens* is a realistic prospect. Another reason is that the concept can embrace a variety of "worldviews." But this, of course, is also the problem with the concept. If it can mean almost anything, it will mean almost nothing. This is why so much effort has been devoted to understanding what it ought to mean.

Dasgupta has done more than anyone else to define the term so as to make it useful for making policy and investment decisions. He saw at once not only that the concept related to his earlier research on exhaustible resources and population (as noted previously), but that it also related to his earliest work on cost-benefit analysis and project evaluation (Dasgupta, Marglin, and Sen 1972). How to know if economic development is sustainable? He showed, first, that the relevant measure is intergenerational well-being. That is, development is sustainable if the integral of discounted social well-being into the distant future is non-decreasing (Dasgupta 2001: 140). He also showed that this condition is equivalent to the requirement that an economy's wealth be non-decreasing.

A project or policy is a perturbation to an economy. Project evaluation is used to answer the question of whether a project or policy should go ahead. It should go ahead if its net present value is positive. Of course, net present value is a measure of wealth, a stock, rather than income, a flow.

A state's wealth comprises its institutions and its capital assets, to include plant and machinery, obviously, but also human capital, knowledge, and environmental and natural resources. An aggregate measure can be calculated by attaching weights to the different assets. The weights are shadow or accounting prices, calculated as the change in social well-being that would result if the amount of an asset were to increase a little bit (Dasgupta and Mäler 2000). Of course, it is the change in wealth that is of primary interest—net investment which, given the above framework, can also be described as genuine investment.

Some matters are rather easily described analytically but are hard to measure. Sustainable development is difficult on both fronts. Institutions cannot be equated to capital; and so cannot be added to the capital base. Population change also creates conceptual challenges. Arrow, Dasgupta, and Mäler (2003) argue that population should be treated as a capital stock. But that means that population change determines well-being, even as sustainable development is being evaluated for the benefit of the population that is changing. Dasgupta (2001) has shown that there are circumstances in which it is reasonable to consider genuine investment per capita as an indicator of sustainable development, but these conditions are rather special.[4] Another problem is how to account for climate change. When a country adds greenhouse gases to the

[4] Wealth per capita is the correct indicator of sustainability if intergenerational well-being is the discounted value of well-being at each time divided by the discounted value of population size at this same time; see Dasgupta (2001: 258–9). You will recognize this as being analogous to the notion of average utilitarianism discussed previously.

atmosphere, should the effect on that country only be reflected in the shadow price, or should the effect on every country be calculated?

Alternative measures that have found popularity are more easily defined and calculated. Ask anyone for a measure of progress, and they are likely to mention GDP per capita. Others may say (total factor) productivity. Still others will cite the Human Development Index. Dasgupta has shown that, if we care about sustainable development, then none of these measures serves as a useful indicator. Based on some crude calculations (drawing from the work by Hamilton and Clemens 1999) of genuine investment, he shows that such indicators can even be of the wrong sign (Dasgupta 2007b). While estimation of genuine savings is still at an early stage, Dasgupta has shown that ignoring the environment and natural resources in national accounting gives a grossly misleading impression. A country can appear to be progressing, and yet be eating into its capital base. What we see as success today may only be a down payment on failure tomorrow.

The greatest estimation problem lies with those shadow/accounting prices that are unobservable. A number of techniques have been developed for inferring such values. The greatest difficulty lies with those values for which even indirect estimation is impossible. In these cases, the only option is to ask people hypothetical questions about their willingness to pay.

In developed countries, application of this technique—called "contingent valuation"—is a virtual industry. There are, however, very few estimates for poor countries (Viscusi and Aldy 2003). In this volume, Rosalina Palanca-Tan makes a useful contribution to this small literature, estimating the value of statistical life of children in metropolitan Manila—a value that would be of great interest for carrying out cost-benefit studies of policies and investments that affect child mortality. Her approach is to estimate willingness to pay for a dengue vaccine that would both save lives and also reduce morbidity. Her approach yields a value of statistical life around $750,000.

In his commentary on Palanca-Tan's chapter, Shantayanan Devarajan supports the approach, but warns that the utility of having such values is limited in a very imperfect world. For example, using such values to support investment in hospitals would not improve the lives of the poor, if the investment calculus neglected the problem of doctor absenteeism. Put differently, for values like the one estimated by Palanca-Tan to be really useful, related market and institutional failures must be corrected.

1.14 INDIA AND THE WORLD

Partha Dasgupta was born in Dhaka, which at the time was part of India, and received his first degree from the University of Delhi before moving to

Cambridge, England, where he met his wife, Carol, and where they both made their home and raised their family. It is hard to think that his work wasn't shaped by both places. How could it not be? Dasgupta's father, the distinguished Indian economist A. K. Dasgupta, was his greatest influence. In England, his PhD supervisor, James Mirrlees, made an indelible impression.

We began this chapter by asking where a researcher gets his ideas. When asked this question in an interview given in 2010, Dasgupta responded, "By observation, I guess." He went on to give an example:

> On one occasion in the early '80s, when passing through Calcutta on my way to visit my parents in Santiniketan, I noticed that the baby of a mother beggar on the sidewalk was being molested by flies. I thought, "That's odd. Why isn't the baby swatting the flies?" Then it dawned on me that the baby was conserving energy. That eventually triggered my joint work with Debraj Ray on malnutrition and the capacity to work.[5]

We are only speculating, but perhaps living in England gave Dasgupta the outsider's sharpened observational powers. Perhaps his childhood memories of India, rekindled by frequent visits, gave him the empathic powers needed to see things from the child's own perspective.

In the penultimate chapter of this book, Amita Shah explains the many interconnections between poverty and natural resources in India. Dasgupta has always stressed the importance of uncovering the pathways that establish cause and effect, and Shah gives a good example of this in irrigation. She notes that people with access to irrigated water fare better, but that, because access to ground water is unregulated poverty may worsen as the ground water is depleted. This is a perfect illustration of how misleading current measures of output such as GDP can be as indicators of intergenerational well-being. As Kanchan Chopra notes in her commentary on Shah's chapter, it is also a prime example of how important institutions are for addressing the connected issues of poverty reduction and natural resource use. The question, she asks, is whether politics in India is capable of correcting the institutional failures that portend a bleak future.

There is reason to be encouraged. Dasgupta was recently invited by the Government of India to chair an expert group on Greening India's National Accounts. In a paper prepared for this group, Dasgupta (2011c) explains how to conceptualize and go about constructing a comprehensive system of national accounts. If India were to adopt such a system, and evaluate its projects, policies, and overall progress in the light of it, intergenerational well-being in India would improve. If other countries adopted the same system, this positive effect would be reinforced. Universal adoption of a system of accounts that reflected the opportunities for, and limits to, substitution of human-made capital for

[5] Bowmaker (2012: 172–3).

natural capital wouldn't by itself prevent development from being unsustainable, but it would make such a bleak future much less likely.

References

Arrow, K. J., P. Dasgupta, and K.-G. Mäler (2003). "The Genuine Savings Criterion and the Value of Population," *Economic Theory* 21(2): 217–25.

Baland, J.-M. and J.-P. Platteau (1996). *Halting Degradation of Natural Resources: Is There a Role for Rural Communities?* Oxford: Oxford University Press.

Bowmaker, S. W. (2012). *The Art and Practice of Economics Research: Lessons from Leading Minds*. Cheltenham: Edward Elgar Publishing.

Chopra, K., G. Kadekodi, and M. N. Murty (1990). *Participatory Development: People and Common Property Resources*. New Delhi: Sage Publications.

Cline, W. R. (1992). *The Economics of Global Warming*, Washington, DC: Peterson Institute.

Dasgupta, P. (1982). *The Control of Resources*. Cambridge, MA: Harvard University Press.

—— (1993). *An Inquiry into Well-Being and Destitution*. Oxford: Clarendon Press.

—— (2000). "Reproductive Externalities and Fertility Behaviour," *European Economic Review* 44(4-6): 619–44.

—— (2001). *Human Well-Being and the Natural Environment*. Oxford: Oxford University Press.

—— (2005a). "Regarding Optimum Population," *Journal of Political Philosophy* 13(4): 414–42.

—— (2005b). "Economics of Social Capital," *Economic Record* 81: S2–21.

—— (2007a). *Economics: A Very Short Introduction*. Oxford: Oxford University Press.

—— (2007b). "The Idea of Sustainable Development," *Sustainability Science* 2: 5–11.

—— (2008). "Common Property Resources: Economic Analytics," in R. Ghate, N. Johdha, and P. Mukhopadhyay (eds.), *Promise, Trust, and Evolution: Managing the Commons in South Asia*. Oxford: Oxford University Press.

—— (2010a). *Selected Papers of Partha Dasgupta, i: Institutions, Innovations, and Human Values*. Oxford: Oxford University Press.

—— (2010b). *Selected Papers of Partha Dasgupta, ii: Poverty, Population, and Natural Resources*. Oxford: Oxford University Press.

—— (2011). "Inclusive National Accounts: Introduction," Paper prepared for the Expert Group for Green National Accounting for India.

—— (2012). "Time and Generations," in R. W. Hahn and A. Ulph (eds.), *Climate Change and Common Sense: Essays in Honour of Tom Schelling*. Oxford: Oxford University Press, 101–30.

—— (2013). "Personal Histories and Poverty Traps," in C. Sepulveda, A. Harrison, and J. Y. Lin (eds.), *Development Challenges in a Post-crisis World: Annual Bank Conference on Development Economics 2011*. Washington, DC: The World Bank, pp. 103–26.

—— and P. A. David (1987). "Information Disclosure and the Economics of Science and Technology," in G. Feiwel (ed.), *Arrow and the Ascent of Modern Economic Theory*. London: Macmillan, 519–42.

—— R. Gilbert, and J. Stiglitz (1983). "Strategic Considerations in Invention and Innovation," *Econometrica* 51(5): 1439–48.
—— P. Hammond, and E. Maskin (1980). "On Imperfect Information and Optimal Pollution Control," *Review of Economic Studies* 47: 857–60.
—— and G. M. Heal (1974). "The Optimal Depletion of Exhaustible Resources," *Review of Economic Studies* (Symposium Issue) 41: 3–28.
—— (1979). *Economic Theory and Exhaustible Resources*. Cambridge: Cambridge University Press.
—— and K.-G. Mäler (1991). "The Environment and Emerging Development Issues," *Proceedings of the Annual World Bank Conference on Development Economics* (Supplement to the World Bank Economic Review and the World Bank Research Observer).
—— and K.-G. Mäler (2000). "Net National Product, Wealth, and Social Well-Being," *Environment and Development Economics* 5(1): 69–93.
—— and S. Barrett (1999). "Intergenerational Equity, Social Discount Rates, and Global Warming," in P. R. Portney and J. P. Weyant (eds.), *Discounting and Intergenerational Equity*. Washington, DC: Resources for the Future, 51–78.
—— S. Marglin, and A. Sen (1972). *Guidelines for Project Evaluation*. New York: United Nations.
—— and E. Maskin (1987). "The Simple Economics of Research Portfolios," *Economic Journal* 97(1): 581–95.
—— and D. Ray (1986). "Inequality as a Determinant of Malnutrition and Unemployment: Theory," *Economic Journal* 96(4): 1011–34.
—— (1987). "Inequality as a Determinant of Malnutrition and Unemployment: Policy," *Economic Journal* 97(1): 177–88.
—— and J. Stiglitz (1980a). "Industrial Structure and the Nature of Innovative Activity," *Economic Journal* 90(2): 266–93.
—— (1980b). "Uncertainty, Industrial Structure, and the Speed of R&D," *Bell Journal of Economics* 11(1): 1–28.
Hamilton, K. and M. Clemens (1999). "Genuine Savings Rates in Developing Countries," *World Bank Economic Review* 13(2): 333–56.
Hardin, G. (1968). "The Tragedy of the Commons," *Science* 162: 1243–8.
Hotelling, H. (1931). "The Economics of Exhaustible Resources," *Journal of Political Economy* 39(2): 137–75.
Little, I. M. D. and J. A. Mirrlees (1969). *Manual of Industrial Project Analysis in Developing Countries: Social Cost-Benefit Analysis*. Paris: OECD.
Malthus, T. R. (1798). *An Essay on the Principle of Population*. London: J. Johnson.
Nordhaus, W. D. (1994). *Managing the Commons: The Economics of Climate Change*. Cambridge, MA: MIT Press.
Ostrom, E. (1990). *Governing the Commons: The Evolution of Institutions for Collective Action*. Cambridge: Cambridge University Press.
Ramsey, F. P. (1928). "A Mathematical Theory of Saving," *Economic Journal* 38(152): 543–59.
Smith, A. (1776). *An Inquiry Into the Nature and Causes of the Wealth of Nations*. London: W. Strahan and T. Cadell.

Stern, N. (2007). *The Economics of Climate Change: The Stern Review*. Cambridge: Cambridge University Press.

Viscusi, W. K. and J. E. Aldy (2003). "The Value of a Statistical Life: A Critical Review of Market Estimates Throughout the World," *Journal of Risk and Uncertainty* 27(1): 5–76.

World Commission on Environment and Development (1987). *Our Common Future*. New York: Oxford University Press.

Part II

Foundations

2

Learning, Growth, and Development: A Lecture in Honor of Sir Partha Dasgupta[1]

Joseph E. Stiglitz[2]

It is a great pleasure to deliver this address to honor my long-time friend and coauthor Partha Dasgupta. Our friendship and collaboration go back some forty-five years to the mid 1960s, when we were both students and research fellows at Cambridge. At the time, it was perhaps the most exciting place in economics in the world. To its own luminaries (Robinson, Kaldor, Meade, Champernowne, Farrell, Kahn, and Sraffa, to name but a few) were added a roster of visiting greats: Solow, Arrow, Radner, Minsky, and Diamond. And a younger generation of economists was just emerging, including future stars like James Mirrlees, Geoff Heal, Tony Atkinson, and Partha Dasgupta

We were all enthralled by growth theory, attempting to understand what makes economies grow and why some economies grow better than others. But there was, at the same time, an ongoing debate about capitalism. There was not then the presumption that prevailed for the three decades beginning with

[1] Slightly revised version of a keynote address that was delivered at the Annual Bank Conference on Development Economics, Stockholm, 2 June 2010, and subsequently published in the publication of the World Bank's Annual Bank Conference on Development Economics 2010: Development Challenges in a Post-Crisis World. Reprinted with permission.

[2] Joseph Stiglitz is University Professor at Columbia University; former chair of the Brooks World Poverty Institute, University of Manchester; and co-president of the Initiative for Policy Dialogue. The author owes a long-term debt to Partha Dasgupta for the ideas discussed here and in the many areas on which we have worked together over more than forty years. I am also greatly indebted to Bruce Greenwald. Much of the research discussed here represents joint work with Greenwald, some of which is reported in our forthcoming book *Creating a Learning Society: A New Approach to Growth, Development, and Social Progress: An Essay in Honor of Kenneth Arrow* (Columbia University Press). The basic ideas were briefly presented in Greenwald and Stiglitz (2006). I am also indebted to Jonathan Dingel, An Li, Sebastian Rondeau, Eamon Kircher-Allen, and Laurence Wilse-Samson for research assistance. Financial assistance from the Hewlett Foundation and the Institute for New Economic Thinking is gratefully acknowledged.

Margaret Thatcher and Ronald Reagan—that markets were efficient and stable. On the contrary, one of the memorable moments was when Frank Hahn first derived his results on the dynamic instability of markets;[3] as he put it, he had put the golden nail in the coffin of capitalism. We were concerned too about the inequality and poverty that seemed to accompany capitalism, and about the problems of development. There was still a hope that planning could replace a flawed market.

Even in those heady days, Partha stood out. He tackled new problems and raised new questions, some of which he would pursue in later years. Not since Edgeworth (1925) had an economic theorist tried to think deeply about population policy (Dasgupta 1969). The environment was not the concern that it is today—this was before the oil price shocks of the 1970s turned everyone's attention to the issues. Partha's pioneering work with Geoff Heal defined the field of the economics of natural resources for a generation (Dasgupta and Heal 1979).

The high hopes all of us shared for Partha's future contributions to economics have been more than realized. Year after year, his papers have presented insights into an increasing range of topics, and he has been joined by an increasingly large constellation of collaborators. But most monumental was his work *An Inquiry into Well-Being and Destitution,* (Dasgupta 1993), which identified the nexus between development, growth, inequality, and the environment. No one who read that work or his subsequent related work (e.g., Dasgupta 2001) could ever approach the problems of development as they had before.

Our interests overlapped in many ways; even when we were not writing together, his thinking influenced me. We worked together on issues of taxation,[4] cost-benefit analysis (Dasgupta and Stiglitz 1974; Dasgupta, Blitzer, and Stiglitz 1981), research and development (R&D) and innovation (the subject of this chapter) (Dasgupta and Stiglitz 1980a, 1980b, 1981a, 1982, 1988a, 1988b; Dasgupta, Gilbert, and Stiglitz 1983), risk,[5] and natural resources,[6] and on research projects that involved intertwining issues of natural resources, innovation, market structures, and uncertainty.[7] At other times, we worked in parallel; for example, on theories of efficiency wages, on markets with imperfect

[3] Later published; see Hahn (1966). Karl Shell and I extended this result in Shell and Stiglitz (1967).

[4] In particular, on the questions of when production efficiency was desirable, the optimal supply of public goods in the presence of distortionary taxation, and "third-best" approaches to optimal taxation when there were constraints on the set of feasible taxes. See especially Dasgupta and Stiglitz (1971, 1972).

[5] See, for instance, Dasgupta and Stiglitz (1977), where we showed that the presumption in favor of tariffs over quotas did not hold in the face of uncertainty and incomplete insurance markets.

[6] This included a large study done for the Department of Energy (Dasgupta et al. 1977).

[7] See Dasgupta, Heal, and Stiglitz (1980); Dasgupta and Stiglitz (1981b, 1981c, 1982); Dasgupta, Gilbert, and Stiglitz (1982, 1983). In many of these studies, we found that the study

information, and on theories of social capital.[8] My most recent project, as chair of the International Commission on the Measurement of Economic Performance and Social Progress (Fitoussi, Sen, and Stiglitz 2010), was in many ways inspired by *An Inquiry into Well-Being and Destitution.*

2.1 ENDOGENOUS LEARNING AND DEVELOPMENT: SCHUMPETERIAN ECONOMICS

It is customary in a Festschrift to write a chapter inspired by the work of the honoree. In this case, there are so many topics I could have chosen. But I shall choose one that I believe is central to development, that has been a source of concern to Partha and me since our days as graduate students, and on which we collaborated extensively in the following years: innovation.[9]

While much of the most widely read work in growth theory of the 1960s assumed exogenous technical progress, that was an assumption of convenience. We spent much time talking about and attempting to model the determinants of the pace of innovation (later called endogenous growth theory).[10]

Solow's seminal work (1957), in which he showed how one could decompose the sources of economic growth, had demonstrated why this task was so important: the vast majority of increases in per capita income were attributable to technological change (the unexplained Solow residual) rather than capital accumulation. To leave unexplained the determinants of technological change was, in short, to leave unexplained most of growth.

In the context of development, the matter was even more compelling. As I have repeatedly noted, what separates developed from less developed countries is not just a gap in resources but a gap in knowledge. The pace at which developing countries grow is largely determined by the pace at which they close that gap. Conventional economics and development theory and practice have given short shrift to these issues. They have focused on how to increase static efficiency; that

of natural resources provided a concrete context within which we could investigate issues of broader concern.

[8] See, in particular, a paper published in a volume edited by Partha in an area in which he has devoted much of his time during the past decade: Stiglitz (2000).

[9] Moreover, the techniques (and second-best reasoning) employed below are those we employed in our joint papers on public finance (see note 4).

[10] Perhaps most notable was the work of Kaldor (1957) and Kaldor and Mirrlees (1962); and that of Karl Shell and William Nordhaus (Shell 1966, 1967; Nordhaus 1969a, 1969b). Also influential were Uzawa (1965), Arrow (1962a, 1962b), and Nelson and Phelps (1965). My own paper with Tony Atkinson (Atkinson and Stiglitz 1969) was influenced by Kaldor. I discuss these developments at greater length in my 1990 paper. For a more recent contribution to the theory of endogenous growth, with some perspectives on the intervening literature, see Stiglitz (2006a).

is, given the state of knowledge within the country, how to move the country closer to its production (or utilities) possibilities curve. This was the focus of the Washington Consensus policies, including trade liberalization. But that meant policy was focusing on something that was, in a sense, of second-order importance: gains in moving to the production possibilities curve (say, as a result of trade liberalization) were one-off. Increases in income attributable to higher investment were dwarfed by those attributable to closing the knowledge gap. If one could only understand how to close that gap more rapidly and how to move the knowledge frontier out at a faster pace, one might be able to design policies that would have far larger impacts on standards of living. Ignoring the most important source of increases in income was bad enough; making matters even worse was that policy conclusions focusing only on static considerations and ignoring dynamics were likely to be wrong and misguided. For instance, if technological change is exogenous (and there are no problems of information asymmetries, no environmental externalities, etc.), the presumption is that markets are efficient and the role for government is very limited. But that may not be the case when technological change is endogenous.[11] One of the major objectives of this chapter is to explore the design of optimal government interventions.

Trade-offs can exist between static efficiency and dynamics. From the perspective of long-term well-being, it may be optimal to maintain static inefficiencies—possibly forever—because of dynamic benefits that might be generated by such seemingly distortionary behavior.

The idea of static versus dynamic trade-offs is familiar: the patent system introduces an inefficiency in the use of knowledge by restricting its free flow (because knowledge is a public good, with non-rivalrous consumption—when provided to an additional individual it does not subtract from that available to others). Moreover, patents reduce competition and in some cases even give rise to (perhaps temporary) monopolies, which in turn give rise to static inefficiencies. We countenance these inefficiencies in the belief that the restrictions incentivize research and that the dynamic gains outweigh the static costs.[12]

These concerns are even more central to development economics, where the focus of attention should be on how to bring about the transformation of the economy and society (Stiglitz 1998). Learning new ways of producing, of doing business, and of organizing economic, political, and social activities is at the heart of development. Dynamics cannot be ignored. Here we focus

[11] Indeed, Arrow (1951) and Debreu (1959), in their proofs of the Pareto efficiency of the market economy (the first fundamental theorem of welfare economics), assumed that technology was fixed, or at least that changes in technology were exogenous. As I explain in this chapter, there are good reasons to believe that when technical change is endogenous, the market equilibrium will not be Pareto-efficient.

[12] Whether and under what conditions that is so is, of course, another matter. Elsewhere, I have argued that intellectual property rights may actually impede innovation, especially if they are not well designed. See Henry and Stiglitz (2010) and Stiglitz (2006b, 2008). The adverse effects may be particularly marked in developing countries. See Stiglitz (2004, 2013).

more narrowly on "economic learning": improving workers' productivity. In this context, the central issue is *how can developing countries maximize these knowledge-related improvements in productivity or, more accurately, balance out the short-run costs and the long-run gains?* Exploring this issue is the central objective of this chapter.

Arrow's (1962a, 1962b) pioneering work provided a framework for analyzing endogenous technological progress: some progress was the result of deliberate allocation of resources to R&D, while much was learning that occurred as one produced or invested (learning by doing).[13] Here, we explore the improvements in productivity that result from learning by doing.[14]

Arrow noted that market structure (i.e., whether there was a monopoly or competition) affected incentives to innovate. But market structures themselves are endogenous, one of the points Partha and I stressed in our joint work. Knowledge can be viewed as a fixed cost; sectors in which R&D or learning are particularly important can be viewed as natural monopolies.

In short, if technological progress is endogenous, there is a raft of market failures: markets are not likely to be perfectly competitive; benefits of research or learning are likely to spill over to others; firms engaged in research will appropriate only a portion of the societal benefits arising from their research; and attempts to strengthen appropriation will introduce further distortions in the economy. Many of these market failures (e.g., those arising from imperfections of competition and the inability to appropriate all the benefits of R&D) may result in underinvestment in research.[15] Yet attempts to correct this problem—for example, through strong patent protection—may result in overinvestment: the private return from obtaining a patent typically exceeds the social return, which is simply the availability of the knowledge shortly before it otherwise would have been available.

Markets may not only invest too much or too little in research, they may invest too much in some kinds of research (me-too patents in the drug industry) and too little in others (especially in basic research).

[13] There is a large empirical literature on the evidence for learning by doing, cited in Arrow (1962a) and Solow (1997). See, in particular, Hirsch (1952), Alchian (1963), and Argote and Epple (1990). For additional theoretical work, see, for instance, Fudenberg and Tirole (1982), Spence, (1981), Cabral and Riordan (1994), and Besanko et al. (2010).

[14] Arrow assumed that learning was a by-product of investment. We simplify by assuming that it is a by-product of production (the input of labor). We comment briefly on how assuming it was a by-product of investment would alter our conclusions. See also Korinek and Servén (2010). Solow (1997) provided an insightful discussion of the Arrow model and its limits, as well as a bibliography of some of the research on learning-by-doing that occurred in the intervening thirty five years, including the work of Levhari (1966, 1967), Sheshinski (1967), and Young (1991, 1997).

[15] More accurately, they result in less R&D or less learning than would occur in the first-best situation; given the lower output associated with monopoly, conditional on the monopoly power persisting, the optimal degree of investment in R&D is lower.

Analyzing the efficiency of the market is a complex task, and at the time Partha and I embarked on our work, a third of a century ago, few attempts had been made to do so. Remarkably, in spite of the constant praise of the market system's "innovativeness," we found no general theorems on the efficiency of markets with respect to the pace and direction of innovation. In a series of papers, we modeled the interactions between industrial structure and the pace of innovation, viewing them as both endogenous and simultaneously determined (Dasgupta and Stiglitz 1980a, 1980b). Only in such a context could one begin to analyze the efficiency of markets.

We were, I think, greatly influenced by the ideas of Schumpeter (1912, 1943), who had been long neglected by the mainstream. Schumpeter had argued—and we agreed—that if there was virtue in a market economy, it lay more with its dynamism, its ability to innovate, than with the kind of allocative efficiency stressed by the standard Arrow-Debreu model. Schumpeter grasped the dynamic/static trade-off.

Economists had long been preoccupied with the dangers of monopolies. Schumpeter dismissed these worries. He observed that in many of the markets in which innovation was most important competition (as conventionally defined) was limited; there was one, or at most only a few, firms. (Modern economic theory, including our joint work, clarified why this was to be expected: the non-convexities associated with research and learning by doing give rise to a "natural" monopoly.) But Schumpeter took a more benign view of monopolies than did the rest of the economics profession. Monopolies could generate the profits necessary to fund research—especially important in an era when financial markets were less developed, and venture capital firms did not exist. Borrowing to finance speculative research was limited because, if the research project failed, there was nothing for the lender to seize. In real estate, at least there is some collateral.

Moreover, in Schumpeter's view, in these dynamic settings conventional competition would be replaced by Schumpeterian competition. Competition *for* the market would replace competition *in* the market, and there would be a succession of monopolies. There were strong incentives for innovation provided by the contest to capture the monopoly rents.

Schumpeter thus countenanced monopoly: he saw it as a small price in static inefficiency to pay for a greater pace of innovation associated with monopoly. Until the development of the modern theory of the economics of information, the presumption in conventional economics was that markets, by themselves, result in efficiency (with well-known exceptions, such as those associated with pollution). Schumpeterian competition seemed to create a similar presumption for dynamic economies, in which the center of attention is on innovation.

As a result of my research on the economics of information, I had less sanguine views of the outcome of these market processes. Knowledge (say, about new technology) can be viewed as a special kind of information. Not surprisingly, then, the economics of information and the economics of knowledge were very similar.[16] Both information and knowledge had public goods properties and large associated externalities.

Markets in which information was endogenous were generally not efficient (see Greenwald and Stiglitz 1986).[17] Given that we had established the inefficiency of market economies in which information was endogenous, it was also clear that economies in which knowledge was endogenous would also be inefficient. There was a presumption *against* unfettered markets.

As a point of departure, we wanted to test the robustness of some of Schumpeter's ideas, which for the most part had not been formally modeled but nonetheless had come to be widely accepted by economists focusing on innovation. At the same time, we wanted to shed light on some key policy debates.

Our analysis called into the question the way Schumpeter had posed the questions. We argued that if market structure itself were endogenous and affected by, say, the technology of technological progress, the right question was not what the effect of monopoly power on innovation was but under what circumstances the market structure that emerged endogenously would lead to efficient allocation of resources to innovation. Or, more broadly, what government interventions would enhance societal well-being? Such interventions could take a myriad of forms: antitrust policies, patent laws, government-funded research, or government incentives for research; for example, through the tax system.

Our results also called into question much of the conventional wisdom and some of what Schumpeter claimed.[18] For instance, Schumpeter too easily dismissed the distortions that arose from monopoly and underestimated the ability of monopolies to maintain their position. Firms had an incentive and the means to deter entry of rivals and maintain their monopoly (Dasgupta and Stiglitz 1980b, 1988b; Gilbert and Newbery 1982). Some of these actions, though privately profitable, were highly socially costly (Stiglitz 1981, 1987b). Monopolization could result in both short-run inefficiencies and a slower pace

[16] This was one of the central points made in my 1974 lecture before the Association of University Teachers of Economics in Manchester (Stiglitz 1975b). In November 1978, I elaborated on the problems arising from the public-good nature of knowledge in a lecture to an InterAmericn Development Bank-CEPAL meeting in Buenos Aires (published later as Stiglitz 1987a). Knowledge is a special kind of public good—a global public good, the benefits of which could accrue to anyone in the world. After developing the concept of international public goods in an address to a UN meeting in Vienna (Stiglitz 1995a), I applied that concept to knowledge (Stiglitz 1999).

[17] Beginning in the late 1960s, I had explored the nature of these inefficiencies. In Stiglitz (1975a), I showed that there could exist Pareto-inferior equilibria, and, in Newbery and Stiglitz (1982), we showed that trade restrictions could make everyone in all countries better off.

[18] For a broad overview, see my introduction to the 2010 edition of Schumpeter's classic *Socialism, Capitalism, and Democracy.*

of innovation.[19] We wrote about this before Microsoft's abuses became well known. In a sense, our work laid out a framework to evaluate claims about the benefits associated with attempts to limit competition, explaining both the private incentives and the high social costs of these anticompetitive practices.

2.1.1 The Infant Industry Argument for Protection

In a later work, we linked this broad conceptual work to our interest in development and, in particular, to the question of industrial policy and whether innovation and learning[20] provided a justification, for instance, for industrial tariffs (Dasgupta and Stiglitz 1988a). While earlier literature had developed the infant industry argument for protection, conventional wisdom in the previous quarter-century had moved against it.[21]

This reaction was partly for reasons of political economy: the infants never grew up, and the argument often seemed more abused than used (America's ethanol subsidies are a case in point). Not content with these political arguments—especially since the most successful countries, those in East Asia, had arguably employed industrial policies with considerable success—many economists attacked the economics itself.

Critics of infant industry protection argued that learning by itself does not imply a market failure. Firms take learning benefits into account in their behavior. They are willing to produce at a loss, knowing that they will be more competitive in the future.

Dasgupta and I provided what was perhaps the obvious answer to this argument: firms faced capital constraints. They couldn't borrow to make up for their shortfall. The retort was that even if capital market imperfections existed, it made more sense to correct those imperfections than to create new ones. If the government couldn't correct the market failure, it should subsidize the firms directly rather than through distortionary tariffs.

But Dasgupta and I provided a novel reply to this retort, based on insights from the emerging field of information economics—one to which the critics of industrial policy have never offered an effective response. We argued that capital market imperfections result from information imperfections, and these

[19] A point I discussed more extensively in chapter 5 of *Making Globalization Work* (Stiglitz 2006b).

[20] Our thinking in this area was greatly influenced by Kenneth Arrow, who first developed the theory of learning by doing in his classic paper (Arrow 1962a). I studied general equilibrium theory under Arrow at MIT, and he visited Cambridge in 1969–70, when Dasgupta and I were both working there.

[21] Dasgupta, in his carefully reasoned exposition of the appropriate role of government in *An Inquiry into Well-Being and Destitution* (1993), seems to express some misgivings as to whether the government should undertake industrial policies.

information imperfections help explain why subsidies may not work. The government may not know which firms to subsidize, just as the market may not know which firms to lend to; it may not know which firms will be most successful in learning or in R&D. But with a tariff or other trade interventions (such as the exchange rate interventions described below), the firms that believe they will be profitable—with their learning—self-select into the market.[22]

Partha and I thus provided a fully articulated rationale for infant industry protection based on information asymmetries and a theory of learning by doing. But while the model provided a convincing refutation of the critique of the infant industry argument, it did not fully answer the question of when and how the government should intervene (putting aside political economy considerations).

One of the reasons countries engage in infant industry protection is that they want to enter the fast-moving high-growth sectors—sectors with significant learning. The industrial sector is subject to faster learning than agriculture, so countries wanted to move into that sector. But industry was not their current comparative advantage; without some government intervention, they could not enter the industrial sector and therefore could not learn. Unfettered markets can keep a country from entering more dynamic sectors, especially if the learning is external to the firm.

But this argument for infant industry protection is not fully convincing,[23] as all countries will benefit from the learning as a result of lower prices, so long as markets remain competitive. Moving into a more dynamic sector does not guarantee a country greater (innovation) rents. And those not in the sector benefitted from the learning going on elsewhere, so long as markets were competitive.

Consider a two-country, two-good model, in which we assume all persons have the same utility function $\ln U = .5 \ln C_1 + .5 \ln C_2$.[24] Each good is

[22] This is not to suggest that self-selection processes would necessarily be efficient. Indeed, in the absence of coordination, there can easily be too few or too many competitors for the patent prize. While the price system may provide an effective way of coordinating production and consumption in a static model, it does not and cannot do the same with respect to innovation. The virtue of such self-selection processes was, however, that the costs of any mistakes fell (for the most part) on those undertaking the research project. Still, markets demand compensation for risk-bearing, so innovation is retarded. For a broader discussion of these issues in the context of R&D, see Stiglitz (2008).

[23] We put aside for the moment the earlier objection—that if firms would eventually have a comparative advantage in the industrial sector, they should have an incentive to invest in learning today. We return to this issue later in the chapter.

[24] What is essential in this example is the unitary elasticity of substitution. There are problems in modeling long-term economic growth with nonunitary elasticity of substitution and differential rates of growth of productivity. With an elasticity of substitution less than unity, the high-productivity growth sector's share of global GDP shrinks to zero; while with an elasticity of substitution greater than unity, it expands to unity. Both limits are uninteresting. At the same time, it is unsatisfactory simply to assume a unitary elasticity of substitution. A finite period model of the kind presented below avoids this modeling dilemma.

produced by labor alone; the two countries are the same size; and country 1 specializes in good 1, while country 2 specializes in good 2. It is trivial to show that half of global income goes to country 1, half to country 2. If country 1 has rapid technical progress (endogenous or exogenous) but goods are produced competitively, prices will fall in proportion to productivity, so that while revenue per unit produced falls in proportion to productivity, revenue per hour remains the same. Country 2 benefits fully from country 1's learning. It should not envy the other country that has specialized in the seemingly more dynamic sector.

A rationale may still exist for encouraging the more dynamic sector, but it lies elsewhere—with the *externalities* the tradable high-learning sector generates, for instance, to the nontradable sector. Here we provide the real answer to the critics of industrial policy. Industrial policy is not focused on picking winners, and it is not predicated on the belief that government can do a better job than the private sector of picking winners. It is based on the notion that learning involves spillovers (externalities) that will be imperfectly internalized in a market economy, and that in circumstances in which learning might largely be internalized—where there is a monopoly—the distortions created by the monopoly itself require government intervention.

I present here a general theory of growth and development based on endogenous learning with endogenous capital constraints derived from underlying market imperfections. It is based on joint work with Bruce Greenwald on what we call the "infant economy argument for protection." The theory offers a policy framework that is markedly different from that of the Washington Consensus, which rests on neoclassical models with well-functioning markets in which technology is either fixed or, if it is changing, the changes are simply assumed to be exogenous, unaffected by anything the government might do. The latter theory focuses on the importance of allocative efficiency given a level of technology. Theories of endogenous learning, by contrast, focus on the determinants of learning.[25] Unlike the standard infant industry theory, the theory presented here examines how a society, not just a particular sector, learns.

The theory shows that in some circumstances Schumpeter's criticism of competition may contain a grain of truth; in general, with full competition, the pace of innovation is suboptimal. There may even be a grain of truth in his perspectives on monopoly: monopolies are more likely to internalize the benefits of learning (R&D), and this factor by itself would suggest a faster pace of innovation. But monopolies constrain production, and that means that they have less incentive to innovate, as Arrow long ago argued. And even

[25] Important inquiries investigating the relationship between learning spillovers, growth, trade, and government policy include Young (1991), Hoff (1997), Hausmann and Rodrik (2003), and Hausmann, Hwang, and Rodrik (2007).

with monopoly, there are likely to be important spillovers to other sectors, the benefits of which the monopolist will not take into account. In short, neither unfettered competitive markets nor unbridled monopolies are likely to lead to socially efficient levels of innovation. Government policies—sometimes called industrial policies—are required. In the context of a highly simplified model, we characterize those policies, identifying both broad-based and sectoral policies that would lead to welfare improvements and a higher level of innovation.

2.2 OUTLINE OF THE CHAPTER

I proceed methodically in the analysis of the infant economy argument for protection based on the theory of learning. I first consider a closed economy, explaining why government intervention is desirable. In the context of a closed economy, I begin by considering a two-period model, and then investigate long-run growth models. Next, I examine the special case of government intervention in the context of monopolistic competition. The remainder of the chapter considers an open economy, asking when countries that are stuck in the less dynamic sectors suffer as a result. To answer that question, I construct a model of dynamic trade equilibrium. First I consider a model that contains only tradable commodities, then I introduce nontradables. The remarkable result is that, in the presence of certain policy restrictions, not only might it be desirable for countries to promote exports and not only might exchange rate policy be an effective mechanism for doing so, but it may even pay countries to permanently maintain an exchange rate that is so undervalued that it creates permanent reserve accumulations.

Like much of the modern economics of the public sector, the nature of the optimal interventions depends on the instruments and powers of government. Whether the government can abolish monopolies or undo their distortionary behavior has implications for the desirable levels of research and learning. It makes a difference, too, if the government can raise revenues to subsidize or support research or learning only through distortionary taxation rather than through lump sum taxes. The economics of the second best is of particular relevance here: R&D and learning give rise to market imperfections, and all policies have to take into account the presence of these imperfections (sometimes referred to as distortions) if they cannot undo them. Well-designed distortions in one market can partially offset distortions in others.

I use the word "distortions" with care: common usage suggests that governments should simply do away with them. But as the term has come to be used, it simply refers to deviations from the way a classical model with, say, perfect information might function. Information is inherently imperfect, and these imperfections cannot be legislated away. Nor can the market power that arises from the returns to scale inherent in research be legislated away. That is why simultaneously endogenizing market structure and innovation is so important. Similarly, the costs associated with R&D (or the "losses" associated with expanding production to "invest" in learning) cannot be ignored; they have to be paid for. Monopoly rents are one way of doing so, but—as I argue here—a far from ideal way. There are ways to impose even distortionary taxes (i.e., taxes that give rise to a loss of consumer surplus) that increase societal well-being and the speed of innovation.

2.3 GOVERNMENT INTERVENTION IN CLOSED ECONOMIES WITH LEARNING BY DOING

When there is learning by doing, today's production has benefits for the future. We must ask, will firms take that into account, and what are the consequences of not doing so?

The answers to these questions revolve around whether the learning is internal to the industry or internal to the firm. If learning is internal only to the firm, then the larger the firm, the lower its cost. Each firm is, in a sense, a natural monopoly. There cannot be competition. And, in general, when competition is restricted, market allocations are not efficient. But now there are two inefficiencies: in addition to the static inefficiencies associated with the exercise of monopoly power, there may be dynamic inefficiencies. These may be complex: products in which firms have more monopoly power will have less production, and the lower production will lead to less learning. Productivity growth in these sectors may, accordingly, be slower.[26] In addition to the static consequence of the loss of consumer surplus from under-production, there is a dynamic cost: the lower learning and higher costs in subsequent periods associated with monopoly today result in lower output in future periods. Of course, labor not used in the monopolized sector gets displaced to other sectors, but if those sectors are sectors with less learning, the overall rate of growth of the economy is reduced. Moreover, monopoly power will result in lower real wages; lower real wages will normally result in lower equilibrium labor supply; and, if learning depends on production (i.e., increases with labor supply), there will be less learning (slower increases in productivity) even if the monopolized sectors did not have an advantage in learning.

[26] Though given the lower level of production, the level of investment in learning/R&D may be optimal.

In short, we will typically see lower societal innovation with monopoly *even in the absence of learning spillovers*—that is, even where the monopolist fully internalizes the benefits of learning—for two reasons: (1) because of underproduction in future periods as a result of monopoly power, the benefits that accrue to the monopolist from innovation are lower than they would be with efficient production; and (2) the lower real wages lead to lower production on average and hence less learning. In addition, the pattern of production will be distorted from what is optimal; that is, the pattern that would emerge from a careful balancing of static costs and dynamic gains. If monopoly power is greater in the more dynamic sectors—because those are sectors where the natural monopoly nature of learning is strongest—resources are displaced from learning sectors to others and, again, there is a presumption that the pace of innovation is lower.

On the other hand, if learning is external to the firm—so much so that others in the industry benefit from its learning as much as it does—the industry can be competitive, but because of the externality, there will be underproduction of goods generating (positive) externalities such as learning.

In short, whether learning is internal or external to the firm, the market equilibrium will not, in general, be Pareto efficient. Government has a role to play in correcting the market misallocations.

While the result on the inefficiency of market equilibrium is robust, the result that a competitive equilibrium can exist if there are full spillovers of knowledge is not. If there are not *full* spillovers, then the firm engaging in learning has a competitive advantage, and the earlier argument about the existence of a natural monopoly is restored. On the other hand, the result that there is always a natural monopoly is also not robust. We can obtain an equilibrium with many firms if the diseconomies of scale are large enough to outweigh the economies of scale in learning.

In the following analysis, we make two important distinctions. The first concerns the structure of the product market. As we have noted, endogenous learning makes some market structures infeasible: in the absence of full within-industry spillovers, a natural monopoly exists. With full spillovers, there can be many firms in the industry; there will be competition, but no firm will take into account the learning benefit its production confers on others. It is possible that the market might best be described as monopolistically competitive, with only one firm in the industry but spillovers to other industries. In this case, we will see two distortions: underproduction as a result of the exercise of monopoly power and underproduction as a result of failing to take into account the learning benefits that accrue to others.

The second concerns the nature of spillovers. Traditional analyses assumed full spillovers within the sector within the country and no spillovers to other sectors or other countries. This is extreme. In fact, the production of any good involves many stages, and some of the stages may involve processes that are

Table 2.1 Spillovers and market structures

	No cross-firm spillovers	Full cross-firm spillovers
Perfect competition	*X* (not feasible)	Underinvestment in learning
Monopolistic competition	Restricted output	Both market distortions

similar to those used in another seemingly distinct sector. The result is that innovations in one sector may benefit other sectors that look markedly different. Inventory control and cash management techniques affect virtually every firm in an economy. Just-in-time production or assembly lines are examples of production processes that affect many industries. Sectors that are similar may, of course, benefit more. (Indeed, the same argument holds within a sector. An innovation in one technology in a given sector may have limited spillovers for other technologies—the spillovers may be greater to other products using analogous technologies.)[27] There are equally important economy-wide "technologies." A financial system developed to serve the manufacturing sector may equally serve the rural sector. In the discussion in this and the next section, we use a general formulation that has as limiting cases no and perfect spillovers.

Table 2.1 outlines the three cases. Most of our attention will focus on the cases with perfect competition and full spillovers, or monopolistic competition and no spillovers.[28]

One of the important methodological implications of the analysis is that not only must one simultaneously consider market structure and innovation (both are endogenous), but the analysis must be conducted within a general equilibrium framework. In a partial equilibrium context, one might conclude—as Schumpeter did—that monopoly was better than competition because it internalized the benefits of learning, without noting adverse general equilibrium effects (in the simple model presented here, arising from the impacts on real wages and labor supply).

[27] Atkinson and I (1969) thus described learning as "localized." Because countries differ, too, some learning that may be relevant in one country may be of limited benefit in other countries. Most changes in technology, however, could confer benefits across borders. And, as we have noted, improvements in skills (techniques) in one sector have spillover benefits to other sectors in which analogous skills are employed. Hidalgo and colleagues (2007) recently characterized the product space, attempting to identify the "capabilities" that different sectors have in common. Presumably, if two products entail similar capabilities, learning that enhances a particular capability in one sector will have spillover benefits to related sectors for which that same capability is relevant.

[28] If there are spillovers across sectors (products), but spillovers external to the firm are not full, there is a natural multiproduct monopoly (under our assumptions of linear technology) as a result of these natural economies of scope. These economies of scope and scale and offsetting diseconomies of scope and scale (e.g., arising from limits of the span of control and the benefits of managerial specialization) help define the boundaries of firms.

2.3.1 Optimal Resource Allocations with Learning: Basic Intuition

It is easy to describe the efficient resource allocations without learning: in each period, the marginal benefit of producing one more unit of a good must equal its marginal cost. In the case of a good produced by labor alone, the marginal rate of substitution between the good and leisure (which should be the same for all persons) should equal the marginal rate of transformation; that is, the marginal product of labor. With learning, producing or investing more today has future benefits—lower future production costs—and this needs to be taken into account. This can easily be done:

(1) The value of the marginal product + *total* future cost savings = marginal cost today.

This contrasts with the competitive equilibrium without learning, where

(2) The value of the marginal product = marginal cost today;

and with the monopolistically competitive equilibrium with learning, where

(3) Marginal revenue product + future cost savings *to the firm* = marginal cost today.

The competitive scenario neglects all the learning benefits; the monopolistically competitive firms underestimate the static benefit of production, ignore learning benefits to other firms, and, because production may be lower, assign a lower value even to firm cost savings.

Understanding the structure of learning and knowledge dissemination is essential to understanding efficient production. We are concerned with societal learning, not just sectoral or firm learning. For example, some sectors may have stronger learning curves; that is, the elasticity of learning may be larger for a firm. But what matters is not just the ability of a firm or sector to learn but also the benefits that sector (firm) transmits to other sectors (firms) and the extent to which it does not appropriate for itself the benefits of the learning.

If learning in one sector generates more externalities to other sectors than do others, production in that sector should be increased (relative to what it would be in the market equilibrium that ignored these learning externalities) at the expense of others. The dynamic (future) benefits need to be offset against the static (short-run) costs.

2.3.2 Part 1: A Two-Period Model

This section is divided into five parts. First, we consider a "direct control" problem in which government can determine the amount of labor allocated to each sector. Second, we provide a price interpretation of this optimum. Third, we examine some special features of the symmetric sectors case. Fourth, we analyze optimal interventions using standard optimal tax theory (i.e., we investigate indirect control mechanisms through taxes and subsidies), assuming that government can levy lump sum taxes. Finally, we analyze government intervention in more realistic contexts, in which government cannot impose such taxes.

2.3.2.1 Optimum Learning

A simple two-period model in which labor is the only input to production suffices to bring out the major issues.[29] Assume (for simplicity) that utility is separable between goods in the two periods and between goods and labor:

$$W = U(x^t) - v(L^t) + \delta\left[U(x^{t+1}) - v(L^{t+1})\right], \tag{1}$$

where $\boldsymbol{x}^t$ is the vector of consumption $\{x_k^t\}$ at time t and L^t is aggregate labor supply at time t. The disutility of work is the same in all sectors, and L^t is aggregate labor input in period t:

$$L^t = \Sigma L_k^t \quad \text{and} \quad L^{t+1} = \Sigma L_k^{t+1},$$

where L_k^t is the input of labor in sector k in period t.

Production is described by (in the appropriate choice of units)

$$x_k^t = L_k^t \tag{2}$$

In this simple model, the more output of good j in period t, the lower the production costs in period $t + 1$. We assume

$$x_k^{t+1} = L_k^{t+1} \cdot H^k\left[\boldsymbol{L}^t\right], \tag{3}$$

where $\boldsymbol{L}^t$ is the vector of labor inputs at time t $\{L_k^t\}$.

The learning functions H^k and their properties are at the center of this analysis. This formulation assumes that there are full within-sector externalities, that is, the amount of learning in sector k depends on the total production (input) in sector k. (Without loss of generality, if there are many firms in a sector and there are imperfect learning spillovers among the firms, we simply

[29] Later, we discuss how the results are changed if learning is related to investment, as in Arrow's original paper.

define the output of the different firms as different commodities, with these commodities being perfect substitutes for each other.)

In the following analysis, two properties of these learning functions will play a central role:

(a) Learning elasticity—how much sectoral productivity is increased as a result of an increase in labor input.

We define

$$h_k = d\left(\ln H^k\right)/d\left(\ln L_k^t\right) \geq 0, \tag{4}$$

where h_k is the elasticity of the learning curve in sector k.

(b) Learning spillovers—the extent to which learning in sector j spills over to sector K, defined as H_j^k.

$\partial H^k/\partial L_j^t > 0, j \neq k$, if there are learning externalities,

while

$\partial H^k/\partial L_j^t = 0, j \neq k$, if there are no learning externalities between sectors j and k.

There may be larger spillovers from one sector to another, and more generally, the extent of cross-sector spillovers may depend as well on the production technologies being employed in the different sectors.

At various points in the discussion, we will find it convenient to focus on two special cases, one with no learning spillovers and one with full learning spillovers. In the special case with no learning externalities,

$$H_j^k = 0 \text{ for all } j \neq k,$$

and we write, for simplicity

$$x_k^{t+1} = L_k^{t+1} \psi_k \left(L_k^t\right). \tag{5}$$

In the other case, with full learning spillovers,

$$H \equiv H^k = H^j, \text{ all } j, k.$$

Optimization of (1) with respect to L_k^j, $j = t, t+1$ yields (in the obvious notation)

$$U_k^t = v'^t - B_k \tag{6}$$

$$U_k^{t+1} H^k = v'^{t+1}, \tag{7}$$

where B_k is the learning benefit from increased output from (input into) sector k:

$$B_k = \delta \Sigma_j U_j^{t+1}\left(x^{t+1}\right) L_j^{t+1} H_k^j \tag{8}$$

The first equation simply says that in allocating labor in the first period, we take into account the learning benefits. The learning benefit is the increased output in *each* of the sectors as a result of increased learning, multiplied by the marginal utility of consumption of that good, all brought back to present values by the discount factor, δ. $B_k \geq 0$ implies that, so long as there are any learning benefits, production the first period goes beyond the level that would have occurred with static efficiency (which entails $U_k^t = v'^t$). Obviously, *sectors with more learning benefits expand production more* (relative to the level of production in the equilibrium with no learning). So too, the smaller δ is, the less we value the future learning benefits.

To see what that entails more precisely, we focus on three polar cases:

(a) *No spillovers*

$$H_j^k = 0 \quad j \neq k.$$

Then

$$B_k = \delta \xi_k h_k U_k^t\left(x^t\right), \tag{9}$$

where

$$\xi_k = \left(U_k^{t+1} x_k^{t+1} / U_k^t x_k^t\right).$$

The magnitude of the learning benefit depends on the discount rate (the larger δ, the more we value future benefits) and the learning elasticity h_k. Indeed, without spillovers, the learning benefit is simply proportional to the learning elasticity.[30]

One might have thought that because of the fixed-cost nature of learning, production in larger sectors would have increased more. But the magnitude of

[30] While this is precisely true in the case of logarithmic utility functions discussed in this chapter, in the more general case, the analysis is somewhat more complicated because of the endogeneity of ξ_k.

expansion of production entails a careful balancing of the marginal benefit of learning (the dynamic gain) and the marginal costs of the first period distortion (the static cost). The formulas derived in this chapter analyze what that entails. In effect, they show that what matters is the learning elasticity and not the scale but changes in the scale between the two periods, captured by the variable ξ_k. The reason for this is that the cost of the distortion (relative to the size of the economy) is related to the size of the sector (relative to that of the economy); but the benefits of the distortion—the learning—accrue to that sector, and that sector only.

Normally, we would expect that, as a result of productivity increases, consumption of each good would increase. In the case of separability with respect to consumption,

$$U = \Sigma_k u_k\left(x_k\right),$$

and the effect on $U_k x_k = u'_k x_k$ of an increase in x_k depends on the elasticity of marginal utility for commodity k, $\eta_{k,}$ where $\eta_k = -d(\ln u'_k)/d(\ln x_k)$:

$$d\left[\ln\left(U_k x_k\right)\right]/d\left(\ln x_k\right) = 1 - \eta_k$$

Because normally $x_k^{t+1} > x_k^t$,[31] ξ_k is greater than or less than unity, depending on whether η_k is greater or less than unity. If η_k is less then unity, marginal utility diminishes slowly, the elasticity of demand is greater than unity, and the value of learning is greater.

In the case of the logarithmic utility function, $\xi_k = 1$, so

$$B_k = \delta h_k U_k^t\left(x^t\right) \tag{10}$$

(b) *Full spillovers*

The case of full spillovers can most simply be analyzed by rewriting our maximization problem as

$$\text{Max}\, W = U\left(x^t\right) - v\left(L^t\right) + \delta\left[U\left(H\left(x^t\right) L^{t+1}\right) - v\left(L^{t+1}\right)\right]. \tag{11}$$

[31] Under normal circumstances, growth (an increase in H, productivity) will lead to an increase in consumption; but matters are slightly more complicated, as first-period consumption is subsidized because of the benefit of learning. If H_o, the increase in productivity with no subsidies, is large relative to $\delta\, h_k$ (the value of the learning benefits), then $x_k^{t+1} > x_k^t$.

For simplicity, we assume homothetic preferences, which allows us to rewrite our utility function $U = U(\varphi(x))$ where φ has constant returns to scale. This generates the first-order condition

$$U'^t \varphi_k - v' = -\delta U'^{t+1} H_k \Sigma_j \varphi_j \left(x^{t+1}\right) L_j^{t+1}$$
$$= U'^t \varphi_k \left[-\delta h_k \xi^* / \gamma_k\right],$$

where

$$\xi^* = U'^{t+1} \varphi^{t+1} / U'^t \varphi^t,$$

$$\gamma_k = d\left(\ln \varphi\right) / d\left(\ln x_k\right) = \varphi_k x_k / \varphi,$$

and where we have made use of the result that with constant returns

$$\Sigma_j \varphi_j \left(x^{t+1}\right) L_j^{t+1} H = \Sigma_j \varphi_j \left(x^{t+1}\right) x_j^{t+1} = \varphi.$$

(The later discussion will make clear that in the competitive equilibrium without learning, $U'^t \varphi_k = p_k v'$, γ_k has a natural interpretation: $\gamma_k = s_k$, the share of income spent on the kth commodity.)

We can now rewrite the first-order condition for first-period consumption:

$$U'^t \varphi_k [1 + \delta h_k \xi^* / \gamma_k] = v'.$$

Again, the learning benefit is proportional to the discount factor and the learning elasticity, and inversely proportional to the "share" of sector k (γ_k). The smaller the share, the larger the relative spillover—the societal benefit relative to the distortion in the sector itself. Obviously, as before, if $U = \ln \varphi$, then $\xi^* = 1$.

(c) *Full spillovers in some sectors and no spillovers in others.*

For simplicity, we focus on two sectors, labeled s for spillovers and 0 for no spillovers. Then our maximand becomes

$$\text{Max}\, W = U\left(x_s^t, x_0^t\right) - v\left(L^t\right)$$
$$+ \delta\left[U\left(H^s\left(x_s^t\right) L_s^{t+1}, H^s\left(x_s^t\right) H^0\left(L_0^t\right) L_0^{t+1}\right) - v\left(L^{t+1}\right)\right],$$

yielding the first-order conditions

$$U_s^t - v'(L^t) = \delta H^{s\prime}(x_s^t)\left[U_s^{t+1} L_s^{t+1} + U_0^{t+1} H^0(L_0^t) L_0^{t+1}\right]$$
$$= \delta h^s(x_s^t)\left[U_s^{t+1}(x_s^{t+1}/x_s^t) + U_0^{t+1} x_0^{t+1}/x_s^t\right]$$

and

$$U_0^t - v'(L^t) = \delta H^s(x_s^t) U_0^{t+1} H^{0\prime}(L_0^t) L_0^{t+1}$$
$$= \delta h^0(x_0^t) U_0^{t+1} x_0^{t+1}/x_0^t.$$

Provided that the learning elasticities are similar, learning induces a far larger expansion in the sector with spillovers than the sector without. For instance, with logarithmic utility functions, $U = \alpha_s \log x_s + \alpha_0 \log x_0$, $\alpha_s + \alpha_0 = 1$

$$U_s^t - v'(L^t) = -\delta h^s(x_s^t)/x_s^t = -\delta h^s U_s^t\left(1 + \frac{\alpha_0}{\alpha_s}\right),$$

while

$$U_0^t - v'(L^t) = -\delta\alpha_0 h^0(x_0^t)/x_0^t = -\delta h^0 U_0^t/\alpha_0$$

If, for instance, $h^0 = h^s$ (i.e., the learning elasticities are the same), the sector with spillovers is expanded much more than the sector without:

$$U^t{}_s = v'/\left[1 + \delta h(1 + \alpha_0/\alpha_s)\right],$$

$$U_0^t = v'/\left[1 + \delta h/\alpha_0\right].$$

2.3.2.2 *Price Interpretation*

The equations describing the optimal allocation of resources have an obvious price interpretation. Let

$U_k^t/v'^t = p_k^t$ = marginal rate of substitution between good k and leisure in period t.

Let q_k^t = marginal rate of transformation between labor and good k in period t.

$$q_k^t = 1 \text{ for all } k,$$

and

$$q_k^{t+1} = 1/H^k, \text{ for all } k.$$

Then (7) implies that

$$p_k^{t+1} = q_k^{t+1} \text{ for all } k. \tag{12}$$

In the first-best allocation, in the second period, the consumer price (equals the marginal rate of substitution) equals the producer price (equals the marginal rate of transformation).

The first period allocation is somewhat more complicated. Equation (6) implies that

$$p_k^t = q_k^t - \Omega_k p_k^t = 1 - \Omega p_k^t = 1/\left(1+\Omega_k\right), \tag{13}$$

where Ω_k is the marginal (normalized by the marginal utility) learning benefit from producing more of good k in the first period (this includes the learning benefits to *all* sectors):

$$\begin{aligned}\Omega_k &\equiv B_k / U_k^t = \delta[\Sigma_j U_j\left(x^{t+1}\right)L_j^{t+1} H_k^j]/U_k^t.\\ &= \delta \Sigma \xi_{jk} d\left(\ln H^j\right)/d\left(\ln x_k^t\right) > 0.\end{aligned} \tag{14}$$

$$\text{where } \xi_{jk} = \frac{U_j^{t+1} x_j^{t+1}}{U_k^t x_k^t}$$

Optimal production entails producing in the first period beyond the point of the static efficiency condition, where the marginal rate of substitution equals the marginal rate of transformation. The extent to which we expand production depends on the direct learning effects *and* on the indirect benefits to other sectors. It is not just the direct learning benefits that count. If a sector has more spillovers to others, we might want to expand its production even if its own learning elasticity is lower.

Consider our two polar cases. First, assume there are no learning spillovers, so $H_j^k = 0$ for $j \neq k$. Then

$$\Omega_k = \delta \xi_{kk} h_k.$$

In the case of a logarithmic utility function, $\xi_{kk} = 1$. The extent to which the marginal rate of substitution is less than the marginal rate of transformation (i.e., the extent to which production is expanded beyond the level of static efficiency) depends on the elasticity of learning. If marginal utility diminishes rapidly, sectors for which there is a lot of learning will have correspondingly smaller values of ξ_{kk}, diminishing the extent to which output is expanded. The higher δ is (the less future utility is discounted), the more important the learning benefits are and thus the higher the level of production in the first period.

Second, consider the case with full spillovers. Then where

$$\xi_{kk} = U_j^{t+1} \cdot x_j^{t+1} / U_k^t \, x_k^t$$

$$\Omega_k = \delta h_k \xi^* / \gamma_k .$$

where ξ^* and γ_k are as defined earlier.

The price interpretation is useful because it provides an easy and direct contrast between optimal resource allocations and the competitive equilibrium without government intervention. (We will discuss the monopolistically competitive equilibrium later.) In the competitive equilibrium,

$$U_k^t / v'^t = q_k^t = 1 \text{ for all } k$$

$$U_k^{t+1} / v'^{t+1} = f q_k^{t+1} = 1 / H^k, \text{ for all } k;$$

that is, production in the first period ignores *all* learning benefits but, conditional on the learning that has occurred, second-period production is efficient. Clearly, there will be underproduction in the first period, especially in those sectors in which learning is important. (Later, we will also contrast the optimal allocation with that generated by monopoly.)

2.3.2.3 *Symmetric Case*

The above analysis derived general formulas for analyzing optimal production/learning if government could directly control inputs/outputs in every sector. We also provided a price interpretation of the optimum. Much of our discussion focused on the desirability of increasing activities that generate learning externalities compared with those that did not.

But there is a broader macroeconomic issue: even if all sectors were identical (symmetric), so that 1/nth of the labor supply ought to (and, in market equilibrium, will) be devoted to each commodity, there may be too little output (labor supply) in the first period. If labor supply is inelastic and the number of goods is fixed at n, in the symmetric equilibrium, 1/nth of the labor force is allocated to each good. It is obvious that the market equilibrium has the efficient amount of learning in each sector; there is no learning distortion, even though there are learning externalities. This is important, for it illustrates the large discrepancy between partial and general equilibrium analysis. (Partial equilibrium analysis would have led us to the conclusion that there was an underinvestment in learning.)

The symmetric equilibrium also provides an easy context in which to compare the market equilibrium with the optimum. For simplicity, we will assume no spillovers across sectors.

The social welfare maximization problem can be easily written as

$$\begin{aligned}\max_{\{L^t,\, L^{t+1}\}} \quad & U^t(L^t/n, L^t/n, L^t/n, \ldots) - v^t(L^t) \\ & + \delta[U^{t+1}(\Psi(L^t/n)L^{t+1}/n, \Psi(L^t/n)L^{t+1}/n, \Psi(L^t/n)L^{t+1}/n, \ldots) \\ & - v^{t+1}(L^{t+1})],\end{aligned}$$

where n is the number of commodities, and where we have assumed separability between labor and goods but not necessarily between goods; where $\psi_k(L_k^t)$ is the learning function giving output per unit input;[32] and where, because of the assumption of symmetry, we can, without loss of generality, drop the subscript on the learning function.

The first order condition can be written

$$\Sigma U_i^t / n - v^{t\prime} = U_i^t - v^{t\prime} = -\delta \Sigma U_i^{t+1} \psi'(L_i^t) L^{t+1}/n = -\delta U_i^{t+1} \psi'(L_i^t) L^{t+1}.$$

In competitive equilibrium

$$U_i^t - v^{t\prime} = 0,$$

so it is clear that (in general) there is too little production the first period. The only exception is the case where L^t is fixed (i.e., cannot be increased). Then, trivially, the market equilibrium is efficient.

The first-order condition for L^{t+1} is

$$U_i^{t+1} \psi(L_i^t) - v^{t+1\prime} = 0.$$

In competitive equilibrium, the price is $1/[\psi(L_i^t)]$, so that, conditional on the state of knowledge in the second period, output is efficient.

If the government were to subsidize first period production by τ, so that the first-order condition is

[32] Recall that in terms of our previous notation, ψ is the special case of H where there are no spillovers.

$$U_i^t - v^{t\prime}(1-\tau) = 0$$

and sets

$$\tau^* = \delta\, U_i^{t+1} \psi'\left(L^t / n\right) L^{t+1} / \left(v^{t'}\right),$$

raising the revenue through a lump sum tax, then the government can replicate the first best optimum.[33]

It is useful to rewrite the above expression as[34]

$$\begin{aligned}\tau^* &= \delta\left[v^{t+1\prime} L^{t+1} / v^{t\prime} L^t\right] h \\ &= \delta \varsigma h,\end{aligned}$$

where ς is our new relative scale parameter, slightly different from that used earlier:

$$\varsigma = v^{t+1\prime} L^{t+1} / v^{t\prime} L^t.$$

For instance, assume constant marginal disutility of work, $v' = 1$ (a constant) and logarithmic utility of goods, $U = \Sigma \ln X_i$. It is easy to show that in the case of symmetry, the results are the same if we had a single consumption good. For notational simplicity, we will assume that, and drop the subscript on X. Then

$$x^t = 1 - \tau^* = L^t$$

and

$$x^{t+1} = \Psi,$$

so

$$L^{t+1} = x^{t+1} / \Psi = 1$$

and

$$\tau^* = \delta h / (1 - \tau^*).$$

[33] $U_i^t - v^{t\prime} = -\tau^* v' = -\delta U_i^{t+1} \psi'\left(L_i^t\right) L^{t+1}$.

[34] The symmetric equilibrium can be treated as if there were a single commodity. Without loss of generality, we then write $U'^t = U_i^t$. From the first-oder condition for L^t, recalling that, in equilibrium, $x^t = L^t$

$$U''\left(L^t\right) - v^{t\prime}\left(L^t\right)\,(1-\tau) = 0,$$

τ^* is thus the solution to the quadratic equation

$$\tau^{*2} - \tau^* + \delta h = 0.$$

For small δh, the solution can be approximated by

$$\tau^* \approx \delta h,$$

as before.

Other special cases can similarly be solved for explicitly. Assume, for instance, that we had a learning function that was linear (rather than constant elasticity), with

$$\Psi = 1 - \vartheta L,$$

where ϑ is a small number (limited learning). Assume constant marginal utility of consumption ($U' = 1$) and quadratic disutility of leisure ($v = .5L^2$).

we can derive $d\ln L^t / d\ln \tau = (\tau/1-\tau)\varepsilon^c_{Lw}$, where ε^c_{Lw} is the elasticity of supply of labor. From the first order condition for L^{t+1}, recalling that $x^{t+1} = H(L^t)L^{t+1}$,

$$HU'^{t+1}\left(HL^{t+1}\right) - v^{t\prime}\left(L^{t+1}\right) = 0,$$

we can derive

$$d\ln L^{t+1}/d\ln H = \varepsilon_{Lw,}$$

from which it follows that

$$d\ln L^{t+1}/d \ln L^t h = h\,\varepsilon_{Lw.}$$

Hence, at $\tau = 0$,

$$v^{t+1\prime}L^{t+1}/v^{t\prime}L^t \approx 1 + (1+v)H_o\varepsilon_{Lw}.$$

$$d\ln\left[v^{t+1\prime}\,L^{t+1}/v^{t\prime}L^t\right]/d\ln\tau = (1+v)\left[h\,\varepsilon_{Lw} - 1\right](\tau/1-\tau)\,\varepsilon^c_{Lw},$$

Hence

$$v^{t+1\prime}\,L^{t+1}/v^{t\prime}L^t \approx \left[1 + (1+v)H_o\varepsilon_{Lw}\right]\left[1 + (1+v)(h\,\varepsilon_{Lw} - 1)(\tau/1-\tau)\,\varepsilon^c_{Lw}\right].$$

It follows that for small h,

$$\tau^* \approx \delta h[1+(1+v)(H_o - 1)\varepsilon_{Lw}]$$

The subsidy increases with h, δ, v, and ε_{Lw}.

Then it is straightforward that $L^{t+1} = \Psi = 1 - \vartheta L^t$, $\Psi' = -\vartheta$, and $L^t = 1 - \tau^*$. Hence,

$$\tau^* = \delta\vartheta[1 - \vartheta(1 - \tau^*)] / (1 - \tau^*),$$

so τ^* is the solution to the quadratic equation

$$\tau^{*2} - (1 + \delta\vartheta^2)\tau^* - \delta\vartheta(1 - \vartheta) = 0.$$

For small subsidies (small ϑ), τ^* can be approximated by

$$\tau^* \approx \delta\vartheta(1 - \vartheta) / (1 - \delta\vartheta^2) \approx \delta\vartheta,$$

again, proportional to the discount factor and the learning parameter.

Even though we can impose lump sum taxes, subsidies distort static allocations. Optimal interventions balance these static losses with the dynamic gains. The above formulas show the outcomes of this balancing.[35]

2.3.2.4 Optimal Learning with Optimal Taxation: Lump Sum Taxation

So far, we have derived the optimal allocation (assuming that government directly controls production and consumption) and analyzed price interpretations of the resulting equilibrium. It may be useful to redo the analysis using more standard techniques in public finance. We begin by assuming that the government can only impose excise taxes and subsidies and lump sum taxes. The government faces an indirect control problem. With lump sum taxation, assuming that first-period subsidies must be paid by a lump sum tax in the first period (i.e., there are no intertemporal budget constraints, so the government cannot borrow from the future to finance this period's deficits), we can write social welfare using the indirect utility function, giving the level of utility as a function of prices and "income":

[35] These formulae provide a characterization of the equilibrium, but it is important to note that, in general, the elasticities can themselves depend on taxes and subsidies. With full spillovers, the learning function is $\Psi = \Psi(L^t/n, L^t/n, \ldots)$ for all sectors. An increase in L^t thus increases learning by Ψ_i. Denoting by Ψ^* the function $\Psi(L^t/n, L^t/n, \ldots)$, with $\Psi^{*\prime} = \Psi_i$, we can write the first-order condition with full spillovers as

$$\Sigma U_i^t / n - v^{t\prime} = U_i^t - v^{t\prime} = -\delta\Sigma\, U_i^{t+1} \Psi^{*\prime}(L_i^t) L^{t+1} / n = -\delta U_i^{t+1} \Psi'^{*}(L^t) L^{t+1}$$

Substituting Ψ^* for Ψ, we obtain exactly the same results, though with a slightly different interpretation. It is likely, because of learning spillovers, that normally $\Psi^{*\prime}$ would be greater than Ψ', implying a higher level of subsidy.

$$V^t\left(\boldsymbol{p}^t,-T\right)+\delta V^{t+1}(\boldsymbol{p}^{t+1},0) \tag{15}$$

$$p_i^t=(1-\tau_i) \tag{16}$$

$$p_i^{t+1}=1/H^i, \tag{17}$$

where τ_i is the first-period subsidy to commodity *j*. Under our normalization, in a competitive market without subsidies, the (consumer) price of all goods would be unity; a subsidy on good *j* of τ_j brings down the competitive price to $1-\tau_j$. In a competitive market, in the second period, the price is just the cost of production.

There are two spillovers from a subsidy on sector *j*:

1. An increase in the subsidy on commodity *j* affects demand (and supply) for commodity *i*. That in turn has two effects: an impact on learning in those sectors (the benefits of which can spill over to other sectors) and an impact on the government's budget constraint; for example, if demand shifts toward highly subsidized products, the government would face a budgetary shortfall, which would necessitate a decrease in the subsidy on some other commodities.
2. The expansion of sector *j* affects learning in sector *i*.

It is easy to establish that, provided the sectors are not too different, it pays to subsidize consumption of every good in the first period. But if sectors are very different, it may pay to impose a tax on a sector, even if there is some learning in that sector. If the learning elasticity of a sector is much larger than that of others, and that sector has large spillovers to others, and there is some sector that is a substitute for the high-learning sector, then it may pay to tax that sector, in order to encourage learning in the high-learning sector.[36]

We can easily derive the optimal tax/subsidy rate[37] :

$$V^t\left(\boldsymbol{p}^t,-T\right)+\delta V^{t+1}\left(\boldsymbol{p}_i^{t+1},0\right)$$

subject to (15) and (16) and to the government's budget constraint,

$$T=\sum\tau_i x_i.$$

The first-order conditions are given by

[36] Since, in the first period (omitting the superscript t), $\Sigma p_i x_i = L + \Sigma\tau_i x_i$, at $\tau = 0$, $\Sigma\, dx_i/d\tau_j = dL/d\tau_j > 0$. Both the income and substitution effects lead to an increased labor supply.

[37] We make use of the fact that $V_{pi} = -V_I x_i$.

$$-V_{p_j}^{t} - \mu[x_j^t + \Sigma\tau_i(dx_i^t / d\tau_j)] - \delta\Sigma_k V_{p_k}^{t+1} \Sigma_i \left[\left(1/H^k\right)^2\right] H_i^k \, dx_i / d\tau_j = 0, \quad (18a)$$

$$-V_I^t - \mu[-1 + \Sigma\tau_j(dx_j^t / dI)] - \delta\Sigma_k V_{p_k}^{t+1} \Sigma_i \left[\left(1/H^k\right)^2\right] H_i^k \, dx_i / dI = 0, \quad (18b)$$

where μ is the Lagrange multiplier associated with the government budget constraint. Using the Slutsky equation[38] we obtain (multiplying (18b) by x_j^t and subtracting (18a))

$$-\mu\Sigma\tau_j(dx_j^t / d\tau_i)_U + \delta\Sigma_k V_{pk}^{t+1} \Sigma_i \left[\left(1/H^k\right)^2\right] H_i^k \left(dx_i / dp_j\right)_U = 0.$$

The term $[\Sigma\tau_j\ (dx_j^t/d\tau_i)]$ reflects the spillovers to the budget constraint: the increase in output of sector *i* affects the aggregate subsidies and, therefore, the aggregate lump sum tax. We define,

$$\delta V_I^{t+1} / \mu = \rho, \quad (19)$$

the intertemporal marginal rate of substitution, reflecting the pure rate of time discount plus the diminution of the marginal utility of income as a result of growth. (Normally, δ is less than unity, and with growth and diminishing marginal utility of income, V_I^{t+1}/V_I^t is less than unity, so ρ is less than one.) Then, using the standard "tricks" of optimal tax theory (combining the Slutsky equation with the symmetry of the compensated price elasticities), we can rewrite (18c) as[39]

$$-\Sigma_j(\tau_j / p_j)(\partial \ln \tau x_i / \partial \ln p_j)_U = \rho\Phi_i + \chi, \quad (20)$$

where $\Phi_i = -[(L^{t+1}/(1+\tau_i)s_i^t L^t]\ \Sigma_k\ \{s_k^{t+1}\ \Sigma_j h_j^k [\partial(\ln x_j^t)/\partial(\ln p_i)]_U\}$ is the total net marginal learning benefit from encouraging the consumption (equals the production in a closed economy) of sector *j*, taking into account potential effects on other sectors, both through induced learning in other sectors (as a result of cross elasticities of demand) and as a result of learning spillovers. The double sums reflect this. An increase in the subsidy on product *i* leads to an increase in consumption of *i*, which affects learning in *i*, but also in other sectors (hence the terms H_i^k); but through cross-elasticity effects, it also affects production in sector *j*, and this affects learning in that sector and every other sector.

$\Sigma_j h_j^k[\partial(\ln x_j^t)/\partial(\ln p_i)]_U$ reflects the total impact of a change in the price of good *i* on learning in sector *k*, taking both of these effects into account. Φ_i weights these learning effects by the relative share of these goods in the second-period

[38] To derive 18(a), we make use of the Slutsky relationship $\partial x_i^t/\partial p_j = (\partial x_i^t/\partial p_j)_U - x_j \partial x_i/\partial I$.

[39] To derive (20), we make use of the symmetry of Slutsky terms.

consumption bundle. Φ_i also reflects the relative scale of the economy in the two periods—if L^{t+1}/L^t is large, Φ_i is large, reflecting the greater value of learning. Finally, we take into account the relative size of sector *i*. If it is small, the cost of the distortion will be small relative to the society-wide benefits.

Equation (20) can be interpreted similarly to the analogous expression in optimal tax theory: in the absence of learning (where $\Phi_i = 0$ for all *i*), the percentage deviation of consumption of good *i* (along the compensated demand curves) should be the same for all goods. Of course, since the only reason for imposing taxes and subsidies is learning, $\tau_i = 0$ for all *i*. Now we will make an adjustment: the percentage deviation should be larger for those sectors with larger marginal learning benefits, but those marginal learning benefits include not just the direct learning benefits but the spillovers to other sectors.

Qualitatively, we can see what is implied by considering the case of separable demand functions with no spillovers:[40]

$$\tau_i = \rho h_i^{\,i} \zeta_i, \tag{21}$$

where $h_i^i = \partial(\ln H^i)/\partial(\ln L_i)$, the (own) elasticity of the learning curve; and

$$\zeta_i = s_i^{t+1} L_i^{t+1} / (s_i^t L_i^t),$$

the ratio in sector i of labor input the second period to that in the first period.[41] ζ_i is itself a function of τ_i. We can use techniques similar to that employed earlier to show that the optimal subsidy increases with the learning elasticity and the elasticity of labor supply, and obviously decreases with the intertemporal price.

(a) A two-sector case

Now let us assume, as before, two sectors: one (denoted by *o*) that has no learning spillover to the other sector and another (denoted by *s*) that has a full learning spillover.

If the two sectors have the same learning elasticity and demand elasticity, we will subsidize (expand) sector *s* (with the spillover), more than sector *0* (without).[42] Similarly, even if sector *j* has a lower learning elasticity,

[40] One must take care in interpreting this and other optimal tax/subsidy formulas in this chapter, because the variables on the right-hand side are typically not constants but functions of the subsidy rate itself. Still, they provide insights into the determinants of the appropriate subsidies for optimally designed subsidies.

[41] With a positive wage elasticity, ζ_j can be shown to be greater than unity, using the technique of footnote 34.

[42] For a fuller analysis, see Greenwald and Stiglitz (2014).

we may wish to subsidize it more. The extent of spillovers is of first order importance.

(b) Symmetric equilibrium

We can simplify further in the special case of symmetry, discussed above. From symmetry, we know that all will face the same price, so we can write our optimization problem as (using the obvious notation)

$$\text{Max } V^t((1-\tau_i),......,-n\tau_i x_i)+\delta V^{t+1}(c_i(\tau_{i,}\tau_{j\neq i}),0), \tag{22}$$

where c is the cost of production, that is, $c_i = 1/H_i$, implying

$$-V_I^t(\tau dx_i^t/d\tau)-\delta V_I^{t+1}\Sigma_i\left[(n-1)x_j^{t+1}\partial c_i(\tau_{i,}\tau_{j\neq i})/\partial\tau_{j\neq i}+x_i^{t+1}\partial c_i(\tau_{i,}\tau_{j\neq i})/\partial\tau_i\right]=0 \tag{23}$$

or

$$\{-V_I^t(\tau/p)+\delta V_I^{t+1}\left(L_j^{t+1}/L_j^t\right)\left[(n-1)h_j^i+h_j^j\right]\}\{d\ln x_i^t/d\ln\tau\}=0, \tag{24}$$

where

$$d\ln c_i(\tau_{i,}\tau_{j\neq i})/d\ln\tau=-[(n-1)(\partial\ln c_i/\partial\ln x_j)_{j\neq i}+\partial\ln c_i/\partial\ln x_i]d\ln x_i^\tau/d\ln\tau x_i^t.$$

There are direct benefits of learning (and $h_j^i = -\frac{\partial\ln c_i}{\partial\ln x_j^t}$, the own elasticity of the learning curve) and indirect benefits (and $h_j^j = -\frac{\partial\ln c_j}{\partial\ln x_j^t}$, the learning spillovers).

There are two solutions. If $d\ln L^t/d\ln\tau = 0$, then (as we argued earlier) there is no reason to interfere with the market. But in the more general case,

$$\tau/1-\tau=\rho\,\zeta\,[(n-1)h_j^i+h_j^j] \tag{25}$$

As before, the higher the learning and the more learning spillovers, the higher the subsidy. If labor supply is very elastic and there is substantial learning, then $L^{t+1}/L^t >>> 1$, so, again, the higher the subsidy. If there are significant spillovers and many sectors, it is the magnitude of the spillovers that really matters.

2.3.2.5 No Lump Sum Taxes

When government cannot impose lump sum taxes, there may still be room for industrial policies. One sector may have more learning benefits, so that a tax on the other sector to finance a subsidy on the learning sector might be desirable.

Consider the following polar model (which will be expanded on in later sections).[43] There is no learning in sector A (the agricultural sector), but sector M (manufacturing) has a learning function $c(L_M)$, and there are full spillovers to sector A. (Greenwald and Stiglitz [2004] argue that it is plausible that not only does manufacturing have a higher learning elasticity ($h^A << h^M$) but that there are larger cross-sector learning spillovers from manufacturing to agricultural than vice versa.) Thus, continuing within the optimal tax framework of the previous section, we seek to

$$\underset{\{\tau_M,\ t_A\}}{\text{Max}}\ V^t((1-\tau_M),(1+t_A),0)+\delta V^{t+1}\left(c(L_M),c(L_M),0\right) \tag{26}$$

where $\tau_M x_M = t_A x_A$, $dt_A / d\tau_M = (x_M / x_A) + \tau_M d(x_M / x_A) / d\tau_M$
where, as before, τ_M is the subsidy on manufacturing and t_A is the tax that must be levied on agriculture to pay for the subsidy. This implies that

$$V_I^t[x_M^t - x_A^t\ (dt_A / d\tau_M)] = -\delta V_I^{t+1} c'(L_M)\left(x_M^{t+1} + x_A^{t+1}\right) dx^t_M / d\tau_M. \tag{27}$$

The LHS of (27) is the cost of the subsidy/tax—the distortion in consumption patterns—while the RHS is the learning benefit. Optimality requires that the (static) marginal cost of a subsidy equal the (dynamic) marginal benefit.

As expected, if $c' = 0$, the solution to (27) entails $\tau_M = t_A = 0$: there is no scope for distortionary taxation. But if the RHS of (27) is positive, it is optimal to tax A (agriculture) to expand M (manufacturing), provided $(\beta_M + \beta_A) > 0$:

$$\tau_M = -\ h\rho\left(L^{t+1} / L_A^{\ t}\right)\beta_M / (\beta_M + \beta_A) \geq 0 \tag{28}$$

where, as before, $\rho = \delta\ V_I^{t+1}/V_I^t$, the discount rate for future income, reflecting both the pure discount factor δ and the normally lower marginal utility of income at $t + 1$ relative to t as a result of growth, and where[44]

[43] This model is, in fact, the limiting case of the two-sector model discussed earlier (with a sector 0 with no spillovers and a sector s with full spillovers), under the special case that $h_0 = 0$: there is no learning in the nonspillover sector. It is straightforward to generalize the results to the case in which there is some learning in the nonspillover sector. In this special case, we relabel the sectors, so $s = M$ (for manufacturing) and $0 = A$ (for agriculture).

[44] Alternatively, we can write $\beta_M = (d\ln x_M/d\ \ln (p_M/p_A))(d\ln (p_M/p_A)/d\ln \tau_M)$, where $d\ln (p_M/p_A)/d\ln \tau_M$ can be calculated in a straightforward way. Similarly for β_A.

$$\beta_M = d\ln x_M / d\ln\tau_M \geq 0, \quad \text{and}$$
$$\beta_A = -d\ln x_A / d\ln\tau_M \geq 0.$$

These are total derivatives, taking into account the indirect effect of the increased price of agricultural goods. Thus, normally we expect the subsidy to increase consumption of manufacturing and reduce the consumption of agricultural goods. It follows that

$$d\ln(x_M / x_A)/d\ln\tau_M = \beta_M + \beta_A.$$

This is the total change in relative consumption of the two goods as a result of the imposition of the subsidy on M paid for by a tax on A, the magnitude of which depends on the elasticity of substitution. If the elasticity of substitution is zero, then $\beta_M + \beta_A = 0$.[45]

When the elasticity of substitution is zero, there are neither benefits nor costs associated with the imposition of the subsidy/tax scheme. If the elasticity of substitutions is greater than zero, the size of the subsidy τ_M decreases with the share of manufacturers in consumption.

Again, we obtain the result that the larger the learning elasticity (h) the larger the subsidy.

Alternatively, the government may be able to borrow, even if private individuals cannot. It can impose taxes in the second period to repay the cost of first-period subsidies. Take the symmetric case. The government seeks to maximize

$$\text{Max } V^t((1-\tau_i),\ldots\ldots,0) + \delta V^{t+1}((1+t_i)c_i(\tau_{i,}\tau_{j\neq i}),\ldots\ldots,0)$$
$$\text{s.t.} \Sigma\tau_i x^t(1+r) = \Sigma t_i x_i^{t+1},$$

where r is the interest rate the government has to pay. In the symmetric case, we can, without loss of generality, simplify by assuming only one commodity; dropping the subscripts, we have $\tau x^t\,(1 + r) = t\,x^{t+1}$ and $c\,(x^t)$.

The first order condition is

$$\tau[V_I^t x^t - \delta(1+r)V_I^{t+1}x^t(1+\beta^t+\beta^{t+1})] + \delta V_I^{t+1}x^{t+1}c' x^t \beta^t(1+t) = 0,$$

where, in the obvious notation,[46]

$$\beta^t = d\ln x^t / d\ln\tau > 0$$

[45] Relative consumptions x_M/x_A is just a function of relative prices $(1 - \tau_M)/(1 + t_A) : x_M/x_A = Q((1 - \tau_M)/(1 + t_A))$. The elasticity of substitution is defined as $d\ln(x_M/x_A)/d\ln(1-\tau_M)/(1+t_A))$, where $dt_A/d\tau_M = (x_M/x_A) + \tau_M d(x_M/x_A)/d\tau_M$.

[46] Both of these are total derivatives, taking into account the direct effect of the change in τ and the indirect effect on the tax in the next period (t).

and

$$\beta^{t+1} = -d \ln x^{t+1} / d \ln \tau,$$

or simplifying

$$\tau\left[1-\rho(1+r)\left[1+\beta^t+\beta^{t+1}\right]\right]+\rho\left(L^{t+1}/L^t\right)h\beta^t=0.$$

$[1 - \rho(1 + r)(1 + \beta^t + \beta^{t+1})]$ is the benefit of borrowing money this period to be paid back next period. It is negative if r is high or ρ is high. We focus on the case where, in the absence of learning benefits, it would not be beneficial to borrow, that is,

$$\rho(1+r)\left(1+\beta^t+\beta^{t+1}\right)>1.$$

In that case, if there is learning, there is an optimal subsidy (financed by borrowing), given by (for small h)

$$\tau^* \approx \rho(L^{t+1}/L^t)h\beta^t / [\rho(1+r)\left(1+\beta^t+\beta^{t+1}\right)-1] > 0.$$

The subsidy is higher the higher the learning elasticity h; the lower the interest rate; and the more sensitive first period consumption (production) is to the subsidy (i.e., the higher β^t is for given β^{t+1}).

2.3.3 Part 2: Long-term Growth

Finite period models have gone out of fashion in economics in favor of infinite period models. To make such models tractable, however, requires much more special parameterizations, so that in practice neither model is really more general than the other. If there is to be a steady state with learning, since the output per unit of labor is increasing steadily, for the labor supply to any sector to be constant, either (a) the labor supply must be inelastic and relative prices must be constant or (b) utility of consumption must be logarithmic. Logarithmic utility functions have the unattractive property that the share of expenditure on each commodity is fixed. Normally, relative prices will be constant only with full spillovers (one of the cases we focus on, but clearly not general). Alternatively, we can focus on asymptotic behavior; for instance, where the fraction of a person's (society's) time spent working in any particular sector approaches some bound. But again, these asymptotes are often of limited interest in the short run (and we are always in the short run), especially since, in the general case of these models, asymptotic allocations of labor to certain sectors go to zero.

The problems posed by learning models are even more complicated in the case of, say, an exponentially growing population. Of course, with a finite earth, such models face a problem of asymptotically infinite density, which is, to say the least, uncomfortable. But more formally, if learning depends on labor input and labor input is always growing, then growth is always increasing, unless there is magically just the right amount of offsetting diminishing returns. One can find parameterizations in which this occurs, but we should not be fooled—they are very special.

Indeed, there is no theoretical reason to expect the episodic large innovations that have transformed our economy—electricity, computers, the automobile—to occur with regular periodicity and appropriate magnitude to sustain anything approximating a steady state.

In our own lifetime, we have seen dramatic transitions in the rate of population growth, to the point where it is even declining in many advanced industrial countries. There is a general consensus that the global population will level off (will *have* to level off) at around nine billion.

In short, we shouldn't take steady-state models excessively seriously. They are meant to help us think through trade-offs. In some cases—for instance, when we are focusing on issues of the demographic transition—more insight might be obtained from looking at N period models, where population is expanding in earlier periods and stationary in later periods. On the other hand, with a high enough discount, the distant future is of little moment, and a model focusing on the short run may provide a good approximation.

In the paragraphs below, we briefly explore special cases in which a steady state exists. We structure the cases so that whatever is optimal at time t is optimal at time $t + 1$; in that case, policy is directed at choosing the optimum steady state. In all the cases, the central result is that it is optimal to permanently impose distorting taxes to encourage production in the learning sector.

In the previous sections, we have explored models in which the government directly controls outputs (inputs), in which it has indirect control through taxes but can impose lump sum taxes, and in which it cannot impose lump sum taxes. We have also explored models in which learning is symmetric or asymmetric. In this section, we investigate only two cases; the results can easily be generalized to the other contexts.

2.3.3.1 Logarithmic Utility Functions

We first assume a logarithmic utility function

$$u^t = \Sigma\alpha_i \ln x^t{}_i, \Sigma\alpha_i = 1$$

and

$$W^t = u^t - v\left(L^t\right),$$

which at each moment of time implies (in static maximization)

$$\alpha_i / x^t_i = p_i v'\left(L^t\right),$$

which in turn implies that

$$x_i^t p_i = \alpha_i / v'\left(L^t\right).$$

Expenditure shares are equal to α_i and don't depend at all on costs. We focus on the direct control problem where the government sets $\{v, L\}$, where v_i is the share of total labor allocated to the production of good *i*. In the short run, as before, we assume the cost of each good is unity. Then

$$W^t = \Sigma_i \alpha_i \ln \upsilon^t_i + \ln L - v\left(L\right) \equiv W_o,$$

from which it follows that static optimization entails $v_i^t = \alpha_i$, and $1 = v'(L^*)L^*$. Note that the short-run optimum *L* does not depend on productivity.

We assume that, as before, productivity at time $t + 1$ is related to productivity at time *t* by a learning function, which we now write as

$$P_i^{t+1} = P_i^t\, H_i^t\, (\upsilon L),$$

where P_i^t is output per unit labor at time *t* and $\boldsymbol{vL}$ is the vector of labor inputs. If *L* and $\boldsymbol{v}$ are the same at *t* and $t + 1$, then

$$u^{t+1} = u^t + \Sigma \alpha_i \ln H_i^t\, (\upsilon L) = u^t + g\, (\upsilon L).$$

$g\,(\boldsymbol{vL})$ is the overall rate of productivity increase (measured here in terms of utility). It should be clear that, given the structure of the model, if $\boldsymbol{vL}$ is optimal for time *t*, it is optimal for time $t + 1$. We can write discounted utility[47]

$$\mathcal{W} = \Sigma\, W^t \delta^t = [W_o + \delta\, g/(1 - \delta)]/(1 - \delta),$$

from which it follows that $\mathcal{W}$ is maximized when

$$\partial W_o / \partial \upsilon_i + \left[\delta / \left(1 - \delta\right)\right] \partial g / \partial \upsilon_i = 0$$

[47] $u^{t+n} = U_o + n\, g . \Sigma n\, g\, \delta^n = \Sigma \delta\, g\, \delta^n / 1 - \delta = \delta\, g / (\,1 - \delta)^2$

$$\partial W_o / \partial L + \left[\delta / (1-\delta)\right] \partial g / \partial L = 0,$$

from which it follows that we expand production beyond short-run utility maximization the most in sectors that increase g the most; in this model, industrial policy is a permanent feature of the economy. Moreover, we increase work (labor supply) beyond the level of short-run utility maximization.

It is easy to derive the implications for some special cases. Assume that there are two sectors, A and M, and there is learning only in the M sector. Then

$$g = \alpha_M \ln H\left(\upsilon_M L\right)$$

and the optimum value of

$$\upsilon_M = \alpha_M \left[1 + h\delta / (1-\delta)\right] / \left[\ 1 + \alpha_M h\delta / (1-\delta)\right],$$

where $h = (d\ln H/d\ln \upsilon_M L)$.

The greater h, the larger the larger the fraction of labor allocated to manufacturing. When $h = 0$, as expected, $\upsilon_M = \alpha_M$. By the same token, work at each date is expanded beyond the static level, to the point where

$$1/L - \nu' = -h\delta\ \alpha_M / (1-\delta) L < 0,$$

(the static marginal disutility of work exceeds the value of the marginal output), or L^{**} now satisfies

$$L\nu' = 1 + h\delta\ \alpha_M / (1-\delta)$$

2.3.3.2 *Fixed Labor Supply, No Lump Sum Taxation*

In the second case, the labor supply is fixed and lump sum taxes are not allowed. There are two sectors, denoted A and M. Here, we have an additional problem in steady-state analysis. If there is differential growth in labor productivity in the two sectors, one sector gets a smaller, with a diminishing share of overall expenditures, except in the special case of unitary elasticity of substitution (the logarithmic utility case just analyzed). Accordingly, we focus on the case with full spillover, so that relative prices remain unchanged, and with homotheticity, so do relative shares. We assume a homothetic utility function of the form

$$U = U(x_M, x_A) = x_A^{-\eta+1} u(x_M / x_A), 0 < \eta < 1,$$

where, as before, η is the elasticity of marginal utility. As before, we impose a subsidy at the rate τ on manufacturing paid for by a tax at rate t on agriculture. We can write the indirect utility function then as $V(1 - \tau, 1 + t, I)$. Static utility maximization entails maximizing V with respect to τ:

$$\begin{aligned} dV/d\tau &= -x_A \tau \left[d(x_M / x_A)/d\tau \right] V_I \\ &= -x_M \left[d\ln(x_M / x_A)/d\ln\tau \right] V_I \\ &= -x_M (\beta_M + \beta_A) V_I \end{aligned}$$

Static efficiency entails, as before, $\tau = 0$.[48] But now assume that there is learning only in the manufacturing sector but perfect spillover to the agricultural sector. Productivity growth is thus $H(x_M)$. Again, we have structured the model so that the optimal subsidy at time t is the optimal subsidy at $t + 1$, and the present discounted value of utility is given by

$$U_o / (1 - \delta H^{-\eta+1}),$$

where U_0 and H are both functions of τ.

The optimal subsidy rate is as before.

2.3.3.3 Cumulative Experience

We now take a somewhat different approach in which changes in productivity are based not directly on current production but on the change in cumulative experience. (Effectively, Arrow's original model was of this form.) That is, we write, in the absence of spillovers,

$$Q^k(t) = H^k(t) L^k(t),$$

where now, say, productivity depends on discounted cumulative experience E according to the function

$$H^k(t) = [E]^{b^k}$$

48 Recall the definitions of β_M and β_A in section 2.3.2.5.

where b^k is the elasticity of productivity with respect to experience in sector k, and where experience E is defined by[49]

$$E = \left[\int_0^t L^k(x) e^{-z(t-x)} dx \right],$$

capturing the notion that experiences a long time ago have limited relevance for productivity today. In steady state, it is obvious that

$$g^k = d \ln Q^k / dt = (b^k + 1) n,$$

where n is the rate of growth of population. Even though learning is endogenous, we obtain the standard Solow result that the long-term sectoral growth rate is determined by the rate of growth of population. The fact that learning is affected by experience is still important, because the aggregate growth rate is affected by the allocation of resources. Assume, for instance, individual logarithmic utility function

$$\mathcal{W}^t = \Sigma (x_j^t) \alpha_i - v(L^t), \quad \Sigma \alpha_i = 1,$$

exponential labor force growth at the rate n, and a social welfare function of the form

$$\mathcal{W} = \int \exp(-r + n) W^t,$$

where r is the discount rate, $r > n + g$, where g is the rate of growth of utility (output, if U has constant returns to scale). In steady state,

$$\mathcal{W} = W^* / (n + g - r).$$

With learning, in steady state, W is increasing at the rate

$$g = \Sigma \alpha^k (b^k + 1) n.$$

Clearly, allocating more labor to sectors with higher learning elasticities will lead to higher rates of growth of utility. As before, let υ_i be the fraction of the

[49] For convenience, we switch to continuous time. Analogous results hold in the discrete time version.

labor supply allocated to sector i. For simplicity, we can express W^* (in steady state) as a function of $\{L, v\}$. Then, we want to choose the allocation that

$$\text{maximizes } W^*\{L, v\}/n + g(L, v) - r$$

implying that we distort the allocation of $\{L, v\}$, relative to static utility maximization, to increase long-run growth.[50] The optimum balances the two effects. Because increasing L increases cumulative experience, it increases productivity, and long-term social welfare maximization takes this into account. Like an increase in the savings rate in the standard Solow growth model, an increase in L does not, however, have any effect on long-term growth rates. The allocation of labor does.

2.3.3.4 Asymmetric Equilibria and the Advantages of Specialization

Learning, as we have noted, introduces nonconvexities, which may make it desirable for countries to specialize. The learning curves introduced in the previous section suffer from diminishing returns and therefore don't capture this effect. If, for instance, there were two commodities, with $\alpha = ½$, then, $v^* = ½$.

Assume that

$$H^k(t) = \left[\int_0^t L^k(x)e^{-z(t-x)}dx\right]^b \text{ if } E \geq E^*$$

$$= \hat{H} \text{ if } E < E^*$$

and $\hat{H}(E)$ is a convex function, such that $\hat{H}(0) = 1$, $\hat{H}(E^*) = E^{*b}$.[51]

Assume further that

$$u^k = \log x^k \textit{ if } x^k \geq 1$$
$$= 0 \text{ otherwise}$$

[50] The full intertemporal maximization problem is somewhat more complicated and can be analyzed using standard techniques.

[51] The simplest form is $\hat{H} = 1$ for $E < E^*$; that is, there is no learning. There is then a discontinuity at E^*.

where now x^k represents individual consumption. (We introduce this assumption because otherwise, as x^k goes to zero, the marginal utility of consumption goes to infinity, and we always produce both goods.)

It follows that if L is small enough, then optimality may require, say, $v_1 = 1$, $v_2 = 0$. The economy specializes in one of the two commodities. As we specialize in commodity 2, H^2/H^1 becomes small (there is no cumulative experience in producing good 2), so it becomes optimal both statically and dynamically not to produce good 1.

2.3.3.5 *Cumulative Learning from Output*

A slight variant of the previous model focuses on output rather than input. The difference arises from that fact that with learning, output grows more rapidly than input.[52] Assume now that the relevant measure of "experience" is

$$E = \left[\int_0^t Q^k(x)e^{-z(t-x)}dx\right]$$

$$H^k(t) = \left[\int_0^t Q^k(x)e^{-z(t-x)}dx\right]^b,$$

so in *steady* state (where the same fraction of labor is allocated to any sector every year)

$$g^k = bg^k + n = n/(1-b),$$

where it will be remembered that $b < 1$. If $b > 1$, faster growth begets faster growth of experience, which begets even faster growth of output. The economy is unstable, with potentially super-exponential growth. While the steady states of this model look very much like those of the earlier models, in which experience is based on labor input, more general versions of this model can give rise to multiple short-run equilibria. Assume that $H^k(E)$ does not have constant elasticity.[53] Then, assuming that at each date, L is fixed,

[52] As we noted in section 2.3.2.1, Arrow's original model focused on learning through investment. But with the capital output ratio fixed, cumulative investment grows with output.

[53] Long-run steady states require asymptotically constant elasticities.

$$g^k = h(E)d\ln E/dt + n + d\ln \upsilon^k/dt.$$

Since E and $d\ln E/dt$ depend on g^k, there can be short/medium rate high-growth scenarios: a high level of expansion of a sector can lead to a higher elasticity of learning (e.g., if there is learning by learning), which supports the higher expansion of the sector. The implications for optimal policy are similar to those discussed earlier: even if two sectors initially appear symmetric, it may be optimal to focus on one of the two sectors to increase learning; but now it is possible that the increased growth induced by the faster learning is further reinforced by a higher learning elasticity.

2.4 MONOPOLISTIC COMPETITION

A similar analysis applies to a model with monopolistic competition. In the previous models, there was competition and learning was external to the firm, so that each firm put no value on the learning generated by its production activities. In this model, there is only one firm in each sector, but there are a sufficiently large number of products that each firm can take the wages and prices of other firms as given. As before, industrial policy depends on the set of instruments available to the government; for example, whether it can undo the effects of monopoly and whether it can impose lump sum taxes. Here, we assume that the government can do nothing about the monopoly power of each firm but that in setting, say, a subsidy for any product, it takes into account that markets are distorted as a result of monopolistic competition.

The major difference between this case and those analyzed in the previous section is that if there are no cross-sector learning externalities, the monopolistically competitive firm internalizes the learning externality. However, the firm still does not internalize cross-sector demand effects. We begin the analysis, however, by focusing on the case in which these can be ignored. The firm sets

$$\left(p_i^t + x_i^t dp_i^t / dx_i^t\right) = 1 - \delta x_i^{t+1} H_i^i / \left(H^i\right)^2 \tag{29}$$

or

$$p_i^t\,(1 - 1/\acute{\eta}_i) = 1 - \delta \zeta_i h_i$$

or

$$p^t{}_i = [1 - \delta \zeta_i h_i]/(1 - 1/\acute{\eta}_i) \tag{30}$$

where (as before) $\zeta_i = L_i^{t+1}/L_i^t$, the ratio of the input into sector j at time t to that at $t + 1$, $h_i = d\ln H^i/d\ln L_i^t$, the (own) elasticity of productivity with respect to labor input (the learning coefficient) and $1/\acute{\eta}_i = -d\ln p_i/d\ln x_i$, the elasticity of demand.

The monopolist obviously doesn't take into account the consequences of his production/pricing decisions on the learning of other firms—either through spillover effects or through market effects. The latter can be important in the case of a nonseparable demand function. But he does take into account his own learning, and so sets a price lower than he would if there were no learning. Firms with more elastic demand functions charge a lower price (and produce more the first period); but firms with a more inelastic demand show a greater sensitivity to learning (i.e., all firms lower their price as h increases, but those with a higher markup—lower price elasticity—lower their price more. They have to, in order to expand output.)

The nature of the overall market distortion is, however, complex. For instance, in the second period, because of the exercise of monopoly power, the benefits of learning will be smaller. But, given the lower level of output in the second period, ignoring spillovers, the firm appropriately values the benefits of learning, which it sees, at the margin, as saving labor.[54]

There can be distortions in both total labor supply in the first period and in its allocation. Consider, for instance, a symmetric equilibrium in which all firms have the same demand and learning elasticities. The effect of monopolistic competition is to change real wages in the first period. If first-period labor supply elasticity is zero, this has no effect on learning. An awareness of the learning benefits drives up the real wage, but that is all that happens. First- and second-period output is unchanged. But if there is a positive elasticity of labor supply, the analysis becomes more interesting. In the case of myopic monopolistic competition (where no weight is given to the value of future learning), first period real wages are lowered as a result of monopoly power, labor supply is lowered, output is lowered, and learning is thereby lowered. *With myopic monopolies, monopoly is unambiguously worse than competition; even though neither takes into account the benefits of learning, growth is higher with competition than with monopoly.*

With nonmyopic monopoly, whether learning (growth) is higher with monopoly depends on whether

$$[1-\delta\zeta_i h_i]/(1-1/\acute{\eta}_i) < \text{or} > 1, \tag{31}$$

[54] In particular, the value of ζ_i is sensitive to the elasticity of demand, the amount of learning in this sector, the elasticity of labor supply, what happens in other sectors, and so on. As we have noted, $p_i^t = (1 - \delta\,\zeta_i\, h_i)/(1 - 1/\acute{\eta}_i)$. On the other hand, $p_i^{t+1} = 1/H^i(1 - 1/\acute{\eta}_i)$. If $H^i = 1/(1 - \delta\,\zeta_i\, h_i)$, the price would be the same both periods. The smaller the elasticity of demand, the higher the mark-up, so the larger the sensitivity of price to any differences between H^i and $1/(1 - \delta\,\zeta_i\, h_i)$.

that is, on whether

$$\delta\zeta_i h_i > \text{or} < 1/\acute{\eta}_i . \tag{32}$$

If the elasticity of demand is low, the elasticity of learning is small, or the rate of discount is high, then monopoly is worse than competition, even though the benefits of learning have been internalized.

The general principles of government intervention should be clear. Government has to correct two market failures and must be careful that in correcting one, it does not exacerbate the other. Focusing only on learning, optimal policy entails encouraging production in the first period by a production subsidy financed (if possible) by a lump sum tax. If a lump sum tax is not possible but the country can borrow, it pays to finance the first-period subsidy with a second-period tax.

Precise prescriptions for the design of optimal intervention depend on what the government can do. For instance, if the government can impose a nondistortionary profits tax and use it to subsidize production in the first and second periods, it can presumably fully undo the effects of monopoly. If it can undo the effects of second-period monopoly, the formulas derived earlier can be used.

If it can only, say, impose a lump sum tax to finance a commodity subsidy in the first period, then it seeks to

$$\underset{\{\tau\}}{\text{Max}}\, V^t(p^t, -\Sigma\tau_i x_i) + \delta V^{t+1}(p_i^{t+1}, 0) \tag{33}$$

where

$$p_i^t = \kappa_i(1-\tau_i) \tag{34}$$

$$p_i^{t+1} = \kappa_i / H^i \tag{35}$$

where

$$\kappa_i = 1/(1-1/\acute{\eta}_i), \tag{36}$$

the monopoly markup over marginal cost. When we introduce a subsidy, we undo the first-period monopoly distortion and correct the underinvestment in production/learning distortion.[55] If we could impose similar corrective taxation in the second period, we could achieve precisely the equilibrium

[55] For instance, in the absence of learning, by setting κ_i $(1 - \tau_i) = 1$, or $(1 - \tau_i) = 1/\kappa_i$ or $\tau = 1 - 1/\kappa_i = 1/\acute{\eta}_i$, we can correct the monopoly distortion.

described earlier for the competition case. If not, we have to take into account the fact that the benefits of learning are lower, because future production is lower. Hence, in general, optimal subsidies will be lower.

The more interesting case is that in which there are two sectors, one (manufacturing) with a full learning spillover and the other (agriculture) with no learning. In this case, it can be shown that not only is a subsidy on manufacturing desirable, there is even some presumption that it should be larger with monopoly than with competition.

We now have

$$\underset{\{\tau_M\}}{\text{Max}}\ V^t(\kappa_M(1-\tau_M),\kappa_A(1+t_A),0)+\delta V^{t+1}(\kappa_M c(L_M),\kappa_A c(L_M),0), \tag{37}$$

where, as before, the subsidy to manufacturing is financed by a tax on agriculture.

$$\begin{aligned} V_I^t & \left[(\kappa_M-\kappa_A)\,x_M-\kappa_A x_A \tau_M d\left(x_M/x_A\right)/\,d\tau_M)\right] \\ & =-\delta V_I^{t+1} c'\left(L_M\right)(\kappa_M x_M^{t+1}+\kappa_A x_A^{t+1}\ )dx_M^t/\,d\tau_M, \end{aligned} \tag{38}$$

where, it will be recalled,

$$dt_A/d\tau_M=\left(x_M/x_A\right)+\tau_M d\left(x_M/x_A\right)/\,d\tau_M.$$

The following differences from the earlier equation (27) are apparent:

(a) The change in relative prices may correct or exacerbate a distortion in relative consumption caused by differences in demand elasticities. In the case where demand elasticities are the same, the LHS of (38) simplifies to

$$-\tau_M(d\left(x_M/x_A\right)/\,d\tau_M)\kappa_A x_A,$$

which is negative.

(b) Lowering costs has a multiplicative effect on prices in the next period, so the benefits of learning are enhanced. In the case where demand elasticities are the same, the benefits are multiplied by a factor $\kappa_M = \kappa_A$ (as are the costs). Moreover, an increase in the subsidy leads to a decrease in the price by a multiple (and an increase in the price of the agricultural good by a corresponding multiple), so that with monopoly, $dx_M^t/d\tau_M$ is much larger than with competition (as is $dx_M^t/x_A^t)/d\tau$). Moreover, under normal assumptions, c' with monopoly is higher but $x_M^{t+1}+x_A^{t+1}$ is smaller, because real wages are smaller and productivity is lower.

2.5 OPEN ECONOMY

The most interesting context for analyzing government intervention is that of a small, open, developing economy. The question is, should it use trade policy (tariffs or foreign exchange intervention)? Such policies change the structure of the economy. Can it do so in ways that will enhance learning and promote welfare? And even if it can, are these the best instruments available?

2.5.1 Two-sector Economy

First, consider a two-sector economy, comprising agriculture and manufacturing, in a Ricardian world in which labor is the only input to production. In the simplest version of this model, the country can produce both goods and exchange some of the tradable goods for imports.

The developing country is small relative to the global economy and is assumed initially to have a comparative advantage in the agricultural good. The agricultural good has no direct learning potential but industrial production has considerable learning potential, and the benefits of learning spill over perfectly to the agricultural sector. This is important, because it means that the relative price of agriculture and industrial goods remains fixed.

In the absence of protection (or some other industrial policy), the small developing country specializes in agriculture and hence has no growth. It stagnates, while the large developed country continues to grow. The gap between the two increases over time.[56]

With protection—say, in the form of quotas—the country produces some of the industrial good, generating some learning, which spills over to the rest of the economy. There is a static inefficiency, but so long as the learning is sufficiently great, the static inefficiency is more than offset by the dynamic benefits.

Assume, for instance, that the labor supply is (in the absence of intervention) fixed at unity (this is just a normalization);[57] that a fraction of the labor force π is assigned to the industrial sector; that the short-term productivity in the industrial sector relative to that in the advanced industrial country is $\gamma < 1$ (where we have normalized productivity abroad at unity); and that a proportion of the production of the agricultural sector λ is traded for industrial goods from the developed country (at a price of unity). Then, at any moment in time,

$$\begin{aligned} U &= \alpha_M \ln M + (1-\alpha_M)\ln A \\ &= \alpha_M \ln(\pi\gamma + (1-\pi)\lambda) + (1-\alpha_M)\ln((1-\lambda)(1-\pi)) = U^*. \end{aligned} \tag{39}$$

[56] It is easy to modify our model to allow a steady-state degree of disparity: all we have to assume is that knowledge diffuses freely from the developed to the less developed country with a lag of N years.

[57] As we noted in section 2.3.3.2, the assumption of a fixed labor supply is, however, not innocuous.

It is easy to show that U is maximized at $\pi = 0$; that is, the country specializes in the production of agricultural goods. This is the conventional static result.[58]

But now we assume that the country's rate of productivity increase is $g(\pi)$, $g' > 0$; that is, the rate of productivity growth increases with the size of the industrial sector. There is full spillover from the industrial sector to the agricultural sector. Because of this assumption (and a similar assumption in the global market), the country's comparative advantage remains with agriculture. The problem facing the country in the next period is essentially the same problem facing the country this year. If consumption of both goods at $t + 1$ is $(1 + g)$ times consumption at t, $U^{t+1} = U^t + \ln(1 + g)$. Hence, if δ is the discount rate, the present discount value of utility is[59]

$$\mathcal{W} \equiv \left\{U^* + \delta\left[\ln(1+g)/(1-\delta)\right]\right\}/(1-\delta). \tag{40}$$

And it is no longer the case that maximizing social welfare ($\mathcal{W}$) entails $\pi = 0$. It immediately follows that

$$\partial U^*/\partial \ln \pi + G\left[g/(1+g)\right]\left[\delta/(1-\delta)\right] = 0, \tag{41}$$

where $G = d\ln g/d\ln \pi$, which implies that, so long as $G > 0$ (there is a marginal benefit to learning) optimality requires that $\pi > 0$: the dynamic benefits of learning exceed the static costs. Industrial policies pay off. The greater the learning elasticity and the higher δ (the lower the discount factor), the higher π; that is, the higher the optimal static distortion.

This framework requires industrial policies that allow for a limited industrial sector, even though the country has a comparative disadvantage in that sector in the short run and, in this model, even in the long run. That is, in our Ricardian model, with full spillovers, technological change does not change

58 $d\,\alpha_M \ln\,(\pi\gamma+(1-\pi)\lambda)+(1-\alpha_M)\ln((1-\lambda)(1-\pi))/d\,\pi$
$= \alpha_M(\gamma-\lambda)/(\pi\gamma+(1-\pi)l)-(1-\alpha_M)/(1-\pi)$

$\alpha_M(\gamma-\lambda)/(\pi\gamma+(1-\pi)\lambda)-(1-\alpha_M)/(1-\pi) \leq 0 \text{ for } \pi \geq 0$ (provided $\gamma < 1$), at $\lambda = \lambda^*$, where λ^* is the solution to

$$d\,\alpha_M \ln(\pi\gamma+(1-\pi)\lambda)+(1-\alpha_M)\ln\,((1-\lambda)(1-\pi))/d\,\lambda$$
$$= \alpha_M(1-\pi)/(\pi\gamma+(1-\pi)\lambda)-(1-\alpha_M)/(1-\lambda) = 0$$

59 $U^{t+1} = U^t + \ln(1 + g)$, and, using the same techniques employed earlier, $\mathcal{W} = \Sigma\, U^*[(1 + t(\ln(1 + g)))]\delta t$, from which (40) follows directly. If U is not logarithmic but exhibits constant elasticity with respect to the scale of consumption (as before), with the elasticity of marginal utility of η, there is a parallel analysis.

the country's comparative advantage. The fact that the country's industrial sector never becomes competitive (the infant never grows up) is not necessarily an argument against industrial policies, when the learning spillovers are great enough.

In this model with a linear technology, the easiest way to implement the desired level of domestic production is through a quota, which ensures that at the equilibrium price, the desired amount of manufactured goods are produced at home. With increasing costs, there exists an optimal tariff, which would result in the desired level of domestic production.

2.5.2 Nontraded Sector

Finally, we consider a variant of the canonical Ricardian model in which there are three goods: exports, imports, and a nontradable good. Government intervention can affect either the price of tradables relative to nontradables or the price of imports relative to exports.

A slight variant of the previous model yields precisely the same results. Let us assume a more general homothetic utility function, with the obvious notation

$$\begin{aligned} U^* &= U(M, A, NT) \\ &= U((\pi\gamma + (1-\pi-\theta)\lambda), (1-\pi-\theta)(1-\lambda), \theta), \end{aligned}$$

where now θ is the fraction of the labor force allocated to the nontraded sector.

We again get the result that U^* is optimized at $\pi = 0$. But again, if the rate of learning is a function of the size of the industrial sector π, the economy should produce industrial goods even though those are not its comparative advantage.

We now consider what happens when international trade agreements restrict the use of industrial policies. The only instrument left is the exchange rate. Lowering the exchange rate simultaneously decreases the price of exports in foreign currency, leading to an increase in the demand for exports, and increases the price of imports (in domestic currency, relative to the price of nontraded goods). It thus encourages substitution away from imported consumption goods. Increased exports and reduced imports lead to a trade surplus.

In a two-period model, this means that the country consumes less than it could in the initial period, offset by increased consumption in the later period.[60]

[60] In our simple model, we assume individuals cannot borrow or lend, and simply solve a period-by-period static utility maximization problem, determining the allocation of current income among the three commodities. But it would be easy in principle (complicated in practice) to generalize the results to cases that include individual borrowing and lending, with precise effects depending on the structure of preferences (e.g., on separability of utility functions.)

As in the earlier models without trade, the static distortion (consuming less than what would normally maximize utility, based on the equality of the marginal rate of substitution and the interest rate) is justified by the dynamic benefits—producing more of the export good, say, leads to more learning, which generates a higher level of consumption in the second period than would otherwise be possible. This is true even though the range of instruments has now been restricted so the social cost of intervention is higher.

But if the learning effects are strong enough, even in an infinite period model, the benefits of expanding exports are sufficiently great that it may be possible that optimal policy requires the country to build up reserves forever, never to use them (essentially like throwing money away). We construct a model in which each period the world looks as it did the previous period, so that if it is desirable to have a surplus at time t, it is desirable to have a trade surplus at time $t + 1$. (Of course, in a more general dynamic model, it may be desirable to have trade surpluses initially, to be spent at later dates.)

Denote the exchange rate by e. Taking labor as our numeraire, and noting that by our choice of units the price of the nontraded goods is also unity (in the absence of taxes and subsidies, which, by assumption, are precluded), the price (and therefore the level of consumption) of the industrial and agriculture good are simply a function of e.

Hence, we obtain

$$U^* = U\left[M(e), A(e), NT(e)\right], \tag{42}$$

where consumption of agricultural goods is equal to production minus exports:

$$A(e) = (1-\pi-\theta)(1-\lambda), \tag{43}$$

where, it will be recalled, λ is the share of production exported, and where consumption of the industrial goods is production plus imports, m,

$$M(e) = \pi\gamma + m \tag{44}$$

Static utility maximization requires

$$(1-\pi-\theta)\lambda - m = S \geq 0, \tag{45}$$

where S is the balance of payments surplus. (Equation (45) is the balance of payments constraint.)

In a static model, U^* is maximized, subject to (45) (the balance of payments constraint), $1 > \lambda > 0$, $1 \geq \pi \geq 0$, and $1 \geq \theta \geq 0$. It is easy to show in the static model (i.e., with no learning) that free trade is optimal and the balance of payments constraint is binding:

$$\pi = 0, \; S = 0, \; \lambda > 0. \tag{46}$$

The equilibrium exchange rate can easily be calculated. In equilibrium, full income is

$$y = \theta + e(1-\theta) = y(e,\theta).$$

$$NT(e, y(e,\theta)) = \theta \tag{47a}$$

$$X = 1 - \theta - A(e, y(e,\theta)) \tag{47b}$$

$$m = M\,(e, y(e,\theta)) \tag{47c}$$

$$X = m \tag{47d}$$

where X = exports, and where $NT(e, y(e, \theta))$, $A(e, y(e, \theta))$ and $M\,(e, y(e, \theta))$ are, respectively the demand for nontraded goods, agricultural goods, and industrial goods, and where, because of the lack of comparative advantage in manufacturing, in the absence of government intervention, the country imports all manufactured goods. Equations (47b) to (47d) can be re-expressed as a function relating e and θ:

$$1 - \theta - A(e, \; y(e, \theta)) = M(e, \; y(e, \theta))$$

or

$$1 - \theta = A(e, \; y(e, \theta)) + M(e, \; y(e, \theta)). \tag{48}$$

Equations (48) and (47a) can be solved simultaneously for e and θ. Equations (47a) through (47d) can then be solved simultaneously for the full equilibrium. We assume the government controls e, and that the rate of growth depends on Q_M, the output of manufacturing goods, which in turn depends on e.

In the dynamic model, we can write again

$$W \equiv \left[U^* + \delta \ln(1+g)/(1-\delta)\right]/\left(1-\delta\right). \tag{49}$$

We now maximize $\mathcal{W}$ with respect to e (recognizing the effect of e on Q_M) to obtain an equation parallel to (41):

$$\partial \ln \; U^*/\partial \ln \; e + G\, g\, \delta \; \left(d \ln \; Q_M \,/\, d \ln \; e\right)/\left(1-\delta\right)\left(1+g\right) = 0. \tag{50}$$

If $\delta\, g\, G\, (d \ln Q_M\, (e)/d \ln e) > 0$, it means that at the optimum e, $\partial U^*/\partial \ln e < 0$.

Once learning is taken into account, it may pay to have a lower exchange rate than the equilibrium exchange rate described earlier. A lower exchange rate will mean that exports will increase and imports decrease, and (with the usual restrictions on demand functions) there is a trade surplus. It pays to perpetually accumulate reserves—to run a surplus—because of the learning benefits. (To repeat: this requires that no other instruments are available to promote learning; e.g., through exports.)

In our Ricardian model, with constant returns to scale, small changes in the exchange rate have no effect on production of the industrial good, given the developing country's comparative and absolute disadvantage in its production. But lowering the (real and nominal) exchange rate enough makes the industrial good competitive. Define e^{**} as the exchange rate at which firms are just indifferent between producing industrial goods and importing them. Assume that at e^{**} the government can choose a level of industrial output, $Q_M^{**} > 0$. Then we can solve for the equilibrium allocation of labor to the nontraded sector:

$$NT(e^{**},\ y(e^{**},\theta^{**})) = \theta^{**}.$$

The equilibrium level of exports is[61]

$$X = 1 - \theta^{**} - A(e^{**},\ y(e^{**},\theta^{**})) - O_M^{**}/\Upsilon),$$

while the level of imports is

$$m = M(e^{**},\ y(e^{**},\theta^{**})) - Q_M^{**}.$$

At every value of Q_M^{**}, we can calculate S:

$$S = X - m.$$

Then the optimal level of Q_M^{**}[62] solves

$$W^{**} = \underset{\{M^{**}\}}{\mathrm{Max}}\left[U\left(M\left(e^{**}\right),\ A\left(e^{**}\right),\ NT\left(e^{**}\right)\right) + \delta \ln\ \left(1+g\right)/\left(1-\delta\right)\right]\Big/(1-\delta) \tag{51}$$

subject to

$$S \geq 0$$

In general, the constraint will not be binding.

[61] Because of the inefficiency in the production, it takes, in effect, $1/\gamma$ units of domestic labor to produce 1 unit of industrial good. Hence, exports are the output of agricultural goods minus the consumption of agricultural goods, where the output of agricultural goods is total labor supply, less the input into nontraded goods and into the industrial sector.

[62] In effect, the supply curve is effectively horizontal at e^{**}.

If $\mathcal{W}^{**} > \mathcal{W}(e^*)$, it pays to lower the exchange rate to e^{**}. The country should run a surplus.

We should emphasize the sensitivity of this analysis to the assumptions that we have imposed to allow for a steady-state analysis. A fuller analysis would take into account the fact that as the country closes the knowledge gap between itself and the advanced industrial countries, learning benefits may decrease, perhaps to the point at which the cost of running a surplus—the lost utility from the foregone consumption—exceeds the learning benefit. The country might then want (as in our two-period model) to consume its accumulated surplus. Other factors would also affect the country's desired level of surplus. A country with an aging population might want to put aside savings and then, as the aging population enters into retirement, reduce that surplus. Such demographic transitions are not analyzed well in steady-state models.[63]

Some countries have been criticized for contributing to global imbalances by accumulating excessive reserves. In static models, it has seemed irrational for developing countries—suffering from capital shortages and with constrained consumption—to do so; just as it has seemed peculiar that the United States, with an aging population, is running long-term deficits. This chapter shows, however, that once dynamic learning benefits are taken into account, with sufficient constraints on industrial policies (such as those imposed by the World Trade Organization), the accumulation of reserves by a developing country (beyond a level required for precautionary reasons to manage global volatility) may be reasonable if the learning benefits are large enough. Interestingly, while this policy leads to a lower level of imports initially because of the induced growth, over the longer run, the country's level of imports is actually increased.[64]

2.6 CONCLUDING COMMENTS

I have argued here that what matters for development is *learning* and, more broadly, technical progress and a developmental transformation. I have

[63] One other interesting aspect characterizes the optimum pattern of reserve accumulation. If, in the earlier stages of development, learning benefits are sufficiently large that the country accumulates a surplus, using the indirect utility function, at the margin, an increase in the price of tradables (a further reduction in the price of nontradables) has a positive effect—it receives more for what it sells; while in later periods, when the country has a trade deficit (using up its surplus), a decrease in the exchange rate (the price the country has to pay for the goods it buys) has a negative effect. This provides further impetus for lowering exchange rates (further below equilibrium levels that would prevail in the absence of intertemporal effects) in earlier stages and increasing them later—exacerbating patterns of "global imbalances."

[64] An analysis of the full global general equilibrium effects of such policies, if pursued by enough developing countries to have systemic effects, is beyond the scope of this chapter.

focused on a simple model of learning, but even within that simple model we have seen how much of recent conventional wisdom about development strategies is overturned. The standard paradigm has focused on eliminating market distortions—ensuring that the economy is on its static production (or, more generally, utility)[65] possibilities curve, based on a given level of knowledge. More important in the long run, however, is moving the possibilities curve outward—for advanced industrial economies by advances in technology; for developing countries by closing the knowledge gap between advanced industrial countries and developing countries; and for all countries by ensuring that all firms are employing best practices[66] as rapidly as possible. Moving toward the frontier (for instance, by eliminating all tariffs and quotas) might entail slowing down the pace of outward movement of the frontier—and slower long-run growth, with the benefit of but a one-time gain.

A full analysis of what makes for a learning economy would take us beyond this short chapter. We can *learn to learn* (Stiglitz 1987c)—we can enhance our learning capacities. Just as what we produce may affect how much we learn, it may affect how we learn to learn. Just as "roundabout means of production" (to use Böhm-Bawerk's terminology) may be more efficient, roundabout means of learning may be more efficient. We can learn more efficiently if we first learn how to learn.[67]

Once one recognizes the importance of learning and developmental transformation (Stiglitz 1998), analysis must go beyond economics. Education can either reinforce norms of *statis* or persuade young people that change is possible and give them tools with which to bring about and cope with change. A variety of institutions and institutional arrangements can either promote or prevent the development of a culture of change.[68]

In this chapter, we have focused on the economics of learning. From the earliest literature on endogenous technological change—when the public-good

[65] The utility possibilities curve gives the maximum level of utility for an individual given the level of utility of others.

[66] As Greenwald and Stiglitz (2014) point out, even in advanced industrial countries, most firms operate well below best practices.

[67] Operationally, we can think of dividing the learning period into two subperiods. In the first, we devote ourselves to improving our learning skills; in the second, we use those learning skills to learn about the subject at hand. (Here, we ignore the problem posed by the possibility of infinite regress: we can learn how to learn how to learn....)

[68] Sah and Stiglitz (1989a, 1989b), Stiglitz (1995b), and Hoff and Stiglitz (2001) show that there can, in fact, be multiple societal equilibria. Hoff and Stiglitz (2010) use recent results in psychology to underpin an analysis of the interactions between prior beliefs and societal change, explaining how some societies can become trapped in a seemingly dysfunctional equilibrium for an extended period, while other societies seem to evolve more smoothly. Politics and economics also interact: repressive and authoritarian societies are, in a fundamental sense, incompatible with the kind of questioning of authority that is associated with a dynamic learning society. See Stiglitz (2010b).

nature of knowledge, the problems of appropriability, and the pervasiveness of spillovers were recognized—it was apparent that markets on their own were not likely to be efficient and that the overall efficiency of the market would depend on market structure in rather complex ways—with monopolies restricting output but internalizing the benefits of learning. Schumpeter recognized that this was a problem in the second best.[69] He tried to defend monopoly on the grounds (in modern language) that it partially solved the appropriability problem and the problems posed by imperfect capital markets. While the question is in some sense not appropriately posed (market structure should be viewed as endogenous, and in the absence of full spillovers, competitive markets may be hard to sustain), this chapter shows that even though monopolists internalize their own learning benefits, the distortion associated with underproduction (monopoly pricing) may lead to less learning than in a competitive market with optimal intervention.

Previously, most of the growth literature has focused on aggregate models in which the scope for allocative decisions was very limited (e.g., sectoral allocations played little role in aggregate growth rates). Insufficient attention has been paid to the design of policy interventions (and the parameters on which they should depend) to correct systemic market failures, especially in the presence of cross-sectoral spillovers. This chapter has provided a simple context in which market distortions—on both the aggregate supply of labor and its allocation—can be analyzed and the kinds of interventions (typically second- or third-best interventions, predicated on the existence of certain restrictions on the set of admissible policies) that might address them.

The chapter thus provides both a case for industrial policies and the beginning of an analysis of the optimal design of such policies. Many of the results are not surprising, though the simplicity of the forms of intervention (at least in some limiting cases) is striking. Simple formulas akin to those arising in the theory of optimal taxation are derived. The size of the static distortions (reflected in subsidies) increases, as expected, with learning elasticities and knowledge spillovers—with the latter taking on a particularly prominent role. Patterns of subsidies are affected, too, in easily understandable ways by patterns of demand interdependence. Intertemporal trade-offs are captured by the pure rate of discount as well as the rate at which marginal utility of income diminishes as a result of increasing productivity (which, in turn, depends on the elasticity of marginal utility and the rate of progress), with the intuitive result that the smaller the value at the margin of future consumption, the less distortion (the smaller the subsidy) to induce

[69] Before the term "second best" had come into fashion through the work of Meade (1955) and Lipsey and Lancaster (1956–7).

learning. But now the intertemporal trade-off is partly endogenous and other factors come to play a role, especially the elasticity of labor supply and a scale parameter reflecting the size of the economy at $t + 1$ relative to time t. Indeed, in the limiting case of symmetric learning and demand functions, we have shown that regardless of the learning elasticity, if the elasticity of labor supply is zero, the market equilibrium may be Pareto efficient. More generally, the magnitude of interventions also depends on labor supply elasticities. A particular complicating factor which we have noted is that, given the nonconvexities naturally associated with learning, optimal intervention may lead to asymmetric equilibria, even when all demand and learning functions are symmetric.

We noted that one of the standard objections to industrial policies in the past has been political: the potential for misuse. This poses an important trade-off. Broad-based measures such as exchange rate interventions require only that the government ascertain that the sectors that would be encouraged by such interventions have more societal learning benefits than the sectors that would be discouraged—and there is ample evidence that that is the case (evidenced by the success of export-led growth strategies). Firms and sectors within the economy self-select, and the expansion of firms and sectors with greater learning enhances the dynamism of the economy. On the other hand, more targeted interventions can lead to even more learning and faster rates of growth. No intervention completely "solves" the political economy problem. Sectors that benefit from exchange rate intervention may lobby for the maintenance of that intervention even in the absence of learning benefits. And some countries have shown that they can manage the political economy problems of more targeted interventions. The East Asian countries did so by using rule-based systems in which interventions were linked to past export success.

In any case, no government can completely absolve itself of the necessity of addressing the issues with which we have been concerned. For while we have focused on the use of taxes and subsidies to alter the structure of production and encourage more learning, different government investments in infrastructure, technology, and education affect different industries differently. In making such decisions, we argue that the government should take into account impacts on societal learning that will shape the country's dynamic comparative advantage.

We have focused on a model with a single factor of production: labor. The early learning literature[70] focused on learning through investment. Obviously, if countries learn through investment, there is an argument for

[70] See, in particular, Arrow (1962a). See also Solow (1997).

encouraging investment, especially in sectors that have a greater learning elasticity and greater spillovers. Standard international trade arguments demonstrate that taxes on imports, if imports are labor-intensive, will drive up wages and lower interest rates, thus encouraging more investment (Korinek and Servén 2010).

We have emphasized the importance of developing policies that maximize effective learning. In our simple model, we have assumed that different sectors have different learning curves, with different spillovers to other sectors. Identifying these learning functions is necessary to design appropriate government policies. Elsewhere, Greenwald and Stiglitz (2014) have discussed some of the factors that contribute to greater learning and greater spillovers. They argue that the manufacturing sector may have both greater learning potential and greater spillovers. Different countries may have different learning elasticities. Countries that are too distant in technology may have more difficulty closing the gap than countries that are somewhat closer, while for some countries there is little gap to close. Hence, learning elasticities (at least in some sectors) may be low for both the least developed countries and those that are near best practices.

Our simplified model also circumvents a central question: learning toward what end? Much of technological change in advanced developed countries has been directed toward saving labor, which is viewed as the "scarce factor." In developing countries, however, labor is in abundance—levels of unemployment are often high. A reduced demand for labor exacerbates the problem of unemployment. To put it another way, in these situations, the shadow wage and the market wage may differ. Innovation responds to market wages; innovation in the advanced industrial countries responds to the high market wages there.

It has long been recognized that technologies that are appropriate for developed countries may be less appropriate for developing countries. This means that developing countries may have less to learn from developed countries than is sometimes supposed;[71] their learning and research should be directed not so much at saving labor (the shadow price of which may be very low) as at saving capital and natural resources, and protecting the environment.[72]

[71] There is an old (and largely forgotten) literature on the determinants of the factor bias of technological change. For a more recent attempt to develop a general theory of the endogenous determination of the factor bias and the equilibrium level of unemployment, using a variant of the efficiency wage model, see Stiglitz (2006a).

[72] Some might argue that with globalization, the price of capital has become the same everywhere in the world. But this view ignores the importance of information and other market imperfections, the effect of which is to make the effective price of capital higher in some countries than in others. See, for example, Greenwald and Stiglitz (2003).

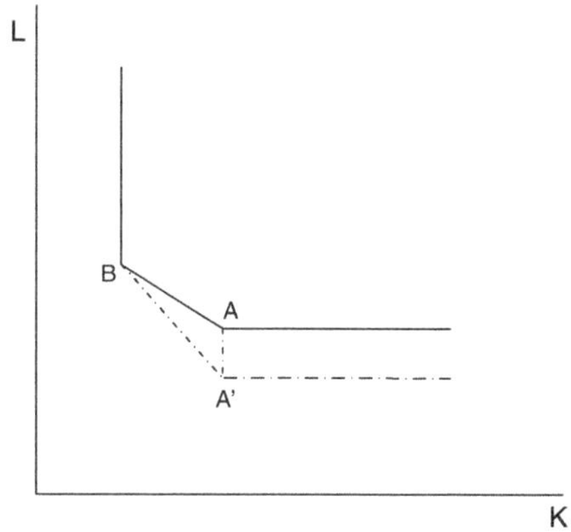

Figure 2.1 An isoquant with two technologies, one (A) appropriate to a high-wage economy, the other (B) appropriate to a low-wage economy

Four decades ago, when we were thinking about these issues at Cambridge, Tony Atkinson and I introduced the concept of "localized technological change" (Atkinson and Stiglitz 1969). Technological change affected only certain production processes. An innovation could improve, for instance, some very advanced technologies but leave traditional technologies largely unaffected. Indeed, as noted earlier in this chapter, the spillovers might be greater to advanced technologies in other sectors than to simple (say, nonautomatic) processes in the same sector.[73] This has an important implication. If developing countries resort to learning and adapting technologies created for circumstances prevalent in developed countries, the advances may be of limited value to their own economies. Emerging markets and developing countries need to develop their own research and learning capacities so they can improve the technologies that are appropriate to their economic circumstances. Thus, the point of industrial policies is not just to catch up to the advanced industrial countries, but to promote advances in technology that are appropriate to their circumstances and enhance their ability to make additional advances in these technologies.

Figure 2.1 illustrates an isoquant with two technologies, one (A) appropriate to a high-wage economy, the other (B) appropriate to a low-wage economy. Advances in technology in the advanced industrial economy move A downward (lower labor requirements per unit of output) but leave B unchanged. If the developing country simply borrows (say, with a lag)

[73] Indeed, that is one of the reasons we have emphasized cross-sector learning spillovers in this chapter.

technology from the advanced industrial country, it initially gets no benefit (if it produces the good at all, it continues to use the unchanged technology B) until the cost savings from lower labor costs are so overwhelming that the country switches to A.

The fact that the country's technology remains unchanged implies that if it did not initially have a comparative advantage in the good (say, the industrial product), its comparative disadvantage may increase over time. But even if the country does not have a comparative advantage in the good and never will, the nontraded sector (or the agriculture sector) might benefit from spillovers.

If, however, the country is able to develop its own learning capacities (e.g., through industrial policies, which might seem inefficient in the short run), it can start improving technology B. Moreover, with capital scarce, the improvements will be directed at saving capital, not labor. Indeed, the improvements in its technology, if rapid enough, could change its comparative advantage. But even if that did not happen, the spillovers to the other sectors—reducing, say, capital but leaving labor inputs unchanged—would have far greater benefits than those generated from borrowing technology from the advanced industrial country.

The distortions in the bias of innovation are even greater when it comes to saving on environmental resources because of the massive mispricing of these resources. With no costs associated with carbon emissions, why would there be any incentive to reduce them? Social costs associated with the macroeconomic variability linked to dependence on imported resources whose prices are highly variable may be far greater than the private costs. This provides another rationale for government policies designed to encourage less dependence on such inputs—and another rationale for industrial policies.[74]

These environmental impacts are important for all countries but especially for developing countries, as Dasgupta's work repeatedly emphasizes.

This brings me back to one of the themes I raised earlier, a theme central to Dasgupta's work. What matters is not GDP but quality of life, well-being, and sustainability.[75] What that entails—and how it can be increased—should and can be the subject of rational inquiry. Dasgupta has led the way in showing us how that can be done. For that, and for all his other contributions, we are grateful.

[74] This is a lesson Europe learned at some cost: it might have been privately profitable to become dependent on Russian oil, but it was socially costly.

[75] This was, of course, the thrust of the *Report of the International Commission on the Measurement of Economic Performance and Social Progress*. See Fitoussi et al. (2010).

References

Alchian, A. (1963). "Reliability of Progress Curves in Airframe Production," *Econometrica* 31(4): 679–93.

Argote, L. and D. Epple. (1990). "Learning Curves in Manufacturing," *Science* 247(4945): 920–24.

Arrow, K. J. (1951). "An Extension of the Basic Theorems of Classical Welfare Economics," in J. Neyman (ed.), *Proceedings of the Second Berkeley Symposium on Mathematical Statistics and Probability*. Berkeley: University of California Press, 507–32.

—— (1962a). "The Economic Implications of Learning by Doing," *Review of Economic Studies*, 29(3): 155–73.

—— (1962b). "Economic Welfare and the Allocation of Resources for Invention," in R. Nelson (ed.) *The Rate and Direction of Inventive Activity: Economic and Social Factors*, National Bureau of Economic Research (NBER). Princeton, NJ: Princeton University Press.

Atkinson, A. B. and J. E. Stiglitz (1969). "A New View of Technological Change," *Economic Journal* 79(315): 573–8.

Besanko, D., U. Doraszelski, Y. Kryukov et al. (2010). "Learning-by-Doing, Organizational Forgetting, and Industry Dynamics," *Econometrica*, 78(2): 453–508.

Cabral, L. and M. Riordan. (1994). "The Learning Curve, Market Dominance, and Predatory Pricing," *Econometrica* 62(5): 1115–40.

Dasgupta, P. S. (1969). "On the Concept of Optimum Population," *Review of Economic Studies I*, 36(107): 295–318.

—— (1993). *An Inquiry into Well-Being and Destitution*. New York: Oxford University Press.

—— (2001). *Human Well-Being and the Natural Environment*. New York: Oxford University Press.

—— (2005). "Economics of Social Capital," *Economic Record*, 81(s1): S2–21.

—— C. R. Blitzer, and J.E. Stiglitz (1981). "Project Appraisal and Foreign Exchange Constraints," *Economic Journal*, 91(361): 58–74.

—— R. Gilbert, and J. E. Stiglitz (1981). "Energy Resources and Research and Development," in H. Siebert (ed.) *Erschopfbare Ressourcen*, vol. 108. Berlin: Duncker and Humbolt, 85–108.

—— and G. Heal (1979). *Economic Theory and Exhaustible Resources*. Cambridge: Cambridge University Press.

—— G. Heal, and J. E. Stiglitz. (1980). "The Taxation of Exhaustible Resources," in G. A. Hughes and G. M. Heal (eds.), *Public Policy and the Tax System*. London: George Allen and Unwin, 150–72.

—— et al. (1977). *An Economic Analysis of the Conservation of Depletable Natural Resources*. Prepared for the Federal Energy Administration, May.

—— and J. E. Stiglitz (1971). "Differential Taxation, Public Goods, and Economic Efficiency," *Review of Economic Studies*, 38(2): 151–74.

—— (1972). "On Optimal Taxation and Public Production," *Review of Economic Studies*, 39(1): 87–103.

—— (1974). "Benefit-Cost Analysis and Trade Policies," *Journal of Political Economy*, 82(1): 1–33.
—— (1977). "Tariffs Versus Quotas as Revenue Raising Devices under Uncertainty," *American Economic Review*, 67(5): 975–81.
—— (1980a). "Industrial Structure and the Nature of Innovative Activity," *Economic Journal*, 90(358): 266–93.
—— (1980b). "Uncertainty, Market Structure and the Speed of R&D," *Bell Journal of Economics*, 11(1): 1–28.
—— (1981a). "Entry, Innovation, Exit: Toward a Dynamic Theory of Oligopolistic Industrial Structure," *European Economic Review*, 15(2): 137–58.
—— (1981b). "Market Structure and Resource Extraction under Uncertainty," *Scandinavian Economic Journal*, 83(2): 318–33.
—— (1981c). "Resource Depletion under Technological Uncertainty," *Econometrica*, 49(1): 85–104.
—— (1982a). "Market Structure and Resource Depletion: A Contribution to the Theory of Intertemporal Monopolistic Competition," *Journal of Economic Theory* 28(1): 128–64.
—— (1982b). "Invention and Innovation under Alternative Market Structures: The Case of Natural Resources," *Review of Economic Studies*, 49(4): 567–82.
—— (1983). "Strategic Considerations in Invention and Innovation: The Case of Natural Resources," *Econometrica*, 51(5): 1430–48.
—— (1988a). "Learning by Doing, Market Structure, and Industrial and Trade Policies," *Oxford Economic Papers* 40(2): 246–68.
—— (1988b). "Potential Competition, Actual Competition and Economic Welfare," *European Economic Review*, 32(2): 569–77.
Debreu, G. (1959). *The Theory of Value*. New Haven, CT: Yale University Press.
Edgeworth, F. Y. (1925). *Papers Relating to Political Economy*, iii. London: Macmillan.
Fields, G. (1987). "Public Policy and the Labour Market in Developing Countries," in D. Newbery and N. Stern (eds.), *The Theory of Taxation for Developing Countries*. Oxford: Oxford University Press, 264–77.
Fitoussi, J.-P., A. Sen, and J. E. Stiglitz (2010). *Mismeasuring Our Lives: Why GDP Doesn't Add Up*. New York: The New Press. Available at <http://www.stiglitz-sen-fitoussi.fr/en/index.htm> (accessed 18 October 2013).
Fudenberg, D. and J. Tirole. (1982). "Learning-by-Doing and Market Performance." CERAS D.P.8, Ecole Nationale des Ponts et Chaussees, 1982.
Gilbert, R. J., and D. M. Newbery (1982). "Preemptive Patenting and the Persistence of Monopoly," *American Economic Review*, 72(3): 514–26 .
Greenwald, B., and J. E. Stiglitz (1986). 'Externalities in Economies with Imperfect Information and Incomplete Markets'. *Quarterly Journal of Economics* 1/2: 229–64.
—— (2003). *Towards a New Paradigm in Monetary Economics*. Cambridge: Cambridge University Press.
—— (2006). "Helping Infant Economies Grow: Foundations of Trade Policies for Developing Countries," *American Economic Review: AEA Papers and Proceedings* 96(2): 141–6.

—— (2014). *Creating a Learning Society: A New Approach to Growth, Development, and Social Progress*. New York: Columbia University Press.

Hahn, F. (1966). "Equilibrium Dynamics with Heterogeneous Capital Goods," *Quarterly Journal of Economics*, 80(4): 633–46.

Hausmann, R., J. Hwang, and D. Rodrik (2007). "What You Export Matters," *Journal of Economic Growth*, 12(1): 1–25.

—— and D. Rodrik (2003). "Economic Development as Self-Discovery," *Journal of Development Economics*, 72(2): 603–33.

Henry, C., and J. E. Stiglitz (2010). "Intellectual Property, Dissemination of Innovation, and Sustainable Development," *Global Policy* 1(1): 237–51.

Hidalgo, C. A., B. Klinger, A.-L. Barabási et al. (2007). "The Product Space Conditions the Development of Nations," *Science*, 317(5837): 482–7.

Hirsch, W. (1952). "Manufacturing Progress Functions," *Review of Economics and Statistics* 34(2): 143–55.

Hoff, K. (1997). "Bayesian Learning in an Infant Industry Model," *Journal of International Economics* 43(3–4): 409–36.

—— and J. E. Stiglitz (2001). "Modern Economic Theory and Development," in G. Meier and J. E. Stiglitz (eds.), *Frontiers of Development Economics: The Future in Perspective*. Oxford: Oxford University Press, 389–459.

—— (2010). "Equilibrium Fictions: A Cognitive Approach to Societal Rigidity," *American Economic Review* 100(2): 141–6. Extended version available as Policy Research Working Paper 5219, World Bank Development Research Group, February 2010, available at <http://www-wds.worldbank.org/external/default/WDSContentServer/IW3P/IB/2010/02/26/000158349_20100226083837/Rendered/PDF/WPS5219.pdf> (accessed 18 October 2013).

Kaldor, N. (1957). "A Model of Economic Growth," *Economic Journal*, 67: 591–624.

—— and J. A. Mirrlees (1962). "A New Model of Economic Growth," *Review of Economic Studies*, 29(3): 174–92.

Korinek, A. and L. Servén (2010). "Undervaluation through Foreign Reserve Accumulation: Static Losses, Dynamic Gains." Policy Research Working Paper 5250, World Bank, Washington, DC.

Levhari, D. (1966). "Extensions of Arrow's Learning by Doing," *Review of Economic Studies*, 33(2): 31–8.

—— (1967). "Further Implications of Learning by Doing," *Review of Economic Studies*, 33: 31–8.

Lipsey, R. G., and K. Lancaster (1956–1957). "The General Theory of Second Best," *Review of Economic Studies*, 24(1): 11–32.

Meade, J. E. (1955). *Trade and Welfare*. London: Oxford University Press.

Nelson, R. R. and E. S. Phelps (1965). "Investment in Humans, Technological Diffusion and Economic Growth." Discussion Paper 189, Cowles Foundation, Yale University, New Haven, CT.

Newbery, D. and J. E. Stiglitz (1982). "The Choice of Techniques and the Optimality of Market Equilibrium with Rational Expectations," *Journal of Political Economy*, 90(2): 223–46.

Nordhaus, W. D. (1969a). "An Economic Theory of Technological Change," *American Economic Association Papers and Proceedings*, 59(May): 18–28.

—— (1969b). *Invention, Growth and Welfare: A Theoretical Treatment of Technological Change*. Cambridge, MA: MIT Press.

Sah, R. and J. E. Stiglitz (1989a). "Technological Learning, Social Learning and Technological Change," in S. Chakravarty (ed.), *The Balance Between Industry and Agriculture in Economic Development*. London: Macmillan, 285–98.

—— —— (1989b). "Sources of Technological Divergence between Developed and Less Developed Countries," in G. Calvo (ed.), *Debt, Stabilizations and Development: Essays in Memory of Carlos Diaz-Alejandro*. Oxford: Basil Blackwell, 423–46.

Schumpeter, J. A. (1912). *Theorie der Wirtschaflichen Entwicklung*. Leipzig: Duncker and Humbolt. Translated in 1934 as *The Theory of Economic Development: An Inquiry into Profits, Capital, Credit, Interest and the Business Cycle*.

—— (1943). *Capitalism, Socialism and Democracy*, New York: Harper.

Shell, K. (1966). "Toward a Theory of Inventive Activity and Capital Accumulation," *American Economic Association Papers and Proceedings*, 56: 62–8.

—— (ed.) (1967). *Essays on the Theory of Optimal Economic Growth*. Cambridge, MA: MIT Press.

—— and J. E. Stiglitz (1967). "Allocation of Investment in a Dynamic Economy," *Quarterly Journal of Economics*, 81(4): 592–609.

Sheshinski, E. (1967). "Tests of the Learning-by-Doing Hypothesis," *Review of Economics and Statistics*, 49(4): 568–78.

Solow, R. M. (1957). "Technical Change and the Aggregate Production Function," *Review of Economics and Statistics*, 39(3): 312–20.

—— (1997). *Learning from "Learning by Doing": Lessons for Economic Growth*. Palo Alto, CA: Stanford University Press.

Spence, A. M. (1981). "The Learning Curve and Competition," *The Bell Journal of Economics* 12(1): 49–70.

Stiglitz, J. E. (1975a). "The Theory of Screening, Education and the Distribution of Income," *American Economic Review* 65(3): 283–300.

—— (1975b). "Information and Economic Analysis," in J. M. Parkin and A. R. Nobay (eds.), *Current Economic Problems: Proceedings of the Association of University Teachers of Economics, Manchester, 1974*. Cambridge: Cambridge University Press, 27–52.

—— (1981). "Potential Competition May Reduce Welfare," *American Economic Review*, 71(2): 184–9.

—— (1986). "Theory of Competition, Incentives and Risk," in J. E. Stiglitz and F. Mathewson (eds.), *New Developments in the Analysis of Market Structure*. Cambridge, MA: MIT Press, 399–449.

—— (1987a). "On the Microeconomics of Technical Progress," in J. M. Katz (ed.) *Technology Generation in Latin American Manufacturing Industries*. London: Macmillan, 56–77.

—— (1987b). "Technological Change, Sunk Costs, and Competition," *Brookings Papers on Economic Activity* 3: 883–947.

—— (1987c). "Learning to Learn, Localized Learning and Technological Progress," in P. S. Dasgupta and P. Stoneman (eds.), *Economic Policy and Technological Performance*. Cambridge: Cambridge University Press, 125–53.
—— (1990). "Comments: Some Retrospective Views on Growth Theory," in P. Diamond (ed.), *Growth/Productivity/Unemployment: Essays to Celebrate Bob Solow's Birthday*. Cambridge, MA: MIT Press, 50–68.
—— (1995a). "*The Theory of International Public Goods and the Architecture of International Organizations*." Background Paper No. 7, Third Meeting, High Level Group on Development Strategy and Management of the Market Economy, United Nations University - World Institute for Development Economics Research, Helsinki, Finland, 8–10 July.
—— (1995b). "Social Absorption Capability and Innovation," in Bon Ho Koo and D. H. Perkins (eds.), *Social Capability and Long-Term Economic Growth*. New York: St. Martin's Press, 48–81.
—— (1998). "Towards a New Paradigm for Development: Strategies, Policies and Processes." Ninth Raul Prebisch Lecture delivered at the Palais des Nations, Geneva, 19 October 1998, UNCTAD. Also in Ha-Joon Chang (ed.), *The Rebel Within*. London: Wimbledon Publishing, 2001, 57–93.
—— (1999). "Knowledge as a Global Public Good," in I. Kaul (ed.), *Global Public Goods: International Cooperation in the 21st Century*, Isabelle Grunberg and Marc A. Stern, United Nations Development Programme. New York: Oxford University Press, 308–25.
—— (2000). "Formal and Informal Institutions," in P. Dasgupta and I. Serageldin (eds.), *Social Capital: A Multifaceted Perspective*. Washington, DC: World Bank, 59–68.
—— (2004). "Towards a Pro-Development and Balanced Intellectual Property Regime." Keynote address presented at the Ministerial Conference on Intellectual Property for Least Developed Countries, World Intellectual Property Organization (WIPO), Seoul, 25 October 2004. Revised and updated version published as Stiglitz (2013).
—— (2006a). "Samuelson and the Factor Bias of Technological Change," in M. Szenberg, L. Ramrattan, and A. Gottesman (eds.), *Samuelsonian Economics and the Twenty-First Century*. New York: Oxford University Press, 235–51.
—— (2006b). *Making Globalization Work*. New York: W. W. Norton.
—— (2008). "The Economic Foundations of Intellectual Property," *Duke Law Journal*, 57(6): 1693–724. Sixth annual Frey Lecture in Intellectual Property, Duke University, 16 February 2007.
—— (2010a). "Introduction," in J. A. Schumpeter, *Capitalism, Socialism and Democracy*. London: Rutledge, ix–xiv.
—— (2010b). "*A Social Democratic Agenda for a More Dynamic Indian Economy: Creating an Innovative and Learning Society*." The 2010 Jawaharlal Nehru Memorial Lecture, New Delhi, 18 November 2011. (Published version forthcoming.)
—— (2013). "Institutional Design For China's Innovation System: Implications For Intellectual Property Rights," in D. Kennedy and J. E. Stiglitz (eds.), *Law and*

Economic Development with Chinese Characteristics: Institutions for the 21st Century. New York: Oxford University Press.

Uzawa, H. (1965). "Optimum Technical Change in an Aggregate Model of Economic Growth," *International Economic Review*, 6(1): 18–31.

Young, A. (1991). "Learning by Doing and the Dynamic Effects of International Trade," *Quarterly Journal of Economics*, 106: 369–406.

—— (1993). "Invention and Bounded Learning by Doing," *Journal of Political Economy*, 101: 443–72.

3

Some Perspectives on Linked Ecosystems and Socioeconomic Systems

Kenneth J. Arrow, Paul R. Ehrlich, and Simon A. Levin

3.1 INTRODUCTION: ECOLOGY, ECONOMICS, SOCIETIES, AND COMPLEX SYSTEMS

Partha Dasgupta has been a pioneer in bridging the gap between two scholarly foci: on the one hand, the human socioeconomic system and its development, and, on the other, the ecosystems on which the former are utterly dependent (Dasgupta 2001; Dasgupta 2003; Dasgupta et al. 2005). In his brilliant book, *Economics: A Very Short Introduction*, Dasgupta summarized the significance of ecosystems (which he categorizes in terms of types of capital assets) as follows: "The services they produce include maintaining a genetic library, preserving and regenerating soil, fixing nitrogen and carbon, recycling nutrients, controlling floods, filtering pollutants, operating the hydrological cycle, and maintaining the gaseous composition of the atmosphere" (Dasgupta 2007: 119). These and many other ecosystem services (Holdren and Ehrlich 1974), such as controlling crop pests, supplying fish from the seas and freshwater sources, and providing cultural, intellectual, spiritual, and aesthetic inspiration, indicate how deeply intertwined are the problems of improving the welfare of humanity, especially the half in need of "development" (basically increased capacity to command consumption), and the problems of maintaining these crucial services.

The importance of natural capital is reinforced by recognition of the accelerating pressures caused by increasing human influence on Earth's ecological systems—the use of land, forests, and animal resources for food and fuel and for space for living, sequestering of "wastes" such as CO2 and other human purposes.

Dasgupta has also been a pioneer in building bridges between ecology and economics, recognizing the similarities inherent in the organization and evolution of ecological and socio-political-economic systems.

Both the human enterprise and ecosystems are complex systems, in both the everyday and the technical senses. The elements of each have many direct and indirect connections. Perturbations in one sector will ultimately have consequences, large or small, on other sectors seemingly far removed. What is more, the consequences in remote sectors in turn affect the sector with the initial disturbance, possibly offsetting it, possibly magnifying it. The similarity of the names, ecology and economics, deriving as they do from a common Greek root, is no accident.

These intertwined systems are actually special cases of complex systems, termed complex adaptive systems (CASs) (Holland 1995; Levin 1998). That is, they are composed of individual agents that adjust their behavior or their relative numbers, with consequences for the system as a whole, and these consequences can in turn affect individual behaviors. There is also in both the notion that the reactions of any element to changes are governed by a motive of increasing utility—profit, power, resilience, security, efficiency, or something else in the human and other animal species, and fitness more generally for all species, including humans, over evolutionary time.

It is not merely that the two complex adaptive systems have many parallel structures. They have direct interactions, and in a profoundly increasing way. The human economy, originally the province of one minor player among many species, has expanded to a position of dominance in the demands on the resources of Earth. Ecosystem services, the benefits humans derive from ecological systems, are under unprecedented assault as a result of a still rapidly growing human population, a considerable increase in per capita consumption, and the development of technologies designed to meet these needs with inadequate concern for their ecological implications (Ehrlich and Ehrlich 2009). In both realms, arguments have been given that the unrestricted and unregulated behavior of the systems leads to outcomes that are optimal for the participants. The doctrine that markets left to their own devices lead to economic outcomes that are efficient with respect to human welfare was held by French eighteenth-century economists (as evidenced by the term, "laissez-faire," brought from French to English) even before Adam Smith enunciated the doctrine of the "invisible hand" (though Smith himself had many qualifications). Similarly, the concept of Gaia (Lovelock 1972; Margulis and Lovelock 1974; Schneider and Boston 1991) in its extreme form is sometimes taken to suggest that the biosphere will self-organize for the good of its inhabitants; such a view flies in the face of our understanding of the mechanisms of evolution.

Either system, left to its own devices, is likely to find some asymptotic configuration, not necessarily equilibrial, but possibly involving fluctuations and even chaos. However, in neither case, as we shall argue, is there any reason to expect that the outcome will optimize the collective good (if defined in any reasonable sense), and certainly not the collective human good. Indeed, many scientists fear that present threats to that good have brought humanity into a largely unrecognized state of emergency. (The view that the welfare of at least sentient non-humans should be taken into account has been defended by such philosophers as Jeremy Bentham and Peter Singer, and informs actual ethical practice in the form of prohibitions against cruelty to animals.) In each case, the individual self-interest that drives the forces of self-organization will have unpredictable and frequently negative macroscopic consequences. Socioeconomic and ecological-environmental systems alike, therefore, require some balance between free running and regulation, whether by government, by "mutual coercion, mutually agreed upon" (Hardin 1968: 1245), or by social norms more generally.

We explore broadly and tentatively these parallels and challenges in this chapter. In Section 3.2, we address socioeconomic and political systems from the point of view of complex adaptive systems. Section 3.3 addresses the behavior of ecosystems and biosphere. In 3.4, we discuss some of the linkages between the socioeconomic and ecological systems, particularly the strain imposed on the ecosphere by the increasing demands of the economy, fueled by the extent to which the price system fails to work with regard to common resources and to the future. In Section 3.5, we study some of the parallels between the socioeconomic and ecological systems, including the role of modularity, the possibility of multiple basins of attraction, and the positive and negative values of robustness and resilience.

3.2 THE ECONOMY AS A COMPLEX ADAPTIVE SYSTEM

The competitive economy is perhaps the first social system to have been analyzed as what today would be called a complex adaptive system (CAS). It is built out of individual units, firms that engage in production by investing capital and buying labor and other materials and households that sell labor or other material possessions and buy the products of the firms. Products are exchanged through market transactions. That is, any given product (including materials bought by firms) is sold at a given price, the same for all participants (whether sellers or buyers).

Every member of the system is assumed to adapt in a way favorable to itself. Capital moves to activities and industries that yield a higher return. For any given output, firms choose factor combinations that will achieve that output at minimum cost. A household will sell its assets (labor, land, or whatever) at the highest price offered compatible with its preferences and will buy the consumption bundle that it judges best among those it can afford with its income. Finally, for any good, the amount desired is equal to the amount available on the market; the prices of the goods adjust until this equality holds. (More precisely, either equality holds or the amount supplied even at zero price exceeds the demand, as, for example, air, or, sometimes, water or land in thinly populated areas.)

This vision of the economic order as a system coordinated through prices and markets was articulated by Adam Smith (1776) and developed further in the nineteenth century, reaching grand syntheses in the works of Léon Walras (1874, 1877) and Alfred Marshall (1890). It was a vision by which an extremely complex series of transactions and activities could make available the commodities that facilitate life and improve its quality. The buyer of the goods need know little of the processes of making them.

Accompanying this understanding of the coordination role of the competitive economy, moreover, was a recognition that the outcomes of the system were in fact "good" for the participants—"good" in the sense of facilitating the accomplishment of the aims of the individual units. What appears as a struggle in which each unit is trying to achieve the best for itself results in an efficient allocation of resources, while being required to compensate others for any damages inflicted upon them.

This picture is not without merit and has served as a useful guide to many policy decisions. The remarkable increase in productivity after the Chinese adoption of markets as a primary form of economic organization is simply the latest manifestation of the principle. But none of the pioneers—Smith, Walras, or Marshall—held that the market allocation was all-sufficient. They all held that there was a major role for the government. As Marshall put it, "So I cry, Laissez-faire: Let the State be up and doing" (Marshall 1907 in Pigou 1925: 336).

The major problem is not the use of markets but rather their non-use—more precisely, their non-existence. The central concept of "capital," which has given its name to our current economic system is that of bridging a gap in time between deciding on production and purchasing inputs and the actual occurrence of the production. But this means that the profitability of an investment depends not on current prices but on the prices that will prevail in the future.

To complete the original intent of the theory, we would need to have markets today for deliveries of goods in the future. These do exist, but only to a very limited extent. For some agricultural goods and minerals, there are so-called futures markets, contracts for purchase and sale for a few years ahead. Much more important are bonds and other securities promising payments in money (the capacity to buy commodities) in the future, sometimes many years ahead. But clearly these are far from providing the coordinating function that makes the market such a satisfactory complex adaptive system.

If markets for the future would be so satisfactory, why do they not exist? One obvious answer is uncertainty. We really do not know what our situation will be in the future. The process of innovation means that manufactured goods that will be available tomorrow, from the same plants being built today, cannot be fully specified. (It is not an accident that such futures markets as exist are confined to goods whose specifications will not be changing: wheat, copper, petroleum, and the like.)

It could be argued that futures markets would be possible if supplemented with markets that offer protection against uncertainties, in effect, insurance contracts against changes in specifications and against other uncertainties arising in economic life. What prevents anything like full or even meaningful protection against business uncertainties of all kinds is the fact that the information needed to specify the contingencies under which payment is to be made is not equally available to all parties. This problem has been addressed in theoretical and applied research in the last half-century under the heading of asymmetric information. The insurance industry has long known this problem under the headings of moral hazard and adverse selection. The first means that motivations are altered by insurance: one insured against fire will have less incentive to take precautions. Similarly, one insured against business failure will have less incentive to work hard; hence, such insurance, in whatever form it may take, will not be found on the market. The failure to have such insurance will in turn inhibit entry into business. Adverse selection occurs when someone desiring insurance knows more about the risks than the insurer does. Hence, the population of insured will not be given by the observable risks in the population, but will be higher to some uncertain extent. If the insurer initially sets rates according to the average risks in the population, those who know they bear greater-than-average risks will buy more insurance and those who know they bear less-than-average risks will buy less. Hence, the insurer will find it is bearing losses and will have to raise its premiums. This in turn will lead to still further shifts in insurance coverage to riskier insured. This process might end in the complete disappearance of insurance coverage or its restriction to a relatively small high-risk group.

It might seem as if the limits on the existence of markets for the future and for risks would mean simply that the market is not as efficient an allocator as a simple reading of equilibrium theory would suggest. But the matter appears to be much worse than that. What this argument has implied is that economic behavior is driven to a major extent by information or, perhaps better put, beliefs. But these beliefs are driven in part by observations on the workings of the economic system. As Oskar Morgenstern (1935) pointed out already in the 1930s, investment is based on a forecast of the economy. But this is based on the investment and other economic activities of others, which, in turn, are based on their forecasts. In short, the belief structures of the different economic agents are dependent on each other. This situation clearly invites instabilities. If some people start to be pessimistic, for whatever reason, this will spread. Hence, the belief systems will be highly intercorrelated and so likely to exhibit unstable behavior. Disturbances are likely to propagate.

The fact that information is dispersed has implications for the behavior of individuals and for the internal organization of firms. Individuals may study the behavior of others as manifest in markets, including the securities markets, to draw inferences. Firms and individuals may engage in costly activities designed to improve their knowledge base. They may need to create incentives for their employees and agents to use the information they have to their advantage. But these incentive systems, though effective most of the time, can never be designed to insure against provoking outcomes that are unfavorable both for the firm and for the entire economy. Some of these issues were discussed in Arrow (1974), and there has been a rich development in the study of incentive mechanisms since. But a full analysis as to how these incentive schemes can produce unfavorable outcomes is still missing.

Indeed, some of the measures designed to create greater security for individuals can increase the instability of the entire system. In view of the limited information, lending is made safer to the lender by requiring collateral. But if there is a downturn so that the borrower defaults, the lender will throw the collateral on the market to recoup his or her losses. This will, however, increase the downward pressure on the securities markets and so create new defaults. To add to the problem, the drawing of inferences from what can be observed becomes increasingly complicated and therefore an additional cost on the economic system.

It was observed early in the history of capitalism that there were sudden inexplicable downturns in economic activity. By the middle of the nineteenth century, the idea that these downturns were a characteristic of the system became widely accepted (Juglar 1862). The study of so-called "business cycles" became standard, but little is known to this day of an explanatory nature. These cycles are sometimes, though not always, associated with crises in the financial sector. (Cycles are also evident in ecological systems, at scales from the forest patch and below to whole ecosystems.)

An example of a possible changed attitude to policy due to complex system thinking might be views on modular design, particularly in international trade, and especially international capital flows. Economists, even those most inclined to favor government intervention, have always tended to favor free trade and, though less strongly, international capital movements. If there are risks, so it is argued, it is best that they be spread widely, so that the advantages of diversification can be achieved.

The physical image is that of a possible flood due to a river overflow. If we try to confine the river with high levees, there will be a concentrated disaster if there is a break somewhere. Hence, it is better to have widespread limited flooding. To those who advocate modular design, the image is rather that of a forest fire, where a small disturbance is multiplied. Here, firebreaks are clearly advantageous.

The Eurozone was indeed strongly supported on the grounds that it would average out disturbances (Mundell 1961). Its existence created an expectation that the consequences of irresponsible fiscal behavior by one member would be covered by the rest. However, it does appear, at least, that separation, in the form of separate currencies might have prevented Greece, after all a relatively small part of the Eurozone, from being in a position to create such havoc. (This is not meant to be a serious analysis of the current situation, but only to point out some connections to complex system analysis.)

3.3 ECOSYSTEMS AND THE BIOSPHERE AS COMPLEX ADAPTIVE SYSTEMS

Perhaps even more disturbing than shifts in socioeconomic systems may be regime shifts in the global ecosystem complex adaptive system, where a historical accident can cause a vast epidemic, trigger an extinction episode greater than the one that wiped out the dinosaurs, or push the climate system into a new basin of attraction. Perturbing phenomena could include such things as political pressure to keep the GDP growing despite market failures and possible resource shortages; pro-natalist policies; resource wars; or simply that humans persist in being animals more comfortable in small groups than in a globalized world of some seven billion people.

Theodosius Dobzhansky wrote that "nothing in biology makes sense except in the light of evolution" (Dobzhansky 1973), and indeed the evolutionary perspective is the most important unifying principle in biology. Genetic lineages adapt to their environments through mutation, recombination, and selection within the context of population structure. Dramatically, they form partnerships with one another that become reinforced over time through genetic integration, leading to the major transitions in evolution, like multicellularity. Bacteria exude extracellular polymers that lead to biofilms, a unique form of cooperation in solving problems of the Commons, and more generally a variety of modes of cooperation within and among species is distributed widely across all of the biological kingdoms.

Still, understanding how and under what circumstances cooperation can arise remain among the great theoretical questions in evolutionary biology, and among the most hotly debated. Ecological systems, at all levels, are complex adaptive systems, as we have already learned, which means that the interests of individual agents may be in conflict with those of the group, or the ecosystem, or the biosphere. The parallel with similar issues in economic systems is not accidental. Ecosystems are economic systems, and vice versa, with competition for resources; the opportunity not only for cooperation but also for exploitation; and the emergence of differentiated systemic roles for different kinds of individuals.

The evolutionary story, at its core, is strongly analogous with the economic story laid out in the previous section. This is of course not surprising, given the similar natures of the two systems, ecological and economic. Agents in nature, from cells to genes to individuals to populations, compete with one another for common resources, and interact with one another directly through competition, exploitation, or mutualism. As the result of these processes, agents receive rewards in terms of differential reproductive success, "fitness," the biological analogue of utility.

Since fitness is differential reproductive success, it seems logical that natural selection will reward the most fit, increasing their representation in future generations, and furthermore that the mean fitness in the population will gradually increase towards a relative peak. This intuition is indeed captured in Sir Ronald Fisher's Fundamental Theorem of Natural Selection, and in Sewall Wright's notion of the adaptive landscape. Fisher demonstrated that, subject to certain assumptions, the mean fitness of the population will increase monotonically over evolutionary time, at a rate proportional to the strength of selection and to a measure of the genetic variance (technically, the additive genic variance) in the population; in Wright's imagery, the population mean fitness is represented by a point that climbs a peak in the fitness landscape. Such landscapes, of course, may have multiple peaks; and so, even in this view, the peak reached is not necessarily the best of all possible peaks (Kauffman and Levin 1987).

The real problem with this description of the evolutionary process, however, is in the assumptions that underlie Fisher's Theorem, and in particular the notion that fitnesses are constant (i.e., that Wright's landscape is static). Environments change, and so adapting to today's conditions is no guarantee of an increase in fitness even in the next generation; uncertainty about future conditions, indeed, is a strong selective force on its own, and perhaps the most important driver of the life history evolution of species. Mutation and sexual recombination, in particular, to some extent have been shaped by the challenges of uncertainty, as ways for genomes to remain adaptive in changing environments. The issues are the same as those addressed earlier in the context of exploitation versus exploration, and the general issue of how agents in ecology and economics alike should balance current versus future success.

We worry today about rapid variation in environmental conditions due to climate disruption, toxification, and other global anthropogenic changes, and about the ability of populations to adapt to those changing environments. The real challenge to the simple view given earlier, however, is not exogenous variation, but variation in fitnesses that arise from the evolutionary process itself. (Indeed, one can argue that climate change is to large extent not an exogenous forcing, but is itself the result of the evolution of the ability of humans to over-exploit their environments; but that is an effect on a much longer time scale.) As organisms with certain genomes exploit particular sets of resources, the depletion of those resources makes those with other genomes more fit. The ability of carriers of some genomes to use a certain resource to best advantage may make other resources more efficient for those with different genomes to use. Or it may lead to selection for mechanisms like nitrogen fixation that provides a selective advantage against those with other genomes. Viral strains that take advantage of the lack of resistance of host cells to their stereochemistries are replaced by other strains that exploit host cells in different ways, ways that previously were competitively inferior.

All of these considerations emphasize that adaptation does not necessarily lead to optimization (Lewontin 1977; Gould and Lewontin 1979). As useful as it is to study biological adaptation from the viewpoint of optimization, we must recognize that evolution is a process that is first of all strongly path dependent (Jacob 1977), historically constrained within a landscape that at any one time has multiple peaks, and secondly that the evolution of any lineage cannot be uncoupled dynamically from the evolutionary and demographic responses of other lineages. When those lineages are within the same species, this phenomenon is called frequency-dependence; when other species are involved, it is termed coevolution (Janzen 1980; Ehrlich and Raven 1964). Within this context, the notion of optimization must be replaced by perspectives from game theory (Lewontin 1961; Slobodkin 1964), which led John Maynard Smith to borrow from economic theory (Nash 1950, 1951) and introduce the concept of the evolutionarily stable strategy—a type that, once established, cannot be displaced from the population (Maynard Smith and Price 1973; Maynard Smith 1982). Dynamically, the situation is even more complicated, since evolutionarily stable strategies may not be reachable within an evolutionary dynamic, and since, conversely, the evolutionary process may lead not to stable strategies but to bifurcations and speciation (Eshel and Motro 1981; Dieckmann and Law 1996; Geritz et al. 1998).

Within this framework, the evolution of cooperation was a puzzle even to Darwin. Cooperation is evident throughout the natural world, including at the extreme the evolution of multicellularity, the ultimate form of cooperation. Our own bodies are consortia of genes and organelles of diverse origins, that each benefited by evolving together into a collective. Early explanations of some extreme forms of cooperation within species relied on genetic relatedness, and the benefits of helping one's kin; but genetic relatedness clearly is not required for cooperation, and there are multiple explanations, from reciprocal altruism and bilateral partnerships, to the more complex arrangements like social norms that sustain large societies (Axelrod 1984).

Here then is the critical nexus between ecological theory and economic theory. What can we learn from evolutionary theory about how cooperation has arisen and been maintained, and what are its limitations as the sizes of groups become larger? William Forster Lloyd elegantly called our attention to the problems associated with common-pool resources, like the grazing commons that are found in most cultures. Garrett Hardin rediscovered Lloyd, and introduced the term that has had such resonance, the "Tragedy of the Commons," in which the collapse of common resource systems can result from a lack of incentive of individual agents to modify their own acquisitive and exploitative behaviors. The problems are reminiscent of those well known to Adam Smith, Walras, and Marshall. The only solution, according to Hardin, was to achieve "mutual coercion, mutually agreed upon" (Hardin 1968: 1245).

Quite simply, this is why the biosphere is in the mess it is today. Whether the agents are individuals or collectives or nations, the interests of the one and the interests of the many can diverge. There are many lessons to learn in dealing with global environmental problems concerning how evolution has resolved, or failed to resolve, these conflicts. Most centrally, we can look at the exquisite functioning of natural systems and feel comfort in the multi-species partnerships that keep nutrients and energy flowing; but that would be misleading, because it ignores the many genotypes and indeed species that disappeared along the way. The biosphere will resolve today's conflicts and find new balance, but there is no guarantee that we, or components we cherish and value, will be part of that balance.

3.4 LINKAGES AND PARALLELS BETWEEN SOCIO-ECONOMIC AND ECOLOGICAL SYSTEMS

The social complex adaptive system is embedded within the CAS of the biosphere—collectively all the world's ecosystems (Levin 1999). The latter is of even greater complexity, and the social CAS is in continual, but often little recognized, interaction with it. For instance, the world market system requires huge amounts of energy, some twenty-fold more than humanity used in 1850, and the signs for rapidly finding a cheap abundant replacement for fossil fuels are not good. There are no obvious new sources of energy, the equivalent of the coal that replaced wood and the oil that added to coal permitted today's degree of global "development," waiting in the wings as fossil fuels are (necessarily) phased out.

While, for example, there is pressure from the social CAS for perpetual growth in GDP and population, that pressure alters the ecosystem CAS and could trigger emergence of nasty consequences from climate disruption that devastates agriculture to epidemics much more severe than those suffered before modern medicine. As mentioned earlier, Gaia theory has often assumed there is a similar invisible hand guiding the evolution of the biosphere (Lovelock 2001), but the flaws in this metaphor are at least as great as they are for the social CAS.

Understanding the properties of complex adaptive systems helps one think about the world, but it will not tell us what will occur. Most of their aspects have not even yet been satisfactorily modeled mathematically, although considerable progress has been made recently at least in identifying early warning indicators of system collapse, like critical slowing down or increasing variance (Scheffer 2008; Scheffer et al. 2009). But understanding the properties that lead to robustness and resilience, of desirable and undesirable states alike, does suggest some lessons that we might internalize as we try to struggle with increasingly dangerous threats to the persistence of civilization (Levin 1999). For example, because a complex adaptive system is prone to emergence of unpredictable phenomena, from AIDS to market meltdowns, policies should be designed with more attention to flexibility and adaptability in response. Resisting change often will not work, but flexibility and adaptability may foster recovery and hence enhance robustness. Similarly, despite the great popularity of large-scale solutions and "globalization," ways should be sought to find small-scale solutions and find an optimal degree of modularity of the world, increasing robustness of desirable large-scale states and patterns. Modularity, of course, just as heterogeneity, has advantages and disadvantages both for human welfare, and for the robustness of systems. Giant electric grids are vulnerable to properties of both the ecosystem CAS (storms, earthquakes, solar storms), and the social CAS (error, terrorism, overloading); housetop solar-electric panels are not, and hence collectively increase the robustness of the entire power grid. More generally, systems that are too interconnected carry systemic risk, the potential for contagious spread of disturbances like bank collapses, infectious diseases, and forest fires. On the other hand, interconnectedness, like the ability to trade goods or provide insurance arrangements, confers benefits both to system performance and robustness. The goal should be to find an intermediate level of modularity that does a satisfactory job of balancing costs and benefits. Indeed, the advantage of some degree of modularity is reinforced by the fact that modularity has been selected for through natural selection, enhancing the process of adaptation and preserving its advances.

As world leaders have belatedly realized that the world's economic system may have flipped into a new basin of attraction, one where we would rather not be, they have attempted unprecedented cooperation, for example in propping up the Euro, reducing modularity as much as is feasible. This is a sensible short-term response, since the goal has been to overcome the robustness of the undesirable state. By the same token, these must be short-term efforts at synchrony; once the system is back in a more desirable state, additional independence and modularity are essential to provide the adaptive capacity needed to sustain the system. Theories of robustness of complex adaptive systems have much to contribute. Economists should be doing more to understand the relationship between markets, culture, and different definitions of freedom (e.g., the freedom we all have to be street people). They should be looking at ways that markets can be restrained from taking us even further from sustainability, and see if their allocative efficiency could be preserved with a goal of individuals seeking adequacy rather than maximizing utility. They should be looking at ways to modularize markets to some degree, so that unfortunate emergent properties can be more readily isolated (e.g., could packaging poor mortgages into Structured Investment Vehicles have been better segregated from the rest of the financial system?) so as to reduce the vulnerability of networks to the propagation of local disaster (Haldane and May 2011). Ben S. Bernanke, addressing this in comments to the Council on Foreign Relations in 2009, expressed what many believe in stating that "First, we must address the problem of financial institutions that are deemed too big—or perhaps too interconnected—to fail." Again, trade offers obvious advantages in spreading benefits and providing insurance against local failures, but these benefits must be balanced against the risks associated with overconnectedness. The recent problems in banking and in sovereign debt illustrate the delicate balancing that must be performed.

Modularity, redundancy, and heterogeneity, in balanced proportions, are all essential aspects of a system's capacity to maintain its functioning in the face of stressors. Redundancy can compensate for the loss of key elements; modularity can contain contagion and systemic risk, and provide building blocks for improvement; and heterogeneity embodies the adaptive capacity of the system to deal with threats (Levin 1999). In ecological and evolutionary systems alike, diversity and heterogeneity are often enhanced by fluctuations (Hutchinson 1961), and hence efforts to suppress short-term fluctuations, like controlled fires or small-scale market corrections, may be misguided. The optimal pathway requires some balance between exploration and exploitation, and this is a lesson that should be heeded by governments, companies, and funding agencies alike.

So it is clear both empirically and theoretically that markets alone cannot create a society that is both just and sustainable. In the rest of this chapter we look more closely at the intertwined social and ecosystem complex adaptive systems, Partha Dasgupta's domain, to seek directions in which humanity might proceed toward the goal of such a society. We also suggest and explore that, because of the similar complex adaptive natures of the two systems and their coupled combination, an evolutionary perspective can be a guide in addressing problems of sustainability. Indeed, an attractive, oft-cited metaphor and model in this regard is the vertebrate immune system, which has evolved to deal with the certainty of unpredictable threats. The immune system combines generalized and immediate responses with longer-term and adaptive ones, illustrating the balance that must be found in the linked social-ecosystem systems between the implementation of known solutions and the adaptive capacity that allows for exploration of new solutions.

3.4.1 Intragenerational and Intergenerational Equity

The great challenge facing society—achieving a sustainable future for our children and our grandchildren—is inherently interdisciplinary. Ecology must meet economics in issues such as the valuation of Earth's biotic resources, and obviously bio-physico-chemical constraints must be addressed as well. At the core, however, ethical issues loom. How should we discount the future (Dasgupta 2008; Arrow and Dasgupta 2009)? How much can we consume now, while heeding the Brundtland Commission mandate to leave for future generations the same options we enjoy today? How should we take account of the inevitable uncertainties necessarily associated with the future (e.g., Arrow 2009)? And of course, intergenerational equity does not stand alone, but must be coupled with its dual, intragenerational equity, and the associated problems of the Global Commons. Both of these issues have been addressed in parallel research in the economic and ecological/evolutionary literature.

The problem of intergenerational transfer of resources is a natural dynastic extension of the problem of optimal resource utililization during one's lifetime (Arrow and Levin 2009). In the ecological literature, this falls under the rubric of life history theory, which addresses issues such as when a plant should switch from growth (consumption) into reproduction (investment), how to allocate reproduction over one's lifetime, and what resources to transfer from parent to children. Life history theory is also largely about the adaptations of organisms to uncertainty, the relative benefits of specialization versus generalization and risk-spreading, and the trade-offs between exploitation and exploration/innovation. The parallels between the ecological and economic issues are obvious, and should not be surprising because of the parallel nature of ecosystems and socioeconomic systems as self-organizing complex adaptive systems, in which individual agents compete for resources.

3.4.2 Optimal Utilization of Multiple Resources

The issue of uncertainty as it relates to the utilization of a single resource extends obviously to the issue of specialization versus generalization in a heterogeneous environment, especially when there is uncertainty regarding which kind of environment will be available. Good and bad environments for growth represent one kind of heterogeneity, but organisms and economic agents alike can modify what "good" and "bad" mean through adaptation and plasticity. Richard Levins (1968) introduced the notion of "grain" into ecology and elegantly demonstrated how temporal correlations in the patterns of environmental variation shaped optimal utilization strategies. In a "fine-grained" environment, an individual's utility or fitness is averaged arithmetically over many different experiences, as if one had picked up a handful of sand on the beach. In contrast, in a coarse-grained environment, utility or fitness emerges from one or a small number of events. Again, there is a strong parallel between ecological and economic systems. For example, plants utilize multiple environmental nutrients, like nitrogen and phosphorus; herbivores feed on multiple plant species; and businesses not only must exploit multiple markets, but also must allocate resources to capital versus labor. In all these cases, the allocation problems are similar, and the optimal patterns of use depend upon predictability and grain.

A central issue in all such determinations is the balance between exploration and exploitation, in ecology the domain of optimal foraging theory (Pyke 1984). The theory deals with the utilization of a known good or a known technology versus investment in less certain alternatives that might have a higher payoff. Animals leave patches where they are feeding to forage for potentially more valuable resource items, paying an immediate price in order to gain information that is not otherwise available. Similarly companies and funding agencies must balance investment in known quantities with speculative forays into research and development of new ideas. Such exploration is key to persistence, especially in a competitive environment, be it ecological or economic.

Exploration is also a way to spread the risks in an uncertain environment, as opposed to investing fully in a pure strategy. Plants disperse seeds, or place them in dormancy, in order to spread them over a variety of environments; investors diversify their investments for the same reasons.

3.4.3 Information, Conflict, Cooperation, and Collective Action

If generalization and risk-spreading are ways individuals deal with heterogeneity and uncertainty, so too is cooperation. Indeed, cooperation is a first step in the evolutionary transition to the formation of complexes, modules that provide building blocks for higher-level evolution. The emergence of multicellularity is a classic evolutionary extension of such transformations, but more generally genetic and phenotypic modules are receiving increasing attention in the evolutionary literature (Hartwell 1999). In socioeconomic systems, modularity is ubiquitous, represented by entities such as tribes, religions, professions, and nations. However, too often, cooperation has arisen as a means to allow groups of individuals to compete more effectively against other groups. For the sustainability of our life-support systems, we must find ways to extend such cooperation to broader scales, raising the unit of focus to the biosphere as a whole. Most likely, that will require a hierarchical approach, for example building cooperation up from polycentric foci (Ostrom 2010; Levin 2013).

3.4.4 Backcasting

Backcasting is a tool that tends to be underutilized in the study of the conjoined complex adaptive systems. Backcasting consists of postulating some desired future state and then working backwards to determine programs and policies, and the timing of their implementation that would be required to reach the proposed goal. Backcasting has an advantage over forecasting in that it allows one at first to largely ignore the potentially disruptive emergent properties (chaotic behavior) of complex adaptive systems, and provides a multi-stage set of concrete targets that need to be met.

A recent example of backcasting was the exercise of the World Business Council for Sustainable Development (WBCSD) examining what would be required to reach a sustainable society by 2050. One of the things not included in the WBCSD exercise was the issue of diminishing marginal product, which is rarely considered in demographic analyses (Ehrlich and Holdren 1971) and has been deeply implicated in the collapse of complex societies, as documented by Tainter (1988). But more important from our viewpoint was that the WBCSD, having done the backcast with the appropriate assumption that the conjoined complex adaptive systems would not generate negative emergent properties that could drastically alter the requirements, did not go further. We believe the exercise should have been extended to develop ways to add robustness and resilience to those requirements, while not neglecting the possibility that trajectories could also be altered by emergence of unexpected positive factors (e.g., a dramatic breakthrough in solar energy technology, or the generation of a mass "shrink your ecological footprint" or "population control movement"). There is a long historical record of both rapid technological change (e.g., following the invention of the internal combustion engine) and social change (American Revolution, civil rights in the US, collapse of the Soviet Union). Finding reasonable ways to work emergence into backcasting is a major challenge for those wishing to plan for a sustainable future.

It is, of course, the interactions of the ecosystem and social complex adaptive systems that determine the carrying capacity of Earth for human beings, and how far (at any given time) the joint system is from that capacity. Here the issue becomes especially difficult because of the problems of factoring emergent properties into both elements. Should the social CAS quickly transition to a state where individuals accept adequacy rather than maximizing consumption as the norm, the carrying capacity would increase. Should the climate shift into a basin of attraction that made many grain-growing regions warm dramatically, carrying capacity would plummet.

3.4.5 Carrying Capacity, Sustainability, and Ecosystem Services

Perhaps the most crucial question facing scholars today is how to create a global society that gives a decent life to all people without doing it at a serious cost to future generation (that is, a society that is "sustainable"). This obviously involves some broad agreement not just on how to define "decent," but also on the distribution above a floor of "decency." Some peoples' standards of living will inevitably be more decent than others. And since the intertwined CASs make predicting the future with great accuracy impossible, societies must consider probabilistic issues when trying to decide on courses of action that might impose costs on our descendants who would violate the sustainability criterion. In short, there is a need for broad social agreement on what is decent, sustainable, and serious—and, most critically, on what is possible or likely. The latter is an issue of the carrying capacity of Earth for human beings (Daily and Ehrlich 1996), where widely disparate guesses have been catalogued (Cohen 1996). But serious estimates under different assumptions are largely lacking (MacKellar 1996), with the outstanding exception of the work of Rees (2001) and Wackernagel (Wackernagel and Rees 1996) on "ecological footprints."

For instance, at the moment there is much discussion of the "need" to increase food production by 70 percent by 2050 in order to provide adequate nourishment to an expected population of some nine billion people. But the demographic projection only represents a population increase by some 30 percent, so that a more realistic (and environmentally cautious) goal might be to attempt to increase production by 50 percent to be used in feeding the newcomers and in improving the diets of the poorest of the poor. Market mechanisms have not developed for adequately feeding seven billion people, as a result of the persistent inability of a billion or so people to command nourishment and thereby generate sufficient demand. If they are to be adequately nourished, it seems a less ambitious and more targeted goal, to strive to increase production by 50 percent and to work hard to institute new policies within the social CAS to increase the demand generated by those now under- or malnourished might have a better chance of success. A related and more limited goal would be to establish the basic investigative apparatus that is required to estimate the long-term carrying capacities of Earth for societies under different assumptions of lifestyle and the robustness and resilience of the ecosystem services required to maintain that lifestyle. The absence of such information, widely shared, is an enormous barrier to the making appropriate policy interventions.

3.5 CONCLUSIONS AND RECOMMENDATIONS

Our most basic conclusion is that policymakers fail to give adequate consideration to some of the most fundamental aspects of the complex adaptive global system they are charged with influencing.

There are a series of evolutionarily inspired topics that badly need a public airing in humanity's attempts to deal with the two intertwined complex adaptive systems. They include their unpredictability —people as a whole must begin to substitute probabilistic thinking for the notion that science can "prove" things or that supernatural forces can supply certainty about ethical issues or the trajectory to the future. Such probabilistic thinking is, of course, central to all standard evolutionary thought, genetic or cultural. In discussions of infrastructure or institutions, much more attention needs to be paid to the issues of robustness and resilience. Considering robustness—how desired aspects of the social CAS can resist change or return to desired states following perturbation—is one of the most ignored aspects of the human predicament. For example, rich nations designed and deployed electric grids that originally were sensible and, with the invention of alternating current, relatively efficient. Now, for economic and political reasons, they are tending toward unreliability and with their great expansion are vulnerable to propagating disaster. In the extreme, a solar storm of the magnitude that occurs every century or so could destroy all the transformers in the North American grid, essentially crippling the civilization of the continent. Without electricity, gasoline and oil could not be pumped; food could not be harvested, dried, or transported; the subways of New York would flood and the skyscrapers would topple; many water systems would collapse; most medical aid would be unavailable; and new transformers could not be manufactured. It would be a catastrophe absolutely unprecedented in scale and death rate, and yet no serious steps have been taken to make the electrical system robust (e.g., modularizing it to one degree or another in the process of transitioning away from fossil-fuel-based generation).

Similarly, it now appears that precipitation patterns will be changing dramatically for at least the next millennium (Solomon et al. 2009), but as yet there is not even broad discussion as to how to convert humanity's water-handling infrastructure so that it is more robust to those relatively unpredictable shifts. Here, as in the evolution of development patterns in organisms, the issue of buffering would necessarily enter the analysis. Just as in development the gene-environment system is buffered in order that minor changes in genes, gene regulation, or environmental impacts do not change the number of heads on an animal, so water systems need to be redesigned so that storage is sufficient and ducting adequate that critical amounts will be available to agriculture where it is essential.

All of this implies that economists should pay much more attention to the allocation of opportunity costs of dealing with the most likely threats embodied in the little-understood instabilities of the linked complex adaptive systems. It suggests that more consideration should be given to establishment and reestablishment of foresight institutions in all nations—for example, in the US replacing the excellent Office of Technology Assessment of the Congress that was foolishly disbanded in 1995, and expanding its mandate. Foresight institutions could provide needed estimates of carrying capacities, capital requirements for revising water-handling infrastructure under different scenarios of climate disruption, necessary revisions of global governance mechanisms, and the like. They could help attack an aspect of the social CAS that demographer Nathan Keyfitz described accurately two decades ago: "If we have one piece of empirically backed knowledge, it is that bad policies are widespread and persistent. Social science has to take account of them" (Keyfitz 1991: 15).

We also believe that at this time of crisis the world desperately needs to start a dialogue on the big issues, since the natural sciences have clearly shown that the ecosystem CAS upon which humanity depends has been significantly degraded. There are numerous and diverse attempts to start organizing the necessary discourse. One example is the MAHB (Millennium Alliance for Humanity and the Biosphere, <http://mahb.stanford.edu/>), which is bringing together natural and social scientists and scholars from the humanities to try to catalyze needed developments throughout society. Another is the Pachacuti movement (<http://pachacuti.com/>), trying to build an online community that would help to shift human cultures and institutions towards environmentally sustainable practices and an equitable and satisfying future. Unless how people perceive and use ecological capital and services changes, the continuity of today's societies, an unchallenged assumption of past thinking, is seriously in question. In any case, special emphasis now should be given to making it clear to people that the issues of human well-being that have been central to Partha Dasgupta's work are also central to creating the required dialogue, however generated.

Any programs or movements trying to rapidly move society toward sustainability, will need to emphasize that many old ideas—such as that infinite growth of the physical economy is possible, that people are rational utility maximizers, that plagues are a phenomenon of the past, that nation states are the final stage of evolution of large political entities—can no longer be solid anchors for thinking about the future. Overall we would also recommend the "precautionary principle" needs to move into the forefront of both policy analysis and the thinking of the general public. This principle states, loosely, that we should avoid following any policy for which there is credible, even though not conclusive, evidence that it may lead to a very serious negative effect. In theory it should be prominent in any properly done cost-benefit analysis, but it normally is not—indeed many of the interactions of the human system with the ecosystem-environmental system (e.g., depletion of natural capital) are classically ignored. It's a big order to apply the principle broadly to the really major issues facing society, but doing so would greatly improve society's ability to buffer the serious threats embodied in the evolution of the two intertwined complex adaptive systems, which have been so central to Partha Dasgupta's research agenda.

Bibliography

Ariely, D. (2009). *Predictably Irrational: The Hidden Forces that Shape Our Decisions.* New York, NY: HarperCollins.

Arrow, K. J. (1974). *The Limits of Organization.* New York, NY: W. W. Norton.

—— (2009). "A Note on Uncertainty and Discounting in Models of Economic Growth," *Journal of Risk*, 38: 87–94.

—— and P. Dasgupta (2009). "Conspicuous Consumption, Inconspicuous Leisure," *The Economic Journal*, 119(541): F497–F516.

—— and S. A. Levin. (2009). "Intergenerational Resource Transfers with Random Offspring," *Proceedings of the National Academy of Sciences*, 106/33: 13702–13706.

Arthur, W. B. (1994). *Increasing Returns and Path Dependence in the Economy.* Ann Arbor, MI: University of Michigan Press.

Axelrod, R. (1984). *The Evolution of Cooperation.* New York, NY: Basic Books.

Cohen, J. E. (1996). *How Many People Can the Earth Support?* New York, NY: W. W. Norton.

Daily, G. C. and P. R. Ehrlich (1996). "Socioeconomic Equity, Sustainability, and Earth's Carrying Capacity," *Ecological Applications*, 6: 991–1001.

Dasgupta, P. (2008). "Discounting Climate Change," *Journal of Risk and Uncertainty*, 37: 141–69.

—— (2007). *Economics: A Very Short Introduction.* Oxford: Oxford University Press.

—— (2001). *Human Well-Being and the Natural Environment.* Oxford: Oxford University Press.

—— (2003). 'Population, Poverty, and the Natural Environment', in K. G. Mäler and J. R. Vincent (eds.), *Handbook of Environmental Economics, i: Environmental Degradation and Institutional Responses.* Amsterdam: Elsevier Science, 191–247.

Dasgupta, S., U. Deichmann, C. Meisner et al. (2005). "Where Is the Poverty-Environment Nexus? Evidence from Cambodia, Lao PDR, and Vietnam," *World Development*, 33(4): 617–38.

Dieckmann, U. and R. Law (1996). "The Dynamical Theory of Coevolution: A Derivation from Stochastic Ecological Processes," *Journal of Mathematical Biology* 34(5–6): 579–612.

Dobzhansky, T. (1973). "Nothing in Biology Makes Sense, Except in the Light of Evolution," *American Biology Teacher*, 35: 125–9.
Ehrlich, P. R. and A. H. Ehrlich (2009). *The Dominant Animal: Human Evolution and the Environment*. Washington, DC: Island Press.
—— and J. Holdren (1971). "Impact of Population Growth," *Science*, 171: 1212–7.
—— and P. H. Raven (1964). "Butterflies and Plants: A Study in Coevolution," *Evolution*, 18: 586–608.
Eshel, I. and U. Motro (1981). "Kin Selection and Strong Evolutionary Stability of Mutual Help," *Theoretical Population Biology*, 19: 420–33.
Friedman, M. (1962). *Capitalism and Freedom*. Chicago, IL: University of Chicago Press.
Geritz, S. A. H., E. Kisdi, G. Meszena et al. (1998). "Evolutionarily Singular Strategies and the Adaptive Growth and Branching of the Evolutionary Tree," *Evolutionary Ecology*, 12: 35–57.
Gould, S. J. and R. C. Lewontin (1979). "The Spandrels of San Marco and the Panglossian Paradigm: A Critique of the Adaptationist Programme," *Proceedings of the Royal Society of London B*, 205: 581–98.
Haldane, A. J. and R. M. May (2011). "Systemic Risk in Banking Ecosystems," *Nature*, 469: 351–5.
Hardin, G. (1968). "The Tragedy of the Commons," *Science*, 162: 1243–7.
Harte, J. (2007). "Human Population as a Dynamic Factor in Environmental Degradation," *Population and Environment*, 28: 223–36.
Hartwell, L. H., J. J. Hopfield, S. Leibler et al. (1999). "From Molecular to Modular Cell Biology," *Nature*, 402 Supplement: C47–C52.
Holdren, J. P. and P. R. Ehrlich (1974). "Human Population and the Global Environment," *American Scientist*, 62: 282–92.
Holland, J. (1995). *Hidden Order: How Adaptation Builds Complexity*. Reading, MA: Addison-Wesley.
Hutchinson, G. E. (1961). "The Paradox of the Plankton," *American Naturalist*, 95(882): 137–45.
Jacob, F. (1977). "Evolution and Tinkering," *Science*, 196(4295): 1161–6.
Janzen, D. H. (1980). "When Is It Coevolution?" *Evolution*, 34: 611–2.
Juglar, C. (1862). *Des crises commerciales et leur retour périodique en France, en Angleterre et aux États Unis*. Paris: Guillaumin.
Kauffman, S. and S. Levin (1987). "Towards a General Theory of Adaptive Walks on Rugged Landscapes," *Journal of Theoretical Biology*, 128(1): 11–45.
Keyfitz, N. (1991). "Population and Development within the Ecosphere: One View of the Literature," *Population Index*, 57: 5–22.
Levin, S. A. (2013). "Comment on 'Voluntary Pledges and Green Growth in the Post-Copenhagen Economy' by Thomas Sterner and 'World Economic Crises: Commodity Prices and Environmental Scarcity as Missing Links' by Ramón López." *The Annual Bank Conference on Development Economics (ABDCE), Papers and Proceedings, 2010, Stockholm, Sweden*. Washington, DC: World Bank, 195–200.
—— (1998). "Ecosystems and the Biosphere as Complex Adaptive Systems," *Ecosystems*, 1: 431–6.
—— (1999). *Fragile Dominion: Complexity and the Commons*. Reading, MA: Perseus Books.

Levins, R. (1968). *Evolution in Changing Environments.* Princeton, NJ: Princeton University Press.
Lewontin, R. C. (1977). "Adaptation," *Encicl Einaudi Turin,* 1: 198–214.
—— (1961). "Evolution and the Theory of Games," *Journal of Theoretical Biology,* 1: 382–403.
Lovelock, J. E. (1972). "Gaia as Seen through the Atmosphere," *Atmospheric Environment,* 6: 579–80.
—— (2001). *Gaia: The Practical Science of Planetary Medicine.* New York, NY: Oxford University Press.
MacKellar, F. L. (1996). "On Human Carrying Capacity: A Review Essay on Joel Cohen's: How Many People Can the Earth Support?" *Population and Development Review,* 22(1): 145–56.
Margulis, L. and J. E. Lovelock (1974). "Biological Modulation of the Earth's Atmosphere," *Icarus,* 21: 471–489.
Marshall, A. (1890). *Principles of Economics.* London, New York: McMillan and Co.
—— (1907). "Social Possibilities of Economic Chivalry," *Economic Journal* (March), in A. C. Pigou (ed.), *Memorials of Alfred Marshall.* London: McMillan and Co., 1925, 323–46.
Maynard Smith, J. (1982). *Evolution and the Theory of Games.* Cambridge; New York, NY: Cambridge University Press.
—— and G. R. Price (1973). "The Logic of Animal Conflict," *Nature,* 246: 15–18.
Morgenstern, O. (1935). "Vollkommene Voraussicht und Wirtschaftliches Gleichgewicht," *Zeitschrift für Nastionalökonomie,* 6: 327–57.
Mundell, R. A. (1961). "A Theory of Optimal Currency Areas," *American Economic Review,* 51(4): 657–65.
Nash, J. F. (1950). "Equilibrium Points in *n*-Person Games," *Proceedings of the National Academy of Sciences,* 36(1): 48–9.
—— (1951). "Non-Cooperative Games," *Annals of Mathematics, Second Series,* 54(2): 286–95.
Ostrom, E. (2010). "Polycentric Systems for Coping with Collective Action and Global Environmental Change," *Global Environmental Change,* 20(4): 550–7.
Pyke, G. H. (1984). "Optimal Foraging Theory: A Critical Review," *Annual Review of Ecology and Systematics,* 15: 523–75.
Rees, W. E. (2001). "Ecological Footprint," in S. A. Levin (ed.), *Encyclopedia of Biodiversity, ii.* San Diego, CA: Academic Press, 229–44.
Scheffer, M. (2008). *Critical Transitions in Nature and Society.* Princeton, NJ: Princeton University Press.
Scheffer, M., J. Bascompte, W. A. Brock et al. (2009). "Early Warning Signals for Critical Transitions," *Nature,* 461: 53–9.
Schneider, S. H. and P. J. Boston, eds. (1991). *Scientists on Gaia.* Cambridge, MA: MIT Press.
Slobodkin, L. (1964). "The Strategy of Evolution," *American Scientist,* 52: 342–357.
Smith, A. (1776). *An Inquiry into the Nature and Causes of the Wealth of Nations.* London: W. Strahan and T. Cadell. Reprinted Indianapolis, IN: Liberty Press, 1981.
Solomon, S., G. K. Plattner, R. Knutti et al. (2009). "Irreversible Climate Change due to Carbon Dioxide Emissions," *Proceedings of the National Academy of Sciences,* 106: 1704–9.

Tainter, J. A. (1988). *The Collapse of Complex Societies*. Cambridge: Cambridge University Press.

Wackernagel, M. and W. Rees (1996). *Our Ecological Footprint: Reducing Human Impact on the Earth*. Gabriola Island, BC: New Society Publishers.

Walras, L. (1874). *Éléments d'économie politique pure, ou théorie de la richesse sociale, Part 1*. Paris, Lausanne, Basel.

—— (1877). *Éléments d'économie politique pure, ou théorie de la richesse sociale, Part 2*. Paris, Lausanne, Basel.

—— (1954). *Elements of Pure Economics; or, The Theory of Social Wealth*. Translated by W. Jaffé. Homewood, IL: Published for the American Economic Association by Richard D. Irwin, Inc.

4

An Institutional Analysis of Development Cooperation

Elinor Ostrom, Clark Gibson, Sujai Shivakumar, and Krister Andersson

Successful development aid generates the appropriate incentives so that the time, skill, knowledge, and effort of multiple individuals create jointly valued outcomes. These incentives come from the institutions—the rules of the games of life and productive coexistence—that development aid helps to create or modify. As a society forms more robust networks of institutions that facilitate individuals to resolve their collective-action problems, it displays the economic and human development characteristics of a wealthy society. Development aid can help to foster and maintain those institutions.

This understanding of development stands in contrast with the traditional role of aid agencies as external mechanisms that infuse the capital and expertise needed to relieve the pathologies of poverty and transform societies. The efficacy of this traditional approach, however, is increasingly being questioned. Most recent studies of development assistance programs conclude that, despite tremendous efforts and good intentions, aid has produced disappointing results in the aggregate (Adam and O'Connell 1999; Burnside and Dollar 2000; Cohen, Grindle, and Walker 1985; Dollar and Easterly 1999; Tsikata 1998; World Bank 1998; Riddell 2007). Seeking to explain this disappointing performance, some bilateral and multilateral aid agencies have indicated that the lack of proper incentives generated by aid itself may be an important factor undermining its sustainability (Easterly 2001, 2003; Martens et al. 2002; Ostrom et al. 2002).

How can we address the challenge of aid if we understand underdevelopment as arising from multiple failures of collective action? When individuals trying to do good find themselves hampered in these efforts, it is important to step back and examine the incentives that they face, and to explore how these incentives might impede rather than enhance development while also reducing the sustainability of critical environmental resources. The tools of institutional analysis developed by scholars at the Workshop in Political Theory and Policy Analysis at Indiana University can help us examine how specific incentives created by extant institutional structures can lead even well-intentioned individuals to produce unintended and even counterproductive results.

The work of Partha Dasgupta has been extremely important to the field of economic development and our understanding of how institutions affect the incentives of officials and citizens, leading to well-being in some instances and poverty traps in others (Dasgupta 1993, 1995). Dasgupta's work on social capital (Dasgupta and Serageldin 2000) is also fundamental to an understanding of how individuals at all levels of a society can create an important form of institutional capital by increasing the trust that they have in one another so as to overcome a diversity of social dilemmas—especially related to resource problems (Dasgupta 2001). Given the foundational work that Dasgupta has contributed to the analysis of development problems, we are honored to contribute this chapter to a book in his honor.[1]

4.1 UNDERSTANDING COLLECTIVE ACTION IN DEVELOPMENT AID

The concepts of collective action and collective-action problems are central to understanding the challenge of development as well as core environmental problems. We define a collective-action situation as a situation that occurs when two or more individuals come together to produce something of value, when it would be difficult to produce it alone. A collective-action problem occurs when a lack of motivation and/or missing or asymmetric information generates incentives that prevent individuals from satisfactorily resolving a collective-action situation. Institutions can overcome these challenges and help individuals achieve higher levels of benefits than if they acted alone. Better institutional solutions endure when they remain adaptive to changing social and physical conditions, as is likely in the context of development aid given to beneficiaries in developing countries (Poteete, Janssen, and Ostrom 2010).

[1] This chapter is based on our earlier work on the political economy of development (Gibson et al. 2005). The original study was commissioned by the Swedish International Development Cooperation Agency (Sida). When preparing the original study, our team spent several months at Sida's headquarters in Stockholm as well as their field offices in India and Zambia. We are deeply indebted to all of the individuals who gave us substantial time when we talked with them or helped to dig out documents, data, and archival materials. We have also benefited greatly by interactions with Professors Matt Auer, Roy Gardner, Michael McGinnis, and Christopher Waller. We thank Eduardo Araral, Shaun McMahon, Esther Mwangi, Amy Poteete, and Enrico Schaar, and Frank van Laerhoven for their useful input. We also thank Joanna Broderick and Patty Lezotte for their excellent editing in helping us prepare this chapter.

Collective-action problems pervade all efforts of international development cooperation. International development cooperation is intended to help the people living in less-developed countries overcome poverty resulting from the wide diversity of often unresolved or poorly resolved collective-action problems (Shirley 2008). Unless development aid properly addresses the incentives of underlying collective-action problems, it will likely be ineffective or, worse, counterproductive. We attribute much of the current lackluster performance of international development cooperation to limited efforts to understand and address the incentives of underlying collective-action problems. The upside of this observation is that with more attention to institutional analysis during all stages of the development cooperation process, performance and sustainability are likely to improve.

The remainder of this chapter is structured as follows: After a brief introduction to the Institutional Analysis and Development (IAD) framework, we discuss the basic collective-action problems that hamper current efforts in development cooperation. Section 4.3 applies the IAD framework to analyze the incentives that are present in several important collective-action situations related to development. Section 4.4 presents the "Aid Octangle," which is a graphic representation of a stylized development cooperation structure that illuminates the incentive structures across different interactions among the core development actors. The Aid Octangle was originally formulated by the four authors of this chapter in a study commissioned by the Swedish International Development Cooperation Agency (Sida) (see Ostrom et al. 2002). Section 4.5 explores how different characteristics and modalities of development cooperation affect incentive structures for different actors. In Section 4.6, we analyze how the growing reliance on contractors in all phases of development cooperation affects the incentives for sustainable outcomes. We conclude with a discussion of how to apply institutional analysis to help achieve improvements in international development cooperation.

4.2 THE INSTITUTIONAL ANALYSIS AND DEVELOPMENT (IAD) FRAMEWORK

Institutional analysts often refer to dysfunctional situations (e.g., see Ostrom, Schroeder, and Wynne 1993; Gibson et al. 2005). These situations can generate counterintentional and counterproductive outcomes for the actors within them and for others affected by them. To help us understand the basic characteristics of such dysfunctional situations and why these problems occur in the first place, we apply the IAD framework. This framework provides a strong basis from which to analyze incentives within dynamic, interactive, and multiple-level phenomena, such as those found in development assistance.

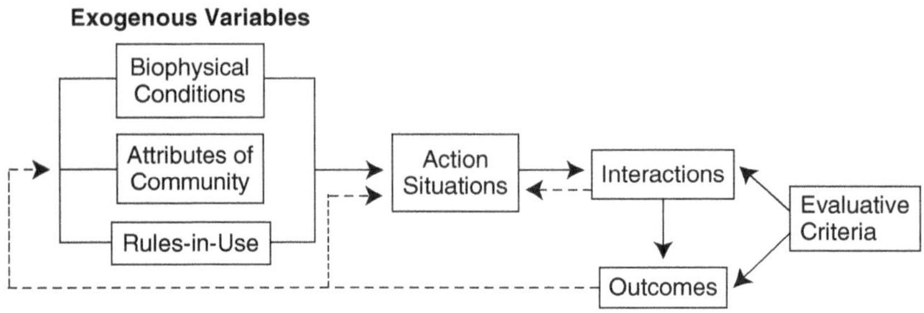

Figure 4.1 A framework for institutional analysis
Source: Adapted from Ostrom (2005: 15)

The IAD framework focuses on the incentives and outcomes generated by actors in particular decision-making settings (Ostrom 2005, 2011; Ostrom, Gardner, and Walker 1994; Kiser and Ostrom 1982; Oakerson 1992). Developed by colleagues at Indiana University, the IAD framework has been employed in a large number of empirical studies, including those that measured the impact of metropolitan-area governance structures on urban service delivery, gauged how institutional incentives affect infrastructure sustainability in developing countries, and explained how ecological conditions combined with institutional structure affect land use change dynamics (see Ostrom, Schroeder, and Wynne 1993; Gibson, McKean, and Ostrom 2000; Andersson 2006).[2] Figure 4.1 provides a graphic representation of the IAD framework.

4.2.1 The Basic Categories of Variables and Their Relationships

As shown in Figure 4.1, the IAD framework draws analytical attention to the following elements:

- The *action situation* is a conceptual unit that defines the inner boundaries of an analysis. As such, it contains one set of variables about the structure of the *action situations* that are under analysis. The analyst must also decide what assumptions will be made about the *actors* that participate in a relevant action situation. An *actor* can be either a single individual or a group of individuals who have a regularized way of making decisions, such as a firm or a government.

[2] The February 2011 issue of the *Policy Studies Journal* is devoted to a discussion of the multiple uses of the IAD framework over time including both development and environmental problems.

- The *context* that frames and affects action situations (including other related and relevant situations). The context provides the initial conditions or "the environment" that structures the efforts to achieve outcomes, including groups of variables that describe the context's physical conditions, rules-in-use, and the attributes of a community. It is within this context that an analyst can identify an *action situation* and its *incentives*.
- The *patterns of interactions* and outcomes that are likely to emerge. Actors behave and interact based on perceived incentives, with their activities, in aggregate, generating patterns of *outcomes*.
- The *evaluation* of the interactions and *outcomes* using multiple criteria designed by participants and by external analysts. For the study of international development cooperation, common evaluative criteria include sustainability, accountability, efficiency, equity, and effectiveness. The criteria used depend on the interest of the analyst as well as the particular goals of the development cooperation under study.

In a nutshell, an IAD-guided analysis involves an identification of critical variables of interest and an examination of their relationships. For example, the three categories of context variables—consisting of working rules, biophysical/material conditions, and community attributes—provide the initial conditions or "the environment" that structures efforts to achieve outcomes. It is within this context that an analyst can identify an action situation and its incentives for an individual's choices. Action situations are composed of the incentives generated by the situation's context, and the incentives of the particular actors involved. Finally, these actors, operating within the incentives produced by action situations, interact and make choices to generate outcomes.

In the context of international development cooperation, all of these relationships are shaped by at least three levels of governance: the constitutional level, the policymaking (or collective-choice) level, and the operational level. One of the strengths of the IAD framework is that it presents a practical method for analyzing how decision-making at any one level of governance is influenced by processes and relationships at other levels.

When individuals interact in repetitive settings that directly affect physical outcomes, they are in an operational situation. All production and consumption activities exist at an operational level of analysis. The construction and operation of a power plant or the planting of an agricultural field are examples of operational situations. The rules that affect the structure of an operational situation are themselves designed and agreed upon in policymaking situations (also called collective-choice situations). Elected officials in legislative or executive bodies in both donor and recipient countries make policy decisions about rules that affect the structure of many operational situations. These policies are themselves made within constitutional rules that affect who will make policy decisions using what type of rules and procedures. Hence, the three levels of governance (operational, collective-choice, and constitutional) link together through the rules-in-use that structure the interactions between individuals at each level.

The focus on multilevel governance dynamics is critical for the institutional analysis of international development cooperation. To the extent that the analysis is limited to just one level—be it the operational, collective-choice, or the constitutional—it is easy to underestimate the complexity of effectively addressing collective-action problems through development cooperation interventions. For example, as a donor trying to help the population of a recipient country, an aid organization's staff members face a diverse set of multilevel action situations. First, they confront the structure of the multiple underlying operational problems existing in the recipient countries. To achieve sustainable development in the recipient countries, the staff members have to affect these underlying situations. To do so requires substantial knowledge about the history and context of these situations as well as about the way operational, policy, and constitutional choices are made in that cultural context. Institutional analysis can help the analyst to identify how observed human behavior at one level is affected by and also affects structure and processes at other levels of governance. Being cognizant of these inter-level relationships and how they affect observed behavior is a first step toward addressing the identified collective-action problems.

In the next section, we review the most generic, pervasive, and unproductive situations at the operational level that frequently characterize developing country contexts (although they may appear anywhere). These can be grouped into two big groups of obstacles to collective action: motivation and information problems.

4.3 MOTIVATION AND INFORMATION PROBLEMS AT THE OPERATIONAL LEVEL

Basic incentive problems result from both the nature of the goods and services involved in development assistance as well as the relationships between actors. Motivation and information problems that give rise to incentive problems can exist at the operational, collective-choice, and constitutional levels. We first focus on motivation and information problems at the operational level. These basic problems need to be solved if the goals of development assistance are to be achieved. Problems of motivation include those involved with public goods, common-pool resources, and the "Samaritan's dilemma" (Gibson et al. 2005).

- *Public good* problems occur when an individual's consumption of a good is not affected by his or her contribution to producing the good. In such situations, an individual has an incentive to *free ride*—to enjoy the good without contribution. Consumption of the good by one individual, however, does not exclude others from consuming the good as well. National defense, radio broadcasts, environmental protection, and education services are all examples of public goods.

- *Common-pool resources* share the difficulty of exclusion with public goods. Unlike public goods, however, one person's use does subtract from the resources available to others. Thus, the problem concerning common-pool resources is that without effective institutions, too many users overharvest (Ostrom, Gardner, and Walker 1994). Many natural resources are common-pool goods, but other goods with which donors are frequently involved have common-pool attributes, like the electricity grid of a country. The government budget is also a common-pool resource since politicians and bureaucrats can consume parts of the treasury at little cost to themselves (Campos and Pradhan 1996). Donor largesse can, in some cases, create a fiscal commons that is ongoing, subject to few constraints and therefore likely to produce inefficient and inequitable outcomes (see Eriksson Skoog 2000).
- The *Samaritan's dilemma* occurs when an actor who is deeply concerned about the well-being of others confronts situations in which other actors are in serious need of help (Buchanan 1977; see also Stone 2008). In Buchanan's formulation, the Samaritan chooses between helping and not helping. The recipient, on the other hand, decides how much effort he or she must make to obtain the Samaritan's help, high or low. If the Samaritan extends help and the recipient exerts high effort, both the Samaritan and the recipient benefit—but the recipient receives even higher benefits when expending less effort. Samaritans face the puzzling problem that their best strategy is always to extend help, but reciprocating with high effort is not the best strategy for the recipient. This dilemma is clearly relevant to development assistance, including the challenge of infrastructure maintenance.

4.3.1 Missing or Asymmetric Information

Missing and asymmetric information also plague development assistance by creating incentives that do not facilitate successful outcomes. With missing information, actors do not know the complete structure of the situation they face. There may be missing information about some of the actions they could take, about the linkages of actions to outcomes, and about material or intrinsic payoffs (Holmstrom 1982a, 1982b; Miller 1992; Moe 1984). This can occur in development assistance, for example, if local knowledge is not included in the design and implementation of a project or program. Asymmetric information also generates poor incentives, including those of principal-agent problems, moral hazard, and adverse selection problems.

- *Principal-agent problems* exist in all hierarchies. They exist within donor agencies as well as within government agencies and ministries in recipient countries. Within such hierarchies, employees who work directly with development activities know more about what they do than the managers to whom they report. Another hierarchy where principal-agent relationships are also common can be seen within the development cooperation arrangement itself. Within this cooperative arrangement, donors and recipient country organizations agree to a set of joint activities, but the real goals of the donor and recipient will often differ. This combination of asymmetric preferences and asymmetric information about a recipient's actions gives rise to inefficient outcomes that increase with the layers of a hierarchy, like all international development agencies (IDAs) and governments. Recipients will not necessarily choose the means or the ends that their donors prefer.
- *Moral hazard problems* exist in a wide variety of settings where individuals are guaranteed a benefit or protected against loss once an initial contract has been entered, regardless of whether they take the proper level of effort to realize the benefit or avoid the loss (Campbell 1995). Governments (or communities) receiving donor financial aid may make solemn promises to reform their own institutions, but may avoid following through. The availability of aid creates a moral hazard, since the aid helps to insulate incompetent governments from the results of their (in)actions, thus weakening their incentive to find alternative revenue sources or better policies (van de Walle 2001; Bräutigam 2000).
- *Adverse selection problems* also occur when information is hidden, leading to the selection of the worst individuals or components. For example, if donors give loans for economic development projects and do not demand repayment of the loans, recipient governments may not work hard to select investment projects that generate high returns needed to repay future obligations. Bad projects can begin to replace good projects.

4.3.2 Overcoming Motivational and Informational Problems

Overcoming motivational and informational problems at the operational level is not easy. Individuals living in donor countries frequently enjoy more favorable institutional conditions to self-organize and to solve motivational and informational problems than individuals living in many recipient countries. In most developed countries, entrepreneurial individuals can solve many collective-action problems within a well-developed property-rights system backed up by effective courts and governance systems at multiple levels. By relying on family, kin, and friends, individuals in developing countries are able to undertake a wide variety of small-scale activities that enhance their economic well-being. These arrangements are often limited to the "informal sector" and to relatively small-scale enterprises. Achieving increasing economic productivity and poverty reduction requires helping those involved and their political leaders to change the structure of the situations they face to counteract effectively the problems of motivation and information.

4.4 CHANGING OPERATIONAL RULES IN POLICY SITUATIONS: WHAT ARE THE INCENTIVES?

Many operational-level problems are solved through informal, face-to-face discussions framed within the basic rules-in-use. They enable the participants to agree upon coordinated strategies and develop shared norms. Coordinated strategies and shared norms are insufficient to solve all collective-action problems because the roots of the particular collective-action problems at the operational level are often linked to processes at the policy, or even constitutional, levels of decision-making. Unless the incentive structures at the policy and constitutional levels are aligned with the incentive structures at an operational level, chances are that local people's efforts to construct and sustain institutional arrangements for collective action will fail (Shivakumar 2005). Development in countries with a high gross national product (GNP) has taken place because many of these basic operational problems are managed within a broad set of institutional arrangements that facilitate a wide diversity of enforceable contractual arrangements.

When embedded in an open public realm that has an effective property-rights system and an accessible and fair court system, individuals can build trusting relationships that enable them to increase the benefits that they can jointly obtain. In aid-recipient countries, however, such institutions are often missing, weak, or bad.

4.4.1 Missing, Weak, or Bad Institutions

When essential institutions, such as effective property-rights systems and fair court systems, are missing, weak, or bad, problem-solving individuals often must deal primarily with their own family and networks of friends and neighbors. In countries with weak or bad institutions, the institutions of the public sector may actually impede the search for collective solutions or even make the problem worse. Missing, weak, or bad institutions are often the result of perverse incentives at the policymaking level where we again find basic problems resulting from motivational and informational sources.

Rules are public goods: the use of a rule by one person does not subtract from the availability of the rule for others, and all actors in the situation receive the benefit in future encounters regardless of whether they spent any time and effort trying to devise new rules. Designing effective rules to solve a wide variety of problems at multiple levels takes substantial time and effort and is often underprovided. Developing countries may face, on the other hand, excessive rules copied from other countries that are difficult to implement.

Rules are rarely neutral in their allocation of resources. Policies in countries with weak government accountability are likely to create benefits for officials while providing perverse incentives at the operational level. Even with public-spirited individuals in powerful positions, the lack or distortion of information from the operational to collective-choice to constitutional levels can generate poor rule choices. When those powerful individuals have to worry about things besides the most efficient policy—such as their own incomes or electoral chances—the rules they create will be that much further away from those needed for effective and sustainable outcomes.

4.4.2 Overcoming Motivational and Informational Asymmetries

A major difference between developed and developing countries is the prevalence of dysfunctional situations in the latter. Many unproductive outcomes in policymaking situations are not evident in the more developmentally advanced societies where participants engage in ongoing efforts to improve performance of outcomes by changing the rules used in these situations.

Given that changes in the rule-structuring situation can also change the distribution of benefits—and in this way greatly advantage some participants while hurting others—the process of changing rules is never a simple path toward more efficient and fair outcomes. The broad trajectory in the more developed countries has been, however, toward creating nested sets of institutional arrangements that together seek to create situations that generate positive outcomes for most participants.

4.4.3 Enter the Donor

When a donor enters a recipient country to try to help, it enters a diversity of operational and policy situations that are already difficult and adds to the complexity of the prevailing incentive structures. Donors must enter a recipient country and interact with officials and citizens in a variety of situations. The donor always adds at least an additional layer to the original action. The donor's presence, whether intentional or not, alters or exacerbates, for better or worse, existing incentives. In many cases, these changes in the incentive structure linger only as long as the donor remains an active player. On the other hand, in some cases, the change may linger for a very long time (Gardner and Waller 2005).

One of the unintentional impacts of development assistance can be the result of moral hazards introduced by the aid process itself. Even the formulae used in determining the appropriate level of aid are not incentive neutral. Many donors have used financing gap models. However, such models give recipient country officials an incentive to maintain or increase the financing gap by encouraging low savings (i.e., high consumption) so as to be eligible for more aid. At a policymaking level, some projects involve aid negotiations or dealings with recipient country officials who, in turn, can decide on the merits of alternative projects. (After all, aid programs often encourage local officials to see themselves as owners of each project.) However, these officials, as agents, can have their own interests at heart.

4.5 INCENTIVES ACROSS SITUATIONS: THE INTERNATIONAL DEVELOPMENT COOPERATION "OCTANGLE"

4.5.1 The System of Development Assistance

Action situations link within a system. Sometimes the system is contained entirely within one organization and is represented in a simplified form by an organization chart. For international development assistance, the set of linked situations cross many organizational and even national boundaries. The effectiveness of a given system depends on the way its action situations are linked together. An effectively structured system of federal governance, for example, links national, regional, and local units so that each can undertake those activities for which it is most efficient.

Development cooperation can similarly be thought of as a system or network of linked action situations. The conventional way of thinking about these linkages is as a "chain of aid delivery." To understand the incentives of development cooperation, it is more appropriate to view it as a set of nested situations that may take on any of a variety of productive or unproductive relationships. We characterize these relationships as the International Development Cooperation Octangle—"the Octangle," for short.

4.5.2 The Octangle

The Octangle features the eight major actors of development cooperation nested within a system: (1) donor government, (2) recipient government, (3) other donors, (4) a donor's IDA, (5) recipient government's ministries and agencies, (6) third-party implementing organizations (e.g., nongovernment organizations [NGOs], private contractors), (7) organized interest groups and civil society organizations within the donor and recipient countries, and (8) targeted beneficiaries. Figure 4.2 presents these actors' most important linkages.

The incentives of officials at all levels need to be taken into account when planning donor-assisted projects and programs. If these are not overtly analyzed, a project that initially looks like it will provide help to needy people may instead be viewed with suspicion and undercut by those who view the activity with a different set of incentives. Exploring the full set of relationships among the major actors involved in international assistance allows the examination of how "the system" as a whole might create positive or negative incentives for individual action.

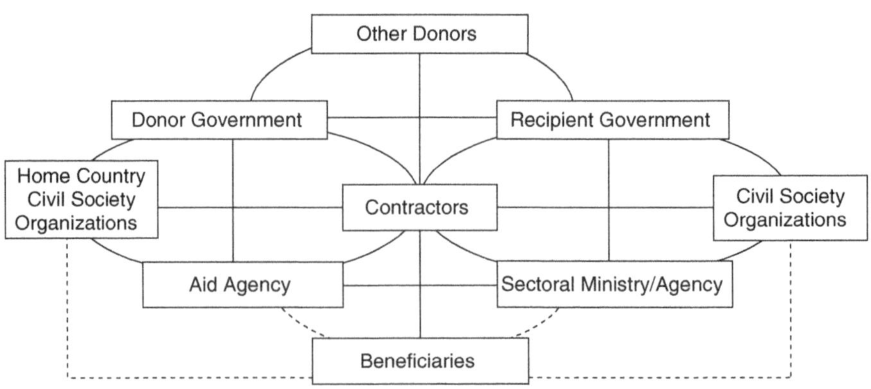

Figure 4.2 The international aid Octangle

Source: Adapted from Gibson et al. (2005: 64)

4.5.3 Relationships within the Octangle

One core relationship is that between donor and recipient governments. In many situations, there is a great asymmetry in their bargaining powers. A weak recipient is one who is dependent on aid and lacks sufficient capacity in economic planning and project administration. Such a recipient may not make much effort to prioritize its needs in seeking assistance and will accept any plans presented by a strong donor. In such cases, negotiations between the two nominal sovereigns can be turned into a principal-agent situation where the donor, as principal, specifies what the recipient country, as agent, must do if it wants to receive development assistance.

In other situations, there is relatively less power asymmetry; that is, a strong donor and strong recipient. The presence of a strong recipient does not necessarily translate into more sustainability. When the recipient country is governed by officials who are primarily interested in seeking out opportunities for private gain, and few institutions are in place to keep these motivations in check, moral hazard problems can become substantial.

If a donor is "enlightened," it will try to designate recipients as owners for each aid intervention. Sweden, for instance, has tried to avoid playing the strong donor–weak recipient game. It has sought to encourage ownership of development projects by recipient governments through establishing country frames for long-term investments, and through providing technical assistance so that recipients can build their own competence over time.

In practice, it is extremely difficult to engage in dyadic negotiation processes where the donor has access to the funds that the recipient really wants while, at the same time, providing full ownership to the recipient. To avoid the Samaritan's dilemma, donor governments need to have more control over the process; this control is in tension with devolving ownership to recipients.

Ownership in development aid, *as generally practiced*, does not contain the four conditions of ownership we argue are necessary for sustainable outcomes:

1. Beneficiary owners need to enunciate a *demand* for aid;
2. Beneficiary owners need to allocate at least some of their own *assets* to the project or program so they have a real stake in the way their own and other actors' assets are used;
3. Beneficiary owners need to obtain *benefits*; and
4. Beneficiary owners need to have clear-cut responsibilities and be able to *participate in decisions* regarding continuance or non-continuance of a project.

4.5.4 Other Principal-Agent Relationships

In addition to the two-sided and three-sided relationships among sovereign governments, a series of principal-agent relationships exist within the ministries of the donor and recipient governments. All of these, in turn, have additional principal-agent relationships within their agencies and with the contractors responsible for carrying out a particular project. In Sweden, for example, the Finance Ministry and the Foreign Affairs Ministry play a major role in developing foreign aid policies and disbursement priorities. In turn, Sida assumes major responsibility for managing development programs. The likelihood of moral hazard problems within the involved donor agency is often more severe than for other public sector bureaucracies as there is often little correlation between the level of individual effort and the effectiveness and sustainability of aid.

The recipient country, correspondingly, may specify a single agency, such as the Indian Department of Economic Affairs in the Ministry of Finance, or authorize several internal ministries or agencies to coordinate its aid policy and to undertake the detailed negotiation and oversight of foreign aid programs and projects. Principal-agent relationships also occur between political leaders and bureaucrats. The political leaders of a recipient country may wish to conduct public affairs in a way that benefits a small clique of influential supporters. Bureaucrats are more likely to be worried about their own careers, especially in countries with small private sectors. In the donor country, politicians may be interested in their political survival and in convincing the public that taxpayer dollars are being spent in a wise and efficient manner. Politicians tend to stress the progress that foreign aid is achieving. Officials in a donor country's IDA face their own incentives related to administering a set of programs for which there are often few known successful technologies or even reliable measures of progress. One of these incentives is to spend allocated budgets, whether this is done efficiently or not, since politicians tend to interpret unallocated funds as evidence of unneeded funds.

Contractors and consultants are often brought in to assist the owner in implementation. The relationship between these third-party implementing agencies and the donor/recipient ministries is another principal-agent relationship where the interests of all parties have some overlap but also have considerable divergence. The initiative, design, and oversight of a project or program may rely heavily on a contractor, leading to considerable information asymmetries between donor, contractor, and recipient.

4.5.5 A Tangle of Relationships

Taken together, the relationships within and across countries, agencies, and their citizens can tangle the principal-agent relationships among the IDA, the recipient owner, and the third-party implementer. For example, whereas the IDA pays for the services of a contractor, the nominal principal is the recipient owner. Meanwhile, the consultant, typically, has more information about ground realities than do officials at the IDA or recipient agencies. Such consultants may in effect take on some of the IDA's administrative responsibilities. In this case, the intended owner may look to the consultant as its de facto principal. The result of this tangle of relationships is that many individuals are responsible for ensuring the effectiveness and sustainability of aid, but no one is really held accountable.

4.5.6 The Weakest Link

While some of the linkages described above are strong, others are relatively weak. Unfortunately, the link with beneficiaries is often the weakest link of all. While improving beneficiaries' welfare is the ultimate goal of project aid, feedback links from the beneficiaries to an IDA—indeed to most other Octangle actors—are weak to nonexistent. In the case of program aid, those who actually receive benefits are only indirectly linked to the donor and recipient governments. Neither donor nor recipient politicians have much accountability to the beneficiaries. The lack of such linkages with beneficiaries excludes valuable information and skills that can foster successful interventions for collective-action problems. Beneficiary organization is generally lacking in most settings.

Interest groups represent a wide variety of preferences, values, and deserved outcomes. Citizens in recipient countries, through their membership in interest groups, may also participate in the aid process. They may be organized in various specific user groups related to particular resources (e.g., forests, irrigation) or broader public interest groups lobbying government officials for particular development policies. Business interests within the donor country have frequently pressured the donor government to negotiate tied aid, whereby the funds given oblige recipient country governments to purchase goods (e.g., tractors, turbines, and other equipment) and/or services (such as training and consulting) from the donor country. Other donors sometimes act as interest groups by advocating certain kinds of aid (e.g., family planning, preserving the environment). Citizens in donor countries, however, rarely hear direct information from the targeted beneficiaries, making this information subject to manipulation by politicians and bureaucrats.

Competition among potential donors can exacerbate incentive problems. When the recipient knows that other donors will step in to fund a project even if one threatens to withdraw based on its recipient's poor show of effort, few consequences exist to put in less effort (or conversely, few incentives to change strategies).

4.6 INCENTIVES IN THE MODALITIES AND CHARACTERISTICS OF DEVELOPMENT COOPERATION

The context within which aid is structured and administered involves a series of interrelated action situations. Understanding incentives within this system of aid requires that we move beyond a focus on a single action situation—that between donor government and recipient government, for example—to consider more complex and configural relationships among a larger set of involved actors (Andersson and Ostrom 2008). Incentives in the interactions among these actors arise within the context of specific rule combinations that emerge, partly, from the presence of given modalities and characteristics of aid. These modalities and characteristics can thus affect the sustainability and effectiveness of donor assistance in solving beneficiary problems of collective action.

Particular aid *characteristics* (credits, grants, and guarantees) and aid *modalities* (project aid, program aid, and sector program support) are constituted by particular sets of rules. These rules, when taken in the context of existing institutions, produce diverse sets of incentives for those involved with aid.

4.6.1 Aid Characteristics

4.6.1.1 Grants

Grants are transfers made from the donor to the recipient in cash, goods, or services for which no repayment is required. Grants are attractive to the recipient since they do not have to be repaid and they are attractive to donors since they appear to enhance recipient ownership. Grants can have significant impacts—some perverse—on incentives. Below, we consider some scenarios where the incentive effects of grant aid are weakened.

The Problem of Fungibility. In some cases, recipient governments swap all or some portion of their *own* contributions to the project with that derived from donor funding. This causes a problem of fungibility. When aid resources are, in effect, shifted away from their intended target by the recipient, prospective owners face little added motivation to maintain the effort needed for project sustainability.

The Problem of Reputation. Responsible ownership of grants—that is, one aligned with an interest in the realization of properly funded outcomes—is enhanced if recipient governments need to maintain credibility with their donors/creditors. However, if the donor faces a Samaritan's dilemma, or if competition exists among donors, recipients have fewer stakes to protect a good reputation.

The Problem of Accountability. Even if officials at the recipient's finance ministry have an interest in maintaining credibility with their donor counterparts, they are often far removed from line ministry officials and other de facto owners further down in the chain of project implementation. These local-level officials, not faced with having to maintain an ongoing relationship with the donor, often suffer fewer repercussions for irresponsible uses of grant aid.

4.6.1.2 Credits

Credits (or loans) are transfers for which repayment is required. There are at least three potential advantages to credit-financed aid over grant aid: First, credits could oblige the recipient country to take greater ownership of projects since accepting credits incurs a debt for the country. Second, the use of market-financed concessionary credits is supposed to lead to larger inflows of capital than grants. Finally, credits are seen as providing a clearer commercial signal to the recipient.

In cases where ownership is separated from the associated responsibility, however, as often is the case in development cooperation, the incentive effect of credits is obscured. In the case of project aid, repayments of credits are usually derived from broad-based domestic taxes rather than the earnings of the project itself. As a result, no direct link exists between the project's success and the success of the loan. The ownership/responsibility links are also weak in program assistance, given that twenty-year (or longer) repayment plans do not match well the recipients' shorter (often politically influenced) time horizons. Often, credit incentives are associated with a recipient making unfulfilled promises to donors.

4.6.1.3 Guarantees

Guarantees facilitate the financing of projects—often relating to infrastructure—that use private sources of capital. Three basic types of guarantees are intended to cover different types of risks: investment guarantees cover the *political* risks in share capital. Credit enhancement guarantees overcome the *credit* risks developing-country borrowers pose. In addition, performance guarantees mitigate the *investor* risks from shortcomings that may exist in regulation, legislation, and project execution. Guarantees reduce the risk involved for firms from donor countries to invest in specific projects in the recipient country, but postpone the need for fundamental institutional reform required of the recipient countries to deal with the presence of these risks in the first place. Thus, donors may find themselves underwriting the recipient government's bad policies and creating a moral hazard problem.

4.6.2 Aid Modalities

Like aid characteristics, the different modalities of aid (such as project aid, program aid, technical cooperation, and research cooperation) also influence incentives. Under each modality, different actors, different linkages, and different rules combine to generate various arrays of incentives.

The scope of project aid is normally distinct and limited, with generally well-defined beneficiaries. The increased specificity of project aid allows a donor government to target more clearly both its domestic and recipient country beneficiaries, which will stimulate both to seek participation. Program aid, in broad comparison, focuses on the recipient country's overall policy objectives and macroeconomic goals. It may be privileged over project aid by a donor agency since it can distribute far greater allocations of an aid agency's budget with less administrative effort. Recipient country officials might also generally prefer the broad nature of program aid, to the extent that it provides them greater discretion over a large amount of resources.

4.7 INVOLVEMENT OF CONTRACTORS

The project development process frequently involves consultants, often even before an initial inquiry is made from the recipient. Indeed, consultants often have strong incentives to "help" the recipient formulate a project inquiry. Not surprisingly, these initial inquiries usually involve problem areas where the consultant has special expertise, relationships with a donor, and/or privileged information.

4.7.1 Contracts for Project Design and Implementation Services Sometimes Go to the Same Firm

It is not uncommon for project design consultants and project implementation consultants to be from the same firm. Such double participation would allow a firm to design projects that cater to their skills and insider knowledge of actors, putting other firms at a disadvantage in the bidding process. Double contracting has the potential to favor consultants' interests over the needs of recipients and beneficiaries, and in this way undermines a recipient's sense of ownership.

4.7.2 Contractors View the Program Developer, rather than the Recipient, as the De Facto Project Owner

Some programs' policies urge that recipient organizations take ownership of projects. Where this policy is applied, recipient owners make key project decisions and serve as principal to the contractors. Here, consultants and recipients often perceive the program developer as the de facto principal. Consultants often face incentives to maximize their efforts on tasks they think will please the donor. Given that consulting firms tend to seek long-term relationships, they strive hard to maintain their reputation and relationship with the donor.

4.7.3 Contractors are Often Motivated by Multiple Goals

Consultants are often motivated to secure well-paying work for their firm. They assume that by performing well on current tasks, additional—and perhaps larger and more lucrative—contracts might be obtained in the future. However, this profit-orientation of their business is only one motivator for doing good work, and is not even necessarily the most important one. Many are committed to developing meaningful, productive partnerships with counterparts overseas. Public praise for their work is an important source of pride and also a means for advertising their skills and experience.

4.7.4 Contractors' Incentives, Ownership, and Sustainability

In sum, contractors' incentives to perform depend on (1) the importance of the donor to the portfolio of the contractor, (2) the nature of the good being contracted (which determines the profit margins), and (3) the extent to which the aid is tied and the extent of competition in the donor country.

While a donor retains a great deal of effective aid ownership by making the crucial decisions, including those related to the amount of funding and the start and termination of projects, consultants can also have strong incentives to exercise ownership over a project. Contractor ownership is enhanced where particular asymmetries of information and/or power exist.

A consultant concerned with possible future contracts with a donor is likely to maximize his or her control over a project, and not pass along control to the intended beneficiaries. Passing along such ownership to the beneficiaries is risky. Beneficiaries do not have the same incentives as contractors. Thus, beneficiaries may not act in the ways that a donor wants. It is rational for contractors to reduce this uncertainty by retaining some degree of control.

As consultants frequently have greater knowledge of what has worked or not worked in the past, it is important to design ways of drawing more effectively on that knowledge while encouraging more recipient ownership. In particular, assigning a greater role to beneficiary organizations (e.g., local user groups) in the hiring, monitoring, and releasing of consultants may be an important step toward combining the local knowledge of beneficiaries with the technical expertise possessed by consultants.

4.8 IMPROVING OUTCOMES IN AID

Most individuals with experience in development cooperation realize that incentives underpin the effectiveness and sustainability of development efforts. Yet, while we may be sensitized to the importance of institutions and the incentives they produce, the knowledge underlying this realization is often tacit and, moreover, is rarely transmitted in a systematic way. An advantage of the IAD framework is that it enables a more systematic understanding of institutions and the incentives that emerge within particular organizational structures, as well as mechanisms for transmitting this knowledge. Applying the IAD approach to the challenges of aid delivery, we believe, can improve donors' mission effectiveness by fostering a keener awareness of project and program design and implementation.

It is important to note that this analytical framework is not a panacea. We doubt that any development cooperation agency can fully mitigate the structures that produce unwanted sets of incentives. Powerful incentives are built into structures over which a development agency often has little control: the structure of political institutions in both donor and recipient countries beget rules that can work directly against effective development aid.

These challenges notwithstanding, we believe that an understanding of the conditions that promote "good" incentives can lead to better aid outcomes. Such rules may be costly to an aid agency in terms of its own time and money, and budget allocations. We would argue, however, that this investment to create better incentive structures will lead to more sustainable outcomes for development assistance.

4.8.1 Assigning Ownership

If devolving ownership is to move beyond rhetoric, it must be systematically approached and implemented, with a sharp eye on the role of institutions.

This is a challenging task when a donor finances projects and programs and thus always remains, in some important respects, a de facto owner. A donor may find itself in a Samaritan's dilemma. Furthermore, a donor must operate within the political imperatives of its own government and society as well as that of a recipient country, which may not be amenable to the aim of promoting sustainable development. Even so, we believe that donor agencies can still take steps to improve a sense of ownership among recipients and beneficiaries.

As a first step, all projects must identify who, in fact, exercises ownership prerogatives, and determine how sustainability can be realized in this context. Project planning documents should clearly identify the intended owners and include an analysis of the anticipated impact that this designation of ownership will have on sustainability. Such documents should also detail how meaningful ownership will be vested and what evidence will be gathered to ascertain success in these goals. This is a formidable task. Development agencies have little time for developing, collecting, and evaluating such evidence (see Gibson et al. 2005: chap. 7). In designing its projects and programs, donor officers must also keep in mind that the greater the number of owners, the smaller the stakes will likely be for any particular owner to ensure success.

In the crucial next step, a donor needs to allow sufficient opportunities for the owner(s) to contribute to the design, implementation, and mid-course corrections of the project or program. A final step is to allow the owner full participation in the final evaluation of a project. That is, beneficiary owners need to (1) enunciate a *demand* for aid, (2) allocate at least some of their own *assets* to the project or program so they have a real stake in the way their own and other actors' assets are used, (3) obtain *benefits*, and (4) have clear-cut responsibilities and be able to *participate in decisions* regarding continuance or non-continuance of a project. Constructing programs that meet these criteria will be another formidable task.

Genuine devolution of ownership may mean less control for the donor and its agent/contractor. While less control is not without its attendant risks, we argue that it is necessary to achieve more sustainable results. More devolution, however, does not mean less involvement in ongoing activities in partner countries. Donor staff can play a crucial facilitative role to ensure that ownership of activities is anchored primarily with beneficiaries, and not taken over by consultants or individuals within recipient organizations (Gibson et al. 2005: chap. 11). The incentive structures that emerge in each undertaking are greatly influenced by interventions, or lack thereof. In general, we think donor staff in the field should not be overstretched in their work to gather and evaluate information about their projects and programs. Devolving ownership may involve greater costs of monitoring for the donor.

4.8.2 Creating Information and Transmitting Learning

Perverse incentives often thrive in the absence of information. As the Octangle illustrates, a desk officer within a donor organization and an intended beneficiary are separated by many intermediary actors, each one facing potential incentives to select and transmit only the information that is likely to benefit him or her privately. Desk officers typically rely primarily on the input of embassy colleagues, consultants, and national government officials. These intermediary actors, however, seldom have direct contact with the ultimate beneficiaries of the development cooperation and also have to rely on secondary sources for beneficiary-level information. The information asymmetries in this multilayered arena make it very difficult for a desk officer to appreciate the reality on the ground.

Identifying and correcting information gaps requires thoughtful analysis before, during, and after a project or program. Mid-term formal evaluations are particularly critical to improving sustainability and should include original staff that has been reassigned. Such evaluations allow project participants to learn more effectively about their own activities and, if needed, adjust strategies mid-project in order to enhance sustainability—or even to disinvest in projects expected to be unsustainable.

All those affected by projects—particularly the beneficiaries—should be involved in the evaluation of projects. This will encourage beneficiaries, donor officials, and contractors to learn of each other's concerns and from each other's experiences (Andersson 2009). Numerous methods exist to evaluate programs and projects, ranging from small samples of the actors involved to surveys of a large number of beneficiaries. The increasingly used method of a randomized controlled trial is a rigorous way to establish the causal effects of an intervention on outcomes. (For a review of the tools of program evaluation in the context of democracy aid, see National Research Council 2008.) To increase learning within a donor organization, staff with past involvement with the project/program should also be invited to project evaluation discussions.

Evaluators should be instructed to examine the level of ownership in a project or program, and the impact of ownership on sustainability should be seriously discussed. Evaluations should be read and discussed formally both with recipient country officials, with beneficiaries where possible, and within the donor organization. They can then be used as guides to future projects. Staff no longer working on a particular project should be encouraged to participate in the discussion of these evaluations. To support this practice, evaluations should be reviewed in conjunction with staff performance reviews.

Gaining information about the specific attributes of development activities and the associated incentives also helps aid agencies avoid the use of panaceas (relying on one type of policy that is thought to be the best for a general type of problem) when supporting local efforts to address particular problems.

The number of variables that affect outcomes obtained in a particular ecology combined with the social structure of those involved is very large. For example, Campbell et al. (2006) point to the diversity of factors that affect the impact of stocking regimes on the sustainability of grazing lands and criticize the efforts of many development agencies to use simple formulae rather than deeper analysis when planning projects to address environmental problems. Using a diagnostic approach (Ostrom 2007) for analyzing complex development and environmental problems, as well as learning from those involved, is more time-consuming and complex than applying "one-size-fits-all" policies, but also is more likely to generate positive rather than negative outcomes.

4.8.3 Developing Institutional Awareness in Recipient Countries

While the learning components of most foreign aid are project/program specific, the process of development is itself complex and broad-based. Local capacity is needed to integrate learning across donor projects with knowledge of indigenous institutions. Donor organizations can help actors in recipient countries increase their in-country ability to create and analyze alternative forms of development and institution-building, based on analyses of incentive structures.

Donor organizations can improve this situation by funding programs that (1) identify scholars interested in development and institutions in major universities in the recipient country; (2) support said scholars for at least one year at competitive salaries; (3) train them in institutional analysis and development, using both in-country and external academics as source persons; (4) help them develop a syllabus for such courses at their own institutions; (5) help them create materials for such a course; (6) support their teaching of this course to undergraduates, graduates, and interested policymakers; and (7) bring these scholars together regularly to create better courses based on their ongoing research and experience. Such a program would serve to give recipients the tools to assess and suggest improvements for the development assistance they receive.

References

Adam, C. S. and S. A. O'Connell (1999). "Aid, Taxation and Development in Sub-Saharan Africa," *Economics and Politics*, 11(3): 225–53.

Andersson, K. (2006). "Understanding Decentralized Forest Governance: An Application of the Institutional Analysis and Development Framework," *Sustainability: Science, Practice, and Policy*, 2(1): 25–35.

—— (2009). "Motivational Dilemmas in Collaborative Learning Processes: The Case of Sida," *Public Administration and Development*, 29(5): 341–51.

—— and E. Ostrom (2008). "Analyzing Decentralized Resource Regimes from a Polycentric Perspective," *Policy Sciences*, 41: 71–93.

Bräutigam, D. (2000). *Aid Dependence and Governance*. Stockholm: Almqvist & Wiksell International.

Buchanan, J. M. (1977). "The Samaritan's Dilemma," in *Freedom in Constitutional Contract: Perspectives of a Political Economist*. College Station: Texas A&M University Press, 169–80.

Burnside, C. and D. Dollar (2000). "Aid, Growth, the Incentive Regime, and Poverty Reduction," in C. L. Gilbert and D. Vines (eds.), *The World Bank: Structure and Policies*. Cambridge: Cambridge University Press, 210–27.

Campbell, B. M., I. J. Gordon, M. Luckert et al. (2006). "In Search of Optimal Stocking Regimes in Semi-Arid Grazing Lands: One Size Does Not Fit All," *Ecological Economics*, 60(1): 75–85.

Campbell, D. E. (1995). *Incentives: Motivations and the Economics of Information*. Cambridge: Cambridge University Press.

Campos, E. and S. Pradhan (1996). "*Budgetary Institutions and Expenditure Outcomes: Binding Governments to Fiscal Performance*," Policy Research Working Paper no. 1646. Washington, DC: World Bank.

Cohen, J., M. Grindle, and S. T. Walker (1985). "Foreign Aid and Conditions Precedent: Political and Bureaucratic Dimensions," *World Development*, 13(12): 1211–30.

Dasgupta, P. (1993). *An Inquiry into Well-Being and Destitution*. Oxford: Clarendon Press.

—— (1995). "The Population Problem: Theory and Evidence," *Journal of Economic Literature*, 33(4): 1879–902.

—— (2001). *Human Well-Being and the Natural Environment*. Oxford: Oxford University Press.

—— and I. Serageldin (eds.) (2000). *Social Capital: A Multifaceted Perspective*. Washington, DC: World Bank.

Dollar, D. and W. Easterly (1999). "*The Search for the Key: Aid, Investment and Policies in Africa*," Policy Research Working Paper No. 2070. Washington, DC: World Bank.

Easterly, W. (2001). *The Elusive Quest for Growth: Economists' Misadventures in the Tropics*. Cambridge, MA: MIT Press.

—— (2003). "Can Foreign Aid Buy Growth?" *Journal of Economic Perspectives*, 17(3): 23–48.

Eriksson Skoog, G. (2000). *The Soft Budget Constraint: The Emergence, Persistence and Logic of an Institution*. Dordrecht, the Netherlands: Kluwer.

Gardner, R. and C. Waller (2005). "A Formal Analysis of Incentives in Strategic Interactions Involving an International Development Cooperation Agency," in C. Gibson, K. Andersson, E. Ostrom et al. (eds.), *The Samaritan's Dilemma: The Political Economy of Development Aid*. Oxford: Oxford University Press, 87–111.

Gibson, C., K. Andersson, E. Ostrom et al. (2005). *The Samaritan's Dilemma: The Political Economy of Development Aid*. Oxford: Oxford University Press.

—— M. McKean, and E. Ostrom (eds.) (2000). *People and Forests: Communities, Institutions, and Governance*. Cambridge, MA: MIT Press.

Holmstrom, B. (1982a). "Managerial Incentive Problems: A Dynamic Perspective," in *Essays in Economics and Management in Honor of Lars Wahlbeck*. Helsinki: Swedish School of Economics.

—— (1982b). "Moral Hazard in Teams," *Bell Journal of Economics*, 13: 324–40.
Kiser, L. and E. Ostrom (1982). "The Three Worlds of Action: A Metatheoretical Synthesis of Institutional Approaches," in E. Ostrom (ed.), *Strategies of Political Inquiry*. Beverly Hills, CA: Sage, 179–222.
Martens, B., with U. Mummert, P. Murrell, and P. Seabright (2002). *The Institutional Economics of Foreign Aid*. Cambridge: Cambridge University Press.
Miller, G. (1992). *Managerial Dilemmas: The Political Economy of Hierarchy*. New York: Cambridge University Press.
Moe, T. M. (1984). "The New Economics of Organization," *American Journal of Political Science*, 28(4): 739–77.
National Research Council (2008). *Improving Democracy Assistance: Building Knowledge through Evaluations and Research*. Committee on the Evaluation of USAID Democracy Assistance Programs. J. Goldstone, L. Garber, J. Gerring et al. (eds.). Washington, DC: National Academies Press.
Oakerson, R. J. (1992). "Analyzing the Commons: A Framework," in D. W. Bromley et al. (eds.), *Making the Commons Work: Theory, Practice, and Policy*. San Francisco, CA: ICS Press, 41–59.
Ostrom, E. (2005). *Understanding Institutional Diversity*. Princeton, NJ: Princeton University Press.
—— (2007). "A Diagnostic Approach for Going beyond Panaceas," *Proceedings of the National Academy of Sciences*, 104(39): 15181–87.
—— (2011). "Background on the Institutional Analysis and Development Framework," *Policy Studies Journal*, 39(1): 7–27.
—— R. Gardner, and J. Walker (1994). *Rules, Games, and Common-Pool Resources*. Ann Arbor, MI: University of Michigan Press.
—— C. Gibson, S. Shivakumar et al. (2002). *Aid, Incentives, and Sustainability: An Institutional Analysis of Development Cooperation*. Main Report, Sida Studies in Evaluation No. 02/01. Stockholm: Sida.
—— L. Schroeder, and S. Wynne (1993). *Institutional Incentives and Sustainable Development: Infrastructure Policies in Perspective*. Boulder, CO: Westview Press.
Poteete, A., M. Janssen, and E. Ostrom (2010). *Working Together: Collective Action, the Commons, and Multiple Methods in Practice*. Princeton, NJ: Princeton University Press.
Riddell, R. C. (2007). *Does Foreign Aid Really Work?* Oxford: Oxford University Press.
Shirley, M. M. (2008). *Institutions and Development: Advances in New Institutional Analysis*. Cheltenham: Edward Elgar.
Shivakumar, S. (2005). *The Constitution of Development: Crafting Capabilities for Self-Governance*. New York: Palgrave Macmillan.
Stone, D. (2008). *The Samaritan's Dilemma: Should Government Help Your Neighbor?* New York: National Books.
Tsikata, T. M. (1998). *"Aid Effectiveness: A Survey of the Recent Empirical Literature,"* IMF Paper on Policy Analysis and Assessment. New York: IMF, Policy Development and Review Department.
van de Walle, N. (2001). *African Economies and the Politics of Permanent Crisis, 1979–1999*. New York: Cambridge University Press.
World Bank (1998). *Assessing Aid: What Works, What Doesn't, and Why*. World Bank Policy Research Report written by D. Dollar and L. Pritchett. New York: Oxford University Press.

Part III

Applications

5

Climate Change, Cookstoves, and Coughs and Colds: Thinking Global and Acting Locally in Rural Nepal[1]

Krishna P. Pant, Subhrendu K. Pattanayak, and Min B. Malla Thakuri

5.1 INTRODUCTION

More than three billion people worldwide depend on solid biomass fuels (e.g., wood, dung, and agriculture residues) to meet their basic energy needs for cooking and heating (WHO 2006). Inefficient burning of biomass fuel creates a dangerous cocktail of hundreds of pollutants such as particulate matter, carbon monoxide, nitrogen dioxide, formaldehyde, and polycyclic organic matter that adversely affect human health—particularly that of women, who are the primary cooks, and their young children (Ezzati and Kammen 2002; Smith et al. 2004). Additionally, traditional cookstoves are energy inefficient: the need to burn large amounts of fuel for a small amount of cooking and heating effectively degrades and draws down forests. Burning biomass also contributes to global warming through emissions of greenhouse gases such as carbon dioxide and greenhouse pollutants like black carbon (Grieshop et al. 2011;

[1] This chapter draws on two studies on household energy in Nepal conducted with technical and financial support of the South Asian Network for Development and Environmental Economics (SANDEE), Kathmandu, Nepal. In this chapter, we focus on the main differences between households using traditional and improved cooking technologies in terms of three outcomes—indoor air pollution, respiratory health, and fuel-wood use. A more comprehensive picture of the study setting and technologies are reported in the working papers published on these projects, which are available from <http://www.sandeeonline.org/publication_search.php>. These projects would not have been possible without the guidance and encouragement of Priya Shyamsundar, Mani Nepal, and the SANDEE Secretariat. We are grateful to Scott Barrett, Marc Jeuland, Jessica Lewis, Joseph Stiglitz and participants at the APHA (San Diego), ABCDE (Stockholm), World Congress of Environmental & Resource Economics (Kyoto) meetings for comments on earlier drafts of this work.

Bond et al. 2004). As Dasgupta (2001) argues, this divergence between private and public costs—that is, local (forest) and global (climate change) externalities from biomass burning—provide justifications in addition to the usual health-based logic for designing and implementing programs that promote improved cookstoves and cleaner fuels.

Unfortunately, policy design and implementation is constrained by a thin empirical literature on the multiple benefits of improved household energy technologies—particularly by the lack of household-level studies that examine more than one class of benefits. We address this challenge by drawing on a pair of multidisciplinary studies in Nepal funded by the SANDEE network from 2006 to 2008 that help fill important gaps in the socioeconomic analysis of household energy technologies (Pant 2008; Thakuri 2009). In Nepal, almost all households use inefficient traditional stoves (*chullahs*) for cooking and 85 percent depend on biomass fuels (Central Bureau of Statistics 2004). Poor people use inefficient stoves and dirty fuels because they are 'cheaper' than modern fuels (liquefied petroleum gas and electricity). For example, these dirty biomass fuels are collected for free from village commons by low cost labor (e.g., women and children). Even though health impacts can be significant, the non-market nature of health impacts are potentially not understood by the rural poor, who often cannot see and therefore link their diseases to the type of stove they use or the fuels they burn. For sure, they disregard the local (forest degradation) and global (greenhouse gas and pollutant) externalities.

The data for these studies came from surveys in the Rasuwa, Syangia, and Chitwan districts of Nepal in 2006 (see Figure 5.1). Socioeconomic surveys of one thousand households were used in conjunction with indoor air pollution monitoring to describe and analyze how cooking technology, kitchen design, and fuel type impact fuel-wood consumption, exposure to particulate matter concentration, and health (Pant 2008; Thakuri 2009). For most parts, we simply draw on the original analysis reported in each study, and occasionally conduct a new analysis (as clarified in the results tables). Both studies look at the potential triple benefits of improved cooking technologies in terms of human health, local forest use, and global climate emissions. However, the studies are different in terms of data collection methods, training of research teams, and the intervention. We present results from both samples to show how variations in the fuel-stove-kitchen type, socio-demographics, and eco-climatic regions impact a set of outcomes related to household energy. This allows us to evaluate external validity by examining contextual factors (Ravallion 2009; Deaton 2010). We readily admit that in doing so we are trading-off statistical power (because of small samples) to make 'plausibility' (not 'probability') inferences about context and the underlying heterogeneity. Thus, we join others in calling for more rigorous economic analysis of this potentially valuable, yet cheap, environmental technology (Ezzati and Kammen, 2002; Larson and Rosen,

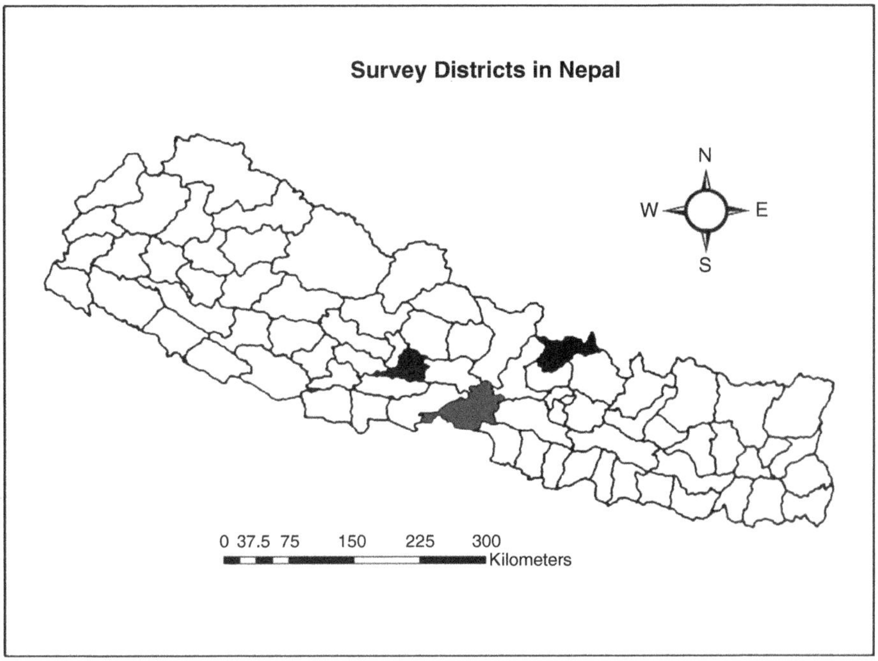

Figure 5.1 Chitwan, Rasuwa, and Syangja districts of central Nepal

2002; Duflo et al., 2008; Mueller et al., 2012; Jeuland and Pattanayak, 2012; Lewis and Pattanayak, 2012).

We find that some improved stoves in some settings can reduce pollution concentration, respiratory illnesses, medical costs, cooking and collection time, fuel-wood consumption, and greenhouse pollutant emissions. These impacts collectively imply high internal-rates-of-return on the use of improved stoves. Why then aren't more households adopting this technology? We conclude with a discussion of the constraints to the adoption and diffusion of household energy technologies, and a presentation of an agenda for future research on this critical topic.

5.2 BACKGROUND: THE ILLUSION OF TRIPLE DIVIDENDS

Although early improved stoves promotion programs focused on (a) reducing fuel-wood consumption to conserve forests (Barnes et al. 1993; Kammen 1995), contemporary programs have highlighted the importance of reducing

(b) respiratory health illnesses and (c) greenhouse gases and pollutants. We briefly summarize the relevant literature on the triple benefits of improved stoves and then highlight the research gaps.

5.2.1 Conservation of Forest and Biological Diversity

Traditional stoves or cooking practices (e.g., open fires) do little to control combustion or improve heat transfer and thus use fuels highly inefficiently. These inefficiencies generate a high demand for fuel-wood that exceeds the supply from natural and planted forests, leading to deforestation pressures (Barnes et al. 1993). In a meta-analysis of drivers of deforestation, 33 out of 152 case studies pointed towards fuel-wood extraction as a proximate cause of deforestation, especially in Asia and Africa (Geist and Lambin 2001). Matthews (2000) suggests that 75 percent of the global fuel-wood demand comes from developing Asian and African countries, and has led to localized deforestation in some areas. Even if fuel-wood extraction from forests does not cause deforestation per se, we can expect forest degradation to negatively impact habitats for species and watershed services. Although most stoves used by households (including the ones in our study sites) fall well below the efficiencies reached by stoves using liquid (kerosene), gas (liquefied petroleum gas) and electricity, technological gains are improving efficiencies to the level that could ease the pressures on forests (Krugman 1987; Kammen 1995; Manibog 1984; Gill 1985). However, economists contend that the relationship is not so straightforward and that improved stoves may not reduce fuel-wood consumption because there might be behavioral 'rebound effects' (Zein-Elabdin 1997) or because the substitution effects of lower effective fuel price are dominated by the income effects such that we see a non-linear (U-shaped or Z-shaped) relationship between income and fuel-wood demand (Pfaff et al. 2004). Nepal et al.'s (2011) review of the recent microeconomic studies on this question is inconclusive. Their own empirical study suggests that improved stoves increase fuel-wood consumption.

5.2.2 Reduction in Respiratory Health Problems

Stove efficiency is inversely correlated with the amount of health-damaging pollutants because traditional stoves convert biomass fuels inefficiently and generate fine 'particles of incomplete combustion'. The exposure to indoor air pollution, especially particulate matter, is a causal agent of respiratory diseases (Pandey 1984a; Pandey 1984b; Pandey et al., 1989; Campbell et al. 1989; Armstrong and Campbell 1991). The main diseases due to indoor air pollutants are acute respiratory infections (ARI), chronic obstructive pulmonary disease (COPD), lung cancer in women, and cardiovascular disease (Bruce et al. 2000; Ezzati and Kammen 2002; Bruce et al. 2006). Many studies emphasize that poor women and children are at greatest risk from the health effects of indoor air pollution (Dasgupta et al. 2006; Dehrani et al. 2008; Kohlin et al. 2011). Moreover, some studies link exposure to indoor smoke to asthma, cataracts, tuberculosis, adverse pregnancy outcomes (in particular, low birth weight), interstitial lung disease, and nasopharyngeal and laryngeal cancers. The World Health Organization suggests that indoor smoke from dirty stoves and fuels is responsible for 1.6 million deaths worldwide annually and 2.7 percent of the global burden of disease. In Nepal, indoor smoke is responsible for the deaths of 7,500 people, 204,400 disability-adjusted life years (DALYs) loss and 2.7 percent of the national burden of diseases in 2002 (WHO 2007).

Though research on exposure to indoor smoke and its impacts on respiratory diseases in developing countries began in the 1960s and 1970s in India, Nigeria, and Papua New Guinea (Ezzati and Kammen 2002), an effective and widely accepted method of reducing such exposure is still illusive. Several studies have attempted to identify the potential determinants of exposure to indoor smoke: fuel type, time spent on cooking, structural characteristics of houses, cooking locations, and household ventilation practices (Brauer and Saxena 2002; Freeman and de Tejada 2002; Dasgupta et al. 2006). For example, Dasgupta et al. (2006, 2008) link the level of indoor smoke with wall and roof permeability as well as the location of the kitchen and its openness to other rooms in the house. However, they also find that different biomass fuels contribute very little towards explaining differences in measured average indoor air pollution. They conclude that fuel choice is less important than ventilation factors when it comes to explaining variation in indoor air pollution among poor households. In contrast, Pitt et al. (2010) conclude that improving ventilation by increasing the permeability of roofs or walls has no significant effect on the health outcomes because the proximity to the stove is a more important exposure factor and is endogenously determined based on intra-household dynamics. In general, indoor air quality depends on the type of cooking devices, type of fuel, hours of burning fire, ventilation, location of kitchen and stove, user's behavior (for example, fuel drying, use of pot lids, good maintenance and sound operation of the stove, and food preparation style). Thus, there is some agreement that improved stoves can be a practical strategy for reducing the indoor smoke in rural households.

5.2.3 Reduction in Emissions that Cause Global Warming

Biomass burning for cooking emits many different greenhouse gases such as carbon dioxide, methane and nitrogen dioxide. In theory, an improved stove in Nepal could reduce one ton of carbon dioxide emissions each year, and therefore qualify for carbon finance (Samson et al. 2006). More recent research argues that too much attention has been given to the global warming commitment of greenhouse gases and too little attention to other greenhouse pollutants such as black carbon (e.g., soot) (Wallack and Ramanathan 2009). These pollutants are potentially more potent in the near term (ten to fifty years) because they create local pollution and warming. More critically, the short-lived nature of the greenhouse pollutants suggests that strong immediate action will generate immediate-term solutions as opposed to reductions of stock pollutants such as greenhouse gases that will need decades of interventions before benefits can be realized (Ramanathan 2007). Approximately 40 percent of greenhouse pollutants can be attributed to biomass burning largely because of incomplete combustion and inefficient cooking technologies (Bond et al. 2004; Venkatraman et al. 2005). This is a particularly big concern in Asia because firewood and crop waste are major energy sources.

Attempts to combat climate change due to biomass burning is emerging as one of the major reasons for financing the adoption of improved cookstoves, at least in the short run (World Bank 2011). For example, the newly formed Global Alliance for Clean Cookstoves is committed to raising $250 million to promote developing countries' use of improved stoves in the near future. In the long run, however, switching to cleaner, greener fuels with a low carbon content is seen as a viable strategy for the carbon offsets market, which might explain a variety of cookstove projects listed under the gold standard market, the voluntary market, and the Clean Development Mechanism (Khopkar and Sills 2012).

5.2.4 Knowledge Gap

As economists, we have both supply (production) and demand (consumption) side concerns regarding the issues of improved cookstoves, forest degradation, human health and global warming. To a large extent, the impact of cookstoves on household health, community forests, and global climate are production side concerns that have traditionally been voiced by epidemiologists, public health practitioners, forest ecologists, environmental engineers, atmospheric chemists, and climate scientists. The triple-dividend argument suggests that mass adoption of improved stoves among the rural poor will make the society better off. But the mechanics for mass adoption of improved cookstoves is still illusive, potentially because the empirical bases for claiming triple dividends is thin. So a clear charge for applied researchers is to go collect more information and attempt to "thicken" the knowledge base, even if the new study essentially re-tests some of the findings of the early literature. Our empirical studies were developed in this vein. Specifically, we respond to Larson and Rosen's (2002) call to improve information on how (a) improved stoves impact air pollution, cooking times, and fuel use, and (b) households value improved health.

In addition, we introduce two other economic perspectives. First, in each realm—household (health), community (forests and biodiversity), and global (carbon dioxide and black carbon)—household choices such as the decision to use improved stoves play a central role (Pattanayak and Pfaff 2009). Ignoring this choice and or the potential feedback between choices, outcomes (e.g., health) and interventions comes at the risk of confounding any analysis as well as any policies that are derived from such analysis. Second, household choices provide a mechanism to value (i.e., derive monetary estimates of) some of the non-market benefits of improved stoves' use—health, energy efficiency, and reductions in global warming potential. The cases that follow illustrate both these uses of applied empirical economics.

5.3 CASE STUDY FROM NEPAL: SETTING AND SAMPLE

This chapter summarizes results based on primary data generated from indoor air monitoring and surveys of approximately one thousand households in rural areas of central Nepal. The studies were conducted in three districts from different physiographic regions--Rasuwa (mountains), Syangja (hills), and Chitwan (*terai* or plains). While many studies on Nepal try to represent the range of eco-climatic regions, it is especially relevant to household energy because topography affects housing conditions and the availability of firewood species. In the mountains that have temperate and alpine conditions, the houses have smaller windows compared to those in hills and *terai*, which have a subtropical climate. Further, households in the mountains will often use the firewood from rhododendron species that burns well, emitting much less smoke compared to most species of firewood available in the hills and *terai*.

Before describing our data collection strategy (sample and instruments), we present a brief overview of how people live in our study area and of the stove interventions that we consider. Most people are smallholder farmers whose livelihood depends on crop and livestock. They live in small one- or two-story farmhouses, with a combined (not separate) area for cooking, dining, and living. Usually they eat two meals a day, prepared with crops that they grow--maize, barley, and potato (mountains); maize, millet, and rice (hills); and rice and wheat (*terai*)—as well as some vegetables, milk, and meat. Cooking maize and millet needs more time and firewood than cooking rice. Cooks are usually females. Because the men are mostly focused on farming and other income-generating activities, they rarely pay attention to traditional cooking practices and the triple impacts on household health, local forests, and global climate. About two-thirds of the population uses firewood as the main cooking fuel; only 13 percent use kerosene, less than 8 percent use liquid petroleum gas, and almost no one uses electricity as the main cooking fuel (Central Bureau of Statistics 2002). Biogas is adopted by no more than 2 percent of the households.

Our study essentially examines three kinds of stove interventions: (1) biogas stoves, (2) improved cookstoves (Chitwan-Syangja sample), and (3) improved cookstoves with smoke hoods (Rasuwa sample). To understand how these represent improvements, consider the fact that most rural Nepali households cook using either an open fire or traditional stoves. Open fires serve triple purposes—cooking, preparing animal food, and space-heating during the winter season (especially in the mountains). Traditional kitchens rarely have exhaust fans, chimneys, or even small openings between the wall and roof.

Biogas is essentially an anaerobic digester that produces cooking gas (methane) from organic wastes like animal dung, night soil, and weeds in the Chitwan-Syangja site. It provides a less polluting, easily controlled source of renewable energy to replace firewood. Given the low density of houses in rural areas, we are more likely to find individual biogas plant of size 5 to 10 m^3 instead of bigger community plants. This technology is more successful in warmer regions (compared to cold regions such as the mountains) because the anaerobic bacteria require warm temperatures.

Improved cookstoves 'improve' combustion efficiency (the proportion of fuel chemical converted to thermal energy) and heat transfer efficiency (the proportion of thermal energy that is transferred to the intended point, for example, a cooking pot); see Grieshop et al. (2011). In essence, these gains are realized by modifying (a) the flow of air, (b) how much heat is retained in the cooking space, (c) the distance between fire and cooking pot, and (d) fuel-wood size. In the Chitwan-Syanjga site, fixed mud stoves were promoted. In the Rasuwa site, metal tripod stoves were set on a mud base.

Additionally, the improved stoves in Rasuwa were promoted with smoke hoods to directly improve ventilation and reduce the pollutants inside the kitchen. The smoke hood is a metal structure, built against the wall in the cooking area, and fitted with a flue to remove the smoke from the cooking area and the house. Further technological details are reported in Pant (2008) and Thakuri (2009).

Pant (2008) conducted surveys of six hundred households from Syangja and Chitwan districts. Similarly, Thakuri (2009) conducted surveys of four hundred households from Rasuwa. Within each district, the sample was stratified to include sufficient number of improved-stove adopters to permit statistical analysis—that is, to obtain enough households who had adopted the technology. Within each village, households were chosen randomly. Household surveys were designed based on SANDEE's protocol of using focus groups, field pre-tests, and enumerator-training to minimize measurement errors and recall bias. Surveys were used to gather information on three sets of outcomes described in this chapter—fuel-wood consumption, and the incidence and costs of diseases related to air pollution—in addition to data on cooking technology, kitchen design, fuel type, time allocation, socioeconomic status, and community infrastructure (e.g., distance to markets, availability of credit). The two main health outcomes are chronic obstructive pulmonary disease (COPD) in adults and acute respiratory illness in children (ARI).[2] Although there is some ambiguity over the nature and size of bias in self-reported health data (Saha et al. 2011, Subramaniam et al. 2009), we include socioeconomic variables such as education and income in the analysis to control for potential biases. The remaining outcome ensues from a unique aspect of these studies: direct measurement of indoor air pollution. Specifically, we measured particulate matter in ninety-nine households in the Chitwan-Syangja sample, and carbon monoxide in two hundred households in Rasuwa.[3] As opposed to proxy measures of pollution (e.g., fuel type, cooking technology, kitchen construction), these indicators directly measure exposure to indoor air pollution.

5.4 EMPIRICAL METHODS AND RESULTS

Below we summarize the findings by comparing main outcomes for improved cookstoves and control using simple statistical tests and regression analysis. The four outcomes described for each subsample include: (a) indoor air pollution, (b) fuel-wood consumption, (c) incidence of respiratory health problems of children and adults, and (d) costs of respiratory health. We consider only the immediate acute health impacts and ignore chronic diseases typically associated with long-term exposure because the intervention had been available in the study area for only a short period of time. We combine the data from Chitwan and Syangja districts for analysis because these data are for the same interventions and from the same study (Pant 2008), whereas we

[2] COPD is measured by cough and phlegm for most days for three months each year. Child ARI includes a combination of the following symptoms: (1) stopped feeding well, (2) abnormally sleepy or difficult to awake, (3) fever or low body temperature, (4) localized chest pain, and (5) cough at first dry and painful, later productive and tenacious with rusty sputum or occasionally frank bloodstained.

[3] In Chitwan and Syangja, laser dust monitoring was used during cooking and non-cooking hours in ninety-nine households to develop an index of particulate matter (PM10) during a twenty-four-hour period. In Rasuwa, an ISC T82 single-gas monitor was used to measure carbon monoxide (CO) in 200 households during a twenty-four-hour period. PM10 was also measured using Buck S.S. pumps, but the sample was limited to sixty households because the process was time-consuming and expensive. Because the CO and PM10 measures were highly correlated (Thakuri, 2009), we only focus on CO in the remainder of the analysis.

separate the analysis of the Rasuwa data because the site represents a different intervention (Thakuri 2009). Furthermore, while the two studies are similar in terms of the questions and outcome they consider, there are some differences in terms of data collection methods, training of research teams, and the intervention (i.e., the fuel-stove-ventilation mix). Thus, any differences across study sites could be attributed to (1) differences in the interventions, (2) differences in data collection process, or (3) differences in sites conditions—climate, socio-demographics, and micro-institutions. We present results from both samples simply to show how variations in the fuel-stove-kitchen type, socio-demographics, and eco-climatic regions impact a set of outcomes related to household energy.

For the analysis, it is critical to recognize that household, community, and environmental factors and the possible correlations between them influence the links between the environmental risk, health outcomes, and behavioral interventions (Pattanayak and Pfaff 2009). For example, the rich may be able to afford better health care and therefore have higher costs. However, simply because the data is observational does not imply that we ignore quasi-experimental methods for reducing confounding caused by omitted variables, selection bias, and measurement errors. Thus, we conduct regression analyses to account for family composition, housing conditions, location, and socioeconomic covariates. In Tables 5.1–5.4, we present these "regression-adjusted" results—that is, differences between the improved stove and control groups, after accounting for covariates. For each table (below the results), we report the exact set of covariates "adjusted" for in each analysis. In general, the findings reported in this chapter draw from and are confirmed by more sophisticated analysis reported in Pant (2008) and Thakuri (2009). For example, Pant (2008) uses an instrumental variable method (where household demographic and community location variables predict improved-stoves use) to address the endogeneity of household stove use—that is, health-status conditions and stove use. For both raw and regression-adjusted mean differences, we consider differences to be statistically significant if the t-statistic is large: 1.65 (10 percent significance), 1.96 (5 percent significance), and 2.57 (1 percent significance). However, we consider evidence as "suggestive" if we find somewhat smaller t-values. Given the lack of empirical evidence on broad questions considered in this study, we believe a more flexible and accommodating review of the suggestive evidence is appropriate—instead of blind adherence to a hard criterion typically used to review findings of biomedical experiments.[4]

[4] Ziliak (2008) makes a related plea in comparing Fisher's and Gosset's (Student) contrasting view of rule-based versus experimentalist approaches to hypothesis testing and inference. We are grateful to Amar Hamoudi for alerting us to this paper. Ultimately, a conservative reader can still choose to ignore the insignificant findings, and focus only on the 10 percent (or lower) "significant" associations reported here.

Table 5.1 shows that indoor air quality—measured in average daily value of particulate matter or carbon monoxide—is worse in households using traditional stoves. Additionally, the levels of air pollutants detected in these households is many orders of magnitudes above the US and international standards. We find that improved stoves can improve air quality by as much as 10–70 percent. Below we speculate on how differences in sites in terms of active stove promotion, socio-demographic, and eco-physiographic factors could explain differences in outcomes in the Rasuwa and the Chitwan-Syangja samples. These results are confirmed by regression adjustments. The regression analyses also reveal that contrary to some recent research (Dasgupta et al. 2004, 2006), kitchen ventilation is not statistically significantly correlated with indoor smoke (see Table 3 in Pant [2008] and Table 3 in Thakuri [2009]).

Table 5.2 shows that fuel-wood consumption—measured in kilograms per year—is statistically significantly lower for users of biogas and smoke hoods, but not for improved cookstoves. The negative t-statistics for differences in means using regressions adjustment (i.e., including covariates) confirm that two of the improved technologies reduce fuel-wood consumption, whereas the evidence is strongly suggestive for the biogas technology. That is, a t-statistic of −1.6 for biogas is strong evidence in small samples of the kinds used in this study.[5] Thus, our findings reject a recent result that improved stoves use more fuel-wood (Nepal et al. 2011).

Table 5.3 shows that respiratory illness—proxied by chronic obstructive pulmonary disease in adults and acute respiratory illnesses in children—is worse in control households, compared to households using smoke hoods and improved stoves (all three districts), but not compared to biogas users. Regression adjustments confirm that smoke hoods and improved stoves reduce the prevalence of respiratory illnesses by 10–30 percent. To further examine this health effect, Table 5.4 shows that the costs of illness are lower for smoke hood-cum-stove users compared to control, but not among biogas and improved-stoves users compared to their control. This finding is confirmed by regression analyses. Below we suggest why micro-institutional, socio-demographic, and eco-physiological factors might be driving the relative effectiveness of the stove-cum-smoke hood technology studied in Rasuwa, compared to the biogas and improve stove technology in Chitwan-Syangja.

In sum, what can we learn from these two studies from three districts in Nepal? First, although it is tempting to compare across the studies, our

[5] Although this seemingly "insignificant" result does not make the Fisherian hard cut-off of 10 percent, it still contains valuable information on a rarely studied topic. For example, a result with a p-value of 0.15 is suggestive of some relationship between the technology and the outcome. That is, as stated above, the failure to reject a false null (no relationship) is 15 percent; or in other words, 85 percent of the time we will be making a reasonable inference about a problem with limited and hard-to-obtain data.

Table 5.1 Indoor air pollution in different intervention groups and tests of statistical differences

	Biogas (BG)	Improved cookstoves (ICS)	Traditional stove (control)	Means differences (t-statistics)			
				BG – control: simple	ICS – control: simple	BG – control: Regression	ICS – control: Regression
Rasuwa (CO ppm)		2.3	9.4		−6.91		−5.34†
Chitwan-Syangja (PM10 µg/m³)	3,250	3,070	3,390	−1.65	−3.05	−1.83‡	−2.97‡

† The differences in means were adjusted for any differences in rainfall, temperature, kitchen size, number of windows, family size, cooking hours, number of cooking sessions, smokers, food type, lighting use (see Table 3 in Thakuri, 2009: 19).

‡ The differences in means were adjusted for any differences in kitchen size, ventilation, and cooking area (see Table 3 in Pant, 2008: 23).

Table 5.2 Annual fuel-wood consumption (kg/year) in different intervention groups and tests of statistical differences

	Biogas (BG)	Improved cookstoves (ICS)	Traditional stove (control)	Means differences (t-statistics)			
				BG – control: simple	ICS – control: simple	BG – control: Regression adjusted	ICS - control: Regression adjusted
Rasuwa		2,170	2,890		−7.2		−10.7†
Chitwan-Syangja	1,140	1,270	1,240	−2.03	0.93	−1.60‡	−2.32‡

† The differences in means were adjusted for any differences in distance to roads, family size, and income (new analysis for this chapter).
‡ The differences in means were adjusted for any differences in percentage of non-agricultural income, ratio of females to males, female-headed household, wealth, location (new analysis for this chapter).

Table 5.3 Prevalence of respiratory infections in different intervention groups and tests of statistical differences

	Biogas (BG)	Improved cookstoves (ICS)	Traditional stove (control)	Means differences (t-statistics)			
				BG – control (simple)	ICS – control: simple	BG – control: Regression	ICS - control: Regression
Rasuwa							
COPD		13%	61%		−8.38		−7.24 †
child ARI		65%	87%		−3.67		−7.55 †
Chitwan-Syangja							
COPD	51%	48%	49%	0.18	−0.46	0.82 ‡	−2.24 ‡
Child ARI	25%	23%	35%	−2.73	−2.32	−1.06 ‡	−2.01 ‡

† The differences in means were adjusted for any differences in distance from health facilities and motorable road, family size, income, number of young children, number of old adults, chronic illness history (see Table 6 in Thakuri, 2009: 21).

‡ The differences in means were adjusted for any differences in percentage of non-agricultural income, ratio of females to males, female-headed household, wealth, location (see Tables 8 and 10 in Pant, 2008: 26 and 27).

Table 5.4 Costs (rupees/year) associated with respiratory illnesses in different intervention groups and tests of statistical differences

	Biogas(BG)	Improved cookstoves (ICS)	Traditional stoves (control)	Mean differences (t-statistics)			
				BG – control (**simple**)	ICS – control (**simple**)	BG – control (Regression)	ICS – control (Regression)
Rasuwa (rupees/year)		170	371		1.60		−5.05†
Chitwan-Syangja (rupees/year)	4,250	5,170	4,010	−0.30	0.95	−0.51‡	0.60‡

† The differences in means were adjusted for any differences in distance from health facilities and motorable road, family size, income, number of young children, number of old adults, chronic illness history (see Table 7 in Thakuri, 2009: 22).

‡ The differences in means were adjusted for any differences in percentage of non-agricultural income, ratio of females to males, female-headed household, wealth, location (new analysis for this chapter).

goals for reporting on both studies was simply to show how variations in the fuel-stove-kitchen type, socio-demographics, and eco-climatic regions impact a set of household energy outcomes because external validity is important (Ravallion 2009; Deaton 2010). While the two studies are similar in terms of the outcomes considered, there are some differences in terms of data collection methods, research training and the intervention (i.e., the fuel-stove-ventilation mix). Thus, any differences across study sites could be attributed to differences in the interventions, data collection, or site conditions.

Second, recognizing the caveat presented in the previous paragraph, our evidence suggests that improved "stove-cum-smoke hoods" in Rasuwa were more effective than either biogas or improved stoves in Chitwan-Syangja. One obvious reason is that ventilation provided by smoke hoods in Rasuwa is in addition to the thermal combustion and heat transfer efficiency of improved stoves. Additionally, the higher efficacy could be because the Rasuwa sample is drawn from the project area of Practical Action, a knowledgeable and committed non-governmental organization that is actively promoting the technology. In contrast, the Chitwan-Syangja sites were chosen opportunistically, and likely lacked active promotion of improved stoves and regular follow-up. It is also possible that socioeconomic factors lead to "fuel stacking" in Chitwan-Syangja such that households are slowly embracing the new technology, while continuing to use the dirty fuel and inefficient stoves (Masera et al. 2000). Or it may simply be that one of the key fuel wood species (rhododendron) in the mountains is a cleaner fuel than the counterpart fuels in the hills and *terai*.

Third, despite these caveats, the overall findings of the statistical (paired) comparisons of households across districts differing in fuel-stove-kitchen types, socio-demographics, and eco-climatic regions show that improved household energy technologies can be beneficial. The technologies can reduce several undesirable outcomes including: (a) indoor air pollution (by 10–70 percent), (b) fuel wood consumption (by 25 percent in one site), (c) acute respiratory illnesses (by 10–30 percent), and (d) medical costs (10–50 percent). The lack of clear findings for some outcomes (e.g., health costs) in the Chitwan-Syangja sample suggests that these gains are uncertain (as discussed below).

5.5 DISCUSSION: DO BENEFITS EXCEED COSTS FOR IMPROVED-STOVES INVESTMENTS?

The previous section suggests that if a household invests in improved stoves, it will likely experience an improvement in health (and reduced illness costs, at least in one site and for one technology) and save costs related to fuel wood collection and consumption. However, will the benefits exceed the costs of investing in an improved stove? We follow the approach used in Jeuland and Pattanayak (2012), who provide additional discussion and references to the literature on estimating stove costs, in illustrating first-order estimates of the cost and benefits of improved-stove adoption in our study sites.

Beginning with the case of Chitwan-Syangja, the average market price of improved stoves and heaters is Rs. 605 (US$ 8.40) with an average lifespan of ten years. To account for credit constraints and otherwise high transaction costs related to multiple market and institutional failures in war-ravaged rural Nepal we assume an annual discount rate of 15 percent. This implies that an improved stoves costs the typical household Rs. 120 per annum.[6] For the Rasuwa site, the amortized costs of smoke hoods that last ten years are Rs. 1,000 per annum. Note the cost of using the traditional three-stone stove is zero for all practical purposes as materials (mud and stones) and knowhow are readily available locally.

Pant (2008) illustrates that we can estimate the benefits in terms of the reduction in annual health costs associated with chronic bronchitis and respiratory illnesses based on the "shadow value" of health outcomes, as advised by Dasgupta (2001) and illustrated by Larson and Rosen (2002). The associated benefits are approximately Rs. 1,200 per annum in Chitwan-Syangja. In contrast, the health benefits—measured in terms of savings in health costs and avoided loss of workdays—are approximately Rs. 2,000 per annum in Rasuwa (Thakuri 2009). Estimates of health benefits are larger in Rasuwa partly because benefits also include estimates of reductions in workdays lost, which is valued at 50 percent of market wages.

While both these analyses show that the health benefits alone exceed the investment costs, they understate the social worth of these investments by ignoring both private energy savings and public reductions in global warming emissions (Dasgupta 2001, 2010). Consider the calculations done by Thakuri (2009) for the improved stoves combined with smoke hoods. First, the data presented in his research report (Thakuri 2009) suggests that the technology results in fuel-wood savings of approximately 3.15 kg per household, which is approximately 1,150 kg per year. Because the households in the study area do not purchase fuel-wood but collect it from nearby forests, we must derive the shadow prices to value the energy savings (Dasgupta 2001; Pattanayak and Pfaff 2009). Based on household survey data summarized by Thakuri (2009), an average trip takes about 6.5 hours and yields 30 kgs of firewood. This suggests a household that uses a more efficient stove will realize savings

[6] The formula we use for the amortized annual value (A) = $[U*i(1+i)^n] / [(1+i)^n - 1]$ where U is the upfront investment cost, i is the annual interest rate (assumed to be 15 percent) and n is the lifetime of the technology (assumed to be 10). A more conservative appraisal—higher interest rate or shorter longevity of the technology—would naturally raise the annualized cost of the technology.

of approximately thirty-one workings days or Rs. 1,550 per year. Additionally, the increased cooking efficiency saves approximately eighty-four hours per year (based on estimates of 14 minutes of cooking saved per day). In monetary terms, these savings of collection and cooking time valued at local wage rates is equivalent to approximately Rs. 525 per year.

Second, we use the global carbon price of Rs. 420 (US$6) for every ton of CO_2 avoided as a shadow value for the global emission reduction benefits. This is a conservative price in the compliance or volunteer carbon markets. In our setting, an average household that reduces fuel-wood use by 1,150 kgs could generate "emission reduction benefits" to the tune of Rs.725 per household per annum by supplying carbon-credits through a CDM type of mechanism.

Thus, the two additional benefits from household energy savings and global emission reductions further tip the benefit-cost ratio in favor of improved stoves. Even without the consideration of the social benefits, these first-order approximations suggest that just the private benefits (health and fuel-wood) of Rs. 3,000 to Rs. 4,000 clearly dwarf the annual costs ranging from Rs. 120 to Rs. 1,200 per year. In the conclusion below, we return to the question of why more households do not adopt seemingly beneficial investments such as improved cookstoves.

5.6 CONCLUSIONS

Improved cookstoves are widely viewed as a relatively cheap and effective way to resolve a major public health problem from indoor air pollution. It is no surprise, therefore, that South Asia, a hotspot for biomass burning, has witnessed concerted research supporting the design and promotion of improved stoves. Much less is known about the co-benefits of improved stoves in terms of reduced fuel-wood use, forest and biodiversity conservation, time savings for women and children, and regional climate benefits (because of reductions in short-lived greenhouse gases and black carbon). We address this gap by drawing on a pair of multidisciplinary studies in the Rasuwa, Syangia, and Chitwan districts of Nepal in 2006, which use socioeconomic surveys of 1,000 households and pollution monitoring to measure cooking technology, kitchen design, fuel type, fuel-wood consumption, time allocation, particulate matter concentration, health conditions, medical costs, and socioeconomic status. Statistical (paired) comparisons of households across districts differing in socio-demographic and eco-climatic dimensions show that improved stoves can reduce particulate matter concentration, acute respiratory illnesses, and fuel-wood consumption. Simple projections of efficient fuel use imply that greenhouse gas and pollutant (e.g., black carbon) emissions will decline. Additionally, improved stoves with smoke hoods can also reduce medical costs and cooking and collection time by 25 percent (Thakuri 2009). These results confirm some findings in the literature (health benefits and time savings), while refuting some others (increased demand for fuel-wood). This is not surprising because the literature on rigorous socioeconomic analysis of stove and fuels is scarce, further strengthening the call for more empirical research on these topics.

The benefit-cost analysis in the previous section suggests high internal-rates-of-return of improved stoves, with private benefits alone substantially exceeding the costs. If that is the case, why aren't more households adopting this technology? The research summarized in this chapter does not have clear answers to this puzzle. Therefore, following Larson and Rosen (2002) and Pattanayak and Pfaff (2009), we recommend that future research should focus on understanding demand for technologies that clean up indoor air. Even though we have not focused on these questions at our research site, our fieldwork and literature review generates the following conjectures about why adoption and diffusion rates are so low.[7]

First, it is possible that the true cost of unsubsidized improved stoves is much higher that we estimate. Given the lack of thriving markets for improved stoves, the transaction costs of acquiring improved stoves could significantly add to the retail price. Second, households likely lack access to cheap credit, which makes it hard for them to pursue investments with high upfront costs and diffused long-term returns in the form of health and human capital. Third, IAP has been described as one of the invisible killers—even though the households see the smoke, they do not see through the smoke and realize that the cocktail of pollutants can significantly harm their health (Pant 2007). Further, even if they see some connection between smoke and health, the uncertainty surrounding this link may be high enough to dissuade a risk-averse household from investing scarce capital in stoves. High discount rates will have the same ultimate effect as risk aversion—the delayed health benefits will seem small compared to significant upfront costs, made larger by credit market failures. Finally, all of these considerations lead to the general point that while we report results in terms of averages, it is likely that costs and benefits vary across the population distribution, and could reflect the differences between the Rasuwa and the Chitwan-Syangja sites, for example. That is, while stove

[7] The first stage of the instrumental variable regressions offers some insights on what drives adoption. However, this is not the focus of the overall project. A systematic review of the socioeconomics literature on adoption (Lewis and Pattanayak 2012) concludes that (a) income, education, and urban location are positively associated with adoption in most but not all studies, (b) the influence of fuel availability and prices, household size and composition, and sex is unclear, and (c) potentially important drivers such as credit, supply-chain strengthening, and social marketing have been ignored. Ongoing research in Bangladesh (Miller and Mobarak 2010) and in India (Saha and Pattanayak 2008) suggests that credit and peer-pressure are key constraints, and that social mobilization campaigns and micro-finance schemes hold tremendous promise.

adoption may look like a good decision for the average household, there may be a significant proportion of the population for whom costs exceed benefits (Jeuland and Pattanayak 2012).

In conclusion, although there are good reasons for the hype surrounding improved stoves and other household energy innovations for poor tropical countries, many scientific uncertainties persist. While the research reported in this chapter plugs some gaps from the environment and development perspectives articulated by Dasgupta (2001, 2013), we also identify a four-pronged research agenda to address some of the unresolved questions. First, simulation analysis may be needed to consider the inherent uncertainty in economic costs and benefits of improved stove use, which depend on unknown combinations of numerous uncertain parameters (Jeuland and Pattanayak 2012). Second, we can also address this uncertainty by conducting replications in different settings to consider the influence of climatic, socio-demographic, market, and institutional factors. However, it is important that such replications are conducted by interdisciplinary teams of economists working with their public health, engineering, and climate science counterparts. Otherwise, we will repeat the problems with the first-generation health impact studies that naively model or worse still simply ignore behavioral and institutional factors, which critically influence program implementation on the ground. Third, researchers will have to be innovative in using experimental and quasi-experimental approaches to improve on current regression-based approaches to establish causality (Pattanayak and Pfaff 2009). One source of persistent challenge is the heterogeneity of household responses, including the basic decision to adopt and appropriately use improved stoves and clean fuels.

Finally, creative study designs will be needed to study what Dasgupta and Mäler (2003) call the fundamental non-convexities inherent in the coupled socio-ecological systems to which smoke-emitting and fuel-wood consuming households belong. Most recently, Dasgupta (2009, 2013) shows how poverty traps result from externalities related to choices concerning nutrition, labor, fertility, and natural resource use, which in turn depend on the initial conditions of the natural environment. We contend that these traps—that is, the inability of households to invest in technologies such as improved stoves and dig themselves out of low levels of health, environmental quality and institutional capacity—are deeper than we had imagined because of epigenetic irreversibilities (Almond and Currie 2011). That is, insufficient investment in technologies that protect against harmful environmental exposures before and during childbirth lead to long-term and irreversible damages to health, education, earning capacity, and development. Thus, if we are to produce meaningful policy advice, then our empirical research on impacts and adoption of improved stoves and clean fuels must adapt the study design to the clearly long, complex, and complicated nature of the persistent puzzles (Rogers 2009).

References

Almond, D. and J. Currie (2011). "Killing Me Softly: The Fetal Origins Hypothesis," *Journal of Economic Perspectives*, 25(3): 153–72.

Armstrong, J. R. and H. Campbell (1991). "Indoor Air Pollution Exposure and Lower Respiratory Infections in Young Gambian Children," *International Journal of Epidemiology*, 20: 424–9.

Barnes, D. et al. (1993). "The Design and Diffusion of Improved Cooking Stoves," *World Bank Research Observer*, 8(2): 119–23.

Bond, T. C., C. Venkataraman and O. Masera (2004). "Global Atmospheric Impacts of Residential Fuels," *Energy for Sustainable Development*, 8(3), 54–66.

Brauer, M. and S. Saxena (2002). "Accessible Tools for Classification of Exposure to Particles," *Chemosphere*, 49: 1151–62.

Bruce, N., R. Perez-Padilla, and R. Albalak (2000). "Indoor Air Pollution in Developing Countries: A Major Environmental and Public Health Challenge," *Bulletin of World Health Organization*, 78(9): 1078–92.

Bruce, N. L., E. Rehfuess, S. Mehta et al. (2006). "Indoor Air Pollution," in D. T. Jamison, J. G. Breman, A. R. Measham., et al. (eds.), *Disease Control Priorities in Developing Countries*, 2nd edn. Washington DC: World Bank. New York: Oxford University Press.

Campbell, H., J. R. Armstrong and P. Byass (1989). "Indoor Air Pollution in Developing Countries and Acute Respiratory Infection in Children," *Lancet*, 1: 1012.

CBS (Central Bureau of Statistics) (2002). "*Population Census 2001*." Kathmandu: Central Bureau of Statistics, National Planning Commission Secretariat, Government of Nepal.

—— "*Nepal Living Standards Survey*." Kathmandu: Central Bureau of Statistics, National Planning Commission Secretariat, Government of Nepal.

Dasgupta, P. (2013). "Personal Histories and Poverty Traps," in C. Sepulveda, A. Harrison, and J. Y. Lin (eds.), *Development Challenges in a Post-crisis World: Annual World Bank Conference on Development Economics, 2011*. Washington, DC: World Bank, 103–26 .

—— (2009). "Poverty Traps: Exploring the Complexity of Causation," *in* J. von Braun, R. Vargas Hill, and R. Pandya-Lorch (eds.), *The Poorest and the Hungry: Assessments, Analyses, and Actions*. Washington, DC: International Food Policy Research Institute, 129–46.

—— (2001). *Human Well-Being and the Natural Environment*. Oxford: Oxford University Press.

—— and K. G. Mäler (2003). "The Economics of Non-convex Ecosystems: Introduction," *Environmental and Resource Economics*, 26: 499–525.

Dasgupta, S., M. Huq, M. Khaliquzzaman et al. (2006). "Indoor Air Quality for Poor Families: New Evidence from Bangladesh," *Indoor Air*, 16: 426–44.

Deaton, A. (2010). "Instruments, Randomization, and Learning About Development," *Journal of Economic Literature*, 48: 424–55.

Dherani, M., D. Pope, M. Mascarenhas et al. (2008). "Indoor Air Pollution from Unprocessed Solid Fuel Use and Pneumonia Risk in Children Aged Under 5 Years: A Systematic Review and Meta-analysis," *Bulletin of the World Health Organization*, 86(5): 390–8.

Duflo, E., M. Greenstone, and R. Hanna (2008). "Indoor Air Pollution, Health and Productivity," *Surveys and Perspectives Integrating Environment and Society*, 1(1): 1–9.

Ezzati, M., and D. Kammen (2002). "Household Energy, Indoor Air Pollution, and Health in Developing Countries: Knowledge Base for Effective Interventions," *Annual Review of Energy & Environment*, 27: 233–70.

Freeman, N. C. G. and S. Saenz de Tejada (2002). "Methods for Collecting Time/Activity Pattern Information Related to Exposure to Combustion Products," *Chemosphere*, 49: 979–92.

Geist, H. J., and E. F. Lambin (2001). "*What Drives Tropical Deforestation? A Meta-Analysis of Proximate and Underlying Causes of Deforestation Based on Subnational Scale Case Study Evidence*," LUCC Report Series No. 4. University of Louvain, Louvain-la-Neuve, Belgium.

Gill, J. (1985). "Stoves and Deforestation in Developing Countries," paper presented to the UK-ISES Conference: Energy for Development–What Are the Solutions? Reading University, 13 December 1985.

Grieshop, A., J. D. Marshall, and M. Kandlikar (2011). "Health and Climate Benefits of Cookstove Replacement Options," *Energy Policy*, 39: 7530–42.

Kammen, D. M. (1995). "Cookstoves for the Developing World," *Scientific American*, 273: 63–7.

Khopkar, A., and E. Sills (2012). "*Woodfuels, Carbon Markets and Black Carbon*," unpublished paper. North Carolina State University, Raleigh.

Kohlin, G., E. O. Sills, S. K. Pattanayak et al. (2011). "*Energy, Gender and Development. What Are the Linkages? Where Is the Evidence?*" Background paper for the World Development Report 2012, commissioned by the Social Dimensions of Climate Change division of the World Bank, Washington, DC.

Krugmann, H. (1987). "*Review of Issues and Research Relating to Improved Cookstoves,*" (IDRC-MR152e). Ottawa: International Development Research Center, Canada.

Jeuland, M. A., and S. K. Pattanayak (2012). "Benefits and Costs of Improved Cookstoves: Assessing the Implications of Variability in Health, Forest and Climate Impacts," *PLOS One*, 7(2): e30338.

Larson, B. A. and S. Rosen (2002). "Understanding Household Demand for Indoor Air Pollution Control in Developing Countries," *Social Science and Medicine*, 55(4): 571–84.

Lewis, J. J. and S. K. Pattanayak (2012). "Who Adopts Improved Fuels and Cookstoves? A Systematic Review," *Environmental Health Perspectives*, 120(5): 637–45.

Manibog, F. R. (1984). "Improved Cooking Stoves in Developing Countries: Problems and Opportunities," *Annual Review of Energy*, 9: 199–227.

Masera, O. R., B. D. Saatkamp, and D. M. Kammen (2000). "From Linear Fuel Switching to Multiple Cooking Strategies: A Critique and Alternative to the Energy Ladder Model," *World Development*, 28(12): 2083–103.

Matthews, E. (2000). "Undying Flame: The Continuing Demand for Wood as Fuel." Excerpted from "Pilot Analysis of Global Ecosystems: Forest Ecosystems". Washington, DC: World Resources Institute.

Miller, G. and M. Mobarak (2010). "Understanding Low Demand: An Experimental Study of Cook-stove Adoption in Bangladesh". Mimeo. Stanford University, Palo Alto, CA.

Mueller, V., A. Pfaff, J. Peabody et al. (2013). "Improving Stove Evaluation Using Survey Data: Who Received Which Intervention Matters," *Ecological Economics*, 93: 301–12.

Nepal, M., A. Nepal, and K. Grimsrud (2011). "Unbelievable but Improved Cookstoves are not Helpful in Reducing Firewood Demand in Nepal," *Environment and Development Economics*, 16(1): 1–23.

Pandey, M. R. (1984). 'Prevalence of Chronic Bronchitis in a Rural Community of the Hill Region of Nepal'. *Thorax*, 39: 331–6.

—— (1984). "Domestic Smoke Pollution and Chronic Bronchitis in a Rural Community of Hill Region of Nepal," *Thorax*, 39: 337–9.

—— et al. (1989). "Indoor Air Pollution in Developing Countries and Acute Respiratory Infection in Children," *Lancet*, 1: 427–9.

Pant, K. P. (2007). "Valuing Interventions to Reduce Indoor Air Pollution-Fuelwood, Deforestation, and Health in Rural Nepal," *The Pakistan Development Review*, 46(4) Part II: 1169–87.

—— (2008). "Estimating Health Benefits When Behaviors Are Endogenous: A Case of Indoor Air Pollution in Rural Nepal," SANDEE Working Paper No 34–08. Kathmandu: South Asian Network for Development and Environmental Economics (SANDEE).

Pattanayak, S. K. and A. Pfaff (2009). "Behavior, Environment and Health in Developing Countries: Evaluation and Valuation," *Annual Review of Resource Economics*, 1: 183–222.

Pfaff, A. S. P., S. Chaudhuri, and H. L. M. Nye (2004). "Household Production and Environmental Kuznets Curves," *Environmental and Resource Economics*, 27(2): 187–200.

Pitt, M. M., M. R. Rosenzweig, and M. N. Hassan (2010). "*Short- and Long-Term Health Effects of Burning Biomass in the Home in Low-Income Countries*'. Mimeo. Brown University, Providence, Rhode Island.

Ramanathan, V. (2007). "Role of Black Carbon in Global and Regional Climate Changes," testimonial to the House Committee on Oversight and Government Reform, Chair: The Honorable Henry A. Waxman. September 2007.

Ravallion, M. (2009). "Evaluation and the Practice of Development," *World Bank Research Observer*, 24: 29–53.

Rogers, P. J. (2009). "Impact Evaluation Design: Matching Impact Evaluation Design to the Nature of the Intervention and the Purpose of the Evaluation," *Journal of Development Effectiveness*, 1(3): 217–26.

Saha, S, S. K. Pattanayak, E. O. Sills et al. (2011). "Under-Mining Health: Environmental Justice and Mining in India," *Health & Place*, 17(1): 140–8.

—— (2008). "Taps, Toilets and Nets: Impact of Micro-Finance and Social Interactions on Prevention Behaviors in Rural India," paper presented at the APHA annual meetings. San Diego, October 2008.

Samson R., C. Ho Lem, S. Bailey et al. (2006). "Improving Methodologies for Using Household Cookstoves under the Clean Development Mechanism," *Partnership for Clean Indoor Air*, Issue 6, January 2006, Resource Efficient Agricultural Production (REAPCanada). Available: <http://www.reap-canada.com/> accessed 8 October 2013.

Smith, K. (1988). "Air Pollution: Assessing Total Exposure in Developing Countries," *Environment*, 30(10): 16–20 and 28–35.

Smith, K. R. (1993). "Fuel Combustion, Air Pollution Exposure, and Health: The Situation in Developing Countries," *Annual Review of Energy and Environment*, 18: 529–66.

—— (1999). "Indoor Air Pollution," *Pollution Management in Focus*, Discussion Note Number 4. Washington DC: The World Bank.

—— (2000). "National Burden of Disease in India from Indoor Air Pollution," *Proceedings of the National Academy of Sciences*, 97: 13286–93.

—— (2002). "Indoor Air Pollution in Developing Countries: Recommendation for Research," *Indoor Air*, 12: 198–207.

—— S. Mehta, M. M. Feuz (2004). "Indoor Air Pollution from Household Use of Solid Fuels," in M. Ezzati (ed.), *Comparative Quantification of Health Risks: Global and Regional Burden of Disease Attributable to Selected Major Risk Factors*. Geneva: WHO (World Health Organization), 1435–94.

Subramaniam, S. V., M. A. Subramanyam, S. Selvaraj et al. (2009). "Are Self-Reports of Health and Morbidities in Developing Countries Misleading? Evidence from India," *Social Science and Medicine*, 68: 260–5.

Thakuri, M. B. M. (2009). "Revisiting the Need of Improved Stoves: Estimating Health, Time and Carbon Benefits," SANDEE Working Paper No 44–09. Kathmandu: South Asian Network for Development and Environmental Economics (SANDEE).

Venkataraman, C., G. Habib, A. Eiguren-Fernandez et al. (2005). "Residential Biofuels in South Asia: Carbonaceous Aerosol Emissions and Climate Impacts," *Science*, 307 (5714): 1424–6.

Wallack, J. S. and V. Ramanathan (2009). "The Other Climate Changers: Why Black Carbon and Ozone Also Matter," *Foreign Affairs*, 88(5): 105–13.

WHO (World Health Organization) (2002). "*Addressing the Impact of Household Energy and Indoor Air Pollution on the Health of the Poor: Implications for Policy Action and Intervention Measures*." Geneva: WHO.

—— (2006). "*Fuel for Life, Household Energy and Health*." Geneva: WHO.

—— (2007a). "*Indoor Air Pollution: National Burden of Disease Estimates*." Geneva: WHO.

—— (2007b). "*Indoor Air Pollution and Lower Respiratory Tract Infections in Children*." Geneva: WHO.

World Bank (2002). "*India: Household Energy, Indoor Air Pollution, and Health*." South Asia Environment and Social Development Unit, Joint UNDP/World Bank Energy Sector Management Assistance Program, November 2002, Washington DC.

—— (2011). "*Household Cookstoves, Environment, Health, and Climate Change: A New Look at an Old Problem*." Washington, DC: World Bank.

Zein-Elabdin, E. O. (1997). "Improved Stoves in Sub-Saharan Africa: The Case of the Sudan," *Energy Economics*, 19: 465–75.

Ziliak, S. T. (2008). "Retrospectives: Guinnessometrics: The Economic Foundation of 'Student's' t," *Journal of Economic Perspectives*, 22(4): 199–216.

6

Comments by Joseph E. Stiglitz on "Climate Change, Cookstoves, and Coughs and Colds: Thinking Globally and Acting Locally in Rural Nepal"

It is a great pleasure for me to participate in this Festschrift session in honor of my longtime friend and coauthor, Partha Dasgupta. Besides his path-breaking work in economic theory, Partha has been a central figure in creating the modern subject of environmental economics. His seminal work[1] is well known; but perhaps less well known has been the role he has played in training a whole generation of environmental economists in the developing world and creating networks of environmental economists within the different regions of the world. The chapters in this volume, all products of young economists affiliated with the South Asian Network for Development and Environmental Economics (SANDEE), are examples of the fruits of that effort.

It is a special pleasure for me to discuss this excellent chapter—the kind of careful and thoughtful empirical research that has the prospect of providing the kind of knowledge that not only enhances our understanding of behavior in poor countries like Nepal, but can also help us design policy interventions that will enhance the well-being and productivity of millions of those living in poverty in the developing world.

It is, in addition, a subject in which I have been interested for more than a dozen years. The first World Development Report during my tenure as Chief Economist of the World Bank was titled *Knowledge for Development* (World Bank 1998). The World Bank was then recasting itself as a "knowledge bank," and emphasizing the role of knowledge in development. What separated developed from developing countries was not just a gap in resources, but also a gap in knowledge.

[1] Examples, in book form alone, include Dasgupta and Heal (1979) and Dasgupta (1982, 1993, and 2001).

One example that influenced our thinking was indoor air pollution. It contributed to respiratory and eye diseases, with obvious adverse effects on the quality of life, health care costs, and productivity. Simple interventions—chimneys and improved cooking stoves—could, at very low cost, reduce indoor air pollution. Those in the developing world typically lacked knowledge of the consequences of existing technologies and practices or the availability of alternatives. Changing knowledge held out the prospect of changing lives.

This chapter demonstrates that the benefits are even greater—but that changing behavior is more complex. It raises key questions such as: how do individuals get information? What affects their choices? And given the huge benefits relative to the costs of more efficient cooking stoves, why hasn't there been more adoption?

At first blush, the subject of cooking stoves might seem too small to be worthy of the kind of intense research that this chapter reflects; but as the authors point out, for people in rural Nepal and in much of the rest of the developing world it is of vital importance. The authors detail the enormous health and environmental benefits from improved cooking stoves that provide more efficient burning and improved ventilation. But the benefits are in fact broader. The authors focus on the reduction in respiratory diseases, but there are also large benefits for the eyes. They quantify the global environmental benefits—reduced emissions—but as I shall comment below, they understate the size of those benefits. There are, in addition, hard-to-quantify but potentially significant local environmental benefits (especially in areas like Nepal facing problems of deforestation): increasing efficiency of cooking stoves may reduce the extent of deforestation, with potentially large benefits in reduced erosion and higher productivity. Finally, as the authors note, greater efficiency reduces the burden on wood-gathering, freeing time for other activities, including work that generates more income or food. Moreover, there is an important gender dimension—both directly and indirectly. Women may suffer more from the indoor air pollution, and they bear the burden of wood-gathering.

Moreover, a study such as this cannot always quantify the full long-term benefits. The full effects of improved cooking stoves may not be felt for a generation: damage to the respiratory system mounts over a lifetime, and can be a complex and non-linear relationship with exposure. By the time a middle-aged woman starts to use an improved cooking device, much of the damage may have already occurred. Moreover, because of the complex interactions with the exposure to other diseases, a weakened respiratory system may make individuals more vulnerable to other health problems.

As an aside, the analysis of this chapter implicitly raises deep questions about the "controlled" experimental approach, which has increasingly come into favor. First, the magnitude of the benefits (relative to the costs) suggests that it is unlikely that any improvement/refinement in estimates from the "preferred" controlled experimental methodology will change the conclusions of the analysis.

Moreover, this study (as well as other studies in this volume—see also my remarks below) has emphasized the importance of peer interactions. Individuals learn from others within their community. But if communities learn from neighboring communities, the appropriate unit of analysis may have to be even larger.

Before turning to the two key questions posed by the chapter, why individuals do not adopt these technologies and what governments should do, I want to make some observations about neighboring Bhutan. These observations are based not on a detailed study, such as the one presented here, but still may be useful.

It appears that the dissemination of improvements in indoor ventilation (including improved cooking stoves) is very widespread there. The commonly used cooking stove is, interestingly, a local "innovation." The production of such products can, itself, be the basis of development—bringing home the importance of integrated approaches to development. (When one thinks of building schools, for instance, one shouldn't necessarily just ask which contractor, domestic or foreign, will do it at lowest cost. School construction may help develop skills, including entrepreneurial/business skills, that are relevant to other construction activities—or which may be of value even more broadly. Anyone concerned about development should accordingly be concerned about international trade agreements that unduly restrict provisions encouraging local procurement or domestic content.)

The widely respected (in some quarters, almost revered) government has played an important role, along with the education system, in the dissemination of knowledge about health. Of course, the improvement in health in recent decades has given considerable credibility to government efforts. But knowledge was only one part of the strategy. The government effectively raised the price of the old technology and lowered the price of alternative technologies.

By creating a widespread understanding of the importance of conservation (one of the pillars of the Gross National Happiness agenda that has played a central role in its development strategy), the Bhutanese government has helped create norms that circumscribe deforestation. At the same time, these norms have aided the implementation of government regulations, which strictly restrict the extent of tree-cutting. Widespread understanding that these regulations are going to be getting tighter motivates a demand for alternatives, such as improved cooking stoves.

The government's provision of electricity (which is remarkably extensive, given the terrain, but still not universal) at low cost has provided an alternative to the use of wood as a source of energy. (The way that electricity bills are paid in some rural areas—a communal exercise—may enhance sensitivity to these issues.)

To return to the impressive results of this chapter: The chapter provides overwhelming evidence that *private* benefits exceed costs by a multiple, posing the question of why adoption isn't more widespread. The answers provide considerable insights into a broader range of developmental issues. One is that the costs are evident and upfront, while the benefits are elusive and occur down the line. With high capital costs and large risk aversion, the cost-benefit calculations may look different. Moreover, for some of the reasons cited earlier—it will take years for the full benefits to be received—there is almost certainly less than full knowledge of the benefits. This may exemplify the importance of "social capital": new norms through peer interactions and trust in government (authority) may make behavioral changes far easier.

The chapter raises another important dimension: what might be called deficiencies in family governance. The decision-maker (the male, responsible for making cash allocations) and those bearing the burden of the costs (both health and the cost of wood-gathering) are different people. Finally, of course, is the fact that social and private costs differ markedly. There is typically no charge in using forest wood.

This list of problems suggests possible government remedies—but also problems with some possible remedies. First, it is desirable to improve information. But that requires "trust" in those providing the information—and it may be difficult to overcome the trust deficit. The issue is of course far broader than just cooking stoves.

Microcredit schemes might lower the cost of capital. But even if the cost of capital were reduced, access would be limited, and it is not obvious that (without explicit constraints) cooking stoves would be at the top of the list. Expenditures that increase incomes and other forms of consumption (weddings) are likely to get priority.

In most countries, controlling the private use of public forests is difficult. Controlling the use of trees on supposedly private land may be impossible.

Government policies changing (or encouraging changes in) household governance would be useful; but these changes occur slowly, and government may have only limited leverage. (Though successes do exist: Bangladesh may provide an example.)

This brings me to the final question: what should donors do? The development community has long worried about the effectiveness of its aid. What are the returns? This chapter provides overwhelming evidence that were donors to provide these improved cooking stoves (and other devices to improve indoor ventilation), the *social* benefit-cost ratio would be enormous. Indeed, this chapter seriously underestimates those benefits. It calculates the annual cost of an improved cookstove at Rs. 120 per year *assuming* a 15 percent interest rate. But for most donor governments, the cost of funds is far, far lower, less than a third of that number, bringing down the annual costs to well below Rs. 100 per year.

On the benefit side, the chapter provides health benefits (including reduced losses in work days) at between Rs. 1,200 and Rs. 2,000 per annum. As I explained above, this underestimates (perhaps considerably) the overall, long-term health benefits.

Time-savings are estimated at Rs. 2,075.

The emission benefits are estimated at Rs. 725, but the calculations deriving this value assume a price of emissions of $6 per ton of carbon. A more reasonable *social* valuation would be ten times higher, or Rs. 7,250 per year.

All of these calculations ignore the ancillary environmental benefits.

Adding all of this together generates a social benefit conservatively estimated at greater than Rs. 9,525 per year, some 100 times the cost.

The chapter asks, given the high private benefit-cost ratio, why households do not make these investments. These calculations suggest an even greater puzzle: given the even higher social benefit-cost ratio (much of which is associated with a universally recognized global public good, global warming), why don't the *donors* make these investments?

References

Dasgupta, P. (1982). *The Control of Resources*. Cambridge, MA: Harvard University Press.

—— (1993). *An Inquiry into Well-Being and Destitution*, Oxford: Clarendon Press.

—— (2001). *Human Well-Being and the Natural Environment*. Oxford: Oxford University Press.

—— and G. M. Heal (1979). *Economic Theory and Exhaustible Resources*. Cambridge: Cambridge University Press.

World Bank (1999). *World Development Report 1998: Knowledge for Development*. New York: Oxford University Press.

7

Red Wells or Green Wells and Does It Matter? Examining Household Use of Arsenic-contaminated Water in Bangladesh[1]

A. K. Enamul Haque, Zakir H. Khan, Mani Nepal, and Priya Shyamsundar

7.1 INTRODUCTION

Bangladesh currently faces a major health calamity because of arsenic contamination of groundwater aquifers. Bangladesh has copious quantities of ground water, but the alluvial aquifers of the Ganges delta are polluted by naturally occurring arsenic (Nickson et al. 1998). Approximately 27 percent of shallow tube wells in Bangladesh are estimated to have arsenic content that exceeds the government's safety standards of 50 mg/liter (Caldwell et al. 2006; BGS and DPHE 2001).[2] Some 46 percent of wells exceed the safety standards set by the World Health Organization of 10 mg/liter (BGS and DPHE 2001).[3] For Bangladesh, this means that an estimated 27 to 60 percent of its population is at risk from arsenic exposure (Smith, Lingas, and Rahman, 2000).

Historically, Bangladesh has been very successful in providing its population with access to safe drinking water. Death due to cholera and diarrheal disease was effectively contained in the seventies and eighties by replacing

[1] The data used in this chapter were collected as part of a research project undertaken by Zakir H. Khan and was sponsored by SANDEE. We are grateful to SANDEE's sponsors for financial support and for SANDEE's advisors who helped with earlier stages of this work. We also thank David Starrett and Scott Barrett for their comments, which helped improve the chapter substantially.

[2] Based on a national sample of 3,534 tube wells.

[3] Air and water quality international standards set by the World Health Organization can differ from national standards. The World Health Organization's arsenic standards apply in several developed countries but many developing countries have set their own standards for practical reasons.

existing sources of drinking water with tube wells, a strategy that was vigorously pursued by the Government of Bangladesh, UNICEF, and other donors. Tube wells were bored to obtain clean water from thirty to hundred feet below the surface. This water did not have to be boiled and was free of many bacterial contaminants. Shallow tube wells were cheap, could be installed close to homes and women found them extremely convenient. Notably, the expansion of tube wells occurred at a period when oral re-hydration treatment was also widely distributed. While, there is evidence that oral re-hydration therapy, more so than the availability of tube-well water, was responsible for the reduction in diarrheal mortality, tube wells grew rapidly as a dominant water source (Caldwell et al. 2006). As of 1997, some 97 percent of the rural population in Bangladesh obtained their drinking water from tube wells (Farouque and Alam 2002). Since the discovery of arsenic in ground water in 1993, Bangladesh has struggled once again with the problem of delivering safe water.

Arsenic poisoning, or arsenicosis, can cause numerous health problems ranging from skin lesions to cancer and cardio-vascular diseases. We discuss some of these symptoms in detail later. Exposure to high concentrations of arsenic can result in rapid onset of diseases, but this is not the case in Bangladesh. Ingestion is mainly through low doses of arsenic in water, resulting in symptoms appearing over a long period of time. Because the presence of arsenic in water is impossible to detect through our normal senses and because health effects are not immediately obvious, it can be difficult to convince households about the threats of arsenic.

Over the last decade, the Bangladesh government, donors, and NGOs have made different investments to provide arsenic-free water and run health campaigns to inform people about the risks of arsenic. The government's main campaign to inform people about the presence of arsenic in drinking water sources is through a binary color-coding system. A green-colored tube well is safe for collecting drinking and cooking water while a red-colored one is not, that is, the arsenic content in red wells is higher than the government safety standards of 50 mg/liter. NGOs have also undertaken door-to-door awareness programs and information has been disseminated through the media. Nonetheless, either due to limited alternative sources of water or for other reasons, many households continue to use water from unsafe tube wells.

It is in this context, that this study examines arsenic exposure and people's responses in two Upazilas[4] in Bangladesh. We seek to understand if providing information on arsenic contamination contributes to reduced exposure. We are particularly interested in the efficacy of different sources of information. We also identify the costs of using arsenic-contaminated

[4] Administratively, Bangladesh is divided into several tiers: Division, District, Upazila, Union and Ward. The local government structure begins at the district level and the Upazila is the second tier of local government.

water. The study attempts to answer three questions: (a) how effective are different sources of information in reducing household use of contaminated water? (b) do households that are able to reduce their exposure to red wells have specific characteristics, that is, are they wealthy or have larger families, allowing them to find alternatives? And (c) what are the costs to households of continuing to use red wells? We try to address these questions by examining the behavior of households that drink water from red (unsafe) and green (safe) wells. We assess how the probability of using red wells is affected by information and other household characteristics. We also examine medical expenditures and sick days that occur as a result of arsenic-related symptoms. Investigating these issues will help us understand the impacts of government and NGO activities and may contribute towards designing better public health strategies.

Information campaigns are a well-tried strategy for regulating pollution and natural resource use (Tietenberg and Wheeler 2001). There is a sizable literature on the viability of information, with several studies examining the effect of labeling, news and media information, and government disclosure of data, on firm, farmer, investor, and consumer behavior (Khanna et al. 1998; Kathuria 2007; Lemos 2008; and Wang et al. 2004). Summarizing this literature, Tietenberg and Wheeler (2001) conclude that information strategies can be effective in changing consumer and firm behavior. However, how information is provided, how much is provided, and what kinds of complementary actions are taken, play a role.

An earlier paper by Madajewicz et al. (2007) offers a careful analysis of the impact of information on health risks in Bangladesh. This study was a joint effort by a large number of scientists and public health specialists in collaboration with professors from Columbia University. Households were provided with information on the health consequences of drinking arsenic-contaminated water and the results of a health exam. The study scientists were also able to run tests on 6,500 wells in one district and inform households about the contamination in their wells. The same households were visited six to twelve months later to assess the effect of information. Household response to the information campaign was quick and significant. Knowing that wells have an unsafe level of arsenic raised the probability that a household switches to a new alternate source of well within a year by 0.37. This switch was done despite a fifteen-fold (4.3 minutes per round trip) increase in the time spent collecting water from alternate sources. An interesting and very important finding from this study is that media communicated general information is as effective (in terms of awareness generation) as expensive house-specific information. However, media campaigns are less able to induce behavioral change and awareness does not necessarily lead to action.

Another study of relevance to our work is Jalan et al. (2009) on the determinants of water-purification behavior among a country-wide sample of Indian respondents. Jalan et al. (2009) treat schooling, media exposure, and the presence of diarrhea as indicators of awareness of health risks. They ask how these indicators influence households to purify water. Using a large dataset, they find that each of these variables has a significant effect on home-purification activities, independent of household characteristics such as wealth. For example, the probability of purification increases by 8 percent points if a female household member reads a newspaper at least once a week. The probability that a household boils water for drinking increases by 5 percent if the household has experienced a previous health shock. The impact of education is also significant. Overall, the effect of "information and awareness" are comparable in magnitude to wealth effects.

Our study is not based on multiple surveys and control and treatment groups as found in Madajewicz et al. (2007) and is more along the lines of Jalan et al. (2009). It also builds on an earlier study by Aziz et al. (2006) that examines the determinants of knowledge of arsenic symptoms and household decisions to switch wells. Like these other studies, we are interested in the role of education versus media versus government and NGO campaigns on water use behavior. The Columbia University study also established the cost of switching wells using information on time costs of collecting water from alternate sources. We attempt to estimate the benefits of switching by looking at medical and time costs resulting from illness.

In the following sections, we first provide background information on the extent of arsenic contamination in ground water in Bangladesh and health effects. We then discuss our study area and the data used to examine the impact of different sources of information. Section 7.4 presents the analyses on the role of information. In section 7.5, we assess the costs of illness associated with arsenic contamination in Bangladesh. Our final section concludes and discusses next steps.

7.2 BACKGROUND

Bangladesh is a very densely populated country with a population of over 140 million (BBS 2009). With a per-capita GDP of USD 444 in 2005 (BER 2005), Bangladesh is also one of the least developed countries in the world. Nevertheless, Bangladesh has made significant strides in accelerating economic and human development. Providing access to clean water is a major development goal of the government. Until the discovery of arsenic, 97 percent of households were estimated to have access to clean water. Because of the presence of arsenic, this number is now down to 74 percent (Khan 2007).

Out of 4.95 million tube wells screened in Bangladesh in 2002 to 2003, 1.44 million or 29 percent were estimated to be contaminated with arsenic above the safe standards of 50 mg/liter.[5] Since several million tube wells are yet to be screened, the official estimate is that nationwide some 20 percent of tube wells or one in five shallow tube wells is contaminated with arsenic above the 50 mg/liter safety standard (DPHE website 2011, UNICEF, Bangladesh 2011).[6] The state of affairs is dire in some parts of Bangladesh. A 2009 situation analyses indicates that only 4 percent of nine million people who live in areas where over 80 percent of wells are contaminated, have arsenic-free water (UNICEF, Bangladesh 2011).

In terms of people affected, according to the Government of Bangladesh's Department of Public Health and Engineering (DPHE), there are some 38,380 arsenic-affected patients in Bangladesh. This is a small number given Bangladesh's current estimated population of over 140 million (BBS 2009). However, this may be the tip of the iceberg since arsenicosis is a slow-growing disease. Screening done by the Bangladesh Arsenic Mitigation and Water Supply Programme, in fact, demonstrates that the figure might be as high as 1.1 cases of arsenicosis per thousand (World Bank 2002).

While the overall number of cases of illness is hard to estimate given lack of data on symptomatic patients, some understanding of exposure is possible. A national sample survey, the Bangladesh Household Survey 2004, found that some 7.9 percent of the sampled population drank from wells that had arsenic over the safety standards of 50 mg/liter (Khan et al. 2007). Using the same safety standards, the Bangladesh Department of Health and Engineering estimates the exposed population to be higher at 30–35 million Bangladeshis (conservatively about 20 percent of the population) (DPHE website 2011). The government's estimates are comparable to UNICEF's estimate of 20 million people who are exposed to high levels of arsenic contamination (UNICEF, Bangladesh 2011). Thus, while there is clear information on the number of wells contaminated with unsafe levels of arsenic, there is uncertainty regarding the exposed population and even more uncertainty about the number of cases of illness.

The primary pathway to arsenicosis is prolonged exposure through drinking arsenic-contaminated water,[7] with symptoms taking five to twenty years to develop. Because of its slow progress, the evolution of the disease is divided into several stages. In the primary stage, an arsenicosis patient may develop several symptoms, sometimes simultaneously, such as blackening of parts of the body (melanosis), thickening and roughness of the palms and soles

[5] These numbers are slightly higher than the estimates referred to earlier by BGS and DPHE (2001).

[6] <http://www.dphe.gov.bd> (accessed 30 August 2011) and <http://www.unicef.org/bangladesh/Arsenic_Mitigation_in_Bangladesh.pdf> (UNICEF media notes, accessed 30 August 2011).

[7] Absorption of arsenic through the skin is minimal. Thus hand-washing, bathing, and laundry done with water containing arsenic does not pose human health risks.

(keratosis), redness of the eye (conjunctivitis), inflammation of the respiratory tract and nausea and vomiting (gastroenteritis). If a patient continues to be exposed to arsenic-contaminated water and if adequate preventive measures are not adopted, the symptoms advance and become more visible: white intermittent dots within blackened areas (called leukonelanosis or Rain Drop Syndrome), nodular growth on the palms and soles (hyper-keratosis), swelling of the feet and legs (non-pitting edema), and peripheral neuropathy as well as liver and kidney disorders. In the tertiary stage, an arsenicosis patient's physical condition deteriorates rapidly and the condition becomes irreversible. Gangrene, cancer of the skin, lungs and bladder, and kidney and liver failure become manifest (Khan 2007).

Numerous studies in Bangladesh have documented the health consequences of arsenic contamination. Chen and Ahsan (2004) estimate a doubling of lifetime mortality risk from liver, bladder, and lung cancer in Bangladesh, because of arsenic exposure through drinking water. A cohort analysis between 1991 and 2000 of 115, 903 people in Matlab Upazila suggests that the death rate due to cancers, cardiovascular disease, and infectious disease increases by a factor of 1.44, 1.16, and 1.30, respectively for patients exposed to contaminated water higher than the Bangladesh safety standards (UNICEF, Bangladesh 2011). In other work, Smith et al. (1999) show arsenic contamination may be mainly responsible for bladder and lung cancer relative to other cancers.

Given the severity of the problem, several Government, NGO and international institutions are engaged in providing technical and financial support for arsenic detection, research, and mitigation projects. However, alternatives to drinking water from tube wells are limited. Dug wells that draw water from close to the surface are an option, but there is fear of microbial contamination. The growth of shallow tube wells was historically a great achievement precisely because it provided people with cheap bacteria-free water. Now, finding a new substitute poses a huge water-supply and economic challenge. Deep tube wells that obtain water from over 150 meters below the ground are a limited option because they are expensive, which explains why there are currently relatively few private deep tube wells. There are also some household-level technologies available for arsenic control, but these are possibly less affordable.[8]

Since all wells in a particular location are not contaminated, well testing and switching is another important strategy. Given the spatial variability of arsenic content in water, well-switching could be a viable in all but 29 Upazilas, where 80 percent of the wells are unsafe (van Geen et al. 2002). However, we note that people also like to use shallow tube wells because the water is conveniently available for bathing and washing; it is only drinking water that poses

[8] There are several processes through which arsenic in water can be reduced to the 'safe' level. Some are at the household level using small filtration units; others are at the community level.

health hazards. It is in this context, that we try to understand the reasons why households continue to drink from unsafe red wells.

7.3 DATA AND STUDY AREA

The data used in this chapter are based on a 2005 survey of 5,563 individuals from 878 households in two Upazilas (sub-districts) of Bangladesh (Khan 2007; Khan and Haque 2011). The data were collected as part of a research project undertaken by one of the authors, Zakir H. Khan, and sponsored by SANDEE.

The study area, Upazilas Matlab and Laksham, are located in the south-eastern part of Bangladesh, which is the most arsenic-prone region in the country. The two Upazilas are located within fifty kilometers of each other. Matlab has had numerous health-related interventions because of work by the International Centre for Diarrheal Diseases Research, Bangladesh, while Laksham seems to have had more government interventions. The government has marked a large number of tube wells (though not all) in this area as red (unsafe for drinking) or green (safe). Data provided by DPHE at the time of the study indicated that only 30 percent of the wells in our study sample fell within the green safety standards of 50 mg/liter.

To identify households for our study, we developed a sampling frame based on a DPHE database. The database contained information on wells, location of wells, and households using the wells. As described in Khan and Haque (2011), a two-step procedure was used to select households. In the first stage, 900 tube wells were randomly chosen (450 from each Upazila) from three Unions[9] in Matlab and four Unions in Laksham. Since the same tube well is shared by several households, at the second stage, one household from each tube-well user group was randomly selected from the DPHE database. The total number of households selected was 878.

The 2005 survey collected data on: (a) household level socioeconomic information; (b) individual health symptoms and demographic information; and (c) workdays lost, income loss, sick days, and averting and mitigating activities both at household and individual levels. Avertive activities refer to actions taken by households to avoid use of contaminated water. Mitigating activities refer to doctor and hospital visits. Survey enumerators were trained to identify different variants of arsenicosis based on symptoms narrated by respondents.

[9] Union is at the third tier of local government and is comprised of ten wards. Each Union has a chair and thirteen elected members (one from each ward plus three women members).

Table 7.1 Household and individual socioeconomic information

	Mean	Mean red well	Mean green well
Household size	6.33 (2.43)	6.41 (2.39)	6.24 (2.48)
Male/female ratio	1.28 (0.98)	1.33 (1.04)	1.22 (0.92)
Age of household head (years)	52.8 (15.3)	53.8 (15.8)	51.5 (14.4)
Age (full sample)	27.49 (20.25)		
Percent of individuals over 7 years illiterate	13.6 (17.9)	15.2 (19.5)	11.5 (15.7)
Percent of individuals over 7 years with primary or secondary education	78.5 (20.7)	78.1 (21.3)	79.1 (20.1)
Education (years)	5.17 (4.15)		
Male (years)	5.6 (4.1)	5.44 (4.03)	5.82 (4.10)
Female (years)	4.8 (3.8)	4.6 (3.75)	4.98 (3.86)
Wealth	51.62 (12.4)	51.8 (12.9)	51.4 (11.7)
Radio ownership (%)	53.3 (49.9)	52.2 (50.0)	55.0 (49.8)
TV ownership (%)	27.1 (44.5)	26.8 (44.3)	27.7 (44.8)

Note: Standard errors in parenthesis

Table 7.1 provides a brief summary of statistics at the individual and household level. The average household size in our study area is 6.3. If we examine the number of working members, households have some 4.5 members over the age of 14. The average age of the individuals in the sample is 28 years and the male to female ratio is 1.28, which is higher than the Bangladesh average. Individuals in our sample have about five years of schooling on average. Women have approximately one year less education than men. Some 14 percent of individuals over seven years of age have no education; while 79 percent of individuals have either primary or secondary education, and about 7 percent of individuals have more than secondary education.

To determine the wealth status of the household, we used a checklist of forty-three assets. Using this list, each household was assigned a number on a wealth index that ranged from 0 to 100.[10] The wealth distribution of the sampled households follows a tight bell-shaped curve (Khan 2007). In terms of assets, ownership of radio and TV are important for understanding the role of

[10] The wealth index for household *i* is given by:

$$WI_i = \left[\frac{A_i - \min(A_k)}{\max(A_k) - \min(A_k)}\right] \times 100$$

where $A_i = \sum_{j=1}^{n} a_{ij}$ denotes the number of assets owned by household *i*, with $a_{ij} = 1$ if household *i* owns asset *j* and $a_{ij} = 0$ otherwise; where $n = 43$; and where $\min(A_k)$ and $\max(A_k)$ denote, respectively, the smallest and largest number of assets held by any household k ($i, k = 1, \ldots, m$) in the sample.

Table 7.2 Drinking water in the study area

	Households %
Percent drink water from tube well	85
Average no. of years of drinking from tube well (among households that drink from tube wells)	11.45
Percent of all water sources owned by individual households	74
Percent aware of arsenic in main source of water	66
Percent drinking water from red wells	55
Percent who follow some form of purification	18
Percent Yes to averting technology	12

information. Table 7.1 indicates that some 53 percent of households owned a radio while 23 percent owned a television.

In order to understand how households were exposed to arsenic, we looked at sources of drinking water. Table 7.2 indicates that 85 percent of the households obtain their drinking water from tube wells. On average, these households had been using the same source of tube well water for over eleven years. Less than 11 percent of households have access to deep tube wells (over 150 meters deep), which are generally arsenic-free. Furthermore, over three-quarters of all water sources are privately owned. Thus, our understanding is that over the last twenty or more years, households have drilled individual tube wells for themselves and use of public sources of water is limited. Very few households use surface water or get water from taps at home, less than 0.5 percent people use filters and only 0.2 percent use water from arsenic removal plants. Most importantly, Table 7.2 indicates that fifty five percent of households still drink water from red tube wells. This shows the extent of vulnerability of the population to arsenicosis.

Table 7.3 shows that approximately 5 percent of the sampled population suffered from arsenicosis. A slightly larger percentage of women (6 percent) versus men (4.6 percent) had symptoms. Interestingly, Madajewicz et al. (2007) also found that some 6 percent of the sample population in nearby Araihazar Upazila showed signs of arsenic impacts. In our sample, some 19 percent of households had at least one person sick from arsenic exposure. If we divide our sample into red well and green well users, we find that a small percentage of green well users are also sick from arsenic. This may be because they were previously exposed and switched water sources over time. If we look at only red well users, 9 percent of the sample females show signs of arsenic contamination.

Most of the individuals who suffered from some form of arsenic exposure were in the early stages of the disease (see Table 7.3). Some 34 percent of sick individuals exhibited signs of kertosis or thickening of the palms and soles. Some 45–50 percent of sick individuals also indicated that they had other symptoms of arsenic poisoning such as redness of the eye and gastro-intestinal problems. Between 2–3 percent of the population exhibited advanced

Table 7.3 Presence of arsenic symptoms

	%
Total individuals with arsenic symptoms	5.3
Male	4.6
Female	6.0
Percent of households with at least one sick from arsenic	19
Distribution of arsenic disease among sick individuals	
Primary Stage	
Melanosis or black spots in the body	8.6
Keratosis or thickening of the palms and soles	34.3
Redness of the eye or conjunctivitis	58.6
Inflammation of the respiratory system	45.7
Gastrointestinal problem	46.4
Secondary Stage	
Hypo-pigmentation or white spots	5.7
Hyper-keratosis or nodular growth	15
Swelling of the feet and legs	12.1
Peripheral neuropathy	17.1
Liver or kidney disorder	7.1
Tertiary Stage	
Gangrene of the distal organs	3.6
Cancer of the skin, lung or urinary tract	2.9
Liver or kidney failure	2.1

conditions of arsenic poisoning. Given that this is a late acting disease that can take twenty-odd years to set in, the distribution of the disease is not surprising.

7.4 THE ROLE OF INFORMATION

In this study, we are interested in the role of information in reducing household exposure to arsenic-contaminated water. Some 66 percent of households in our sample indicated that they were aware of the presence of arsenic in their wells. These numbers echo results from Aziz et al. (2006) who found that some 70 percent of their sample of households in Matlab Upazila were aware of the arsenic problem in their water. As Table 7.4 shows, the main sources of arsenic-related information amongst our study households are: NGOs (43 percent of households), DPHE (25 percent) and other government sources, including health facilities (17 percent). Some 32 percent of households had attended awareness programs organized by NGOs. Not surprising, since NGOs activities cover nearly 50 percent of the rural Bangladeshi population. Some 15 percent of households got their information from a TV or radio. It is possible

Table 7.4 Sources of information and reasons for drinking contaminated water

	Households %
Main Source of information on arsenic contamination came from:	
DPHE	24.5
TV/Radio	14.6
Newspaper	0.59
Government	16.7
NGO	42.9
Other	0.24
Reasons for drinking from red wells (among those who reported drinking from red wells (n = 485 HHs))	
Safe or arsenic free source of water unavailable	47.42
Taste of the water is good	14.02
Shortage of money	5.57
Do not know the effect of drinking from red wells	27.01
Other	5.99

that households got information from multiple sources. Our survey, however, probed and obtained data on the "main" source of information.

One of the questions we try to address in this chapter is whether different sources of information available through the government, NGOs, or the media has an impact on household use of arsenic-contaminated water. As previously noted, many wells in this area are painted red or green but households continue to use both kinds of wells. There are clearly various reasons why households continue to use contaminated "red" wells but the most important reason identified is lack of alternate sources (see Table 7.4). However, as Table 7.1 shows there are no systematic differences in terms of wealth or demographics between red-well and green-well users. Indicators such as household size, age, male-to-female ratio and wealth do not vary much across people who imbibe from red wells versus green. Green-well users are slightly more educated. We think the main reasons for why some households may use red versus green may be two-fold: (a) geological, that is, because of their location some households have better access to red wells; and (b) behavioral—because of information available some households may have switched to green wells.

To examine this question of why some households use red wells versus green more carefully we ask what factors affect the probability of a household using a "red" well. In particular, we ask if different sources of information in the form of TV or Radio, NGO awareness activities and information by the Department of Public Health have influenced the use of red wells. We are also interested in the role of education.

We use the following model to assess factors that influence household use of red versus green wells:

$$Y_1 = \sum \beta_i X_i + \gamma_2 Y_2 + \eta_k + u_1 \quad (1)$$

where Y_1 is a binary variable (1 for drinking from red, 0 for drinking from other sources, including green tube wells), *X*'s are a set of independent variables including information sources, Y_2 is the number of household members affected by arsenic in a household, and η_L is a Union fixed effect.[11] We estimate equation (1) to assess the impact of different sources of information on the probability of drinking from red wells. We discuss below our empirical strategy for addressing the endogeneity problem posed by the inclusion of Y_2.

Drinking from red wells is expected to be affected by household characteristics such as wealth, the relative number of females in the household, which reflects knowledge about water sources and ability to carry water, and whether the well is owned privately. We hypothesize that wealth increases access to alternate sources of water or purification technologies, and the percent of females in the household decreases the probability of drinking from red wells. Whether the well is privately or publicly owned is an interesting variable. Our hypothesis is that if a household owns the private well that it has access to, it may be reluctant to switch because of investments already made. This hypothesis builds on results by Madajewicz et al. (2007), who find that well-switching is negatively related to well ownership. If the household doesn't own the well, switching may be more likely. Since we are not able to link household use with household specific ownership rights, we are unable to hypothesize on the sign of the coefficient on private well ownership.

The right-hand side variables in the above model include three information-related indicator variables: (a) whether the household obtained arsenic information from various government sources (mainly from the health sector); (b) whether the household obtained its information from the electronic media such as TV or Radio, and (c) whether the household obtained its arsenic information from NGOs. In the empirical estimation of Y_1 in equation (1), the coefficients of these variables are ascertained relative to the default position of the households obtaining information from DPHE. We do this because we partly want to assess whether the role of DPHE is as important as other information campaigns. We are also interested in the effect of education as this could be considered an indicator of awareness of health risks (Jalan et al. 2009).

Following Jalan et al. (2009), we hypothesize that households are less likely to use red wells if they already have sick people in the household. As previously noted, some 19 percent of the households have at least a member who is sick with arsenicosis. We hypothesize that health shocks are likely to make the household more aware of sources and use of alternate water. We also hypothesize that, given cultural biases, if there are more men than women in

[11] Union is a lower-level political unit in Bangladesh and includes groups of villages.

the household that are sick with arsenicosis, this decreases the probability of drinking from red wells.

The inclusion of arsenic patients in the household as an "awareness" indicator creates an endogeneity problem while estimating equation (1). The presence of arsenic patients in the household (Y_2 in equation (2) below) is itself dependent on drinking water from red wells (Y_1). In order to remove this potential endogeneity in our model, we use a two-stage instrumental variable approach. In the first stage, we estimate the number of arsenic-affected people in a household (Y_2). Since the number of arsenic-affected people is a discrete non-negative integer; we use a negative binomial model to estimate equation (2). When the left-hand side variable is a count of one kind or the other, it is appropriate to model this information assuming that the data follows a Poisson or negative binomial distribution. The first-stage results are presented in Table 7.10 of the appendix, which shows that the coefficient *alpha* (the negative binomial variance parameter) is significantly different from zero, indicating that the negative binomial is better suited than the Poisson model. Thus, we use the negative binomial model for the first-stage estimation.

In the first-stage regression, we use two instrumental variables (Z_j), chronic illness and use of tube wells, which are assumed to be correlated with the presence of sick people with arsenicosis, but not correlated with drinking water from red tube wells. Both of these instruments are indicator variables. Since the arsenic effect on the human body depends on the immunity levels of individuals, we use chronic illness as an instrument. Since arsenicosis is linked to drinking of water from shallow-aquifer-based tube wells, we use drinking from tube wells as another instrument. We recognize that these variables are imperfect instruments, but we are constrained by data limitations.

In order to verify the relevance of the instruments, we perform statistical tests. We first run the first-stage regression and perform the joint significance test of the instruments. This joint significance test indicates that coefficients of these two instruments are jointly significant, indicating that they are correlated with the endogenous variable. This suggests that our instruments are good enough to address the endogeneity issue.

Following the first-stage estimation, in the second stage, we estimate a logit regression in which the dependent variable (Y_1) is a binary variable with Y_1= 1 if the household drinks water from tube wells marked as "red" and 0 otherwise. In equation (3) $\widehat{Y}_2$ is predicted from equation (2) as given below:

$$Y_2 = \sum \beta_i X_i + \sum \delta_j Z_j + \eta_k + U_2 \tag{2}$$

$$Y_1 = \sum \beta_i X_i + \gamma_2 \check{Y}_2 + \eta_k + u_3 \tag{3}$$

Table 7.5 Summary statistics of variables used in information regression

Variable	Definition	Mean	SD	Min	Max
DRINK_RED_ WATER	1 if drinking from red well	0.55	0.5	0	1
ARS_AFFECT	Number of household member(s) affected by arsenic-related diseases	0.34	0.89	0	10
PVT_OWNER	1 if the households is using a private water source	0.74	0.44	0	1
FEMALE	Ratio of female members to all household members	0.49	0.17	0	1
INFO_GOVT	1 if main source of information on arsenic was from government	0.16	0.37	0	1
INFO_TVR	1 if main source of information on arsenic was from TV/radio	0.15	0.35	0	1
INFO_NGO	1 if main source of information on arsenic was from NGOs	0.42	0.49	0	1
INFO_DPHE	1 if HH's main source of information on arsenic was from DPHE	0.4	0.49	0	1
F_MORE	1 if more female members relative to male members are arsenic-affected in sampled HHs	0.91	0.29	0	1
EDU1_10	1 if at least one member of the household had an education between 1 to 10 years	0.79	0.21	0	1
HEDU	1 if at least one member of the household had education over 10 years	0.08	0.15	0	1
WINDEX	Wealth index	51.62	12.41	0	100
TUBE WELLS	1 if source of drinking water is tube wells	0.84	0.36	0	1
CHRO_Ill	1 if a member of the household has been suffering from any other chronic illness	0.26	0.55	0	4

Table 7.5 presents the summary statistics of the variables used in the two-stage estimation. The results are presented in Table 7.6. Column 1 of Table 7.6 represents the results from a basic logit model without instrumenting for arsenic patients in the household. Column 2 presents the coefficients of the

Table 7.6 Fixed-effect logit regression for the full sample (DepVar: drink from the red tube wells)

VARIABLES	Model 1	Model 2	
	Un-instrumented	Instrumented	
	coefficients	coefficients	Marginal effects
PVT_OWNER	0.494*** (0.176)	−1.695*** (0.316)	−0.01352
FEMALE	−0.802* (0.443)	−1.544*** (0.476)	−0.01231
INFO_NGO	0.00204 (0.314)	−5.510*** (0.729)	−0.04393
INFO_TVRADIO	−0.270 (0.348)	−2.176*** (0.425)	−0.01735
INFO_GOVT	0.263 (0.359)	0.992** (0.389)	0.007907
F_MORE	0.0563 (0.323)	6.652*** (0.844)	0.053034
EDU1_10	−1.096** (0.469)	−5.880*** (0.757)	−0.04688
HEDU	−1.805*** (0.598)	−9.724*** (1.133)	−0.07753
WINDEX	−0.00315 (0.00595)	−0.0306*** (0.00706)	−0.00024
ARS_AFFECTED	0.0478 (0.142)		—
ARS_AFFECTEDP		−7.315*** (0.866)	−0.05832
OBSERVATIONS	878	878	
NUMBER OF UNION	7	7	
LR CHI SQ (10)	21.21**	104***	

Note: Standard errors are within parenthesis. ***, ** and * indicate significant at 1 percent, 5 percent, and 10 percent level respectively.

logit equation after instrumenting the number of arsenic patients. These logit equations are estimated after controlling for unobserved heterogeneity at the 'Union (local government)' level. There are twenty-five Unions in Laksham and twenty-two in Matlab. While a number of investment decisions, including those related to water and sanitation, are made at the Union level, we do not have this information. Therefore, we use a Union fixed effect model to account for heterogeneity among Unions. As results from alternative specifications are stable,[12] we restrict our discussion below to results from the two-stage model presented in column 2 (coefficients) and column 3 (marginal effects) of Table 7.6.

As Table 7.6 shows private ownership of wells has a negative impact on the probability of drinking from a red well as does the percentage of women in the family.[13] More women in the house may reflect a higher capacity to carry safe drinking water from a distance. As expected, wealth, which reflects access to alternate water sources and purification possibilities, reduces the probability of drinking from red wells.

Two of the three information variables (TV/radio and NGO information) reduce the probability of a household using a red well relative to information obtained from DPHE. Information coming from NGOs seems to be the most effective. The probability of drinking from red wells decreases by 4.4 percent more when the information comes from NGOs relative to DPHE. Information from the media is significantly more effective than DPHE information but not by a huge degree. Information from other government agencies seems to be less effective than information from DPHE, as indicated by the positive marginal effect of the variable INFO_GOVT. Overall, our analyses suggests that information on arsenic in water provided by non-government sources, including the electronic media, is, at least, if not more effective than information provided by government sources. This is useful to know because government provision of information may be more costly relative to other sources.

Education plays an important role in reducing exposure to arsenic. These results are on par with Jalan et al. (2009) and Aziz et al. (2006), who find that education is significant in inducing behavioral change that reduces health risks. Table 7.6 shows that the marginal effects of higher education (7.8 percent) and studies up to 10th grade (4.7 percent) are both negative. As expected, higher education has a bigger impact on reducing the probability of drinking from red wells. Notably, Madajewicz et al. (2007) find that secondary and higher education increase the probability of well-switching while primary education does not. In our analyses, higher education has the biggest effect relative to all other variables that may induce households to switch from red to green wells.

If the household has more male members affected from arsenic compared to females, then this reduces the probability of using a red well. Thus, even though females may be the managers of water in the household, the likelihood of switching to clean water is higher if more male members are sick as a result

[12] We also estimated an alternative model without wealth index as an explanatory variable, and results are comparable in terms of sign and statistical significance.

[13] It is possible for the variable 'private ownership of tube wells' to be highly correlated with the wealth index. If these variables are highly correlated, we cannot use them together as explanatory variables. In our sample, the correlation coefficient between these two variables, however, is very low (less than 0.08). This is not surprising because, while the well may be privately owned, not all households in our sample own the well from which they obtain water.

of exposure. It may be the case that male members of the households have more influence in deciding where to obtain drinking water.

The coefficient on the number of arsenic-affected household members is positive in the basic model but switches sign and is negative in the two-stage model. Thus, once we correct for endogeneity, it is clear that the number of arsenic patients in the household sends a signal and lowers the likelihood of using a red well. Interestingly, the marginal effect of a health shock on the probability of sickness in our analyses (6 percent) is not that different from the results obtained by Jalan et al. (2009), who find that a health shock increases the probability of households boiling water for drinking purposes by 5 percent.

In general, however, our data and analysis suggest that providing information to households about arsenic contamination in wells—even if this information is very specific—is not sufficient. Fifty-five percent of the wells used by the sample households were contaminated with arsenic at higher than safe levels; yet households continue to use these wells. Education and information campaigns do reduce use, but lack of access to alternate safe sources of water results in households exposing themselves to arsenic poisoning continuously.

An interesting issue that emerged in reviewing our data was that the two Upazilas Laksham and Matlab are quite different from each other. T-tests of mean differences were significant for a number of variables such as higher education, households with members sick with arsenic disease, information sources, water purification behavior and so on. This may be because they are in two neighboring districts, but we note that Matlab also hosts a major field center for diarrheal research in Bangladesh and has had significant NGO presence.

Because the underlying characteristics and access to information in Matlab and Laksham are different, we also ran separate regressions on data from these two sub-districts. These results are presented in Table 7.7. The results from Matlab (column 2) reinforce our overall understanding of what affects the probability of drinking from red wells (obtained from Table 7.6). Thus, as Table 7.7 shows, in Matlab, wealth, percentage of females, arsenic patients in the household, and education have a negative effect on drinking from red. The same information variables (TV/radio and NGO campaigns) have a significant impact. However, the results from Laksham are not as clear. While wealth and education certainly reduce the use of arsenic-contaminated water, the only information variable that is significant is government information (from departments such as health services), which is less effective (positive sign) than the information provided by DPHE. This likely reflects the lack of NGO presence in Laksham and perhaps a stronger role by DPHE.

Table 7.7 Fixed-effect logit regression for two Upazilas (DepVar: drink from the red tube wells)

VARIABLES	MatlabUpazila		LakhsamUpazila	
	Un-instrumented	Instrumented	Un-instrumented	Instrumented
PVT_OWNER	0.0547	−0.391	1.105***	1.223***
	(0.241)	(0.281)	(0.279)	(0.308)
FEMALE	−0.704	−2.360***	−0.751	0.515
	(0.593)	(0.800)	(0.691)	(0.753)
INFO_NGO	−0.0789	−3.450***	0.883	0.296
	(0.388)	(1.135)	(0.783)	(0.859)
INFO_TVRADIO	−0.240	−44.29***	−0.0302	0.384
	(0.532)	(14.21)	(0.482)	(0.509)
INFO_GOVT	0.241	0.379	1.052	3.729***
	(0.464)	(0.470)	(0.779)	(0.980)
F_MORE	0.292	3.286***	0.00864	2.649***
	(0.516)	(1.167)	(0.445)	(0.732)
EDU1_10	−0.887	−2.135***	−1.187*	−3.185***
	(0.656)	(0.766)	(0.708)	(0.845)
HEDU	−1.554*	−6.917***	−1.521*	0.621
	(0.828)	(1.894)	(0.899)	(0.999)
WINDEX	−0.00905	−0.0217**	0.00267	−0.0271**
	(0.00825)	(0.00930)	(0.00894)	(0.0109)
ARS_AFFECTED	0.266		-0.0319	
	(0.295)		(0.153)	
ARS_ AFFECTEDP		−2.041***		−5.374***
		(0.659)		(0.980)
OBSERVATIONS	436	436	442	442
NO OF UNION	3	3	4	4
LRCHISQ(10)	9.1	18.7**	24.73***	64.4***

Note: Standard errors are within parenthesis. ***, ** and * indicate significant at 1 percent, 5 percent, and 10 percent level respectively.

7.5 COST OF ILLNESS

The next question we ask is what kind of a burden households bear as a result of exposure to arsenic contamination. Are households willing to pay to make the switch to clean water and to what extent are they already paying in the way of health costs and workdays lost? In order to address this question, we follow a simple health production function model to estimate health costs. Here, we build on earlier work by Dasgupta and Ray (1986, 1987) on the importance of nutrition for employment and poverty reduction. Dasgupta and Ray (1986, 1987) discuss a context where malnourished workers are less productive, earn less, and are, therefore, simply unable to become more productive. Such workers are caught in a poverty trap. Similarly, we assert that sickness due to arsenic can reduce wage income available to households because of losses in productivity and due to medical expenses. This may well contribute to leaving such households trapped in poverty.

Following Freeman (1993), most health cost studies start with a utility maximizing individual, whose utility function is defined as:

$$U = U(X, L, S) \tag{4}$$

where, X represents a composite market good, L denotes leisure, and S represents sick days or the health condition of the individual. The partial derivatives are expected to be $(\partial U/\partial X) \geq 0, (\partial U/\partial l) \geq 0,$ and $(\partial U/\partial S) \leq 0.$

The individual's health is determined by her exposure to pollution (P), the actions she takes to reduce exposure or her avertive actions (A) and medical treatment taken to improve health (M). Thus, the sickness or health production function is given by:

$$S = S(A, M, P) \tag{5}$$

The individual's utility maximization problem therefore is:

$$\text{Max } U(X, L, S(A, M, P)) \tag{6}$$

Subject to

$$I + w(T - L - S) = X + P_a A + P_m M \tag{7}$$

where I is non-wage income, T is the total available time to the individual, p_a is the unit cost of avertive activities, p_m is the price or unit cost of medical treatment and X is treated as the numeraire with normalized price. The individual chooses X, L, A, and M to maximize her utility.

The simultaneous solution to the first-order conditions of this utility maximization problem establishes the demand for X, L, M, and A. For example, the demand functions for avertive activities (A) and medical treatment (M) would be:

$$A = A^*(I, w, p_a, p_m, P) \tag{8}$$

$$M = M^*(I, w, p_a, p_m, P) \tag{9}$$

Further, as Freeman (1993) shows, by maximizing (6), the individual's willingness to pay (*MWTP*) to reduce pollution can be deduced. This can be shown to equal the sum of four terms:

$$MWTP = w\frac{ds}{dp} + p_a\frac{\partial A}{\partial P} + p_m\frac{\partial M}{\partial P} - \frac{U_s}{\lambda}\frac{dS}{dp} \tag{10}$$

Thus, the *MWTP* for health benefits from a reduction in pollution is the sum of the resulting reduction in the time costs of illness plus the costs of any avertive actions taken plus medical and treatment expenses plus the monetary equivalent of the disutility of illness.

Most health cost studies estimate the health production function *S*, along with the avertive actions (*A*) and mitigating activities (*M*) function to obtain the *MWTP*. The dis-utility of illness is difficult to capture and is often ignored. Because the price of avertive actions and unit costs of medical treatment are difficult to establish, *A* and *M*, are usually estimated as expenditure functions. In our study, we estimate the sickness or dose-response function and the demand function for mitigating activities. Mitigation activities refer to actions undertaken to reduce the effects of arsenic-related sickness and include medical expenses, fees paid to doctors or pharmacists, and travel costs. We do not have data to estimate averting costs.

Survey data shows that arsenic-affected patients have very few sick days, when they fully stop working, and limited medical expenditures. Only eighty-two individuals, out of more than 3,260 individuals with some form of sickness, reported workdays lost due to sickness. In our sample of 5,563 individuals, only eighty-eight reported medical expenditures related to arsenic, even though 296 suffered from arsenic-related diseases. Consequently, instead of using continuous data to estimate the dose-response and mitigating functions, we use binary variables. Sickness takes the value of 1 if the individual reported arsenic-related sickness and 0 otherwise. Similarly, mitigating activities take the value 1 if an individual has any medical expenditure and zero otherwise. Using probit models, we estimate the probability of sickness and the probability of incurring mitigating expenditure due to exposure to arsenic.

A vector of independent variables is hypothesized to affect sickness and mitigating expenditures. These variables include: (a) individual level information such as age measured in years, education and the gender of the individual; and (b) a binary variable indicating the presence of arsenic in drinking water (which equals 1 if the tube well is labeled red or 0 if labeled green). Using a probit model, we determine the marginal effect due to a change in the source of drinking water (from red to green). The marginal effect measures the benefit of switching the source of water to a safe mode. The summary statistics of the variables used in the estimation of the dose-response and mitigating activities regressions are

Table 7.8 Summary statistics for sickness and mitigating costs function

Variable	Mean	SD	Min	Max
Sickness (days)	0.053	0.224	0	1
Medical cost (Taka)	280.04	2,469.75	0	80,000
Age (years)	27.5	20.2	0	110
Education (years)	5.2	3.9	0	13
Male (1=male)	0.503	0.5	0	1
Drink red (1= drink red)	0.559	0.497	0	1

Table 7.9 Estimation of the sickness and mitigating cost functions

Variables	Sickness		Medical_cost	
	Coeffcient	Marginal effect	Coefficient	Marginal effect
Age	0.0536***	0.0042***	0.0427***	0.0009***
	(0.0055)	(0.0004)	(0.0086)	(0.00017)
Age_Squared	-0.0005***	-0.00004***	-0.0003***	-0.000007***
	(0.00006)	(0.000005)	(0.00009)	(0.0000)
Education	-0.0342***	-0.00859*	0.0760	0.0016
	(0.0081)	(0.0006)	(0.0128)	(0.0003)
Male	-0.108*	-0.0086*	0.076	0.0016
	(0.0614)	(0.0049)	(0.0985)	(0.0021)
Drink_Red	0.517***	0.0397***	0.465***	0.0097***
	(0.0665)	(0.0049)	(0.111)	(0.0023)
N	5,549	5,549	5,549	5,549

Standard errors in parenthesis. * $p < 0.05$, ** $p < 0.01$, and *** $p < 0.001$.

presented in Table 7.8. The estimated probit equations and the marginal effects are shown in Table 7.9.[14]

Column 2 of Table 7.9 shows that the probability of sickness is associated with changes in age, and education. Since arsenic is a bio-accumulative element, the probability of arsenicosis increases non-linearly with age at a decreasing rate. Years-of-schooling is negatively associated with the probability of sickness. This reinforces our understanding that education is an indicator of health awareness; it may also be picking up some wealth effects. Finally, the impact of switching from red to green sources of water reduces the probability of sickness by 4 percent, by far the largest gain in terms of reducing sickness.

Column 4 of Table 7.9 shows the marginal effects of the mitigating expenditures regression. The probability of incurring health expenditures

[14] We also estimated these two probit equations jointly and did not find any difference in the results.

increases if the water source is red. Age, as in the previous case, has a non-linear effect.

The next step is to estimate the willingness-to-pay of households for switching to cleaner water sources. We estimate the marginal willingness-to-pay in the following manner:

$$MWTP = w \times \overline{WDL} \times P(S \mid \Delta P) + \overline{M} \times P(M \mid \Delta P) \tag{11}$$

$$= (A) + (B)$$

where $P(S|\Delta P)$ is the marginal effect or change in the probability of sickness (related to arsenic poisoning) for an individual due to changes in the level of arsenic poisoning, ΔP is the change from red to green well; w is average wage of the adult working population, $\overline{WDL}$ is the mean workdays lost, $\overline{M}$ is the mean mitigating expenditure per individual when he/she is affected with arsenic-related diseases and $P(M|\Delta P)$ is the change in the probability of incurring mitigating expenses due to changes in the level of exposure at the individual level. (A) measures the marginal impact in terms of income loss due to changes in the level of exposure to arsenic and (B) measures the marginal effect on mitigating expenditure due to changes in the exposure to arsenic poisoning.

Based on equation (11), and the coefficients from Table 7.9, we calculate the mean cost of illness for an individual from continuing to drink from red wells to be Taka 219 (USD 3) per year. Thus, to avoid sickness to all household members, a household would, on average, have to pay Taka 1,386 (USD 20) per household per year. However, if we consider that all household members are currently not sick, the lower limit on this number (taking into account the percentage currently sick or probability of sickness) is Taka 70 (USD 1) per year. These numbers provide a range for annual household willingness-to-pay for switching from red to green sources of water.

It is useful to compare our estimate of the benefits of switching with some other recent studies on willingness-to-pay (WTP) for clean water in Bangladesh. An earlier study by Ahmad et al., (2002) estimates the WTP for safe water to be Taka 2,831 per household per year. They use contingent valuation based on an understanding that households would have access to clean water either through home connections or stand posts. Madagewicz et al. (2007) estimate the lower bound for WTP based on an assessment of additional time taken by women to walk to alternative water sources. The implied WTP from their study is 90 Taka per month or Taka 1,080 per household per year. It is interesting to note that the time costs to households who switch wells in Madagewicz et al. (2007) is so much higher than the productivity and medical costs accrued by the average household in our study. So at the household level, the benefits of switching may be lower than the costs. This may partly explain why at least some households continue to use red wells.

7.6 CONCLUSIONS

Our analysis of water use in Matlab and Laksham Upazilas in Bangladesh suggests that a majority of households continue to drink from arsenic-contaminated red wells. Fifty-five percent of our sample households indicated that they used red wells, despite the fact that many were aware of arsenic contamination of their main source of water. We note that some 70 percent of the wells in the two Upazilas contain water with arsenic levels higher than the Bangladesh government's safe standard of 50 mg/liter.

There are many factors that constrain households from switching to safer water sources. In nearby Araihazar Upazila, Madajewicz et al. (2007) report that an information campaign lead 60 percent of people who learned that their well was unsafe to switch to a safe well within a year. In our study area, the red-well/green-well strategy is a way of providing households with similar information. Yet, a large percentage of households continue to drink from red wells. It is possible that many households switched to green wells when this information was originally provided by DPHE, but limited access to clean water prevented the remaining population from switching. Madajewicz et al. (2007) find that private well owners share their water mainly with relatives. Thus, there may be both social and distance or opportunity costs-related issues that prevent well-switching. These are topics that need to be further probed.

Higher education is the most important factor that reduces the probability of households drinking from red wells (it is far more important than wealth, for example). There is also an important role for information campaigns in reducing exposure to arsenic contaminated water. We find that information from TV/radio and NGO campaigns are more effective in reducing exposure to arsenic relative to information provided by the official agency DPHE. These effects are independent of other variables that may affect the household's decision to drink from red wells. Our overall conclusion is that non-government and private sector media sources of information are at least, if not more, effective than government sources. This is useful to know because the costs of delivering information through electronic media and NGO operations will differ from costs associated with government strategies.

Some 5 percent of our sampled individuals showed symptoms of arsenicosis. Most patients exhibited early stages of the disease. While this number seems small, the burden of arsenic contamination is clearer at the household level since 19 percent of households have at least one person sick from arsenic. Arsenic is a slow-growing disease. Thus, with continual exposure, we expect the number of sick individuals to continue to grow.

Households pay for their use of unsafe water by the sickness they experience. However, monetary payments in terms of wages lost or medical costs borne are low. We estimated a lower bound to the costs sick individuals bear as a result of arsenicosis and find that this is Taka 219 per year. Given that the per capita GDP in Bangladesh in 2005 was USD 444, the health costs of arsenic exposure amount to about 1 percent of annual income (for sick individuals). This percentage, however, is an underestimate since income in rural districts is likely to be lower than the Bangladeshi average and because we are only able to estimate the costs partially. The stress, the difficult choices households face, the general malaise from using bad water, and the costs of any avertive actions taken are not accounted for in our analyses.

Previous research (Khan 2007) suggests that there are technologies available to remove arsenic that cost less than 1000 Taka to buy and would cost about the same per year to maintain. These seem to be too expensive relative to medical and productivity losses currently sustained by households. UNICEF estimates that an investment of USD 200 million is required to provide arsenic-free water to the most exposed 20 million of the population (assuming 20 people share one tube well) (UNICEF Bangladesh 2011). This suggests an investment cost of USD 10 per person or approximately USD 50 per household. Any such investment may be viable because it would bring benefits that go beyond reductions in arsenicosis. Plus, as we previously noted, the costs of continued exposure to arsenic will increase over time. However, like so many governments in developing countries, the Government of Bangladesh is constrained by resources and ability in terms of the public investments it can rapidly make.

Finally, we note that we are unable to say for sure what factors lead to the actual switch from red wells to green wells. We do not have before-and-after information to answer this specific question. We have also yet to ascertain the independent effect of different types of information awareness campaigns. Further, our results hinge on the use of somewhat imperfect instruments. Thus, there are several issues that require further analyses. Arsenic contamination is a serious long-term issue in Bangladesh. This chapter is mainly an effort to raise awareness about the issue and identify areas for future economics research.

Appendix

Table 7.10 First-stage negative binomial regression

Dep Var: ars_affect	Coef.	Std. Err.	z	P>z	[95% Conf.	Interval]
Tube wells	-0.531	0.163	-3.260	0.001	-0.850	-0.211
Chro_Ill	0.378	0.082	4.630	0.000	0.218	0.538
Cur_owner	0.069	0.194	0.350	0.723	-0.311	0.449
Female	-0.849	0.241	-3.530	0.000	-1.321	-0.377
NGO_Arsenic_related	-0.107	0.201	-0.530	0.595	-0.502	0.288
News	-16.445	0.759	-21.660	0.000	-17.934	-14.957
Info_DPHE_survey	-0.428	0.215	-1.990	0.046	-0.848	-0.007
F_more	1.978	0.435	4.550	0.000	2.831	1.125
Edu1_10	-1.754	0.446	-3.930	0.000	-2.628	-0.879
Hedu	-3.574	0.403	-8.880	0.000	-4.363	-2.785
WINDEX	0.002	0.005	0.360	0.717	-0.008	0.011
Cons	2.543	0.372	6.830	0.000	1.813	3.273
Alpha	1.303	0.425			0.688	2.469

References

Aziz, S., K. J. Boyle, and M. Rahman (2006). "Knowledge of Arsenic in Drinking-water: Risks and Avoidance in Matlab, Bangladesh," *Journal of Health, Population and Nutrition*, 24 (3): 327–35.

BGS AND DPHE (British Geological Survey and Department of Public Health and Engineering) (2001). *Arsenic Contamination of Groundwater in Bangladesh*. D. G. Kinniburgh and P.L.Smedley (eds.), British Geological Survey Technical Report WC/00/19, Keyworth: British Geological Survey.

BBS (Bangladesh Bureau of Statistics) (2009). *2008 Statistical Year Book of Bangladesh*,28th edn. Planning Division, Ministry of Planning, Government of the People's Republic of Bangladesh. Available at <http://www.bbs.gov.bd> (accessed 18 October 2013).

Caldwell B. K., W. T. Smith, K. Lokuge et al. (2006). "Access to Drinking Water and Arsenicosis in Bangladesh," *Journal of Health, Population and Nutrition*, 24(3): 336–45.

Chen Y. and H. Ahsan (2004). "Excess Risk of Internal Cancers due to Arsenic Exposure from Drinking Water in Bangladesh," *American Journal of Public Health*, 94(5):741–4.

Dasgupta, P. and D. Ray (1986). "Inequality as a Determinant of Malnutrition and Unemployment: Theory," *Economic Journal*, 96(4): 1011–34.

—— (1987). "Inequality as a Determinant of Malnutrition and Unemployment: Policy," *Economic Journal*, 97(1): 177–88.

Farouque, H. S. M. and S. Alam (2002). "State of Arsenic Contamination in Bangladesh," Dialogue on Food Water and Environment: International Water Conference, Hanoi, Vietnam.

Freeman, A. M. III, (1993). *The Measurement of Environmental and Resource Values: Theory and Methods*. Washington, DC: Resources for the Future.

Jalan, J., E. Somanathan, and S. Chaudhuri (2009). "Awareness and Demand for Environmental Quality: Survey Evidence on Drinking Water in Urban India," *Environment and Development Economics*, 14: 665–92.

Kathuria, V. (2007). "Informal Regulation of Pollution in a Developing Country: Evidence from India," *Ecological Economics*, 63(2–3): 403–17.

Khan, M. M. H., K. Aklimunnessa, M. Kabir et al. (2007). "Determinants of Drinking Arsenic-contaminated Tube Well Water in Bangladesh," *Health Policy and Planning*, 22(5): 335–43.

Khan, Z. H. (2007). "*Managing the Arsenic Disaster in Water Supply: Risk Measurement, Costs of Illness and Policy Choices in Bangladesh*," SANDEE Working Paper No. 27. Kathmandu, Nepal: SANDEE.

—— and A. K. E. Haque (2011). "Red Wells, Green Wells and the Costs of Arsenic Contamination in Bangladesh, in M. N. Murty, A. K. E. Haque, and P. Shyamsundar (eds.), *Environmental Valuation in South Asia*. New Delhi: Cambridge University Press, 477.

Khanna, M., W. Quimio, and D. Bojilova (1998). "Toxic Release Information: A Policy Tool for Environmental Protection," *Journal of Environmental Economics and Management*, 36 (3): 243–66.

Lemos, M. C. (2008). "What Influences Innovation Adoption by Water Managers? Climate Information Use in Brazil and the United States," *Journal of the American Water Resources Association*, 44(6):1388–96.

Madajewicz, M., A. Pfaff, A. van Green et al. (2007). "Can Information alone Change Behavior? Response to Arsenic Contamination of Ground Water in Bangladesh," *Journal of Development Economics*, 84: 731–54

Nickson, R., J. McArthur, W. Burgess et al. (1998). "Arsenic Poisoning of Bangladesh Groundwater," *Nature*, 395: 338.

Smith, A. H., E. O. Lingas, and M. Rahman (2000). "Contamination of Drinking Water by Arsenic in Bangladesh: A Public Health Emergency," *Bulletin of WHO*, 78:1093–103.

Smith, A., M. L. Biggs, and L. Moore (1999). "Cancer Risks from Arsenic in Drinking Water: Implications for Drinking Water Standards," in W. R. Chappell, C. O. Abernathy, and R. L. Calderon (eds.), *Arsenic Exposure and Health Effects, Proceedings of the Third International Conference on Arsenic Exposure and Health Effects, 1998, San Diego, California.*

Tietenberg, T. and D. Wheeler (2000). "Empowering the Community. Information Strategies for Pollution Control," in H. Folmer, H. L. Gabel, S. Gerking et al. (eds.), *Frontiers of Environmental Economics*. Cheltenham: Edward Elgar Publishing, 85–120.

UNICEF, Bangladesh. (2011). "Arsenic Mitigation in Bangladesh." Available at <http://www.unicef.org/bangladesh/Arsenic_Mitigation_in_Bangladesh.pdf> (accessed 18 October 2013).

van Geen, A., H. Ahsan, A. H. Horneman et al. (2002). "Promotion of Well-switching to Mitigate the Current Arsenic Crisis in Bangladesh," *Bulletin of the World Health Organization*, 80(9):732–7.

Wang, H., J. Bi, D. Wheeler et al. (2004). "Environmental Performance Rating and Disclosure: China's Green Watch Program," *Journal of Environmental Management*, 71(2): 123–33.

8

Comments by David Starrett on "Red Wells or Green Wells and Does It Matter?"

I am not in the best position to comment on this chapter. I know next to nothing about arsenic-related diseases and the last regression I ran was about forty-five years ago at the National Bureau of Standards using punch cards. However, the lure of being present to celebrate the stellar career of my friend and colleague Partha Dasgupta was too great to resist, so here goes.

I like this study. There is a lot of evidence in the health literature that prevention is more cost-effective than treatment. This chapter studies the prevention issue by examining which factors are most effective at getting households to switch from more to less arsenic-contaminated water sources. The study finds that accurate information is a significant contributor and further that the method in which it is conveyed matters. It is perhaps not surprising to find that direct contact is more effective than government campaigns, but it is nice to see it quantified here. It is also interesting to see the importance (or lack thereof) of the wide variety of demographic factors the authors consider.

The study goes on to estimate the willingness to pay for clean water sources. The authors assume that households maximize utility and calculate the marginal improvement that could be achieved through an increment in better water quality. I found the functional form used to be rather restrictive. In particular, the way in which the sickness measure enters the utility function has to be exactly the same as the amount of labor time lost to sickness. This is especially unfortunate since the evidence they gather shows that very little labor time is actually lost to sickness.

Fortunately, however, the reduced form exhibited in equation (10), which is subsequently used in the cost estimates, turns out to be quite robust and would result from a wide variety of structural formulations.

To illustrate this, I suggest a quite different model with this property:

$$\text{Max } U(I + w(T - L) - p_a A - p_m M, P)$$

$$\text{Subject to } S(L, A, M, P) \leq S^*.$$

Here pollution (P) enters the utility function directly (not just through sickness), leisure is not valued directly and sickness enters as a constraint with S^* representing the maximal level of sickness that can be tolerated. I do not offer this as necessarily a better version of the problem faced but rather to indicate that structural formulations with significant differences lead to the same reduced form (10). Indeed it is not necessary that all households look at the problem in the same way as long as each represented formulation is consistent with (10).

It is important to note that the numbers presented in Table 7.9 are an underestimate of the full cost since they leave out terms in equation (10), in particular the cost of avertive activities and the disutility of being sick. In addition, from society's point of view they would leave out any externalities associated with arsenic diseases.

One surprising finding of this study is that households are not using available technologies for improving water quality even though these sometimes cost less that the lower bounds calculated using Table 7.9. This is a bit disturbing since it suggests that the utility maximizing framework of the paper might be misspecified. After all, if the treatment options were included in the choice set, why wouldn't household adopt them?

I see two possible answers here. First, there is at least one way in which the model of this chapter is oversimplified (therefore misspecified): The model is static whereas the reality is dynamic—costs are upfront whereas benefits from reduced sickness are down the road. Consequently, if households discount the future sufficiently, this could explain their reluctance to adopt. However, the time frame may not be sufficient to justify this explanation.

There is a second possible explanation. Households may not be willing to try something new even if it can be demonstrated to be superior on paper. This might be particularly true when the costs are concrete and upfront whereas benefits are hypothetical. One possible way to counter this inertia is to set up demonstration projects. A recent successful project of this type was conducted in rural Uganda. There, Eco-San toilets were installed and the urine collected used to fertilize crops. Users could see for themselves that the toilets were safe and clean; further they could observe firsthand the effectiveness of urine as fertilizer. Perhaps something similar could be done with arsenic reduction treatments in Bangladesh although documenting the benefits in a convincing way may be more difficult.

9

Forest Degradation in the Himalayas: Determinants and Policy Options

Jean-Marie Baland, Sanghamitra Das, and Dilip Mookherjee

9.1 INTRODUCTION

Deforestation and forest degradation in the Himalayas are a major concern for social scientists and policymakers because of the large common property externalities involved at both the global and the local levels. At the global level, the Himalayan range is one of the most unstable and fragile mountain areas in the world (Ives and Messerly 1989). Deforestation speeds up global warming and tends to accentuate the disastrous consequences of earthquakes, and is a significant contributing factor to landslides and flooding. This has a serious impact on the equilibrium of the Ganges and Brahmaputra river basins, and heightens the frequency of flooding in Bangladesh (Metz 1991).

At a more local level, the alpine zone of the Himalayas is home to populations who rely mainly on agriculture and livestock-rearing for their livelihood. Their livelihoods rely strongly on the forests adjoining their villages. Firewood, timber, fodder and leaf-litter for livestock are collected from these forests. The forests are also used for grazing livestock. Environmental degradation reduces the amount of available resource and increases the time required for their collection. A number of studies have argued that these losses adversely affect the poor in a number of ways, for example, health, nutrition, and child education (Amacher et al. 2004; Cooke 1998; Dasgupta 1995; Dasgupta and Mäler 1995; Kumar and Hotchkiss 1988).

Other concerns include the likely impact of economic growth in poor countries on environmental resources (Arrow et al. 1995; Dasgupta and Mäler 1995, 2009; Dasgupta et al. 2000). As developing countries catch up with the rest of the world, what will be the impact on the world's forests?

Our project which was initiated in the late 1990s had a number of objectives. The first was to empirically assess the extent and the nature of deforestation or forest degradation in the Himalayas, using ground-level forest ecology surveys. The second objective was to use this data along with detailed household surveys in areas adjoining the forests to empirically investigate the role of different underlying causes commonly alleged by academic researchers, policymakers and environmental groups. These include local poverty, inequality and its deleterious effects on local collective action, economic growth and commercialization pressures, demographic changes comprising rapid population growth, household fragmentation and migratory patterns, property rights over forests and ineffective management of state-owned forests. We also sought to measure effects on standards of living of rural communities living near the forests, identify suitable policy options and estimate their effectiveness.

The primary hypotheses concerning factors driving environmental degradation in developing countries can be roughly classified as follows. At one extreme is the Poverty-Environment Hypothesis, originally proposed by the 1987 United Nations Brundtland Commission, asserting that poverty is the root cause of environmental problems, as degradation arises owing to exploitation of common property resources particularly by the poor (Barbier 1997; Duraiappah 1998; Jalal 1993; Lele 1991; Lopez 1998; Mäler 1998). According to this view, solutions to environmental problems require first and foremost reduction in local poverty, either via economic growth or other state-initiated anti-poverty programs. At the other extreme is the view that environmental degradation owes to economic growth, which raises the demand for environmental resources in tandem with private goods (e.g., views expressed in the media, 2006 Summit Report of the World Economic Forum, or World Bank reports on deforestation in India).[1] An intermediate hypothesis referred to as the "Environmental Kuznets Curve", is that economic growth may initially aggravate environmental problems in poor countries at early stages of development, but will eventually ease them once the level of per capita income passes a threshold (Barbier 1997b; Grossman and Krueger 1995; Yandle, Vijayaraghavan, and Bhattarai 2002).

Other viewpoints stress the importance of local institutions such as monitoring systems and community property rights (Baland and Platteau 1996; Bardhan 2005; Bardhan and Dayton-Johnson 1997; Dasgupta and Mäler 2009; Jodha 2001; Somanathan 1991; Varughese 2000). Some argue that deforestation in the past owed primarily to poor control and monitoring systems: once local communities are assigned control they will be successful in regulating environmental pressures, implying there is not much role for external state interventions. And some argue that local collective action is undermined by social and economic inequality within neighboring communities.

[1] See *Economist* magazine, "No Economic Fire Without Smoke," 8 July 2004, Books and Arts section; <http://www.economist.com/node/2896990> and World Bank (2000).

These hypotheses present different perspectives on the environmental consequences of development, and the role of policy. Yet there is remarkably little systematic micro-empirical evidence on their validity. Efforts to test these hypotheses have been cast mainly on the basis of macro cross-country regressions. There are only a handful of recent efforts to use micro-econometric evidence concerning behavior of households and local institutions governing use of environmental resources (Chaudhuri and Pfaff 2003; Foster and Rosenzweig 2003; Somanathan, Prabhakar, and Mehta 2009).

Accordingly we started by using household-level surveys (with World Bank Living Standards Surveys) in Nepal to address these questions. These household level surveys were not designed to address detailed questions concerning deforestation. We therefore subsequently conducted surveys of forests, village communities, and households in two northern Indian states in the same mid-Himalayan region between 2000 and 2003. Anthropological surveys in six villages in the sample were also commissioned, in order to test and/or corroborate our empirical findings. Resource and time limitations necessitated our relying on a single cross-section round of surveys, with limited use of recall data to estimate historical patterns of deforestation. This imposes inevitable restrictions on the econometric analysis and the nature of reliable inferences that can be drawn. However we have recently had the opportunity to access a panel dataset for Nepal from the LSMS surveys in collaboration with Francois Libois, from which preliminary results indicate that the main results of the cross-section analyses continue to hold (Baland, Libois, and Mookherjee 2011).

This chapter provides an overview of the main findings so far. We first describe in Section 9.2 what we learnt regarding pressure on the Indian Himalayan forests on the basis of our forest ecology surveys. As we shall see, the key problem appears to be forest degradation owing to firewood and fodder collected by neighboring households, rather than deforestation. Local collective action constraining forest use is conspicuous by its absence, implying that self-interested behavior of households drives firewood and fodder collection. Section 9.3 thereafter describes our findings concerning determinants of household firewood collection activities. Section 9.4 focuses on community property rights, where we assess the performance of the differing regimes of property management in Uttaranchal. Section 9.5 concludes.

9.2 DEGRADATION OF THE HIMALAYAN FORESTS

9.2.1 The India survey

Our analysis is based on household, community, and forest ecology surveys of a random sample of 165 villages divided equally between Himachal Pradesh and Uttaranchal, carried out by our field investigators between 2000 and 2003. On the basis of census data, villages were stratified on the basis of altitude, population, and distance to the nearest town. Villages were then selected randomly within each stratum. A random sample of twenty households was selected in each village, on the basis of a stratification procedure combining landholding and caste-distribution in the village.

Three sets of questionnaires were used to conduct surveys in each village: (a) a household questionnaire administered to the twenty sample households dealt with the socioeconomic structure of the household and its dependence on forests; (b) a village questionnaire was designed to secure information on a host of village-level characteristics such as demographic size, access to physical and social infrastructure, the market environment, and institutions of local governance; (c) an ecology questionnaire intended to gather quantitative and qualitative evidence on the condition of the forest stock accessed by the villagers.

The forest surveys were carried out by trained ecologists who first identified local forest zones accessed by each village in the sample, which were mapped by interacting with the villagers. Random transects (100 meters in length) were laid in each forest area and measurements were recorded at three equidistant plots (of 5.63 meters radius) on the transect to record the species composition, canopy cover, basal area, heights and girths of trees above 3 meters in height as well as regeneration characteristics. Qualitative assessment of grazing, lopping, leaf-litter accumulation, timber extraction, and evidence on natural calamities such as fire and snowfall damage to trees was also recorded at each plot in terms of a predetermined qualitative scale. We collected detailed information on 619 forests by taking measures in 3,512 forest plots (as the number of transects varied with the size of the forest). The second part of the ecology surveys interviewed three to four members of each village (chosen randomly within each village) with regard to their perceptions of changes in forest stock over the past quarter-century and the nature of institutions governing access and use of the forest.

In the context of Nepal we utilized only the World Bank Living Standard Measurement Surveys carried out in 1995–1996 and 2002–2003. While these surveys contain very little information on forests and village ecology, they have detailed information at the household level, particularly relative to household consumption, income, and firewood collection. We will also, when possible, compare the results for Nepal and India.

9.2.2 Measuring Himalayan Forest Degradation

The few quantitative studies available are based on satellite imagery and indicate substantial degradation of the Himalayan forest over the last decades.

Prabhakar et al. (2006) estimate that 61 percent[2] of forests in two districts of Uttarankhand are severely deteriorated (defined by crown cover of under 40 percent). This observation suggests that the present trend differs substantially from past developments, which were characterized more by deforestation, that is, a decline of forest area. Myers (1986) calculates for example that, in Nepal between 1947 and 1980, forest cover of national territory dropped from 57 percent to 23 percent. By contrast, Foster and Rosenzweig (2003) find that, for India as a whole, the proportion of land covered by forests (measured on the basis of satellite images) has increased significantly over the past three decades.

In our own survey, we used physical measurements taken directly in the forests, rather than rely on aerial satellite images. Our view is that important dimensions of forest quality can best be assessed by ground-level ecology studies. Various measures have been devised by forest ecologists for assessing the state of a forest. The conventional forest management indicators measure the available tree stock. These include *canopy cover* (the amount of ground area covered by the canopy through which direct light passes),[3] which measures the density of foliage, and *basal area* (the total area covered by the cross-sectional area of tree trunks per hectare), which measures the density of standing trees per hectare. The latter measure depends on tree-felling for timber by villagers. Another set of measures captures, for a given stock of trees, the quality and the state of the standing trees. These measures, which include *lopping* (the proportion of a tree trunk that has been lopped) reflect another type of pressure on the forests coming from firewood and fodder collections. At a stationary equilibrium, these various measures should be correlated, with residual variations being explained by factors such as the type of soil, natural hazards, exposure to light, or tree species. The problem however stems from the fact that, when fodder and firewood collections increase while timber-felling remains constant, the basal area does not correctly reflect forest degradation, at least in the short run. The other measures are much more sensitive to these changes.[4]

Table 9.1 below shows the median values and the correlations obtained between these variables. We have also included the firewood collection time, which measures one of the direct impacts of forest degradation on households. Here, collection time corresponds to total collection time, which includes the time it takes to walk to the forest.

This table invites three comments. First, the correlation between the different measures is weak, which justifies paying attention to all three to evaluate

[2] The 90 percent confidence interval is equal to 48–73 percent.

[3] This is, in fact, a similar measure to the *crown cover* indicator used by Prabhakar et al. (2006), but as seen from ground level, rather than an aerial view.

[4] In Baland et al. (2010b), we also measured the volume of wood per hectare (basal volume), which is another conventional measure of biomass and regeneration capacity (number

Table 9.1 Correlation coefficients between measures of forest quality in India[5]

	Canopy cover (%)	Basal area (m^2/ha)	Lopping (%)	Collection time (hr)
Canopy cover (%)	1.00			
Basal area (m^2/ha)	0.32	1.00		
Lopping (%)	−0.59	−0.21	1.00	
Collection time (hr)	0.06	0.13	−0.02	1.00
Median (standard errors)	**37.5**	**41.3**	**67.1**	4
	(11.1)	(24.6)	(13.2)	(1.2)

Source: Baland et al. (2010b).

the state of a forest. Secondly, there is little correlation between collection time and the other measures. The low correlation is partly explained by the fact that collection times are not a good measure of forest degradation within a village. Indeed, as villagers choose their collecting places on the basis of the time they expect to take, collection times across forests within a village should be equalized, and would therefore be independent of the degree of degradation of a particular forest. Comparisons of collection time across forests adjoining a given village over time would be more informative of differences in degradation.

Finally, the median value of canopy cover is very low while that of lopping is alarmingly high. By comparison, the natural thresholds indicating a completely non-degraded forest have been estimated around 80 percent for canopy cover, 40 m^2/ha for the basal area and 15 percent of tree height for lopping (Thadani 1999). We illustrate the distribution observed for each of these measures in Figures 9.1 to 9.3 below. We also use a vertical broken straight line to show the level corresponding to a *severely degraded* state of the forest, corresponding to thresholds of 40 percent for canopy cover, two-thirds of tree height lopped, and 35 square metres per hectare for basal area (Thadani 1999).

More than half of the forests evidence a severely degraded canopy cover (less than 40 percent) and the extent of lopping exceeds two-thirds of tree height. On the other hand, as shown in Figure 9.3, the tree biomass, measured by the basal area, shows significantly less deterioration. This means that most of the degradation is linked to excessive short-run exploitation, which is not yet visible in terms of a reduction in the volume of standing wood in the forest. In other words, even though the quantity of trees is satisfactory, they are in a particularly poor state: most of their branches have been lopped or torn off and their canopy

of saplings above a height of 0.5 metre per hectare), which declines in the case of illegal felling or frequent grazing. Further measures of biological diversity or quality of tree species could be included. However the main issue here is more the quantity of available wood, which explains our choice of the aforementioned measures.

[5] This table is based on the sub-sample of the forests in Uttarakhand. A similar picture emerges when using the Himachal forests.

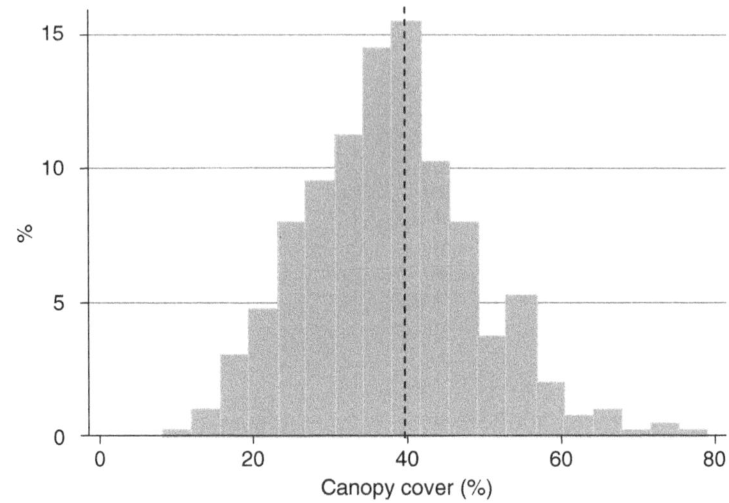

Figure 9.1 Percentage distribution of forests based on their canopy cover (Indian Himalayas, 2002–3)

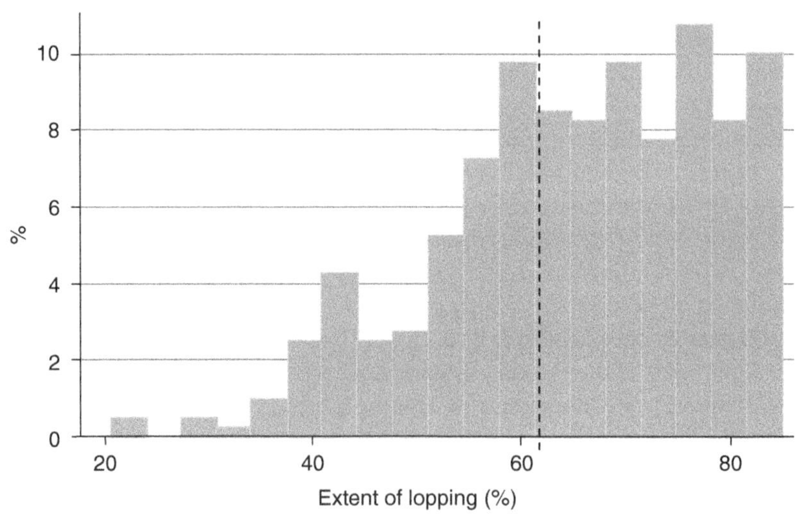

Figure 9.2 Percentage distribution of forests based on the extent of lopping (Indian Himalayas, 2002–3)

density is much too low. The unhealthy quality of trees threatens their growth potential and their resistance to natural calamities (such as frost or drought). It drastically reduces the forest's capacities for future biomass production.

The household surveys conducted confirm these trends. Over the last twenty-five years, the average firewood collection time increased by 60 percent

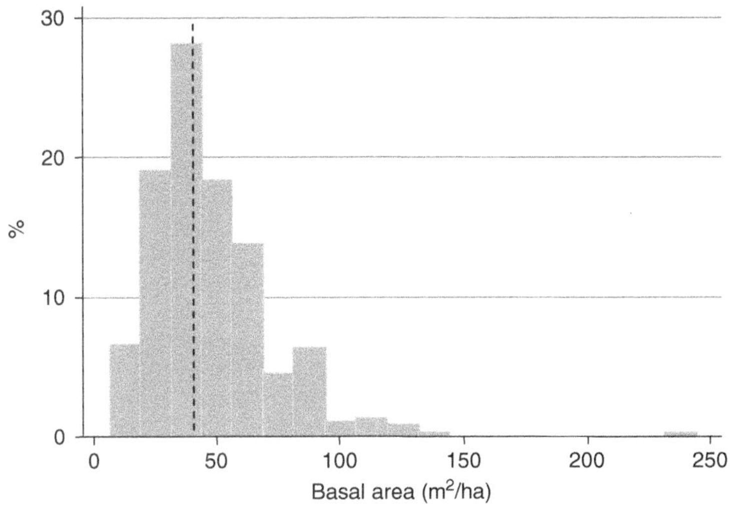

Figure 9.3 Percentage distribution of forests based on basal area (m^2/ha) (Indian Himalayas, 2002–3)

(from 2.36 to 3.84 hours per firewood bundle), whereas distance to the forest increased by only 10 percent (from 2.06 to 2.31 kilometres). These differing trends suggest that the cause of increased collection time is not so much the conversion of forest areas into agricultural land or pastureland, as the degradation of forest quality.[6] More than 80 percent of the village respondents said they felt that forest quality was in decline. Forest degradation rather than deforestation thus seems to characterize current changes in the Himalayan forest.

9.2.3 Proximate Causes of Himalayan Forest Degradation

We thus set about examining the causes of this degradation. These can be natural, such as fire- or snowfall-related damage, or anthropogenic. Among the man-related causes, a distinction should be made between those linked to the use of firewood, fodder collection, and grazing, and those relating to tree-felling for commercial purposes or to timber removal. Table 9.2 illustrates the relative importance of these causes in each of the forest plots

[6] The household surveys show that the level of clearance for agricultural purposes is relatively negligible. Moreover, clearance mostly involves non-forested commons (60 percent). Clearance of forested areas only concerns 5 percent of cases.

Table 9.2 Extent of degradation of forest lots according to each possible cause (India 2002–3)

Type of degradation (within a plot)	Percent of plots in each category (n = 3512)	
	Low impact %	High impact %
Grazing: low if the only sign of interference is a livestock trail	30	70
Lopping: low if lopping is less than 30%	20	80
Wood-cutting: low if less than 3 tree stumps from wood-cutting	57	43
Forest fires: low if less than 3 tree stumps from burning	62	38
Snowfall: low if less than 3 tree stumps ripped by snow	81	19

visited.[7] Although all the measures are not strictly comparable, anthropogenic pressures, particularly in the context of firewood collection, play a crucial role in the observed degradation.

It is somewhat difficult to obtain reliable data on timber removal, chiefly because this activity is strictly controlled and commercial exploitation is mostly forbidden. This said, our household surveys show the equivalent of one tree of timber is used by a household every five years for construction purposes. Assuming an average three-ton weight per tree, and an average of eighty households per village, this represents forty-eight tons of timber per year per village. This compares with a little over 450 tons of firewood collected per year per village. In terms of biomass, timber removal for household usage accounts for scarcely 10 percent of the total mass of wood removed from the forest. Lopping for fodder and particularly for firewood is thus the foremost cause of forest degradation.

9.2.4 Forest Ownership and Use Rights

All forests are classified as state forests; with exceptions noted below they are governed by the forest department. The department has a hierarchical administrative structure. The lowest rung is occupied by a forest guard who is responsible for monitoring use on a day-to-day basis. A legacy of the colonial past, the department manages and monitors vast expanses of forests under its control. The main motive behind the forest department's operations is conservation, though some commercialization objectives also exist. For instance,

[7] The size of each plot is equal to $100m^2$.

while there is a ban on green felling, the forest department can sell timber acquired through salvaging operations where the forest stock has been damaged due to natural calamities or alternatively timber acquired through silviculture operations. In some pine forests, the department can extract and sell resin, an important ingredient in the manufacture of turpentine.

Locals have "rights" to access state forests for their livelihood needs. However, they have to abide by rules of extraction and use prescribed by the forest department. Violation of such rules is a legal offence. The forest guard is the main interface between the locals and higher authorities in the department, whose main role is to watch over the forest for detecting violations and imposing penalties on the accused. For historical reasons in the past, state forests have been classified into "un-demarcated" and "demarcated" patches. Un-demarcated forests known as "unclassed forests" in Himachal and "civil soyam" forests in Uttaranchal, are recorded as forests by the forest department but these are not marked by boundary pillars. The department cannot impose prohibitions on these patches as regards rights of access and use. In contrast, a demarcated forest is marked by boundary pillars, an area notified under the Indian Forest Act of 1927. Locals can access such forests unless restrictions are imposed by the forest department. When a forest is declared as a "sanctuary area" all rights are completely denied. Demarcated forests are further categorized into "demarcated protected forests" and "reserved forests." As the name suggests, reserve forests are subject to the most stringent restrictions on use.

However, the forest department faces many obstacles in enforcing these restrictions. Households revealed in the course of their survey responses the ineffectiveness of the forest guard in monitoring violations or imposing penalties. Our ecology surveys indicated no significant differences in degradation between demarcated and un-demarcated forest patches, with regard to canopy cover, lopping, and basal area.

In Uttaranchal the management of some forests have been turned over to local Van Panchayats, or self-governing forest user groups. We discuss these further below.

9.2.5 Local Collective Action Constraining Forest Use

A random sample of four local inhabitants in each village was asked to provide oral histories of local forests on the basis of a structured questionnaire. A large majority of them (88 percent) agreed that there was a general sense in their villages that the forest stock was shrinking. Yet only 45 percent reported that there was any alarm or concern regarding this in their communities. Only in a handful of cases did they report that concrete steps had been taken to arrest the process.[8] This was corroborated in the more detailed anthropological studies of select villages.

Consistent with the lack of spontaneous collective action to control firewood collections within these villages, cross-village analyses of the relationship between land inequality and firewood collections using the Nepal LSMS data for 1995–1996 failed to find any significant correlations, controlling for average holdings of land and other relevant village characteristics (Baland et al. 2007b). As mentioned earlier, a large theoretical literature has speculated that local inequality may be an important determinant of effective collective action; this consideration ceases to be relevant when collective action is absent.

This raises the question of the reasons for failure of local communities to engage in some form of collective action. Could the failure to act collectively to arrest the deforestation process more widely reflect lack of knowledge of appropriate forest management practices? This appears unlikely as villagers seemed well aware of methods of ensuring sustainable forests prescribed by the forest department (collection of dry wood, rotational methods of lopping), but restricted their practice to their own private tree holdings and sacred groves in the village. The collective failure to arrest forest degradation could neither be explained by a lack of capacity for local collective action per se. We found numerous instances of collective action in other areas relevant to current livelihoods, such as agriculture, water management and credit, besides women's groups, youth groups, and temple committees.

Spontaneous collective action with respect to forests therefore seems basically absent. In many villages, however, some of the village forest is managed by a formal forest committee (Van Panchayats, eco-vikas, forest management committees). These have been created and/or recognized by the government. They are more widespread in Uttaranchal where forty-five out of eighty-three villages had a Van Panchayat. However, the actual area under the control of these formal village committees remains limited: according to Sarkar (2008), Van Panchayat forests represent 11 percent of the total forest area in Uttaranchal. The experience of these committees is described as mixed, with some committees functioning effectively and succeeding in protecting the part of the forest under their command. We provide a more systematic analysis of their effectiveness in controlling firewood collections in Section 9.3 below.

[8] In a few villages in Uttaranchal some un-demarcated state forests were reported to have been closed for regeneration. Village inhabitants of Rogi village in Kinnaur district and Gojra in Kullu district of Himachal, closed some local forest patches due to severe threat of landslides that has damaged their fields in the past.

9.3 ANALYZING HOUSEHOLD DEMAND FOR FIREWOOD

9.3.1 Modeling Household Choices

At the beginning of this project we thought that understanding patterns of collective action would be important, and how it interacts with the state of the common property resource as well as with a number of village characteristics, such as leadership and inequality. But with the community surveys and anthropological evidence indicating virtual absence of spontaneous collective action, as well as extremely weak control over firewood use in state forests, it became evident that we needed to model household collections as resulting from self-interested household choices, unconstrained by social norms or penalties for collections. The only relevant costs of collecting firewood and fodder were the opportunity costs of the time spent in these activities. Hence our analytical efforts shifted from modeling collective action in villages to private household production-cum-consumption models where production, energy, and household consumption activities are jointly determined.

The household surveys showed that firewood continues to be the main source of household energy in the Himalayas. In the zone under study, firewood is used for cooking energy in summer by 90 percent of households, and gas by 9 percent. For cooking and heating in winter, firewood is used by 99 percent of households (Baland et al. 2007a). In Nepal, according to 1995–1996 LSMS, villages use firewood as the prime source of energy, when it is available: 82 percent of households in 1995–1996 and 75 percent in 2002–2003. The second source of energy used was gas (in 2002–2003) (Baland et al. 2010a).

In most villages there are no markets for firewood at the village level, though some marginal amounts are commercialized at the nearby market centers. This implies that, for a typical villager, the collection and the production of firewood cannot be separated. Going back to our initial question as to what extent income growth is related to forest degradation in this region, there are two effects at play. The first is the wealth effect, wherein increasing wealth increases consumption of goods and energy, assuming their relative costs are unchanged. The wealth effect can however be negative for firewood if it is an inferior good, for example, if it is associated with less social prestige or if the household seeks to reduce its exposure to pollution by switching to alternate cleaner but more expensive fuels. Hence the direction of the wealth effect in the case of firewood is not clear a priori. The second is the cost effect: insofar as firewood is mainly collected by households, wealthier households have a higher opportunity cost of time spent collecting it, which makes the firewood more expensive. Our surveys indicated negligible use of purchased firewood, hired labor, or technology to substitute for family labor in collection of firewood. Hence the cost channel implies that increasing wealth and income will reduce the demand for firewood. The net effect is therefore ambiguous, if firewood is a normal good, with the wealth and cost effects operating in opposite directions. If it is an inferior good, then both effects would cause firewood consumption to decline in wealth. Hence empirical work is needed to discover the effect of rising wealth on firewood collection, and disentangle the wealth and cost effects.

This task is complicated by the fact that conventional tools of demand analysis that assume exogeneity of income, consumption, and prices are inapplicable. Hence the economic cost of firewood cannot be separated from other household characteristics, incomes, or consumption. In most of the existing literature, there are no attempts to estimate wealth and cost effects associated with increases in income (or the underlying productive assets). Given the lack of longitudinal data (except in our most recent work on this topic), we examine cross-sectional variations in household firewood collections with ownership of different assets. In so doing we confronted a number of formidable methodological problems associated with endogeneity of income, measurement error, omitted variables, and endogenous censoring, which we now discuss.

The most important problem is endogeneity of income or consumption, the most commonly used measures of household living standards. There are many possible unobserved household traits that affect both consumption and firewood collection that could bias estimated Engel elasticities. In addition, both income and consumption are prone to significant measurement errors, especially in a rural society dominated by farming and livestock-related occupations. Reliable instruments for income and consumption that do not affect firewood collections are rarely available. We proceed on the premise that endogeneity and measurement error problems are less acute for underlying household assets (land, livestock, household size, education, etc.) than income or consumption. Based on a model of household decision-making concerning labor supply, fuel choice and consumption for a given composition of assets owned, we develop two estimation strategies. The first (called the semi-structural form (SS) approach) aggregates stocks of different assets into a single scalar measure of wealth (called "potential income"). For this purpose we estimate a household production function, following the approach of Jacoby (1993) to overcome problems with endogeneity of labor supply. Apart from allowing us to estimate household potential income as the measure of wealth, this yields an estimate of household shadow wages, which can be used to value the opportunity cost of time spent collecting firewood. At the second step these are used as measures of household wealth to estimate the wealth effects, while cost effects are estimated using interactions of these estimated shadow wages with reported firewood collection times. Firewood consumption is regressed both on potential income and the interactions of shadow wage with collection time, so that controlling for the other the regression coefficient of these variables can be interpreted as the wealth and cost effects respectively.[9]

The second estimation strategy (which we refer to as the reduced form (RF) approach) relates firewood collection directly to the entire vector of household assets, and their interaction with collection times. While the results of this approach are more complex and harder to interpret than the SS results, they are more reliable owing to avoidance of errors in estimating potential income and shadow wages. Moreover, it avoids the assumption implicit in the aggregation procedure underlying the SS approach that the wealth effects of each asset are proportional to their respective effects on household income. Wealth effects could differ from income effects in a heterogenous fashion if different assets are associated with distinct occupations, locations of work, or networks of coworkers, which affect awareness of household members concerning health effects of firewood vis-à-vis alternate fuels, or accessibility to the latter.

Other econometric problems pertain to omitted variables and endogenous censoring. Geography or climate variations may jointly affect firewood availability, asset ownership and living standards. We control for such village-specific characteristics with village fixed effects, effectively focusing on intra-village variations of firewood collections with household wealth. This also controls for factors such as inequality or social norms that have been argued to be important determinants of common property resources use. In addition we control for various other household characteristics available in the LSMS data, such as household demographics. In the context of Nepal we see a sizeable fraction of households not using firewood at all, so the estimation procedure has to incorporate endogenous censoring. Similar problems arise in the Indian context in studying the role of variations in the cost of LPG gas, since only a small fraction of households use LPG gas.

Problems that we cannot address owing to the nature of the data include the following. The amount of firewood collected is measured in terms of the number of "*bharis*" or headloads that the household report collecting. As the size of a headload varies across individuals, this introduces a potential bias. It is possible that richer households are better fed and tend to carry larger *bharis*, resulting in an underestimate of the impact of living standards on actual firewood collection. Additionally, households confronted with longer walking times carry lighter or smaller headloads. The impact of collection time on the amount of firewood taken may thus be underestimated. Collection time is also based on individual reporting by the household, and may vary with various

[9] To elaborate further, the estimated coefficient with respect to wealth can be interpreted as the effect of increasing wealth of the household in a context where collection times are negligible, as the cost effect would then not come into play. Conversely, the regression coefficient of the interaction of the shadow wage and collection time indicates the effect of rising collection time and how it differentially affects households with varying shadow wages, controlling for their respective wealth levels.

characteristics. To partially address this problem, we compute the average of individual collection times at the village level, and use the latter as a more "objective" measure of collection time. The other advantage of this is that this measure can also be used for villagers that do not collect firewood. This procedure is valid as long as villages are not too dispersed so that all villagers face the same distance to the forests.

Yet other shortcomings of our approach arise from our assumption that all household members are identical with regard to their skills and are thus perfect substitutes in production. In particular, it implies that all members face the same shadow wage in collecting firewood, and share collection tasks equally. This ignores the possibility of specialization of tasks within the household, with resulting disparities in shadow wages across different members.

The hypotheses discussed in the Introduction are all based on a specific assumption as to the predominance that one of the effects has over the other. For example, the environmental Kuznets curve can be interpreted as the claim that the wealth effect is positive and dominates the cost effect at low levels of income, while at higher incomes the wealth effect becomes smaller relative to the cost effect, and may even turn negative. Unfortunately, rigorous studies separating out wealth and cost effects are few and far between: many studies suffer from major methodological weaknesses, owing to their neglect of the issues discussed above.[10]

Among the methodologically rigorous studies, Chaudhury and Pfaff (2003) use a large sample of households in Pakistan to evidence a clear transition from traditional to modern fuels as per capita income rises. It is important to note that they find this transition happening mainly in urban areas, where substitutes to firewood are more readily available. Foster and Rosenzweig (2003) find a small (but statistically significant) negative relationship between firewood consumption and income in a large household sample of rural households in India. However, the Himalayan-village context is different from the all-India context, mainly due to the easy access to firewood, higher levels of poverty and lack of access to alternate energy sources.

9.3.2 Firewood Engel Curves

We start by describing the relationship between income and firewood consumption in Nepal and the Indian Himalayas (Baland et al. 2007a, 2010a)[11] using simple Engel curves. These show the relationship between the amount of firewood collected by the household compared to the village average (in the

[10] A detailed literature review is provided in Baland et al. (2010a).

[11] We use collection and consumption interchangeably, given the virtual absence of firewood markets.

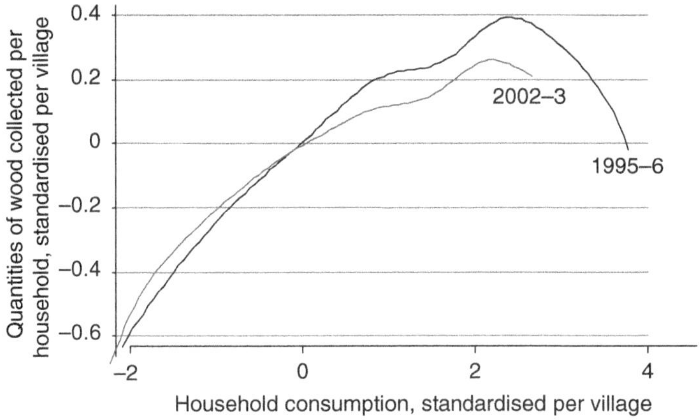

Figure 9.4 Engel curve for firewood collection in Nepal in 1995-6 and 2002-3. Each axis presents deviations from the village mean, divided by the village standard deviation.

Source: Baland et al. (2010a)

number of standard deviations), and household income compared to the village average (in the number of standard deviations, income being measured by consumption expenditures). In this way, we actually compare the amount of firewood collected by different households within the same village (i.e., by comparing with the village average) non-parametrically, with no other controls. Figure 9.4 represents the Engel curve obtained for Nepal in 1995–1996 and 2002–2003, Figure 9.5 the curve obtained for the Indian Himalayan villages.

The Engel curves show an essentially increasing relationship between firewood collection and household income. In the Nepalese villages, this relationship is concave, with the wealthiest households showing a turning point in the tail of the distribution (above the 95 percentile). On average, a 10 percent increase in income is associated with a 4 percent rise in firewood collection. The income effect thus seems to be largely positive and dominates the substitution effect. The results are very similar for India. It should be noted that the concavity of the Engel curves could imply, all other things being equal, that villages in which income disparities are lower consume more wood. The concavity measure in the present instance remains relatively weak, which means that this effect is probably not of great importance. This is corroborated by lack of direct evidence of any significant effect of local land inequality on household firewood collection, in a paper which estimated village fixed effects at the first step and then examined how the estimated village effects varied with measures of inequality (Baland et al. 2007b).

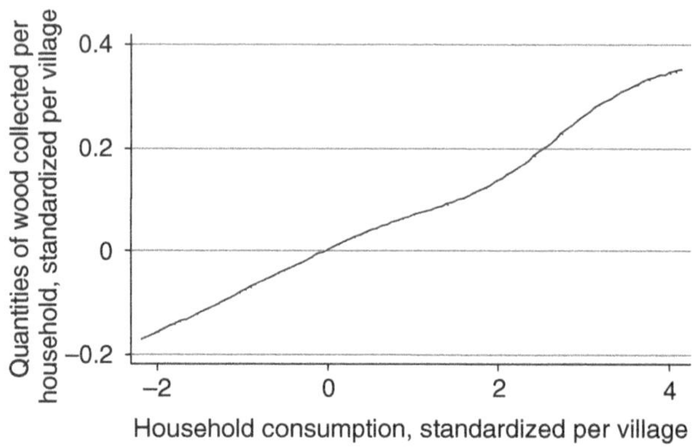

Figure 9.5 Engel curve for firewood collection in the Indian Himalayas (rural zone) in 2002–3. Each axis presents deviations from the village mean, divided by the village standard deviation.

9.3.3 Reduced Form and Semi-Structural Approaches to Estimating Household Demand for Firewood

Households maximize utility by choosing firewood, leisure, and consumption expenditures subject to a time budget constraint. Productive assets, demographics, and the time taken to collect firewood are taken as given. This maximization yields the household demand for firewood as a function of income (or some measure of wealth), collection cost (the product of shadow wage and collection time), and household size.[12] We thus have:

$$F_i = f(W_i, w_i \cdot tc_i, n_i) \tag{1}$$

where F_i represents the amount of firewood collected and consumed, W_i a measure of income or wealth, tc_i the time spent collecting one unit of firewood, w_i the shadow wage and n_i, the labor stock in the family, or family size. It is natural to suppose that collection time depends on occupational patterns, which themselves depend on the composition of assets owned. We therefore assume:

$$tc_i = t(\gamma + \Sigma\gamma_i A_i) \tag{2}$$

where t represents collection time in the village, and A_i represent the assets operated by household i. Linearizing by a first-order Taylor approximation, we obtain:

$$F_i = \alpha_1 W_i + \alpha_2 w_i{}^{*}t(\gamma + \Sigma\gamma_i A_i) + \alpha_3 n_i \qquad (3).$$

[12] It is relatively immediate to also include the price of the closest substitute source of energy, such as gas (Baland et al. 2010a).

This expression represents the basic regression equation estimated in our semi-structural (SS) approach, controlling for village fixed effects and endogenous censoring. As explained above, the coefficient α_1 is a measure of the wealth effect while α_2 is a measure of the cost effect.

The critical problem here is how to measure wealth and the shadow wage. One possibility is to directly use the level of consumption expenditures as a measure of wealth and as a proxy of the shadow wage. However, both are endogenously determined. Omitted household characteristics such as industriousness, location, or illness could simultaneously affect consumption, shadow wages, and firewood collections, resulting in biased estimates. Measurement error in consumption compounds this problem.

To address these, an alternative strategy is to use an asset-based measure of household wealth, under the assumption that most assets are inherited and less subject to endogeneity and measurement error. So we develop a wealth measure called *potential income*, defined as the self-employment income that the household is expected to earn from its assets if it were to fully utilize its labor stock. We therefore estimate in a first step a Cobb-Douglas production function in which the household income is predicted by its productive assets and the number of labor hours worked. Since labor choices are potentially endogenous, we instrument labor hours by household size (the number of adults available for self-employment), a method used earlier by Jacoby (1993).[13] We then use the estimated elasticities of the household production function from the first stage to estimate its potential income, by calculating the income it would have earned if the entire labor stock in the household were fully utilized. We can also estimate the shadow wage of the household by estimating the marginal product of labor hours from the production function. As it turns out, potential income per head is highly correlated with estimated shadow wages, reflecting underlying variations in asset ownership. At the second step, we then estimate equation (3) using potential income as a proxy for wealth W_i and either potential income or shadow wages as a proxy for w_i.

However, this method of using estimated production function parameters inevitably creates some errors of measurement in potential income and shadow wages, with attendant attenuation biases. They may also involve aggregation biases if the assumption underlying the aggregation (that the wealth effect generated by different assets should be proportional to their respective effects on income) is not valid. These problems can be avoided in the reduced form approach, which relates consumption and shadow wages directly back to household characteristics. Wealth is a function of household assets (which

[13] This strategy ignores the possibility that more productive households might attract relatives to join the household. Moreover, the exclusion restriction rules out the possibility that controlling for total hours employed, a larger household may be more productive, by taking better advantage of the division of labor or complementarity of skills across members.

includes household labor stock). The shadow wage is a function of household assets and collection costs. Combining these, we obtain the (RF) specification in which F is expressed as a function of household assets, household size and collection time interacted with household assets (since the collection cost is the product of collection time with the shadow wage in the household).

The results of these various strategies are given in Tables 9.3, 9.4, and 9.5. Table 9.3 gives the results of the semi-structural approach in the context of the Nepal 1995–1996 LSMS data. The results presented in Table 9.3 separate the effect of rising assets into wealth and cost-of-collection effects. Estimated wealth effects are statistically insignificant at the 10 percent level when potential income is used as the measure of wealth. However, they are significant when consumption and income are used instead. Cost-of-collection effects do not differ much across different measures of wealth. Rising collection time itself (interacted with the shadow wage) has a significant negative effect. The computation of the elasticity of firewood consumption to collection time cannot be directly estimated, as we have to take into account the interaction terms with the household productive assets. We discuss this further below.

We also estimated firewood collection in India using a similar semi-structural approach. The estimated elasticities for an average household are given in the Table 9.4. It shows that in the Indian sample firewood use is inelastic with respect to income growth, irrespective of whether it arises from productivity increases or asset accumulation. For the average household, firewood use per capita falls 0.06 percent following an increase in potential income of 10 percent. The elasticity with respect to growth of any asset is uniformly below 0.02 in absolute value. Compared to our estimates for Nepal, the estimates for the

Table 9.3 Firewood collection: semi-structural estimates for Nepal (1995–6 LSMS)

Dependent variable: firewood collection (log of number of bharis per year)	Using potential income	Consumption	Actual income
Log potential income	**1.961** (1.599)	—	—
Square of log potential income	-0.083 (0.076)	—	—
Log consumption expenditures	—	2.289** (1.138)	—
Square of log consumption Expenditures	—	-0.118** (0.056)	—
Log actual income	—	—	0.959* (0.482)
Square of log actual income	—	—	-0.049* (0.025)
Log(collection time)* Log(shadow wage)	-0.165** (0.079)	-0.150** (0.070)	-0.134* (0.071)

Household size and triple interactions between collection time, shadow wage, and productive assets are included. Village fixed effects are included. Standard errors are given in parentheses. *: significant at 10%, **: significant at 5%, ***: significant at 1%. The number of observations is 2190 households in 201 villages.
Source: Baland et al. (2010a)

Table 9.4 Predicted effects of 10 percent asset growth on yearly per-capita firewood use of average household in Indian mid-Himalayan region

Predicted % change in firewood collection for an average household resulting from:	
Increase in potential income by 10%	−0.06
Increase in land by 10 %	−0.08
Increase in big livestock by 10%	0.15
Increase in small livestock by 10%	0.01
Increase in education by 10%	−0.19
Increase in non-farm business assets by 10%	−0.01

Source: Baland et al. (2007a)

Table 9.5 Elasticity of firewood collection: reduced form estimates for Nepal, 1995–6 and 2002–3

Productive asset	Wealth effect elasticity		Cost effect elasticity		Total elasticity	
	1995–6	2002–3	1995–6	2002–3	1995–6	2002–3
Land	0.22	0.36	−0.19	−0.25	0.03	0.12
Livestock	N.S.	−0.25	0.50	0.50	0.50	0.25
Education	0.57	N.S.	−0.39	−0.19	0.18	−0.19
Non-farm business Assets	0.18	0.13	N.S.	N.S.	0.18	0.13

NS: not significant at the 10% level.
Source: Baland et al. (2010a)

Indian Himalayan region using the potential income approach yields substantially smaller elasticities.

We also estimated firewood collection using the reduced form approach for Nepal in 1995–1996 and 2002–2003. Table 9.5 shows the results, which distinguish between the wealth and cost effect of changes in various assets.

The reduced form elasticities are generally statistically significant, though of smaller magnitude than indicated by the estimates in Table 9.3 based on the semi-structural form using potential income. The improved statistical significance may owe to the reduction in measurement error associated with using assets directly rather than potential income. The results also indicate substantial mis-specification in the semi-structural form: for example, disparate productive assets do not have a homogenous impact on firewood collection. For example, livestock ownership is associated with a positive cost effect, indicating complementarity between livestock-rearing activities and firewood collection. On the other hand, land, education, and non-farm business assets to some extent are associated with negative cost effects. The wealth effects of different assets are not proportional to their effects on potential income in the first stage regression in the semi-structural approach, as would be required for the latter approach to be valid.

The reduced form estimates are therefore more reliable. The failure of the SS approach has some constructive implications, however. It indicates that the future impact of economic growth for the forest in Nepal crucially depends on the type of asset underpinning this growth. Growth based on modern assets, such as education and non-farm business assets, reduces firewood collection (on the basis of 2002–2003 estimates), with a total net elasticity of -0.06: if these two assets were to double, the demand for firewood is expected to decline by around 6 percent. On the other hand, growth associated with doubling of land and livestock is expected to lead to increased collection of firewood by 37 percent.

Moreover, total elasticity of firewood collection, the sum of the elasticities of all the assets, is relatively high: 0.89 in 1995–1996 and 0.31 in 2002–2003. An overall growth of all the assets, which leads to an equivalent growth in household income (economies of scale proved constant in our estimates), is thus expected to produce a significant increase in the demand for firewood. The Engel curves presented in Figure 9.4 already illustrated this phenomenon.

These results for Nepal indicate the need to estimate firewood demand in India using the reduced form approach rather than the semi-structural approach. This still remains to be done.

To summarize we do *not* find any evidence from within-village variations in support of the Poverty Environment Hypothesis. If anything, we find some evidence for the Environmental Kuznets curve in Nepal, whether one relies on the pure wealth effect or its combined effect including the induced changes in collection costs. But the upward rising portion of the Kuznets curve prevails for over 90 percent of the distribution, with some flattening and decline at the very top end. The impact of wealth or income increases on firewood collection is either negligible (as in our SS estimates for India) or positive (as in the RF estimates for Nepal), except at the very top end of the respective distributions.

Finally, consider the implications of the preceding results for effects of demographic changes, consisting of population growth and changes in household size and composition. The average household size in both India and Nepal indicates that most families are nuclear already and there is little scope for further fragmentation of households. Within villages we also find little variation in household size with per capita potential income. So it is reasonable to assume that household size will remain fixed in the near future, irrespective of economic growth. This implies that population growth will consist mainly of an increase in the number of households. Unless there is substantial out-migration from villages, it is reasonable to suppose that population will grow by at least 10 percent in the next decade. Since our estimates pertained to demand per household, a 10 percent increase in the number of households in the village would give rise to a 10 percent rise in *total* firewood and fodder collections from the neighboring forests. This is a sizeable effect, comparable to the effect of doubling of non-farm business assets in Nepal, and bigger than the effect of doubling of education and non-farm assets with land and livestock remaining unchanged (as implied by the elasticities in Table 9.5). Demographic changes may thus be just important as economic growth in determining the rate of forest degradation over time. Absent significant increases in migration out of these villages, the pressure on forests may be expected to rise approximately in proportion to the rise in population. Hence calculated benefits of policies that reduce fertility rates and encourage migration out of these rural communities should include their effects on forest degradation.

9.3.4 Local Impact of Forest Degradation: Estimating the Local Externality

Continued forest degradation will impact the lives of neighboring villagers primarily by raising the time it takes them to collect firewood and fodder. If trees are more severely lopped, the villagers will take longer to collect a single bundle, either by searching longer for trees that still have branches that can be lopped, or walking further into the forest parts that have not yet been harvested. This is the principal source of the local externality: higher collections today by any single household will raise collection times for all households in surrounding villages in the future.

Precise quantification of the magnitude of this local externality requires knowledge of the rate at which future collection times will rise in response to current collection levels. We have not attempted to estimate this so far. Instead we will try to provide some bounds for the magnitude of the externality by considering the effects of an increase in collection time by one hour per bundle.

The effect of a small increase in collection time on household welfare can be approximated by calculating the shadow cost of additional time required to collect the same number of bundles of firewood selected by the household prior to the increase in collection time. We therefore compute the shadow wage corresponding to the rise in time required to collect the same amount of firewood over a year. In the case of Nepal in 1995–1996, a one-hour increase in the time required to collect on bundle of wood corresponds to an estimated loss of income of around 2 percent.[14] In the case of India, this figure is slightly lower, standing at around 1 percent. The direct impact of the local externality

[14] The data we use is an average firewood collection of seventy-nine bundles per household per year, a median shadow wage of Rs 6.4 per hour, and median consumption expenditure of Rs 30,675.5 per year. The total time spent collecting firewood in Nepal in 1995–6 represented around 400 hours per household per year.

on the villagers' welfare is thus weak, which is certainly part of the explanation for the lack of collective action at the local level.

Assessments of future degradation would require estimates of the extent to which increased collection times resulting from current degradation would induce a reduction in firewood collections. This requires an estimate of the elasticity of firewood consumption to collection time. The regression specification using village fixed effects makes this difficult, as collection times are partially absorbed by the village fixed effect. We estimated only the extent to which differences in asset ownership interact with collection time at the village level to affect firewood collections. Better data on variations in collection time across households within the same village would be needed to estimate the overall effect of increased collection time, and thus assess the extent to which current degradation patterns would generate a self-correcting tendency for household collections to decrease in the future.

9.3.5 Household Substitution between Alternate Energy Sources

To the extent that policy interventions are deemed desirable to limit firewood collections, it is natural for economists to think of corrective taxes and subsidies. Since monitoring firewood collection by the government does not appear to be feasible option, a natural alternative policy instrument would be subsidies on alternate energy sources (see, for instance, Pitt 1985). We studied this question in the case of India in Baland et al. (2007a).[15] The most commonly found substitute fuel is gas in cylinders (LPG). In the villages where this is available, the elasticity of firewood collection with respect to the price of gas is fairly high. Given an average price of Rs. 300 per cylinder, the estimated impact of a Rs. 100 subsidy on household firewood collection is reported in Table 9.6. As might be expected, the reduction in firewood consumption is larger during the summer than in winter (27 percent and 19 percent respectively), averaging to a 22 percent decrease in annual consumption. The effects are substantial at all income levels: even amongst the poorest households (in the first quartile of the income distribution), demand for firewood drops by 19 percent. Our estimates imply a Rs. 200 subsidy would reduce firewood consumption by 40 percent.

Our household-level estimates also enable us to estimate the fiscal cost of subsidies. As we show in Baland et al. (2007a), this subsidy encourages 37 percent of the households to use an average 1.07 cylinders per person, which represents a subsidy of Rs. 107 per using household. With an average per capita

[15] It was more difficult to design a similar approach for Nepal where the use of gas in 1995–6 was much less common. The 2002–3 data has yet to be analyzed.

Table 9.6 Estimated effect of a Rs. 100 decrease in the price of an LPG cylinder

Season	Income level	% change in the amount of wood collected
All year	Mean	−22%
	First quartile	−19%
	Second quartile	−22%
	Third quartile	−22%
	Fourth quartile	−26%
Summer	Mean	−27%
Winter	Mean	−19%

Source: Baland et al. (2007a)

consumption expenditure of Rs. 8,646 per year, this corresponds to around 1.2 percent of their total consumption expenditure. For the overall consumption expenditures of all the villagers, this subsidy corresponds to an annual tax of 0.4 percent. At a relatively low cost, this policy can thus lead to a significant decrease in firewood consumption, particularly during the summer months.

9.4 DECENTRALIZATION, COMMUNITY MANAGEMENT, AND FOREST QUALITY

9.4.1 Decentralization Movements in India and Nepal

For several years, policies have been adopted in both Nepal and India to transfer part of the rights relating to state forest management and use to local communities. This policy approach is grounded in the idea that degradation of common property resources result from an inadequate institutional framework, which does not provide rural households with suitable incentives for rational and sustainable resource management. While it is true that centralized state management, which often focuses on regulating resources, yields mitigated results in terms of environmental management (Ostrom 1990), the performance of decentralization policies concerning natural resources management by user communities has been called into question by many authors (Baland and Platteau 1996). Whereas local user organizations are often able to develop complex mechanisms for allocating and distributing products from these resources, they often seem to be inadequate when it comes to setting up systems to protect such resources. This is particularly true when market expansion and population pressures come into play. Certain authors also criticize the idealized image of village "communities" put forward by some literature, drawing on case studies. They lay greater emphasis on the shortcomings of community participation programmes, underlining phenomena such as capture by village elites, the absence of accountability and monitoring procedures, or insufficient knowledge and preparation of users (Abraham and Platteau 2001; Mansuri and Rao 2004). In the context of Himalayan forests, an important question thus concerns the relative effectiveness of local community management vis-à-vis centralized state management.

In Nepal, a large-scale programme for forest resources management was launched in 1993. The programme's objective is to transfer the management of all accessible forests to local communities, via Forest User Groups (FUGs). This includes controls on access to the forests, the right to tax forest products, hire forest guards, and launch plantation programmes. Incomes generated by forest-related activities can be used by these groups to finance local projects (such as roads, schools and temples).[16] This programme expanded very swiftly and it was estimated that 38 percent of the population was involved in an FUG by January 2007.

In India, local forest management structures (known as Van Panchayats) were first created in 1931, primarily in Uttaranchal by the colonial British government in order to guarantee local communities the exclusive use of demarcated forest areas. This policy was vigorously pursued after independence, and by 1998, more than one third of the region's villages had their own Van Panchayat. An estimated 10 percent of existing forests are now under Van Panchayat control. Currently, three types of common property management regimes coexist in Uttaranchal. State forests (*Reserve Forest* and *Demarcated Protected Forests*) are forests protected and managed by the state. Access and use of these forests are subject to many restrictions, the Forest Department being responsible for their enforcement. Open access forests (*Civil Soyam*) are forest patches with unrestricted rights of access (except that tree-felling for commercial purposes remains prohibited). They correspond to open access commons. Finally, the forests managed by the Van Panchayats are clearly demarcated forest patches, the use and exploitation (including plantation programmes) of which are defined by the local Van Panchayat, sometimes with state support.

Since 2001, there has been a dramatic increase of Van Panchayats, as shown in Table 9.7. Under pressure from the Indian government, the number of Van Panchayats has almost doubled in five years. New rules were introduced to make it easier to create Van Panchayats (for example, approval by only 1/5 of the population is now required to create a Van Panchayat, instead of the previous 1/3). The programme includes various infrastructure and plantation projects, which are a source of employment for the villagers.

[16] Certain legal restrictions are set for the use of these funds. For example, 25% of revenue must be reinvested in work aimed at developing the forest.

Table 9.7 Number of Van Panchayats in Uttaranchal, India

Year	Number
1947	429
1993	3,635
2001	6,777
2006	12,089

Source: Sarkar (2008)

Some observers, however, have pointed to the villagers' lack of interest in these recently created community-managed forests, once the casual jobs related to the plantation and infrastructure work disappear. Some of the new Van Panchayats no longer meet and, in fact, only exist on paper (Sarkar 2008). This situation seems to differ from that of the Van Panchayats that were set up much earlier, which involved greater mobilization and active involvement of local communities.

9.4.2 The Impact of Decentralization Policies in India and Nepal

Most existing surveys (Somanathan 1991) that compare state-managed forests with those managed by local communities underline the relative effectiveness of the latter but also the great disparities in their functioning and performance. These studies have three major shortcomings. Firstly, they often only cover very narrow geographical areas (Ostrom 1990; Somanathan 1991; Gibson, McKean, and Ostrom 2000; Jodha 2001; Varughese and Ostrom 2001; Shivakoti and Ostrom 2002). Moreover, they often base their evaluations on how the management councils operate (existence of regulations, penalties, forest guards and so on) or how the villagers perceive the state of the forests, rather than objective indicators of forest quality. Finally, they typically do not take into account problems of selection: a Van Panchayat is formed by villagers' decisions, which gives rise to a potentially significant selection bias. For example, it is possible that villages facing a more deteriorated forest environment have more to gain by creating active Van Panchayats to protect their forests. If forest quality is compared across villages with and without Van Panchayats, a positive correlation would be observed between the existence of a Van Panchayat and forest degradation.

The studies discussed below attempt to get around these problems. In Baland et al. (2010b), we compare different types of forest areas accessed by the same village. Somanathan et al. (2009) compare adjoining forests of different status. Edmonds (2002) compares villages where a community-managed forest is about to be created with villages in which this type of forest has just been created.

Edmonds (2002) followed the implementation of an FUG programme in Nepal. He uses the fact that these groups are gradually set up to compare those villages where the programme was already in place in 1995–1996 with the villages where it had not yet been implemented, in a region with relatively similar ecological conditions. After controlling for a large number of household and village variables, he finds that setting up an FUG causes a 10 to 15 percent reduction in the amount of firewood collected by neighboring households. This estimate is robust to a set of alternative methods and controls. This suggests the programme had a moderating effect on the quantities of firewood used.[17] Tree plantation and timber sales are also a key part of the programme, but a rigorous evaluation of this component is not yet available.[18]

Somanathan et al. (2009) evaluate forest quality using data from satellite images in two regions of Uttaranchal. They compare crown cover of forests across three types of forest management regimes: Van Panchayat forest, open access forest (unregulated), and state forest. They show that on average the crown cover of Van Panchayat forests is significantly higher than open access forests (12 percent for broad-leafed forests), and similar to state-managed forests. This is all the more remarkable as the Van Panchayats do not have the same rights as the Forest Department, especially as far as timber sales are concerned. In their comparisons, the authors take important factors into account such as population density, closeness to the villages and the geographical attributes of the forests, state forests having a better aspect and being further from the villages than the other types of forest. The authors compare these results with forest management costs: the costs of state management are thirteen times higher per hectare of forest than those for Van Panchayat management.[19]

In Uttaranchal we collected detailed information on different types of forest management regimes in the villages surveyed (i.e., 399 forests in eighty-three villages). We were thus able to study how ground-level measures of forest quality varied across different management regimes. We will report here results for three measures: canopy cover, basal area, and lopping (for further details, see Baland et al. 2010b).

Table 9.8 reports the results of the various regressions measuring the impact of the management regime on these three measures of forest quality. These

[17] This is the case, even though the observations were made only three years after the formation of the FUGs. It is therefore likely that the long-run effects are greater.

[18] According to a recent estimate, sale of wood could represent on average two-thirds of overall revenue generated by the FUGs in Nepal (Pokharel 2008).

[19] In 2002–3, management costs per hectare were equal to Rs. 862 for a state-managed forest, as opposed to Rs. 65 for a Van Panchayat-managed forest (Somanathan et al. 2009).

Table 9.8 Impact of management regime on forest quality

Difference between	Canopy cover (%)	Basal area (m^2/ha)	Lopping (%)
Van Panchayat and state forest	5.27	-4.14	-13.18***
Van Panchayat and open-access forest	2.06	-5.20	-4.01
Old Van Panchayat and state forest	9.35**	2.47	-18.26***
New Van Panchayat and state forest	0.06	-12.56**	-6.70**

Note: **: significant at 5%, ***: significant at 1%.
Source: Baland et al. (2010b)

regressions, similar to those of Somanathan et al. (2009), use a large number of control variables (in particular, aspect, distance from the village, or altitude), as well as village fixed effects. What we compare are thus the differences observed between forests patches managed by different regimes but adjoining the same village.

While the results show absence of significant differences between open access forests and state forests, the forests managed by Van Panchayats displayed significantly lower rates of lopping. The collection of firewood and leaf-litter for fodder is less pronounced when the forest is managed by a Van Panchayat.[20]

This more rational use of forests mainly typifies the older Van Panchayats created before 1980. They are also characterized by a higher biomass, measured by canopy cover. On the other hand, the more recently formed Van Panchayats have a smaller basal area. This latter result may indicate that Van Panchayats tend to form when the concerned forests have a poorer quality to start with.[21] The high performance of the older Van Panchayats possibly reflects superior management, being grounded in effective community participation. Reduced rates of lopping over long periods of time also are likely to explain why older Van Panchayat forests achieve superior biomass than state forest.

These findings thus reinforce similar results of Somanathan et al. (2009) based on aerial satellite images. Moreover, they indicate a connection between measures of biomass in the long run and rates of lopping. They are also consistent with the results of Edmonds (2002) for Nepal that creation of an FUG reduces household firewood collection. In our study of firewood collection in India (Baland et al. 2007a) based on household surveys we also observed a

[20] It should also be noted that we did not observe any effect of increased firewood or fodder collection in neighboring forests.

[21] As in Somanathan et al. (2009), everything seems to indicate that the more degraded forests are more likely to be converted into a Van Panchayat forest.

significant decline in firewood collection in villages with a larger fraction of neighboring forests under Van Panchayat management. These estimates indicate that firewood collection levels would decline by an order of 20 percent if all village forests were converted from state into Van Panchayats forests.

Although setting up a formal community management structure therefore appears effective in terms of improving forest quality, it has important effects with respect to redistribution, as it changes the rules for using and sharing forest produce. In Nepal, some studies suggest that the local elite often dominate the FUG executive committee and sway its decisions to their own benefit. More particularly, the substantial funds generated by timber sales are invested chiefly in projects that are advantageous to this elite[22] (Banjade et al. 2006; Malla et al. 2003; Pokharel 2008; Timsina 2003). This is reminiscent of the results obtained by Banerjee et al. (2001) in the sugar cooperatives of Maharashtra, in which the richest members secure rents for themselves by manipulating producer prices and using cooperative's profits for their personal benefit (see also Dasgupta 2010, 2012).

In the same vein, in a study of some twenty villages in Gujarat, Agarwal (2007) shows how the creation of a forest management council (similar to the Van Panchayats) has excluded women—who are traditionally users of the forest—from participatory and decision-making structures and deprived them of their access rights to the forest. The women express their feeling of expropriation and exclusion as follows: "If you were to attend meetings, the men will say, oh you haven't cooked my meal on time. What happened to my tea?...The meetings are considered for men only....No one ever listened to my suggestions....People don't like it when we speak, they think women are becoming very smart." (Agarwal 2007: 288–9) Agarwal concludes that women bear a large share of the costs linked to community forest management, whereas they only benefit very indirectly from the related advantages, "How will we cook if we don't get wood from the forest? What do they expect us to do?" (Agarwal 2007: 291).

9.5 SUMMARY AND POLICY IMPLICATIONS

Without some kind of effective government intervention, the future of Himalayan forests appear somewhat bleak. Forest degradation in this region is related to the unregulated extraction of firewood and fodder, which has led to an alarming decline in the quality and resistance of trees in the region. The pressures on the Himalayan forests are increasing due to population

[22] Pokharel (2008) estimates that around three-quarters of the available funds are allocated to projects that benefit wealthier households.

growth: over the last twenty-five years, the average number of households per village has doubled. In addition, the demand for firewood has risen owing to rising standards of living and reduced levels of poverty, though this tends to be moderated if growth is associated with rising education and increasing incidence of non-agricultural activities.

However, it is unclear that local inhabitants perceive this degradation as an important problem, or that they are acting on it to self-regulate local collection activities. Local collective action among local inhabitants is conspicuous by its absence, in the absence of formal efforts by the state to grant rights to local forest user groups. This reason perhaps explains the irrelevance of local land inequality to matter as a determinant of firewood collection levels (e.g., in Baland et al. 2007b), contrary to a large and mainly theoretical literature emphasizing the role of collective action. Part of the reason for lack of spontaneous collective action may be the negligible magnitude of the associated local externality. The relevant externality is therefore essentially non-local in nature, with forest degradation in the Himalayas contributing to landslides, siltation, and floods, and possibly also to global climate change. These necessitate some kind of external state interventions.

Two types of policy interventions can be considered. The first involves encouraging the development of community-based methods of forest management. The experience of Uttaranchal shows that local community management helps ensure a better quality of forest than that obtained through the most protected state forests. The measures for setting up these community management mechanisms nonetheless have a crucial impact on the extent of their success, and it is not clear how state or central governments can encourage genuine grass-roots mobilization and involvement in forest management groups. Moreover, it may take a long time for such groups to become effective in improving the condition of the forest.

The second policy intervention would involve subsidies on LPG, the principal form of alternate energy. Our results on household substitution between firewood and LPG in response to the price paid for LPG are encouraging in this respect, suggesting this to be a cost-effective and reliable method to induce reduced firewood collections.

Third, our analysis indicates that the *composition* of growth matters. To the extent that growth is associated with decline in traditional livestock-based occupations, and rise of education and non-agricultural occupations, pressures on the forest would be ameliorated. Improvements in transport and communication would be likely to raise the value of non-agricultural occupations and expand accessibility to low-cost alternate fuels. Policies encouraging out-migration and reductions in fertility would also be expected to reduce the pressure on the forests.

Many important questions need to be addressed in future research. We need to re-estimate household demand equations in the Indian context using the reduced form approach, and reassess our findings concerning growth projections and elasticities with respect to alternate energy costs. The availability of longitudinal studies of forests and collection behavior of neighboring communities would represent a big step forward, in allowing for more refined controls and accurate projections for the future. Our recent exploration ((Baland, Libois, and Mookherjee 2011) using a small panel from the Nepal LSMS spanning 1995–1996 and 2002–2003 generates results concerning the effects of changes in levels and composition of household assets that are similar to those obtained from earlier cross-sectional analyses that we have described in this chapter. The availability of larger and more comprehensive longitudinal surveys would enable more detailed examination of the inter-connections between development and forest degradation. Even using the data in hand, there is scope for assessing future sustainability of the Himalayan forests using simulations of a dynamic model of interaction between forest quality and firewood collection patterns, calibrated to fit the observed patterns in the data.

References

Abraham, A. and J.-P. Platteau (2001). "Participatory Development in the Presence of Endogenous Community Imperfections," *Journal of Development Studies*, 32(2): 104–36.

Agarwal, B. (2007). "Gender Inequality, Cooperation and Environmental Sustainability," in J.-M. Baland, P. Bardhan, and S. Bowles (eds.), *Inequality, Cooperation and Environmental Sustainability*, Princeton, NJ: Princeton University Press, 274–314.

Amacher, G. S., L. Ersado, D. Grebner et al. (2004). "Disease, Microdams and Natural Resources in Tigray, Ethiopia," *The Journal of Development Studies*, 40(6): 122–45.

Arrow, K., B. Bolin, R. Costanza et al. (1995) "Economic Growth, Carrying Capacity, and the Environment," *Science*, 268: 520–521.

Baland, J.-M., P. Bardhan, S. Das et al. (2010a). "The Environmental Impact of Poverty: Evidence from Firewood Collection in Rural Nepal," *Economic Development and Cultural Change*, 59(1): 23–62.

—— et al. (2010b). "Forests to the People: Decentralization and Forest Degradation in the Indian Himalayas," *World Development*, 38(11): 1642–56.

—— et al. (2007a). "Managing the Environmental Consequences of Growth: Forest Degradation in the Indian Mid-Himalayas," *Indian Policy Forum*, 3: 215–66.

—— et al. (2007b). "Inequality, Collective Action and the Environment: Evidence from Firewood Collection in Nepal," in J.-M. Baland, P. Bardhan, and S. Bowles (eds.), *Inequality, Cooperation and Environmental Sustainability*. Princeton, NJ: Princeton University Press, 246–73.

—— F. Libois and D. Mookherjee (2011). "Evolving Patterns in Firewood Collection in Nepal: A Household Panel Analysis 1995–2003," mimeo, University of Namur.

—— and J.-P. Platteau (1996). *Halting Degradation of Natural Resources: Is There a Role for Rural Communities?* Oxford: Oxford University Press.

Banerjee A., D. Mookherjee, K. Munshi et al. (2001). 'Inequality, Control Rights and Rent-Seeking: Sugar Cooperatives in Maharashtra," *Journal of Political Economy*, 109(1): 138–90.

Banjade, M. R., H. Schanz, and C. Leeuwis (2006). "Discourses of Information in Community Forest-user Groups in Nepal," *International Forestry Review*, 8(2): 229–40.

Barbier, E. B. (1997a). "Introduction to the Environmental Kuznets Curve Special Issue," *Environment and Development Economics*, 2(4): 369–81.

Barbier, E. B. (1997b). "The Economic Determinants of Land Degradation in Developing Countries," *Philosophical Transactions of the Royal Society*, 352: 891–9.

Bardhan P. and J. Dayton-Johnson (2002). "Inequality and Conservation on the Local Common: a Theoretical Perspective," *Economic Journal, Royal Economic Society*, 112(481): 577–602.

Bardhan P. (2005). *Scarcity, Conflict and Cooperation*. Cambridge, MA: MIT Press.

Chaudhuri S. and A. S. P. Pfaff (2002). "*Economic Growth and the Environment: What Can we Learn from Household Data?*" Department of Economics, Columbia University.

Cooke, P. (1998). "The Effects of Environmental Good Scarcity on Own-Farm Labor Allocation: the Case of Agricultural Households in Rural Nepal," *Environment and Development Economics*, 3: 443–69.

Dasgupta, P. (1995), *An Enquiry Into Well-Being and Destitution*. New York: Oxford University Press.

—— (2010). "Trust and Cooperation among Economic Agents," *Philosophical Transactions of the Royal Society B*, 364: 3301–9.

—— (2012). "Dark Matters: Exploitation as Cooperation," *Journal of Theoretical Biology*, 299: 180–7.

—— S. Levine, and J. Lubchenco (2000). "Economic Pathways to Ecological Sustainability," *Bioscience*, 50(4): 339–45.

—— and K.-G. Mäler (1995). "Poverty, Institutions, and the Environmental Resource-base," in J. Behrman and T. Srinivasan (eds.), *Handbook of Development Economics*,iiiA, Amsterdam: Elsevier, 2371–463.

—— (2004). "*Environmental and Resource Economics: Some Recent Developments*,' in K. Chopra and V. Dayal (eds.), *Handbook of Environmental Economics in India*. New Dehli: Oxford University Press, 17–68.

Durraiappah, A. K. (1998). "Poverty and Environmental Degradation: A Review and Analysis of the Nexus," *World Development*, 26(12): 2169–79.

Edmonds, E. (2002). "Government Initiated Community Resource Management and Local Resource Extraction from Nepal's Forests," *Journal of Development Economics*, 68(1): 89–115.

Foster, A. and M. Rosenzweig (2003). "Economic Growth and the Rise of Forests," *Quarterly Journal of Economics*, 118: 601–37.

Gibson C., M. McKean, and E. Ostrom (eds.) (2000). *People and Forests: Communities, Institutions and Governance*. Cambridge MA and London: MIT Press.

Grossman G. and A. Krueger (1995). "Economic Growth and the Environment," *Quarterly Journal of Economics*, 110: 353–77.

Ives, J. D. and B. Messerly (1989). *The Himalayan Dilemma: Reconciling Development and Conservation*. London: Routledge.

Jacoby, H. (1993). "Shadow Wages and Peasant Family Labour Supply: An Econometric Application to the Peruvian Sierra," *Review of Economic Studies*, 60(4): 903–21.

Jalal, K.F. (1993). *Sustainable Development, Environment and Poverty Nexus*. Manilla: Asian Development Bank Economics and Development Resources Center Occasional Papers 7.

Jodha, N. S. (2001). *Life on the Edge: Sustaining Agriculture and Community Resources in Fragile Environments*. New Delhi: Oxford University Press.

Kumar, S. K. and D. Hotchkiss (1988). *Consequences of Deforestation for Women's Time Allocation, Agricultural Production and Nutrition in Hill Areas in Nepal*. Washington DC: IFPRI, Research Report 69.

Lele S. M. (1991). "Sustainable Development: A Critical Review," *World Development*, 19(6): 607–21.

Lopez R. (1998). "Where Development Can or Cannot Go: The Role of Poverty-Environment Linkages," in B. Pleskovic and J. Stiglitz (eds.), *1997 Annual World Bank Conference in Development Economics*. Washington DC: World Bank.

Mäler K. G. (1998). "Environment, Poverty and Economic Growth," in B. Pleskovic and J. Stiglitz (eds.), *1997 Annual World Bank Conference in Development Economics*. Washington DC: World Bank.

Malla, Y. B. (2000). "Impact of Community Forestry Policy on Rural Livelihoods and Food Security in Nepal," *Unasylva*, 51(3): 37–45.

Mansuri, G. and V. Rao (2004). "Community-based and -driven Development: a Critical Review," *World Bank Research Observer*, 19(1): 1–39.

Metz, K. G., (1991). "A reassessment of the Causes and the Severity of Nepal's Environmental Crisis," *World Development*, 19(7): 805–20.

Myers, N. (1986). "Environmental Repercussions of Deforestation in the Himalayas," *Journal of World Forest Resource Management*, 2: 63–72.

Ostrom, E. (1990). *Governing the Commons: The Evolution of Institutions for Collective Action*. Cambridge: Cambridge University Press.

Pitt, M., (1985). "Equity, Externalities and Energy Subsidies: the Case of Kerosene in Indonesia," *Journal of Development Economics*, 17: 201–17.

Pokharel, R. K. (2008). *"Nepal's Community Forestry Funds: Do They Benefit the Poor?"* Kathmandu: SANDEE Working Paper No. 31.

Prabhakar, R., E. Somanathan, and B. S. Mehta (2006). "How Degraded are Himalayan Forests?" *Current Science*, 91(1): 61–7.

Sarkar, R. (2008). "Decentralised Forest Governance in Central Himalayas: A Re-evaluation of Outcomes," *Economic and Political Weekly*, 43(18): 54–63.

Shivakoti, G. and E. Ostrom (eds.) (2002). *Improving Irrigation Governance and Management in Nepal*. Oakland: Institute for Contemporary Studies Press.

Somanathan, E. (1991). "Deforestation, Property Rights and Incentives in the Central Himalayas," *Economic & Political Weekly*, 26: PE 37–46.

—— R Prabhakar, and B. S. Mehta (2006). "How Degraded are Himalayan Forests?" *Current Science*, 91(1): 61–7.

—— (2009). "Decentralization for Cost-effective Conservation," *Proceedings of the National Academy of Sciences of the USA*, 106(11): 4143–7.

Thadani, R. (1999). "*Disturbance, Micro Climate and the Competitive Dynamics of Tree Seedlings in Banj Oak Forests of the Central Himalaya*," PhD thesis, Yale University.

Timsina, N. P. (2003). "Promoting Social Justice and Conserving Montane Forests Environments: A Case Study of Nepal's Community Forestry Programme," *The Geographical Journal*, 169(3): 236–42.

Varughese, G. (2000). "Population and Forest Dynamics in the Hills of Nepal: Institutional Remedies by Rural Communities," in C. Gibson, M. McKean, and E. Ostrom (eds.), *People and Forests: Communities, Institutions and Governance*. Cambridge, MA: MIT Press.

Varughese G. and E. Ostrom (2001). "The Contested Role of Heterogeneity in Collective Action: Some Evidence from Community Forestry in Nepal," *World Development*, 29(5): 747–65.

Yandle B., V. Maya, and B. Madhusudan (2002). "*The Environmental Kuznets Curve: A Primer*." Montana: Political Economy Research Center, Center for Free Market Environmentalism.

10

Comments by Geoffrey Heal on "Forest Degradation in the Himalayas"

Baland, Das, and Mookherjee tackle an interesting and important issue and provide some nice insights. They show that in the region of their study, the Himalayas, forest degradation through lopping and partial clearing matters more than full-blown deforestation. This is important: most of the data that we have on the status of the world's forests reflects the extent of deforestation, which can be readily measured from satellite images, but not that of degradation, which is harder to measure without a physical presence in the forest. As they say, this degradation is not yet visible in the volume of standing wood in the forests. This suggests that global numbers on deforestation could be underestimating the seriousness of damages to the world's forests.

The authors also show the extent of the dependence of local communities on forests for energy for cooking and heating, and the considerable impact that forest degradation has on their time budgets. Clearly providing alternative sources of energy could be a relatively simple and effective route to forest conservation. The authors mention gas as an alternative cooking fuel in their region: in fact some of the most interesting developments currently involve using solar heating to cook, though in different areas of India. They also show that the pattern of economic growth is important in understanding the implications of growth for the status of forests: not surprisingly, growth based on agriculture is likely to be harmful for forests, whereas that based on education and non-farm businesses is likely to be positive.

Another interesting fact to emerge from the data presented is that degradation and deforestation are no better in state-managed forests than in open access forests, whereas forests managed by local Forest User Groups fare better, a fact that has interesting implications for governance.

10.1 FORESTS AS NATURAL CAPITAL

These issues are important because forests are a crucial element of our natural capital stock. It's hard to place an economic value on them, but we can look at the World Bank's numbers to get some ideas of an order of magnitude (World Bank 2010). The Bank's estimates suggest that for low-income countries natural capital is the most important component of their total capital stock, which includes constructed or conventional capital, human and intellectual capital. For low-income countries that are not resource-rich, forests are frequently the most important element of natural capital. So understanding the dynamics of forests and the factors driving their exploitation is of great significance. The chapter by Baland et al. is an important step in this direction.

Why are forests a crucial part of natural capital? They play a fundamental role in managing the climate, both locally and globally. They shelter and support biodiversity. And they are often an integral part of watersheds: in hilly areas, such as Nepal and Northern India, a part of their watershed role is to stabilize soils and prevent them from running off during intense rain. As an illustration of this, in 1998 China suffered some of the worst floods in its history along the Yangtze valley. Research revealed that the main cause was deforestation of the steeply sloped watershed, which led the Chinese government both to ban the deforestation of watersheds and also to engage in an intense reforestation campaign in the upper reaches of the Yangtze. In addition, forests of course provide timber for construction and wood for energy, the main focus of the Baland et al. chapter.

Using sunlight to generate electric currents, that is, using solar power, the trees in forests split water molecules into hydrogen and oxygen and combine the hydrogen with carbon dioxide from the air to produce carbohydrates. Oxygen, which we and all other animals breathe, is a by-product released into the air. So trees are managing the balance between carbon dioxide and oxygen in the atmosphere, regulating the amount of the principal greenhouse gas and ensuring that we can breathe. Forests and the soil beneath them absorb about a quarter of all emissions of carbon dioxide. In fact preserving and growing forests is one of the most cost-effective ways of reducing the concentration of greenhouse gases in the atmosphere, which is why there is a great deal of interest in paying tropical countries to keep their forests intact as in the REDD (Reducing Emissions from Deforestation and Degradation) proposal from the Coalition for Rainforest Nations[1] that has been accepted in principle by the UNFCCC.

Trees also affect the climate locally, releasing water into the atmosphere, one of the reasons why rainforests have rain. A large forest releases so much water that it affects the climate locally and generates rain. We have known for a long time that clearing forests reduces humidity and rainfall, and a major concern in a country like Brazil that has huge forests and also vast agricultural areas is that deforestation will reduce rainfall and hence the productivity of

[1] <http://www.rainforestcoalition.org> (accessed 17 October 2013).

the agricultural areas. In fact some scientists believe that deforestation of the Amazon region would dry the climate as far north as the US.

Forests also play a major role in managing the flow of fresh water to human societies. Watersheds are often forested, with the forests being an integral part of the natural capital that manages stream flow and water purification. So we owe both the oxygen we breathe and the water we drink to forests, and much of our climate too.

10.2 THE VALUE OF FORESTS

Can we put a value on these services? An acre of forest in the US may capture between one and four tons of carbon dioxide each year, with an average of about 2.5 tons. In the tropics, the numbers are much higher: a hectare of moist tropical forest may capture as much as 50 tons of carbon dioxide each year.[2] The US government recently assessed the social cost of carbon dioxide emissions as about $35 per ton, due to rise up to $65 by 2050 (Greenstone et al.). Using this as the value of capturing and storing a ton of CO2, the present value of this service provided by forests in the US using US sequestration rates is worth about $3,000 per acre. In other words, a typical acre of US forest is worth three thousand dollars for its carbon-capture services, using the US government's carbon price. In the tropics the value is dramatically greater, close to $24,000.

There is another way of approaching the carbon-capture value of forests, from the top down rather than from the bottom up. By bottom up I mean that the calculation I just went through takes a typical acre, works out how much carbon it captures, and values this service per acre. We end up with a value per acre but not a total value for all forests. But instead we can start with some facts about carbon sequestration at the global level. Global carbon emissions are about 30 billion tons CO2 per year. Forests absorb about 25 percent of this or 7.5 billion tons each year. If we value the removal of CO2 at $35 per ton, that's worth $262 billion per year. So if we focus on the CO2 capture role alone and take the US government social cost of carbon, the world's forests are worth $262 billion each year. This is neglecting the other contributions that forests make to welfare—via managing watersheds, and providing timber and energy. Clearly for the communities studied by Baland et al. the provision of energy is of fundamental importance.

If we let the social cost of carbon rise as suggested in the US government report, the present value of the stream of services from the world's forests is

[2] <http://www.fao.org/newsroom/en/focus/2006/1000247/index.html> (accessed 17 October 2013).

$9.5 trillion, over half of the national income of the US. However you look at it, forests are immensely valuable assets. In these calculations we've been using the US government's social cost of carbon, their estimate of the external costs of the emission of carbon dioxide. This is a well-researched number, but my sense is that it is too small. I think they've used too high a discount rate in their calculations, and that they have underestimated some of the costs of climate change, in particular those associated with the impact of a hotter world on food production (the mathematical models they used had not taken into account the most current research results) and those linked to the loss of biodiversity, on which they placed no value. So it is likely that these numbers, huge as they are, are underestimates.

10.3 GOVERNANCE

The services provided by forests are important and valuable, but nevertheless not easy to capture in the marketplace—they are not easily monetized. The reason is that they are either public goods, or positive external effects—or in some cases both. This means that providing the right incentives for proper forest management requires thought. As Baland et al. note, the interdependencies between households induced by the local public good aspects of forests are not sufficiently strong to provide incentives for efficient management. Furthermore, the most important external benefits from forest conservation are those associated with their role in the global carbon cycle, and these are benefits that accrue to the global community. They can only be internalized by global action, and the proposal known as REDD and mentioned above is an attempt to do just this.

An interesting issue is whether the payments for forest conservation proposed under REDD would in fact provide sufficient incentive for the villagers whom Baland et al. study to conserve their forests rather than allow then to deteriorate because of lopping for firewood. A number of studies, including those carried out for the Stern Review (Stern 2006), suggest that cutting for firewood is one of the lowest value destructive uses of forests, and that the opportunity cost of foregoing this use is low, and translates into $5 or less per ton of CO2. This is significantly less than estimates of the social cost of carbon emissions, and less even than the prices of emissions rights in the European Union's Emissions Trading Scheme. On this basis, internalizing the global externalities associated with forest conservation would solve the local governance problem too.

10.4 CONCLUSION

Forests really matter. They matter locally, affecting the living standards of local communities, and they matter globally, effecting the carbon cycle and hence the global climate. Conserving or extending them is one of the most cost-effective ways of tackling global warming. But this is a *global* problem, and forests are destroyed or degraded at a *local* level. We need to find ways of linking the local to the global to solve this problem. Baland, Das, and Mookherjee's findings, helping us to understand the local issues, are a useful step in this direction.

References

Greenstone, M., E. Kopits, and A. Wolverton (2011). *Estimating the Social Cost of Carbon for Regulatory Rulemakings: A Summary and Interpretation*. MIT Center for Energy and Environmental Policy Research WP 2011-006

Stern, N. (2006). *The Stern Review on the Economics of Climate Change*. Available at <http://webarchive.nationalarchives.gov.uk/+/http:/www.hm-treasury.gov.uk/independent_reviews/stern_review_economics_climate_change/stern_review_report.cfm> (accessed 17 October 2013).

World Bank (2010). *The Changing Wealth of Nations: Measuring Sustainable Development in the New Millenium*. Washington, DC: World Bank.

11

An Optimal Contract for Monitoring Illegal Exploitation of Co-Managed Forests in Benin

Albert N. Honlonkou and Rashid Hassan

11.1 INTRODUCTION

In Benin, natural forest reserves are under serious threat from legal and illegal loggers, poachers, hunters, farmers, herders, and wood traders. High population growth and technological change have led to increased exploitation of, and excessive pressure on, these resources. Available statistics show that one thousand square kilometers of forests are destroyed every year against only ten square kilometers of reforestation (MEHU 1993).

Until the late 1980s, public policymakers adopted a command-and-control approach to protecting the country's forests. Clearly this approach was ineffective, as the pressure on forest resources steadily increased and local populations continued to ignore all regulations applying to protected forests. This traditional protectionist approach also clashed with the argument that the sustainable management of natural resources did not require that they be fully preserved. Finally, it ignored the growing evidence that state and communal management regimes could be combined into hybrid systems, yielding better solutions than alternative, "pure" systems (whether state, communal, or private property). This provided the basis for co-management systems that promote decentralization of controls and active involvement of the local populations in the management of natural resources (Ostrom 1990; Eggertsson 1993). Common property management[1] is defined by Baland and Platteau (2002) as the collective regulation of both membership and the use of rights

[1] The literature makes a distinction between open common pool resource and closed common pool resource (Furubotn and Richter 2005) and we refer here to the latter.

supported by monitoring and sanctioning procedures, to effectively enforce the set rules. It offers an alternative to impersonal markets and coercive states (Dasgupta 2008).

Since 1990, the government of Benin introduced co-management as an institutional device to promote the sharing of power and responsibility among local forest resource user communities and resource management agencies. It was expected that this would promote more collaborative and coordinated actions among resource users and enhance adaptive management of natural forest reserves. The forest co-management system used by the government creates different roles for the various partners. The principal (the government) designs and executes contracts with cooperatives of local populations for monitoring local users who produce private and public goods aimed at protecting the forests (e.g. controlled logging and firewood collection, coal and honey production, and fishing). The role of the monitoring cooperatives is to protect the forest from poaching, illegal logging, illegal farming, and fires (PAMF 2002).

Contracts between the government, local cooperatives, and users display the traits of a typical agency relationship (Seabright 1993), and are plagued accordingly by problems of incentives and commitment common to agency relations. In the context of asymmetric information, agency theory deals with the structuring of contracts between the principal and his agents to manage the trade-off between risk sharing (when the principal and the agents have different attitudes towards risk) and incentives (to align the conflicting goals of the principal to that of the agents; Holmstrom 1979; Eisenhardt 1989). For example, local people retained as monitors in a forest co-management project have more information about the forest endowment in wild animals and timbers than the officials. This confers on them bargaining power, which they may use to continue to allow poaching (collusion with local users) while still benefiting from the government's support. Thus, some cooperatives may not fully cooperate with project officials if the contract between them and the community/government is not optimally designed. If this happens, the co-management system will fail to attain the stated objective, which is the sustainable management of the forests.

This chapter draws on agency theory literature to analyze the optimality of the typical contract between the government, local cooperatives, and users. In the following section we show some connections between common resource management and agency theory. We then present a model to analyze the agency relations among the parties. In Section 11.4, we employ the theoretical results from the previous section to evaluate the experience of common resource management in Benin. The last section distills key findings and implications of the study.

11.2 COMMON RESOURCE MANAGEMENT AND AGENCY THEORY

Since publication of the influential paper "The Tragedy of the Commons" by Hardin (1968), studies on common property resources have become widespread. The key lesson of these studies is that the outcomes of actual experiences with common property management are mixed; and there is a general concern about the reasons for these varying levels of performance among user-managed resource systems. Baland and Platteau (2003) argue that the support of the state impacts the efficiency of common management. There are two main ways in which the government can impede village-level management of common property resources. The first is by not providing services, such as technical expertise, conflict-resolution mechanisms, and legal support; the second is by interventions, deliberate or not, that undermine villagers' ability or willingness to cooperate. Dasgupta (2008) asserts that in studying common property resources, we are not only in the realm of natural resources, but institutions. Furubotn and Richter (2005) argue that even "self-organized and self-governed common property resources need an institutional structure that takes care of appropriation, provision, monitoring, enforcement, conflict resolution, and governance activities—as does the private ownership economy." In fact, any organization can be seen as a network of overlapping or nested principal-agent relations (Tirole 1986).

Faure-Grimaud et al. (2003) analyzed two types of agency relations. In a centralized organization, the principal can communicate and contract with both the supervisor and the agent. These two agents can then collude against the principal. In a decentralized organization, the principal only communicates with the supervisor, who in turn subcontracts with the agent. They show that the two organizations achieve the same outcome. Laffont and Rochet (1997) argue that the assumption made in the standard principal-agent model (that the cooperation of agents desired by the principal is induced by the contracts he offers to the agents, whereby each can maximize his own welfare according to the behavior of the other agents) is unrealistic. The principal is supposed to have complete control of the game played by the agents, so that unwanted communication or side contracting between agents can be prevented. Under asymmetric information, when the principal structures the contracts so as to minimize the informational rents given up to the agents because of their informational advantages, it is quite natural to expect a collective reaction on the part of the agents to protect their rents. Thus it becomes important to understand how agents can react to the rules of an organization and how a principal who is aware of potential collusion (formation of horizontal and vertical cliques) should design an incentive contract.

The delegation of monitoring to a supervisor, making the agency model a principal-supervisor-agent relationship (delegated principal-agent relation), is accompanied by the threat of collusion between the supervisor and the supervisee (agent) to "exploit" the principal. The principal then faces a double hazard problem and needs to create two types of incentives: one for the agent and the other for the supervisor. Paradoxically, Strausz (1997) succeeded in showing that with two contracts (principal-supervisor, principal-agent), the principal can regulate behaviors more accurately. This enhances the incentive effect of double contracting in delegations as explained below.

Because monitoring signals are private information, the supervisor has to decide if he should withhold them or make them public. Then, it is optimal for the principal (in the case of mediated relationship) to use a carrot and stick approach to incentives. This creates a commitment effect on the delegation of monitoring. In a direct (one-shot) relationship, the principal has an incentive to withhold information revealing that the agent has high performance, because this will force him to hand out carrots. But under this relationship, the reward structure creates incentives by letting the agent receive a greater reward when evidence of his performance is inconclusive than when it shows it to be high. This operates as a punishment for the principal and induces him to monitor. However, this higher monitoring has the drawback of reducing incentives for the agent to work harder than contracted. With delegation, this condition disappears. But against the incentive and commitment effects of delegation, the principal has to pay the cost to ensure that collusion between the supervisor and the agent does not occur. Nevertheless, Strausz (1997) showed that the incentive-effect is powerful enough to make delegation profitable even in the absence of the commitment-effect. Melumad and Mookherjee (1989) showed that in the presence of incomplete contract, delegation may perform better than centralized arrangements.

Even if an agency contract is optimal, the challenge remains to measure the output of the agents by investing in information systems. Monitoring (creating additional layers of management) is then necessary when effort and output are not observable and/or not verifiable. Based on the theoretical literature, it is possible to isolate some factors determining the choice of optimal contract in the presence of asymmetric information. When the contract designer needs to pay great attention to the incentives of the agent, the outcome is measurable, and the principal is risk averse, then an outcome-based contract is optimal. But when investments in information systems are available to verify the behavior of the agent, the outcome is uncertain, and the agent is risk averse, there will be a conflict in goals between the parties. In such cases, the behavior-based contract is preferred. Generally, however, full observation of actions is either impossible or prohibitively costly. In such situations, interest centers on the use of imperfect estimators of actions in contracting (Holmstrom 1979). At any rate, to devise optimal incentive contracts in a PAR, all available information should be used. This "sufficiency condition" creates demands for monitoring (Mirrlees 1999; Strausz 1997; Hart and Holmstrom 1987; Eisenhardt 1989; Shavell 1979; and Tirole 1986).

Instead of using absolute performance measure, outcome-based or behavior-based, it is possible to use relative performance measure. Nalebuff and Stiglitz (1983) explore the role of competition measured by relative (instead of absolute) performance as an incentive device. But the problem with penalties is that they can become self-perpetuating. The losers become demoralized, fail to continue competing, and thus continue to lose. Furthermore, in large groups, prizes alone are ineffective in motivating effort as the expected prizes are too small to stop shirking. Worse, the presence of a sure loser destroys everyone's incentive to work hard. For competition to work, participants should be similar. Handicapping is possible to equilibrate relative different abilities; but this may be harder, and inequitable to implement (Miller 2005).

This brief review of the literature shows that agency theory may help construct socially powerful incentives, supported by external enforcement, in situations where mutual affection, pro-social disposition and long-term relationship are lacking or insufficient (Dasgupta 2008). We have used this theoretical framework to develop an analytical model to study the experience of villages' forest commons management in Benin.

11.3 THE ANALYTICAL MODEL

In this section, we set up a model to analyze the role of incentives in the management of a villages' forest common. We also analyze the effect of some parameters on the behavior of agents involved.

11.3.1 The Model

Our setting consists of a village common. This is a forest to which villagers (users) have historical rights but no deed that can be enforced by a court. This is a common situation in developing countries (Dasgupta and Mäler 2004). Prior to government intervention, the forest common was managed by the villagers who set up an organization to control utilization of the forest and exclude outsiders. Typically, the government will intervene using the argument that the forest is misused. The government's first intervention would be to consolidate multiple village forests into a single area. While some use rights would still be granted to the communities, compliance with rules would now be monitored by an official forest police force, in charge of detecting and punishing any misuse of the forest. This policy has proven inefficient in Benin as it has resulted in continuing battles and/or collusion between the forest police and community users. After the second United Nations' Conference on Environment and Development in Rio de Janeiro (Brazil), government policy shifted to promote co-management of forests. We will now model the organization instituted by the new policy. By doing so, we will be able to appreciate if the incentives created are conducive to a more effective management of the forests.

The new co-management organization involves complex relationships between the government (the public project officials and forest police), the forest cooperatives, and the community of users—agency relationships that are difficult to model. But from this complexity, we can isolate the main contract: a principal-supervisor-agent hierarchy involving three players whose objectives are to maximize their expected payoffs.

The first player is a risk-neutral government (*G*). This is actually a group of players, comprised of public officials and project agents. We are then assuming that all of these players have the same objective defined below, and succeed in solving any free rider problem. Note that in the agency relationship, G is the uninformed principal.

The second player is a risk-neutral supervisory agency (*S*). This is also a group of players, made up of forest police and local cooperatives of hunters. In the spirit of co-management principles, the new organization uses the former local supervisory device to detect illegal users; and while the forest police and the local cooperative of hunters are not collapsed into a single agency, their objective is congruent. The spotting and reporting of cheating to forest guards as social fencing is practiced for example, in India (Lise 2005). The cooperative of hunters is hired by the principal to detect and report any forest misuse to the forest police. The latter is the only legal structure entitled to punish illegal users.

The third agent is a risk-neutral user of the forest (*A*)[2]. Here again, we have a group of users, which may be divided into two categories. The first is a proportion ρ of users, called strategic users, who are potential violators of the forest use rules—violating only when it is rational to do so. The second category is comprised of the proportion $(1 - \rho)$ of users who never violate (conformists). Their behavior may be determined by their full internalization of the former social norm that prescribes a friendly use of natural resources. The categorization of the users into conformists (habitual compliers) and strategists is a way to incorporate explicitly ethical standards (normative valuations and obligations) as parameters in the analysis. This allows us to study the effect of their erosion. Some people (especially in traditional society) routinely obey rules not based on cost-benefit analysis, but because of overriding norms (see Graetz et al 1986, for the case of tax compliance).

The simplification described above conforms to the three axioms of Tirole (1986) necessary to model a three-level hierarchy:

[2] A potential violator should not be risk averse.

1) The principal (here the government) lacks time and knowledge for a direct supervision of the agents (forest users). Strausz (1997) criticized this assumption as reminiscent of why the principal needs an agent in the first place. But this criticism does not hold because in our case study local users are already present within or in close proximity, and direct government supervision (forest police) has failed in the past.
2) There is a unique supervisory agency. The co-management system we describe involves many villages but at each village level, there is only one supervisor (a combination of the forest police and a local cooperative).
3) The supervisory agency lacks either the time or the resources to run the vertical structure directly (axiom trivially implied)[3].

Furthermore, we add the assumption that while our model analyzes potential collusion between the agent and the supervisor, it ignores the free-riding problem within groups of players. We also assume away complications like common agency and repeated relations (Arrow 1986; Bernheim and Whinston 1986).

Let us now describe the actions of the players and the information structure of the game.

Two-agent (A) types: the conformist user and the strategic user. The conformist user always plays legal low harvest (*L*). The strategic user, a potential violator, has the choice between illegal high harvest (*H*) and legal low harvest (*L*). We normalize *L*, the low rate of individual use of the forest, to be 0. We assume that the value of the forest and its provisioning services are converted into monetary values. The low harvest may mean an allowed right to gather wood, fodder, and fruits in the forest. We suppose that the cost of harvesting is 0. This is a reasonable assumption in a setting where the opportunity cost of labor is close to 0 (Lise 2005). We suppose that the strategic user plays *L* with probability a, and H with probability $(1 - a)$. If the user chooses H and is caught, he pays a fine w_h that draws his payoff below 0. The harvest of the agent is not observable. We assume that the user has access to an external (non-forest) income *I*.

The supervisory agency (S) chooses to monitor with probability s or not to monitor with probability $(1 - s)$. We assume that a costly monitoring technology is available, controlled by the supervisor, and can be implemented at cost c. This could be the cost of a number of trips per month to the forests to monitor illegal users. The efficiency parameter of the technology is λ, such that, after monitoring, the supervisor observes the true action with probability λ and nothing with probability $(1 - \lambda)$. Then $c = c(\lambda)$ and $c(.)$ is assumed to be increasing and convex in λ. The monitoring technology is imperfect, but there is no

[3] Strausz (1997) asserts that monitoring is profitable because of two assumptions: 1) monitoring is not verifiable and therefore non-contractible, and 2) monitoring signals are private information.

type II error (the probability of assuming that a user violates when he doesn't) in the sense that any result is hard evidence against the agent's behavior. The monitoring procedure itself is not verifiable. The evidence is private information for the supervisor; but if it is revealed, it can be verified by a third party.

Since the monitoring signals are private information, the supervisor can conceal information. Thus, if the supervisor claims that he observes nothing, this may be the outcome of one of three possibilities: the supervisor did not monitor at all (N); he effectively monitors (M) but obtains no results; or he effectively monitors (M), obtains results but decides to conceal them by colluding with the agent. The only verifiable states of the world are therefore (1) state H, where the supervisor reveals that the harvest is H; (2) state L, where the supervisor reveals that the harvest is L; and (3) state N, where the supervisor reveals nothing. In cases where S knows the true harvest and finds that it is high, he chooses to reveal it with probability r and to conceal it with probability $(1 - r)$.

The supervisor will conceal information when he succeeds in reaching an agreement with the strategic user to share the gain from violation. In this case, they share the gain from collusion (w_h), a part βk for S and a part $(1 - \beta)k$ for the strategic user. As in Strausz (1997), we assume that collusion is accompanied by a transfer from the strategic user to the supervisor, conditional on the supervisor's report. k is a transaction cost parameter ($0 \leq k \leq 1$). The higher the value of k, the lower the cost of transaction. The reasons for introducing transaction cost are that side transfers have to be given in stealth, that a mechanism has to be designed to ensure enforceability and the inefficiency of bargaining, that the supervisor and agent may have moral costs (shame and social embarrassments) or fear detection of higher order supervision (see also Laffont 2000)[4]. β ($0 \leq \beta \leq 1$) depends on the bargaining power of the strategic user relative to the supervisor (Baiman et al. 1991). Furthermore, only the coalition between the supervisor and the agent matters because of its possibility to lower the expected utility of the principal (Tirole 1988).

The government (G) offers contract w to the agent (A) and contract t to the supervisor (S). We assume that $w = (w_l, - w_h, w_n)$ and $t = (t_l, t_h, t_n) \geq 0$. For w, w_h stands as penalty or fines for damages for high-level (illegal and non-sustainable) harvesting. Because we normalize the low harvest to 0, we shall assume that $H - w_h < 0$; otherwise, violators lose nothing (and in fact gain) by playing high. We further normalize w by assuming that the principal pays nothing to the agent when he does not play H, and nothing to the supervisor when he reveals nothing. That is $w_l = w_n = t_n = 0$. With this normalization $w = (0, -w_h, 0)$ and $t = (t_l, t_h, 0) \geq 0$. The rationale behind these normalizations of the payments to the agent is that the latter is not punished when the

[4] As usual in the relevant literature, we do not model the bargaining nor address the enforceability of the side contract.

supervisor reveals nothing. Here, "the benefit of doubt" may be invoked as in the judiciary system. As usual we assume that the supervisor is more encouraged to spot violation than to spot conformism, that is, $t_h > t_l$.

We assume that the net revenue of the user cannot be very negative, so that $H < w_h \leq H + I$, where I is the non-forest income. This assumption also permits avoidance of a situation whereby no violation can be obtained with small proportion of conformists and small probability of monitoring by setting an infinite fine.

The timing of the game is defined by the following seven stages:

(1) G offers a contract w to A and a contract t to S;

(2) S accepts or rejects the contracts;

(3) Nature chooses the type of user: the strategic user with probability ρ and the conformist with probability $1 - \rho$;

(4) A and S play a simultaneous move game: A chooses the level of harvest (H or L) and S chooses to monitor (M) or not (N);

(5) If S monitors, Nature reveals the true harvest with probability λ;

(6) In cases where S knows the true harvest and finds it to be high, he chooses to reveal or to conceal it;

(7) Payoffs are realized.

Useful notations and definitions are compiled in Table 11.1.

The extensive form of the game is represented in Figure 11.1.

We analyze the relevant part of the game where the government proposes a contract and the supervisor accepts it. Using the different assumptions and notations, we can now compile the expected payoffs of the players in Table 11.2.

For the different outcomes' scenarios, the expected payoffs of the three agents are given in Table 11.3. We assume that protecting the natural forest resource (public good) has a monetary value of G (social benefit). The protection is financed through t and w, which represent, respectively, payments by the principal to the supervisor, and to the agent, from some government (public) budget.

From Table 11.3, we can now sum up and record the expected payoffs of the three agents.

Government's expected payoff U_G:

The government's expected payoff from the contract is:

$$U_G(w,t,a,s,r) = [1-\rho(1-a)s\lambda(G-t_l) + \rho(1-a)s\lambda r(G-H-t_h+w_h)] + \rho(1-a)(1-s\lambda r(G-H) + [(1-\rho)(1-s\lambda) + \rho a(1-s\lambda)]G \quad (1)$$

Table 11.1 Notation and definitions for the extensive game

Name	Notation	Definition
Government, the principal	*G*	The group of players made of public officials and project agents
Supervisory agency	*S*	The group of players made of forest police and local cooperative of hunters
Forest user	*A*	The group of forest users
Proportion of strategic users	*P*	The group of potential violators of the forest-use rules. Then 1 – ρ is the proportion of users who never violate (the conformists)
Legal low harvest	*L*	The level of harvest that causes no forest degradation
Illegal high harvest	*H*	The level of harvest that degrades the forest
The supervisor's action of monitoring	*M*	Pure strategy
The supervisor's action of not monitoring	*N*	Pure strategy
Strategist's behavior strategy of playing *L*	*A*	The strategist's probability of playing low harvest. Then (1 – *a*) is the probability of playing high harvest
Supervisor's behavior strategy of monitoring	*S*	The supervisor's probability of monitoring. Then 1 – *s* is the probability of not monitoring
The supervisor's strategy of revealing information when he gets a strategist playing *H*	*R*	Thus 1 – *r* is the probability of concealing information when the supervisor gets a strategist's user
External (non-forest) income of the user	*I*	
The cost of implementing the monitoring technology	*C*	The cost to monitor the illegal users inside the forest
The efficiency parameter of the monitoring technology	*Λ*	The probability of observing the true action of the user when monitoring. Thus 1 – λ is the probability of observing nothing

(Continued)

Table 11.1 (Continued)

Name	Notation	Definition
Transaction cost parameter	K	The proportion of the proceeds from collusion between the supervisor and the agent kept by the supervisor. $1- k$ is the proportion kept by the strategist user.
The proportion of the gain from collusion going to the supervisor	B	Thus $1 - \beta$ is the gain from collusion going to the strategic user
The fine paid by a strategic user to the Government when caught	w_h	
The payment of the principal to the agent when he plays low harvest	w_l	
The payment of the principal to the agent when the supervisor observes nothing	w_n	
The payment vector to the agent	W	$w = (w_l, - w_h,)$
The payment of the principal to the supervisor when he observes and reveals that the strategic user is playing high	t_h	
The payment of the principal to the supervisor when he observes and reveals that the strategic user is playing low	t_l	
The payment of the principal to the supervisor when he observes or reveals nothing	t_n	
The payment vector to the supervisor	T	$t = (t_l, - t_h, t_n)$
The expected payoff of player i	U_i	Examples: U_G, U_S, U_A

Agent's expected payoff U_A:
The agent's expected payoff is

$$U_A(w,t,a,s,r) = \rho(1-a)[s\lambda r(I+H-w_h) + s\lambda(1-r)(I+H-w_h + (1-\beta k w_h) + (1-s\lambda)(I+H) + (\rho a + (1+\rho))I \tag{2}$$

It is important to note that the expected payoff of a random user who is playing low is $[1-\rho(1-a)]I$[5]. Obviously, the aggregate probability of playing low and the associated expected payoff decreases with ρ and increases with a.

[5] To obtain this, add outcomes 1, 2, 3, 8, 9, and 10.

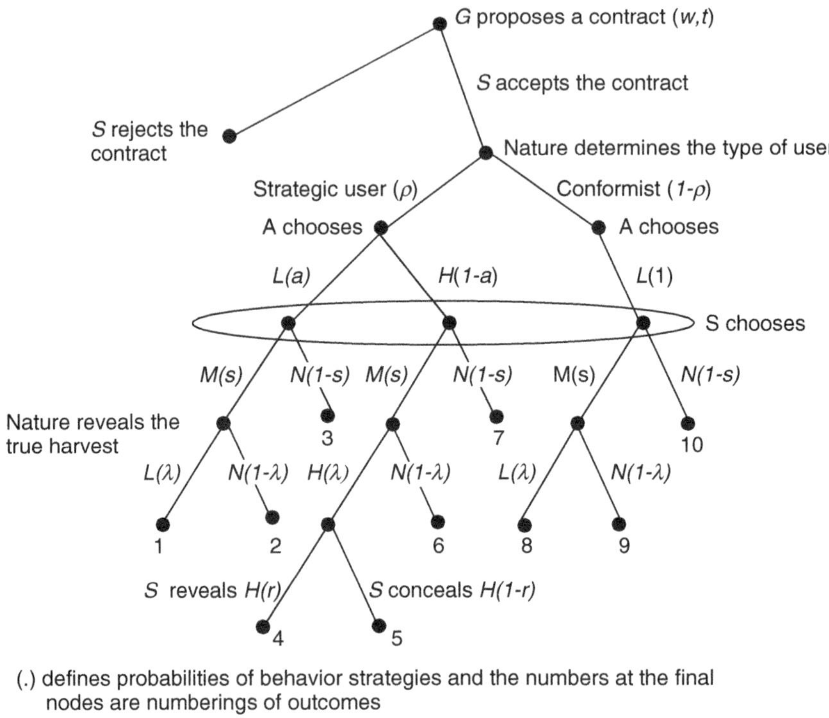

Figure 11.1 The principal-agent game in extensive form

Table 11.2 Extensive game outcomes' scenarios

Outcome number	Strategic user (ρ)	A chooses L (a)	S monitors M (s)	Nature reveals the true harvest (λ)	S reveals H (r)	Outcome
1	YES	YES	YES	YES	—	$\rho as\lambda$
2	YES	YES	YES	NO	—	$\rho as(1 - \lambda)$
3	YES	YES	NO	—	—	$\rho a(1 - s)$
4	YES	NO	YES	YES	YES	$\rho(1 - a)s\lambda r$
5	YES	NO	YES	YES	NO	$\rho(1 - a)s\lambda(1 - r)$
6	YES	NO	YES	NO	—	$\rho(1 - a)s(1 - \lambda)$
7	YES	NO	NO	—	—	$\rho(1 - a)(1 - s)$
8*	NO	YES	YES	YES	—	$(1 - \rho)s\lambda$
9*	NO	YES	YES	NO	—	$(1 - \rho)s(1 - \lambda)$
10*	NO	YES	NO	—	—	$(1 - \rho)(1 - s)$

* *Note that for outcomes 8, 9, and 10, a =1 for the conformist user.*

Table 11.3 Expected payoffs of the three agents (L is normalized to 0 and hence does not appear in Table)

Outcome number	A	S	G
1	$\rho as\lambda^{*}I$	$\rho as\lambda^{*}(t_{l}\_c)$	$\rho as\lambda^{*}(G-t_{l})$
2	$\rho as(1-\lambda)^{*}I$	$\rho as(1-\lambda)^{*}(0-c)$	$\rho as(1-\lambda)^{*}G$
3	$\rho a(1-s)^{*}I$	$\rho a(1-s)^{*}0$	$\rho a(1-s)^{*}G$
4	$\rho(1-a)s\lambda r^{*}(H+I-w_{h})$	$\rho(1-a)s\lambda r^{*}(t_{h}-c)$	$\rho(1-a)s\lambda r^{*}$ $(G-H-t_{h}+w_{h})$
5	$\rho(1-a)s\lambda(1-r)^{*}$ $(H+I-w_{h}+(1-\beta)\text{k}$	$\rho(1-a)s\lambda(1-r)^{*}$ $(\beta kw_{h}-c)$	$\rho(1-a)s\lambda(1-r)^{*}$ $(G-H)$
6	$\rho(1-a)s(1-\lambda)^{*}(H+I)$	$\rho(1-a)s(1-\lambda)^{*}(0-c)$	$\rho(1-a)s(1-\lambda)^{*}(G-H)$
7	$\rho(1-a)(1-s)^{*}(H+I)$	$\rho(1-a)(1-s)^{*}0$	$\rho(1-a)(1-s)^{*}(G-H)$
8	$(1-\rho)s\lambda^{*}I$	$(1-\rho)s\lambda^{*}(t_{l}-c)$	$(1-\rho)s\lambda^{*}(G-t_{l})$
9	$(1-\rho)s(1-\lambda)^{*}I$	$(1-\rho)s(1-\lambda)^{*}(0-c)$	$(1-\rho)s(1-\lambda)^{*}G$
10	$(1-\rho)(1-s)^{*}I$	$(1-\rho)(1-s)^{*}0$	$(1-\rho)(1-s)^{*}G$
Total	U_{A}	U_{S}	U_{G}

Supervisor's expected payoff U_S:
The supervisor's expected payoff is

$$U_S(w,t,a,s,r)=\rho s\lambda[a(t_l-c)+(1-a)r(t_h-c) \\ +(1-a)(1-r)(\beta kw_h-c)](1-\rho)s\lambda(t_l-c)-s(1-\lambda)c \quad (3)$$

11.3.2 Analysis of Incentives

We now study the (possibly mixed) sub-game "perfect equilibria" with imperfect information described above.

First of all, before the supervisor accepts to be engaged, the payments t_l, t_h, the cost (c), and the efficiency parameter (λ) of the supervision technology, should be such that $U_s \geq 0$, that is,

$$\rho s\lambda[a(t_l-c)+(1-a)r(t_h-c)+(1-a)(1-r)(\beta kw_h-c)]+s(1-\rho)\lambda(t_l-c)\geq s(1-\lambda)sc$$

Or,

$$\rho s\lambda(1-a)[rt_h+(1-r)\beta kw_h]+s\lambda[1-\rho(1-a)]t_l\geq sc$$

This equation asserts that the supervisor accepts the contract if the expected income from supervision is at least equal to the expected cost of supervision. It is also important to note that even if the payments of the principal to the supervisor are 0, there is a penalty level w_h at which the supervisor may accept a contract and expect to collude systematically with violators ($r=0$). That is the case if:

$$\rho s\lambda(1-a)\beta k w_h + \lambda[1-\rho(1-a)]t_l \geq c$$

The odds that this will happen increase with higher proportions of the following: strategic violators, the level of efficiency parameter of the supervision technology, and the extraction power of the corrupt supervisor (β). The odds also increase when the transaction cost of collusion is low (k high).

Using backward induction, we start with the supervisor who has the choice of revealing that a strategic user is in violation, or concealing this and colluding with the user. This is an important issue because managing common property resources involves cooperation which is beneficial (Dasgupta 2008), or side contracts as collusion which are detrimental, especially when the contracts are incomplete (Itoh 1993; Tirole 1988). In such a relationship, the reporting agent (the supervisor) has an incentive to misrepresent because transfers between the parties depend on his report (Moorkherjee and Png 1989; Tirole 1988).

The choice of the supervisor to collude or not to collude depends on the sign of the derivative of his payoff (equation 3) with respect to r. We have:

$$\frac{\partial U_s(.)}{\partial r} = \rho s\lambda[(1-a)(t_h - c) - (1-a)(\beta k w_h - c)$$

or,

$$\frac{\partial U_s(.)}{\partial r} = \rho s\lambda[(1-a)[(t_h - \beta k w_h] \quad (4)$$

Equation (4) establishes important relations between t_h and w_h. To avoid the capture of the co-management system by users and supervisors ($r = 0$), the government should set the payment of the supervisor higher than the expected bribe ($t_h > \beta k w_h$). This is an important requirement because this means that the government should pay the supervisor more than the proceeds of violation when he succeeds in catching a violator.[6] Otherwise, the supervisor will turn his information of low

[6] Since we are not modeling a multi-period setting, we exclude the perverse situation where the supervisor may pay the user to violate more, either to increase the proceeds from violations to be shared, or to induce the government to increase the supervisor's payment. It is shown that if the supervisor obtains additional private information before contracting with the principal, he can increase his informational rent (Melumad et al. 1995). Indeed, the government can counteract this by increasing the fine and then reversing the power relation between the supervisor and

or high level of harvesting into "observe nothing." A supervisor is totally useless if his independence can be compromised with relative ease, that is, the collusion costs are small (Khalil and Lawarrée 2006). It is important not to forget that given the rules, together with the punishment and reward structure for transgressions, the actual responses are determined by the participants' behavioral characteristics (Hurwicz 1973). Solutions lie in recruiting honest supervisors (low *k* or high transaction cost), or using higher order supervision (external auditing). But these solutions also entail agency problems (adverse selection) and costs.

From here on, we assume that the supervisor will always reveal any violation ($r = 1$) if he knows it. The different payoffs become:

$$U_G(w,t,a,s,r) = [1-\rho(1-a)s\lambda(G-t_l) + \rho(1-a)s\lambda r(G-H-t_h+w_h)] + \rho(1-a)(1-s\lambda)(G-H) + [((1-s\lambda)+(1-\rho(1-a))]G$$

or,

$$U_G(w,t,a,s,r) = G-[1-\rho(1-a)]s\lambda t_l - \rho(1-a)s\lambda(t_h-w_h) - \rho(1-a)H \quad (1')$$

$$U_A(w,t,a,s,r) = \rho(1-a)[H - s\lambda w_h] + I \quad (2')$$

$$U_S(w,t,a,s,r) = \rho s\lambda[a(t_l-c)+(1-a)(t_h-c)] + (1-\rho)s\lambda(t_l-c) - s[\rho(1-\lambda)+(1-\rho)(1-\lambda)]$$

or,

$$U_S(w,t,a,s,r) = [1-\rho(1-a)]s\lambda t_l + \rho s\lambda(1-a)t_h - sc) \quad (3')$$

Assuming that the values of other outside options of *A* and *S* are 0, (a, s) is feasible if:

$$U_A(w,t,a,s) \geq 0 \; and \; U_S(w,t,a,s) \geq 0 \quad (5)$$

A Nash Equilibrium (a^*, s^*) of the sub-game induced by the contracts proposed by the government is given by the following two maximizing programs:

$$P1: a^* \in \arg \underset{a\in[0,1]}{Max}\, U_A(w,t,a,s^*) \; and \; s^* \in \arg \underset{s\in[0,1]}{Max}\, U_S(w,t,a^*,s) \; subject \; to \; (5) \quad (6)$$

the user. Moreover, the possibility that the principal bribes the supervisor to retain information that is favorable to the agent (in order to pay the latter a lower wage) can be made innocuous by an adequate organizational design (Tirole 1988).

A contract (w,t) is feasible where there exists a viable Nash Equilibrium between the agent and the supervisor.

Following Strausz (1997), the optimal contract $(w^{**},t^{**},a^{**},s^{**})$ is the subgame perfect equilibrium of the game, and is given by the maximizing program *P2*:

$$P2:(a^{**},s^{**},w^{**},t^{**}) \in \arg \underset{a^*,s^*,w,t}{Max}\, U_A(w,t,a^*,s^*) \; subject\ to\ (6) \tag{7}$$

The solutions to *P1* are given by the following first-order conditions (ignoring the feasibility constraints):

$$\frac{\partial U_A(.)}{\partial a} = \rho[s\lambda w_h - H] \leq 0,\ a=0\ if\ \rho[s\lambda w_h - H] < 0,\ a=1\ if\ \rho[s\lambda w_h - H] > 0 \tag{8.1}$$

Equation (8.1) says that the agent will never comply (*a=0*) if the expected fine is less than the expected gain from violation, and will always comply in the contrary situation.

$$\begin{aligned} \frac{\partial U_S(.)}{\partial_S} &= [1-\rho(1-a)]\lambda t_l + \rho\lambda(1-a)t_h \leq c, \\ & s=0\ if\ [1-\rho(1-a)]\lambda t_l + \rho\lambda(1-a)t_h < c\ and \\ & s=1\ if\ [1-\rho(1-a)]\lambda t_l + \rho\lambda(1-a)t_h > c \end{aligned} \tag{8.2}$$

Equation (8.2) says that the supervisor will never supervise ($s = 0$) if the expected marginal income from supervision is less than the expected marginal cost of supervision, and will always supervise in the contrary instance.

If the inequalities are strict, then $a = 0$ for (8.1) and $s = 0$ for (8.2).

If an optimal contract exists, 8.1 and 8.2 should bind in equilibrium. If not, since U_A and U_S are respectively linear in *a* and *s*, this would mean that the participation constraints (5) are not satisfied. Furthermore, if $s = 0$, $a = 0$, the strategic user will always violate, and the hiring of a supervisor is useless. In the sequel, we will then assume that 8.1 and 8.2 are binding and derive a^* and s^* accordingly. The fact that $0 < a^*, s^* < 1$ makes auditing random (see Mookherjee and Png 1989).

$$a^* = 1 - \frac{c - \lambda t_l}{\rho\lambda(t_h - t_l)} \tag{9}$$

and

$$s^* = \frac{H}{\lambda w_h} \tag{10}$$

To be sensible, equation (9) implies that $c - \lambda t_l \geq 0$, or $t_l \leq (c / \lambda)$, that is, the payment for discovering low users should be less than the effective cost of the technology. To understand this, suppose the contrary. Then equation (8.2) shows that $[1 - \rho(1-a)]\lambda t_l + \rho\lambda(1-a)t_h > c$, so that the supervisor will supervise with certainty. The same reasoning shows that $\lambda w_h \geq H$ or $\lambda w_h \geq (H / \lambda)$ (the effective rent from violation), because otherwise the agent will always play high, that is, violate.

We will then suppose that $1 > a^* > 0$ and $1 > s^* > 1$ so that equation (9) and (10) will be used to characterize the structure of the payments made by the principal to the supervisor and agent.

These equations give some insights concerning the double interpretation of the infinite reward scheme analyzed in the monitoring literature (Strausz 1997). First, an infinite punishment ($w_h \rightarrow +\infty$) will induce the agent to comply with certainty (equation 8.1) with almost no monitoring (equation 10). Indeed, unbounded payment schemes can be used to induce any sort of behavior (Border and Sobel 1987). Second, an infinite payment to the supervisor ($t_h \rightarrow \infty$) will induce the agent to play low harvest with certainty (equation 9). Those results mean that even if relatively efficient reward schemes can be constructed, an optimal contract does not obtain (see Strausz 1997; Mirrlees 1999). Any structure of rewards' scheme will always be surpassed by a better one capable of ensuring that a^* and s^* are close to 1.

One implication of these findings is that the possibility of collusion between the agent and the supervisor is especially plausible when the contract approaches efficiency (w_h very large). In fact, a wedge between w_h and t_h suffices to trigger corruption practices between the agent and the supervisor. Clearly an incentive contract with a harsh punishment of the offender and low compensation for the monitor is counterproductive. If the punishment should fit the crime, the compensation of the monitor should also fit the crime.

11.3.3 Comparative Statics Analyses

We perform in this section a comparative statistics' analysis of the influence of some key parameters in the model (assuming interior solutions, i.e., $0 < a^* < 1$ and $0 < s^* < 1$). Given the payments of the principal to the agent and the supervisor, a change in the environment (parameters) triggers the reactions of the latter who compute new reactions functions (9 and 10). Knowing these new reactions, the principal updates the payments to assure optimality for himself.

Finally, the agent and the supervisor incorporate the new payments. Given the structure we have given to the model, this involves deriving the comparative statistics for five variables w_h, t_l, t_h, a, s, and five parameters ρ, λ, h, c, and G[7]. This amounts to twenty-five comparative statistics. This is clearly a daunting task. Nevertheless, we can garner some results by assuming that the agent and the supervisor take the payments of the principal as given, that is, as parameters fixed by an administrative or legislative body. This is a realistic assumption because the government rarely alters the payments as a response to environmental change. But then, we are no closer to the equilibrium than we would be from our former game. Table 11.4 gives the results based on the differentiation of equations (9) and (10) with respect to the relevant parameters.

Some results displayed by Table 11.4 may seem counterintuitive. For example, parameters supposed to have effects on one player might affect another player instead. But we should remember that the results depend on the interaction between the agent and the supervisor.

The belief that deteriorating social norms increase the likelihood of degradation of common resources makes the effects of change in the proportion of strategic users (ρ) particularly interesting. An increase in the proportion of strategic users decreases the compliance rate of the strategic users and has no effect on the supervision rate. An increase in ρ has no direct impact on individual strategic users. It increases the proportion of dishonest users and then the productivity of supervision: the discovery of illegal users and the reception of higher payments t_h. So the supervision rate increases. Then a increases, triggering a decrease in s. In equilibrium, s remains constant and a decreases.

Table 11.4 Some comparative statics' results (the payments to the principal are given)

Parameters	a^*	s^*
ρ	–	0
λ	+	–
h	0	+
c	–	0
w_h	0	–
t_l	*	0
t_h	+	0

0=no effect,+ = positive effect,–= negative effect, * = undetermined/ ambiguous

[7] The non-forest income does not appear in the first-order conditions and then is irrelevant for comparative statics analysis.

Then our model shows that when social norms deteriorate, this is likely to increase the misuse of natural resources.

An increase in the efficiency of the supervision technology (λ) (independent of its cost) decreases the supervision rate and increases the rate of compliance. When λ increases, noncompliance is easily detected so that a increases. But then supervision becomes less profitable, and s decreases. The decrease in s triggers a decrease in a. Our model shows that the net effect on s is negative and the one on a is positive. The main insight is that when the supervision technology is improved, care should be taken so that the effort in supervision is maintained. This will reinforce the direct effect on compliance rate.

When the stake of noncompliance (H) is high, supervision is high, but this has no effect on the violation rate. An immediate effect of an increase in H is a decrease in the compliance rate a. But then s will increase, triggering an increase in a. The net effect is an increase in s and no effect on a. These results show that rich forests are not always associated with higher violation rates than the poor ones, so long as adequate incentives are given to the supervisors.

An increase in the cost of the supervision technology (c), independent of its efficiency, has a negative effect on a, but no effect on s. An increase in c has no direct effect on a, but decreases the payoff from more supervision, so that s decreases. A decrease in s will induce a decrease in a, then an increase in s followed by an increase in a. The net effect of c shows that a massive investment in the supervision technology (by giving subsidies) may be the relevant policy to encourage supervision and deter noncompliance. But care should be taken to sustain the supervision rate.

An increase in the fine (w_h) has no effect on the compliance rate (a), but decreases the rate of supervision. This is at odds with the literature on crime, which consistently found that the level of fines has a negative effect on the violation rate (Becker 1968; Graetz et al. 1986; Davis 1988). To be sure, an increase in w_h has a positive direct effect on the compliance rate (see equation 8.1), but the rise in a is followed by a decrease in s. This decrease in s in turn implies a decrease in a. Our model shows that the net effect is to keep a constant. This result should remind us that it is insufficient to keep the level of fines high if one wants to deter crime. This should be accompanied by an effort to maintain the level of supervision aimed at detecting and punishing violators.

An increase in payment for detecting the compliance of a user has an ambiguous effect on the level of compliance, but none on the supervision level. An increase in t_l increases the return from the supervision of compliers (strategic users or natural compliers), and then has a positive effect on the level of supervision. This is followed by an increase in a, followed by a decrease of s. This result shows that the performance of supervision should not only be measured by and rewarded according to the level of the crime rate, but also by the rate of population that may be certified to be conforming.

Finally, an increase in payment for detecting violators (t_h) has a positive effect on a, but no effect on s. This is in conformity with what is ordinarily believed and applied: a prize for those who can catch criminals. An increase in t_h increases the return from supervision. An increase in s implies an increase in a, compensating for the former increase in s. This cancellation effect is accompanied by a decrease in a. The net effect of the increase of t_h on a is positive. But placed in relation to the preceding result on t_p, we set forth the argument that the effort to "certificate" compliance, and that of succeeding in spotting criminals, should be properly rewarded.

The following section demonstrates to what extent this analytical framework is applicable to co-management experiences in Benin.

11.4 EVALAUATING FOREST CO-MANAGEMENT EXPERIENCES IN BENIN

In this section we apply the agency analytical framework described above to Benin's experience in co-management of its forest reserves. We evaluate against this the features of the contracts designed by the government to support common resource management in the forests of Benin. We will show below that the standards are not adhered to, yielding a poor performance.

11.4.1 Case-study Description

The classified forests of Agoua, Kouffé Mounts, and Wari-Maroare, located in the Center–West of Benin, total 370,000 hectares, spread over several regions (Collines, Donga, and Borgou). Traditional relationships between local populations, the forest, and the state are in conflict. While there is some tolerance of communities' use of the forest products, they have to sustain some vagaries of the forest police. They are often charged and fined if they are convicted of some misuse. Nevertheless, there is some kind of informal sharing of the forest among the local villages. The traditional management of a village's forest is organized around the Chief of the village's land and the Chief of the hunter's brotherhood. In the village hierarchy, the Chief of the village's land is at the top, in charge of distributing the land and ruling on disputes. The hunters' brotherhood assures the security of the village (including human beings and forests) against intruders, under the auspices of a local divinity named "Ogu", the god of iron. Thus, while the state does not recognize ownership rights of the village community to the forests, the local populations develop security measures against inside and outside aggressions. So, *"whatever the source of the authority that underpins the ownership structure, the local commons are not open to outsiders: they are not "open access resources"* (Dasgupta and Mäler 2004).

But, with population pressure and increasing conflicts between local populations, outside intruders and the forest police, it became urgent to improve the system of management of the forests. Following the new paradigm of including local populations in the management of their "own resources", a local non-governmental organization (NGO) tried to organize the village brotherhoods into a confederation with the help of donors. The idea was to make the local populations sensitive to the sustainable use and protection of forests beyond village-level interests. But when donors' assistance ceased, this initiative was abandoned.

The Beninese government then stepped in, elaborated, financed, and implemented a project (the "Projet d'Aménagement des massifs Forestiers") with funding from the African Development Bank. Among the main interventions of the project is the implementation of a system of forest co-management involving local populations.

In the setup of the co-management system, local populations are encouraged to create cooperatives, through which they receive support and payments from the environmental project. The support they end up getting depends on the activities they undertake. Thus, we can distinguish three types of cooperatives.

The first type produces private goods that can be sold in markets independently of the project (honey, oil, intensive farming, non-conventional animal breeding, etc.). These activities are encouraged to reduce the pressure on forests. Because of their private nature, the income generated by these activities is directly linked to the efforts that the members of the cooperatives provide.

The second category of cooperatives produces semi-private/semi-public goods (seedling nurseries) that they sell directly to the project to develop the forest. Because of the limited market for these products, the income generated depends strongly on the price fixed by the project officials.

The third category of cooperatives produces public goods such as reforestation, control of illegal users, intruders/poachers. For these activities, the cooperatives are employed by the project/public officials as wage-workers to supervise the use of the forests. Here we have an agency including the government as the principal, the hunters' brotherhood as the supervisor, and the local users as agents.

Since the local users are too unorganized to impact the principal, we can employ the traditional principal-agent theory (enriched by the presence of a supervisor). This lack of organization among local users led the project to focus on making the relation between the government and the supervisor a proper principal-agent relation on its own. In the case-study forests, there are thirty-three hunters' brotherhoods organized in a three-level confederation: local (village) level, inter-district level and inter-forest level. Our analysis concentrates on the performance of supervisors (the brotherhoods) on which we have data.

The elements of a typical contract between the government and the supervisor read as follow:

- Contract holder: village hunters' brotherhood
- Object: Surveillance and protection of forests against late fires, transhumance, illegal wood exploitation, poaching, and land development
- Amount: CFA 1,639,440 (US$ 3,279)
- Duration: 12 months
- The contract is executed with the assistance of the forest police

It is clear that nothing is said in this contract about performance measurement. Later on, however, a relative performance measure was developed and used to award prizes to the five best hunters' brotherhoods. That is the relation we are going to analyze after presenting its performance results.

11.4.2 Hunters' Brotherhood Performance Results

Given that data are scarce, we present only two results here: the relative performance measure for two years, and the results of our interviews of agents on the present state of the forests following the project's culmination in 2008. The performance measure is constructed using governance indices, equipment, and activities. Table 11.5 presents the results of two years of relative performance of the supervisors.

Table 11.5 shows that response results to the introduced incentive (prize) system are very volatile, implying randomness of the ranking, as winners change from year to year. Of the five hunters' brotherhoods that received prizes in 2006, only one survived the following year (2007). This helps to avoid the problem of a sure winner, but makes the average prize very small compared to the gain from collusion as we show below.

From interviews with local community members and key informants we found a general agreement that illegal use of the forests had increased after the project ended. Two explanations were given. The first was to attribute increases to the disappearance of incentive compensations to hunters (having ended with the project), confirming the importance of some form of external intervention. The second put forth that, with the help of the project, hunters were now better informed of the areas of the forests that are wealthy in woods and well stocked with game. Endowed with that better information, hunters were now serving as guides for illegal poachers and loggers for discovering these rich areas. This is a very disappointing result of a project aimed at protecting the forests through a promotion of co-management. In fact, when

Table 11.5 Ranks of some hunters' brotherhood in two successive years ($N = 33$)

Hunters' brotherhood	Rank in 2006	Rank in 2007	Annual Prize (US $)
1	1	>5	2,000
2	2	1	1,600
3	3	>5	1,200
4	4	>5	800
5	5	>5	400
6	>5	2	0
7	>5	3	0
8	>5	4	0
9	>5	5	0
Expected prize			182

>means greater than
Source: compiled from PAMF reports (2006, 2007)

people are uncertain of their rights to a piece of property, they are reluctant to protect and improve it and may even overuse it (Dasgupta 2008; Runge 1981).

The question now becomes: how can the agency help to explain these results? Some answers to this question are attempted in the following section.

11.4.3 Analysis of the Hunters' Brotherhood Performance Results

The unit of analysis in agency theory is the contract. We use the theoretical results to see if the project had designed the efficient contract. We hold the view that if the suitable incentive system is not chosen, the performance will be low; but we are not testing efficiency directly.

Given that a main component of the performance measure is the value of the equipment seized from poachers and illegal users, some brotherhoods claimed that this ranking is unfair. Their argument is that if you are efficient in chasing away illegal users from your forest, you will have no equipment to seize and thus you will get a low ranking. This suggests some kind of ratchet effect: an agent with a high performance today will be expected to achieve more tomorrow. He should thus be reluctant to convey favorable information too early in the relationship (Laffont and Tirole 1988). There is also a kind of hold-up problem, because each village has only one hunters' brotherhood. Once each brotherhood is properly equipped by the Government, its bargaining power to extract rents from any side (government and illegal users) increases and may be used to effect illegal collusion at the expense of the government.

These results show that the composition and constituents of the performance indicator are crucially important in ranking for an effective incentive system. Furthermore, for relative performance to be valuable as a signal for relative effort, individuals should be similar and face similar risks (Miller 2005). It is well known that the village forests are unevenly rich. The expected prize[8] is US$182, while from corruption practices local monitors may gain many times that amount. The value of illegal logging from each village forest is estimated at $2,100. From those figures, we can safely infer that the compensation of monitors doesn't fit the crime. This is clearly in contrast with what our comparative statics' results reveal: that to control illegal use of the forest, detection of violators, and certification of compliance by the supervisors should be properly rewarded.

The agency relation implemented by the project is both outcome-based (supervisors) and behavior-based (forest users). So when providing the right incentives for supervisors, investments in information systems are necessary to verify behavior over a long period of time. Within the time length of a project (six years for the project), these are not guaranteed if no provision is made to assure institutional continuity. The exploitation of the forests may be integrated in the co-management system to insure that continuity. Since it is understood that a classified forest should not be exploited, the development plan should be implemented before delving into a co-management experience. Without that provision, the success of co-management is not guaranteed.

Agency problems may then be one explanation for why some local commons have degraded in many parts of the poorer world despite massive state intervention to encourage co-management. Natural resource degradation persists due to unclear institutional arrangements, and the breakdown of norms and incentives that give meaning to those institutional arrangements. For these, governments are largely to blame for creating perverse incentives (Dasgupta and Mäler 2004; MEA 2005; Bromley 1991).

11.5 CONCLUDING REMARKS

When the government intervenes to co-manage a resource with local users, it creates an agency relationship with its associated problems and available solutions. In this chapter, we analyzed theoretically and empirically just such a relationship for the co-management experience of forest reserves in Benin. We showed that the contract devised by public officials was ill-designed—and, in particular, that the compensation of monitors didn't "fit the crime." We propose that the forest reserves co-management regime of Benin be revised based on agency theory principles. In particular, we recommend that the following

[8] We consider the contest to get a prize in a tournament between 33 competitors with equal chance of winning. Then the probability of getting any rank is 1/33 and the expected prize is (2, 000+1,600+1,200+800+400)/33=$182.

steps be considered: 1) recognize the agency relations between agents; 2) ensure development of the commons before setting up the co-management regime, to guarantee institutional continuity; and 3) devise sound incentives for agents involved.

These steps are necessary to achieve the combined public and private goals of environmental protection and enhanced welfare of local communities. It is especially important to avoid a situation whereby interventions by the state damage local institutions and turn common property resources into open access resources.

References

Arrow, K. J. (1986). "Agency and the Market," in K. J. Arrow and M. D. Intriligator (eds.), *Handbook of Mathematical Economics*, iii. Amsterdam: North-Holland Publishing Company, 1183–95.

Baiman, S., J. H. Evans III, and N. J. Nagarajan (1991). "Collusion in Auditing," *Journal of Accounting Research*, 29(1): 1–18.

Baland, J.-M. and J.-P. Platteau (2003). "Economics of Common Property Management Regimes," in *Handbook of EnvironmentalEconomics*, i. Amsterdam: Elsevier, 127–90.

Becker, G. S. (1968). "Crime and Punishment: An Economic Approach," *Journal of Political Economy*, 76(2): 169–217.

Bernheim, B. D. and M. D. Whinston (1986). "Common Agency," *Econometrica*, 54(4): 923–42.

Border, K. C. and J. S. Sobel (1987). "Samurai Accountant: A Theory of Auditing and Plunder," *The Review of Economic Studies*, 54(4): 525–40.

Bromley, D. W. (1991). *Environment and Economy: Property Rights and Public Policy.* Oxford: Blackwell.

Dasgupta, P. (2008). "Common Property Resources: Economics Analytics," in R. N. S. Jodha and P. Mukhopadhyay (eds.), *Promise, Trust and Evolution: Managing the Commons of South Asia*. Oxford: Oxford University Press, 19–50.

—— and K.-G. Mäler (2004). *Environmental and Resource Economics: Some Recent Developments*, mimeo. Stockholm: Beijer International Institute of Ecological Economics.

Davis, M. L. (1988). "Time and Punishment: an Intertemporal Model of Crime," *Journal of Political Economy*, 96(2): 383–90.

Eggertsson, T. (1993). "*Economic Perspectives on Property Rights and the Economics of Institutions,*" Beijer discussion paper series N° 40. Stockholm: Beijer International Institute of Ecological Economics.

Eisenhardt, K. M. (1989). "Agency Theory: An Assessment and Review," *The Academy of Management Review*, 14(1): 57–74.

Faure-Grimaud, A., J.-J. Laffont, and D. Martimort (2003). "Collusion, Delegation and Supervision with Soft Information," *The Review of Economic Studies*, 70(2): 253–79.

Furubotn, E. G. and R. Richter (2005). *Institutions and Economic Theory: The Contribution of the New Institutional Economics*. Ann Arbor, MI: University of Michigan Press.

Graetz, M. J., J. F. Reinganum, and L. L. Wilde (1986). "The Tax Compliance Game: Toward an Interactive Theory of Law Enforcement," *Journal of Law, Economics, & Organization*, 2(1): 1–32.

Hart, O. and B. Holstrom (1987). "The Theory of Contracts," in T. F. Bewley (ed.), *Advances in Economic Theory*. Fifth World Congress. Cambridge: Cambridge University Press.

Holmstrom, B. (1979). "Moral Hazard and Observability," *The Bell Journal of Economics*, 10(1): 74–91.

Hurwicz, L. (1973). "The Design of Mechanisms for Resource" *The American Economic Review, Papers and Proceedings of the Eighty-fifth Annual Meeting of the American Economic Association*, 63(2): 1–30.

Itoh, H. (1993). "Coalitions, Incentives, and Risk Sharing," *Journal of Economic Theory*, 60: 410–27.

Khalil, F. and J. Lawarrée (2006). "Incentives for Corruptible Auditors in the Absence of Commitment," *The Journal of Industrial Economics*, LIV(2): 269–291.

Kuhn, H. W. (1953). "Extensive Games and the Problem of Information," in H. W. Kuhn and A. W. Tucker (eds.), *Contributions to the Theory of Games*, ii. Princeton, NJ: Princeton University Press, 193–216.

Laffont, J.-J. (2000). *Incentives and Political Economy*. Oxford: Oxford University Press.

—— and J.-C. Rochet (1997). "Collusion in Organizations," *The Scandinavian Journal of Economics*, 99(4): 485–95.

—— and J. Tirole (1988). "The Dynamics of Incentive Contracts," *Econometrica*, 56(5): 1153–75.

Lise, W. (2005). "A Game Model of People's Participation in Forest Management in Northern India," *Environment and Development Economics*, 10: 217–40.

MEA (Millennium Ecosystem Assessment) (2005). *Ecosystems and Human Well-being: Synthesis*. Washington, DC: Island Press.

MEHU (Ministère de l'Environnement, de l'Habitat et de l'Urbanisme) (1993). *Plan d'Action Environnemental du Bénin*, Document final, Cotonou, Bénin: MEHU.

Melumad, N. D., D. Mookherjee, and S. Reichelstein (1995). "Hierarchical Decentralization of Incentive Contracts," *The RAND Journal of Economics*, 26(4): 654–72.

—— (1989). "Delegation as Commitment: The Case of Income Tax Audits," *The RAND Journal of Economics*, 20(2): 139–63.

Miller, G. J. (2005). "Solutions to Principal-agent Problems in Firms," in C. Menard and M. M. Shirley (eds.), *Handbook of New Institutional Economics*. Dordrecht: Springer, 349–70.

Mirrlees, J. A. (1999). "The Theory of Moral Hazard and Unobservable Behaviour: Part I," *The Review of Economic Studies*, (*Special Issue: Contracts*), 66(1): 3–21.

Mookherjee, D. and I. Png (1989). "Optimal Auditing, Insurance, and Redistribution," *The Quarterly Journal of Economics*, 104(2): 399–415.

Nalebuff, B. J. and J. E. Stiglitz (1983). 'Prizes and Incentives: Towards a General Theory of Compensation and Competition," *The Bell Journal of Economics*, 14(1): 21–43.

Ostrom, E., (1990). *Governing the Commons: The Evolution of Institutions for Collective Action*. Cambridge: Cambridge University Press.

PAMF (Projet d'Aménagement des Massifs Forestiers) (2002). *Mieux comprendre le projet d'aménagement des massifs forestiers*. Cotonou, Bénin: PAMF/DFRN/MAEP.

Runge, C. F. (1981). "Common Property Externalities: Isolation, Assurance, and Resource Depletion in a Traditional Grazing," *American Journal of Agricultural Economics*, 63(4): 595–606.

Seabright, P. (1993). "Managing Local Commons: Theoretical Issues in Incentive Design," *The Journal of Economic Perspectives*, 7(4): 113–34.

Shavell, S. (1979). "Risk Sharing and Incentives in the Principal and Agent Relationship," *The Bell Journal of Economics*, 10(1): 55–73.

Strausz, R. (1997). "Delegation of Monitoring in a Principal-Agent Relationship," *The Review of Economic Studies*, 64(3): 337–57.

—— (1997). "Collusion and Renegotiation in a Principal-Supervisor-Agent Relationship," *The Scandinavian Journal of Economics*, 99(4): 497–518.

Tirole, J. (1988). "The Multicontract Organization," *The Canadian Journal of Economics/Revue Canadienne d'Economique*, 21(3): 459–66.

—— (1986). "Hierarchies and Bureaucracies: On the Role of Collusion in Organizations," *Journal of Law, Economics, & Organization*, 2(2): 181–214.

12

Comments by Eric Maskin on "An Optimal Contract"

This is an interesting and well-executed effort to use optimal contract theory for illuminating why the policy of co-managing forest reserves in Benin has failed to stop those forests from being degraded. Co-management—wherein local communities have considerable autonomy in how they use a natural resource (in this case, forests)—had been hailed internationally as an improvement over the conventional "command-and-control" model, in which the government dictates how the resource is to be used. Thus, its failure in Benin has been a shock and a disappointment.

The authors make a good case that the Benin story is not an argument against co-management *per se*, but rather a demonstration of what goes wrong when incentives are not designed properly in such an arrangement. To do that, they first develop a theoretical contract model, consisting of a *principal* (who, in the model's application to Benin, becomes the government), a *supervisor* (the "hunter's brotherhood" in the application), and an *agent* (the community using the forests). In the model, the principal hires the supervisor to monitor the agent's action, which can be either "appropriate" or "inappropriate." Monitoring is costly, and so the supervisor may only pretend to monitor. But even if he monitors for real, he may choose not to report the evidence acquired about the agent's action. If he *does* make a report to the principal and the action was inappropriate, the principal can then impose a fine on the agent (though there is a limit to how high this fine can be).

If the contract between the principal and supervisor is designed optimally, the principal will pay the supervisor a fee contingent on the evidence reported (assuming there is a report). This contingent fee, when properly set, will give the supervisor the incentive to undertake monitoring and to report any evidence discovered. Furthermore, it will dissuade the supervisor from "colluding" with the agent (in a collusive arrangement, the supervisor would agree not to report the agent for acting inappropriately—or perhaps not to monitor at all—in exchange for a bribe). Finally, a well-chosen fine will induce the agent to act appropriately.

The authors do a nice job of formulating the model and analyzing it. I have just two comments and questions about their theoretical work:

(1) The model provides for the agent to be fined if she is reported to have acted inappropriately, but it assumes nothing happens to her otherwise. Yet, given that there is a restriction on how severe the fine can be, wouldn't incentives be more powerful if the agent were also *rewarded* by the principal for a good report, that is, for having acted appropriately? This would give the agent greater motivation to choose the appropriate action and would also reduce the temptation for collusion between the agent and the supervisor.

(2) It is assumed that the agent and supervisor collude by dividing up the fine w_H the agent would have paid had the supervisor reported that she acted inappropriately. But this assumption doesn't seem quite right because if the supervisor chooses not to report the agent, he loses the contingent fee t_H he would otherwise get (assuming that he undertakes monitoring). So, the net surplus to be divided appears to be $w_H - t_H$, not w_H. For collusion to be deterred, I believe it is sufficient that the principal should set w_H and t_H so that $w_H \leq t_H$ (presuming, again, that the supervisor has the incentive to monitor).

As for applying this model to the case of Benin, the authors interpret acting inappropriately as acting *illegally*, for example, poaching. They make the valuable point that a major shortcoming of the incentive contract actually used by Benin's government was that the supervisor (the hunter's brotherhood) was rewarded for providing evidence only of inappropriate action and not also of appropriate behavior. This limitation had the perverse property that if the brotherhood had somehow managed to stop all illegal activity, then it would have got paid nothing—and so would have had no compensation for its monitoring. The authors persuasively argue that this was a serious flaw in contract design. Furthermore, it is one that could easily have been fixed.

Left open in the author's discussion is the question of how the contract might have been designed to take account of legal but suboptimal actions by the forest-using community. Perhaps the authors will wish to study this issue in future work. If so, it will be interesting to see what they come up with.

13

Why Cooperation is Better: The Gains to Cooperative Management of the Argentine Shortfin Squid Fishery in South America

Sebastián Villasante, U. Rashid Sumaila, and Manel Antelo[1]

13.1 INTRODUCTION

Rockström et al. (2009) argue that human activities could potentially push the Earth system outside the stable environmental state of the Holocene, with catastrophic consequences. According to these authors, largely because of a growing reliance on fossil fuels and increasing production, humans are the most significant drivers of global environmental change, propelling the planet into a new geological epoch called the *Anthropocene*.

[1] This work is an outcome of research developed under the project "Exploring Cooperative and Non-cooperative Fisheries Management of the *Illex argentinus* Fishery in the Patagonian Large Marine Ecosystem: An Economic Perspective", financially supported by the Latin American and Caribbean Environmental Economics Program (LACEEP), the Canadian International Development Research Center (IDRC) and the Swedish International Development Cooperation Agency (SIDA). Sebastián Villasante is also grateful to the Norwegian Research Council and The Beijer Institute of Ecological Economics (Sweden) for being awarded the Karl-Göran Mäler Scholarship. Rashid Sumaila acknowledges the Sea Around Us Project, a Partnership of the Pew Charitable Trusts, and the Lenfest Ocean program. Manel Antelo wishes to express his appreciation for the financial aid received from the Galician Autonomous Government (Xunta de Galicia) through Project GPC 2013–045.

The authors are grateful to a number of people for their encouragement and fruitful comments. Special thanks are due to Professor Scott Barrett (Columbia University) for his generosity in sharing his knowledge, and to Professor Peter Hammond (University of Warwick) for his insightful comments on this chapter. Thanks are also due to Francisco Alpízar and Juan Robalino (LACEEP, CATIE), Allen Blackman (Resources for the Future), Juan C. Estévez (University of Santiago de Compostela), Nancy Olewiler (Simon Fraser University), Norma Brunetti (INIDEP), David Agnew (Imperial College), William Cheung (University of East Anglia), Julio Martínez-Portela (Instituto Español de Oceanografía), Vladimir Laptikhovsky (Falklands Islands Fisheries Department), and

Marine social-ecological systems are key components of the Earth system, providing an enormous and diverse array of use and non-use environmental goods and services (fishery resources, tourism, recreational activities, etc.), in addition to helping to regulate the Earth's climate. Marine social-ecological systems are also characterized by intervals of both gradual and rapid change, and non-linear dynamics (Levin 1999).

In South America, the Patagonian marine social-ecological system supports one of the world's most productive fishing grounds, with important commercial shared fish stocks such as the Argentine hake (*Merluccius hubbsi*) and Argentine shortfin squid (*Illex argentinus*) (Bisbal 1995; Agnew et al. 2005). The Argentine shortfin squid is exploited by different local and foreign fleets that operate within Argentina's Exclusive Economic Zone, in the seas around the Falkland (Malvinas) Islands, and in the high seas. Vessels from European (mainly Spain) and Asian (Taiwan, South Korea, China, and Japan) countries participate in this large fishery (Villasante and Sumaila 2008), creating a stock externality—a situation in which one state's catch negatively impacts the other countries (Sumaila 1999).

The biological and management aspects of this issue have been studied extensively (Basson et al. 1996; Agnew et al. 2005). However, little research has been carried out on the economic dimensions of this important squid fishery. The core problem is creating incentives for countries to cooperate, when each is tempted to free ride (Walker et al. 2009). The objectives of this chapter are (i) to reconstruct the biomass and recruitment series of the Argentine shortfin squid fishery; and (ii) to develop an empirical game-theoretical simulation model by estimating the ecological and economic benefits of this fishery for non-cooperative and cooperative scenarios.

Our aim is not to explore the negotiation and implementation of agreements between national governments. Rather, we present empirical results that can be interpreted as representing the outcome of a non-cooperative game between Argentina and the Falkland (Malvinas) Islands. The research also quantitatively demonstrates that, in a cooperative outcome, both players, Argentina and the Falkland (Malvinas) Islands, would obtain better economic benefits—fishing effort would be reduced, the stock would be higher, and fishing costs would be lower.

The remainder of the chapter is organized as follows. Section 13.2 provides an overview of the literature on the management of shared fish stocks. In Section 13.3, we describe the management of (transboundary) stocks in the Patagonian marine social-ecological systems. Section 13.4 outlines the model used to

Antonio Cordeiro for comments and suggestions. Useful feedback was also received from assistants to the IIFET 2010 Conference in Montpellier. The authors are also grateful to Elinor Ostrom (Indiana University) and Robert Solow (Massachusetts Institute of Technology) for valuable discussions and productive comments during the ABCDE World Bank Conference "Development Challenges in a Post-Crisis World" held in Stockholm, 31 May–2 June 2010.

estimate profits under a cooperative and a non-cooperative scenario, describes the data required to solve the model, and presents estimates of the parameters. Section 13.5 offers the main numerical results from the sensitivity analysis of the model to changes in the more relevant parameters. Section 13.6 discusses the main policy implications of the results obtained. Finally, Section 13.7 concludes.

13.2 MANAGEMENT OF SHARED FISH STOCKS: AN OVERVIEW

One main concern has been the management of transboundary resources (Munro 1987), a problem complicated by the need to look upon fishery resources as a form of natural capital (Clark and Munro 1994). The United Nations Convention on Law of the Sea addresses the management of these stocks through Articles 63 and 64 (Exclusive Economic Zone), and Article 87 (Freedom on the High Seas) in conjunction with Articles 116–120 (Conservation and Management of the Living Resources of the High Seas). The United Nations Convention on the Law of the Sea does not define the term "straddling stocks" but it refers to them in article 63(2) as "the same stock or stocks of associated species [which] occur both within the economic exclusive zone and in an area beyond and adjacent to the zone" (United Nations 1982). Hence, "straddling fish stocks" is a catch-all term for fishery resources (such as demersal or large pelagic stocks) that cross the exclusive economic zone boundaries of countries into the adjacent high seas (Hanneson 1995; Kaitala and Munro 1997).

Article 63(1) refers directly to the management of straddling stocks: "Where the same stock or stocks of associated species occur within the exclusive economic zones of two or more coastal states, these states shall seek, either directly or through appropriate sub regional or regional organizations, to agree upon the measures necessary to coordinate and ensure the conservation and development of such stocks without prejudice to the other provisions of this Part [V]" (United Nations 1982). Therefore, the United Nations Convention on Law of the Sea imposes a duty upon the relevant coastal states to negotiate arrangements for transboundary stock management but it does not require that they reach an agreement (Burke 1989). If the involved states are unable to reach an agreement, then each state shall manage that portion of the transboundary stock occurring within its exclusive economic zone (Munro et al. 2005). If they do so non-cooperatively, then they are not necessarily in violation of the United Nations Convention on Law of the Sea provision (Munro et al. 2005).

On the other hand, the high seas fishing regime established in the United Nations Convention on Law of the Sea, Section 1 of Article 87, affirms every state's right to fish on the high seas "subject to the conditions laid down in Section 2 [of Part VII]" (Article 87 (1) (e)) (United Nations 1982). The high seas regime in the United Nations Convention on Law of the Sea also states, in Article 116, that all states have the right to fish on the high seas subject to: "i) their treaty obligations; ii) the rights and duties as well as the interests of coastal states provided for, *inter alia*, in Article 63, paragraph 2, and Articles 64 to 67; and iii) the provisions of this section" (United Nations 1982). Article 116, Part VII, requires that states harvesting highly migratory [as well as straddling stocks] on the high seas adjacent to the exclusive economic zone take into account the rights, duties, and interests of relevant coastal states.

In addition, under the framework provided by the 1995 United Nations Fish Stocks Agreement, coastal states and interested states fishing on the high seas should pursue cooperation in relation to these stocks either directly or through Regional Fisheries Management Organizations or similar arrangements (United Nations 1995). Unfortunately, these property rights management instruments have been only partially successful (Barrett 2007).

13.3 SHARED FISH STOCKS IN THE PATAGONIAN MARINE SOCIAL-ECOLOGICAL SYSTEM

The Argentinian shortfin squid is a neritic-oceanic species found from 54° to 23° South (Brunetti et al. 2000). The population has a life cycle of around one year (Hartfield 1991). Its biomass can vary greatly from year to year (Agnew et al. 2005).

The Argentinian shortfin squid is found off the coast of Argentina, usually at bottom temperatures of 4–12°C (Brunetti 1990). Off of southern Brazil, juveniles are found in warmer waters (see Figure 13.1). Brunetti (1990) identifies three main spawning stocks in the southern range: the Summer-Spawning Stock, the South Patagonic Stock, and the Bonaerensis-Northpatagonic Stock. The most commercially important population is the South Patagonic or winter-spawning stock, found between 28°S and 38°S (Laptikhovsky et al. 2001).

In 1987, the United Kingdom government established a system of fisheries jurisdiction referred to as the Falklands Interim Fisheries Conservation Zone. Its purpose was to ensure the conservation of marine resources. This was done through the Declaration on the Conservation of Fish Stocks and Proclamation No. 4 of 1986, covering a 150-mile zone, as well as through the declaration of the Falklands Outer Conservation Zone, which was introduced in December 1990. This new zone extends beyond the Falklands Interim Fisheries Conservation Zone to the north, east, and south of the Falkland (Malvinas) Islands to 200 miles, measured from coastal baselines. It is about 527,000 km^2 in size.

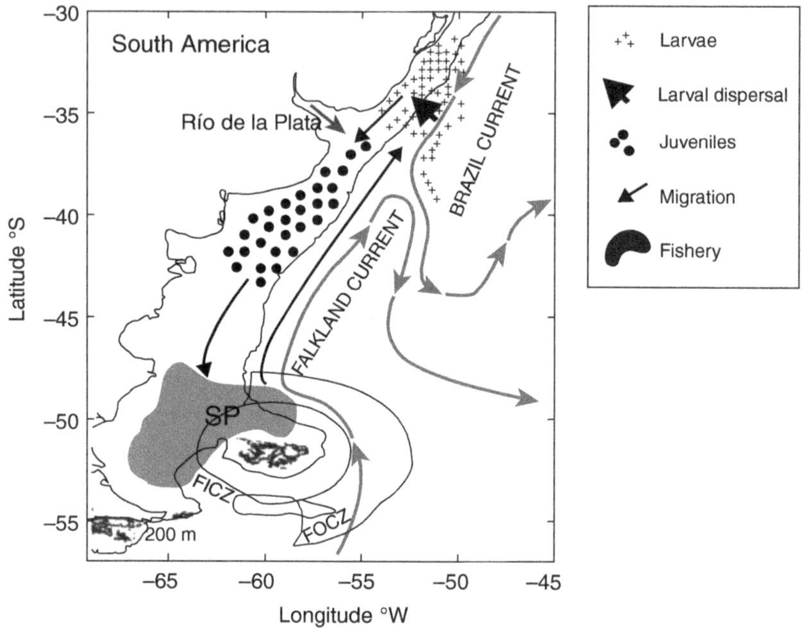

Figure 13.1 Life history and migration pattern of the South Patagonian stock of the Argentine shortfin squid in the Southwest Atlantic Ocean
Source: Agnew et al. (2005).

In both the Falklands Interim Fisheries Conservation Zone and the Falklands Outer Conservation Zone, fishing effort is controlled by issuing a limited number of licenses that allow fishing for a certain period of time. The main goal of this fishery policy is to minimize the risk of recruitment overfishing by defining a minimum threshold of the spawning stock biomass (Basson et al. 1996). The level of fishing mortality is adjusted to ensure that 40 percent of proportional escapement remains above the minimum threshold. The fishery currently operates a minimum target escapement of 40,000 tonnes (Agnew et al. 2005).

According to the *Sea Around Us* Database, total catches in the Patagonian large marine ecosystem increased from 170,153 tonnes in 1970 to 1.37 million tonnes in 2006, peaking at 1.79 million tonnes in 1997. The catches of distant-water fishing nations increased from 1,500 to 610,000 tonnes from 1975 to 1999.

Catches by distant-water fishing nations increased dramatically in the 1980s (with 3.8 million tonnes being caught over the decade) and 1990s (when 4.2 million tonnes were caught; see Figure 13.2), with catches peaking in 1998 (752 thousand tonnes). The Spanish freezer fleet is one of the most important fleets operating in the area. It operated on an irregular basis between 1960 and

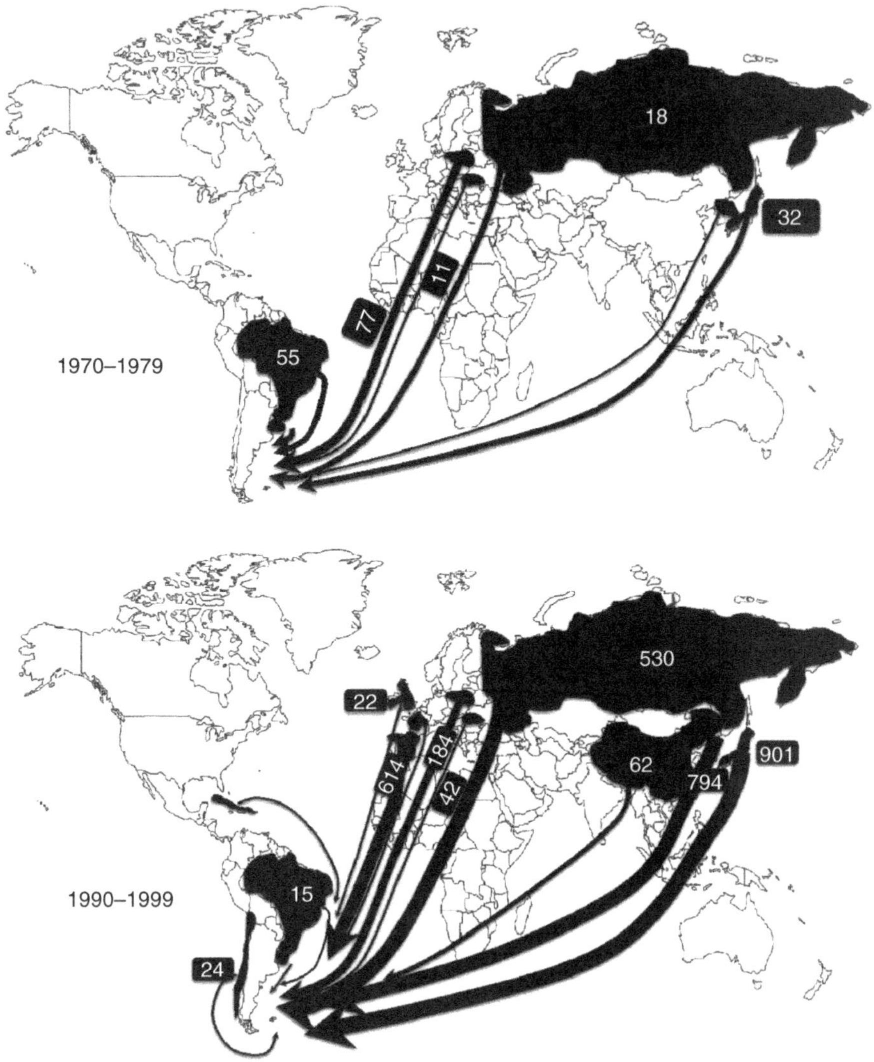

Figure 13.2 Catches of distant-water fishing nations and other coastal states from the Patagonian marine social-ecological system (in thousands tonnes).

Source: Own elaboration from Sea Around Us Database. Note: The thickness of the lines indicates the intensity of foreign fishing fleet activity in terms of catches. The numbers refer to the total catch by country for each decade.

1983, and increased its fishing effort gradually after that. Indeed, it reached its highest level in 1990 when the Namibian fishing ground was closed (Portela et al. 2005). At this time, the number of vessels operating in the Patagonian marine ecosystem increased by 50 percent. In the last three decades (1970–2006), catches of Argentinian vessels in the high seas experienced a significant decrease. In fact, their share of the total catch fell from 26.9 to 11.5 percent over this period; see Figure 13.3a.

The most important resources harvested in the high seas are the shared fish stocks, which represent 77 percent of the 25.4 million tonnes of fish caught over the 1970–2006 period (Argentine shortfin squid for 39 percent, Argentine hake accounted for 11.7 percent, Southern blue whiting for 4.8 percent, and Patagonian squid for 3.6 percent); see Figure 13.3. Moreover, the importance of these fishery resources increased over time. To illustrate, the catch volume increased from 6,800 tonnes in 1970 to about 513,000 tonnes in 2006; catch value increased from \$5.2 million to \$620 million in value (Villasante and Sumaila 2008; see Figures 13.3 c–d).

Nowadays, the Falklands (Malvinas) fisheries fleet is made up of trawler-jiggers, jiggers, long liners, and trawler vessels, most of them foreign flagged (especially Spanish vessels flagged to the Falklands (Malvinas)), and vessels owned by joint ventures with Falklands (Malvinas) companies (Cordeiro, pers. comm.). In 2007, fifty-eight jiggers received licenses to fish,

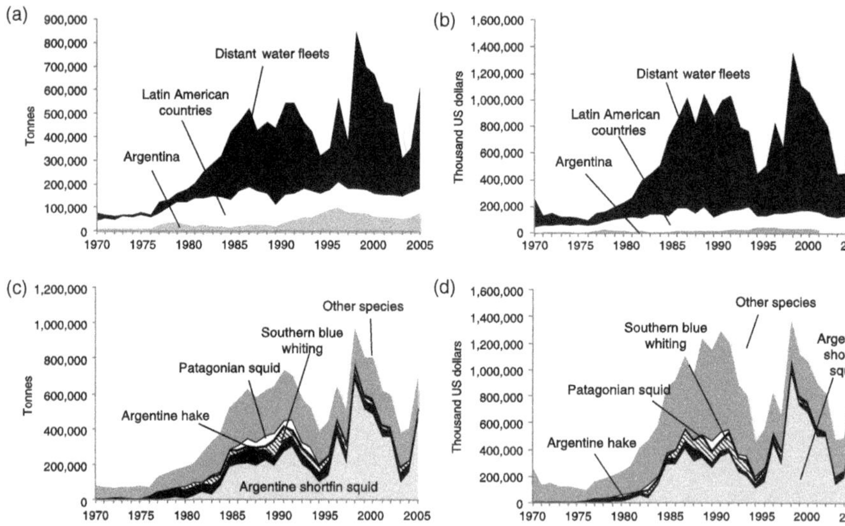

Figure 13.3 Catch and catch-value trends in the high sea area of FAO (41), Southwest Atlantic Ocean, 1970–2006. (a) Aggregate catches (in tonnes) by three groups of countries: Argentina, Latin American countries (including Brazil and Uruguay), and distant-water fishing fleets (from Bulgaria, China, Estonia, Germany, Italy Japan, Lithuania, Latvia, Poland, Portugal, South Korea, Spain, Taiwan, USSR/Russian Federation, and Ukraine); (b) Catch value (in thousands of 2000 US dollars) achieved by these groups; (c) Catches (in tonnes) of the main commercial species (Argentine hake, Argentine shortfin squid, Patagonian squid, Southern blue whiting); and (d) Catch value (in thousands of 2000 US dollars) for these same species.

Source: Own elaboration from *Sea Around Us* Database.

generating more than $12.4 million for the local economy, a value significantly lower than in previous years ($20.9 million in 2001) (FIFD 2008). Catches in Argentine waters have also dropped over the last years: from 338,000 tonnes in 1999 to a low of 233,000 tonnes in 2007.

The stock of the Argentine shortfin squid is currently fully exploited; the state of Argentine hake (found and caught mostly within the Exclusive Economic Zones) is reported as being overexploited or depleted (with a harvest rate below maximum sustained yield due to the stock being below the level needed to sustain this yield), while the biomass of the southern blue whiting (Wölher et al. 2007a) and pink cusk-eel is diminishing (Cordo 2006). The biomass of the Argentinian grenadier is increasing, thanks to four good years of recruitment (1993, 1995, 1996, and 1998) (Wölher et al. 2007b).

As regards the Argentine shortfin squid fishery, Figures 13.3c and 13.4 show that the best catch record registered in Falklands (Malvinas) waters was in a previous period (1997–1999), when daily catches per vessel increased due to the reduction in the number of licensed vessels. However, from 2001 to 2002, catches in Falkland (Malvinas) waters plummeted from 150,631 tonnes to 13,411 tonnes. Catches recovered after that, rising to 103,375 tonnes in 2003. Nevertheless, they dropped again in 2004 to 1,720 tonnes before rising to 7,936 tonnes in 2005 (see Figure 13.4). In 2004, recruitment, total catches in the Falkland (Malvinas) and Argentine waters, and observed spawning biomass were all the lowest on record (Villasante and Sumaila 2008).

This poor performance during 2005 represents the third lowest catch since the creation of the Fisheries Interim Conservation and Fisheries

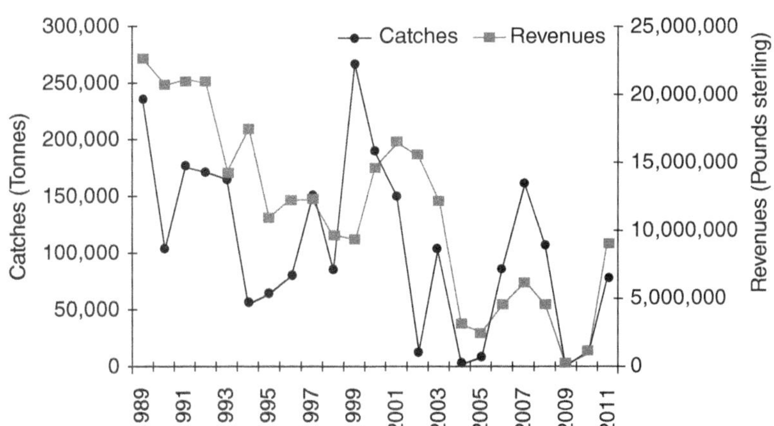

Figure 13.4 Catches in tonnes (black line) and annual revenue in pounds sterling (nominal values, gray line) of the Argentine shortfin squid fishery in Falkland (Malvinas) Islands conservation zones.

Source: Falkland Islands Fisheries Department.

Outer Conservation Zones. Stock collapses, due to overfishing and/or environmental factors, are likely to negatively impact both the Argentinian and Falkland (Malvinas) Islands economies (Barton et al. 2004; Agnew et al. 2005). This can be seen by the reduction in the volume of and economic benefits derived from licenses for catching Argentine shortfin squid from 1989 to 2007.

13.3.1 Fisheries Economics and Game Theory

Two types of analytical tools are available for analyzing the exploitation of fish stocks. The first are bioeconomic models, used in the study of stocks managed by a single state. These include the Schaefer model in discrete time (Schaefer 1954, 1957), the Ricker model in continuous time (Ricker 1954), and the cohort models developed by Beverton and Holt (Beverton and Holt 1957)). The second are game theoretic models, used to analyze shared stocks, described in detail below.

Game theory is a mathematical tool used to examine strategic interaction among players (individuals, firms, states, or any other agents). In the context of the current work, its relevance lies in the fact that it provides methods for analyzing strategic choices among agents who share a common fish stock (Sumaila 1999). Munro conducted pioneering work on the application of game theory to shared fishery resources, both before and after the United Nations Convention on Law of the Sea era (Munro 1979, 1987). In the 1990s, a large number of studies analyzed cooperative management of common pool resources (Ostrom 2000; Vincent 2007; Dasgupta 2009; Polasky et al. 2006; Walker et al. 2009), with particular emphasis on shared fish stocks (Kaitala and Munro 1993; Sumaila 1995; Ostrom 2000; Kronbak and Lindroos 2007; Bailey et al. 2010; Wang and Ewald 2010).

International disputes regarding marine resources may arise when one state catches a stock in its Exclusive Economic Zone, while another harvests from the same stock on the high seas. The theory focuses on the characteristics of each player's strategy, and allows researchers to predict possible solutions to the game (Bailey et al. 2010).

In a non-cooperative game, players are assumed to be motivated entirely by self-interest (Dasgupta and Heal 1979; Ostrom 1990). The literature shows that non-cooperative management leads to significant over-exploitation of a given resource (Munro 1979). Clark (1980) argues that, if the players are symmetric, the outcome will be similar to that encountered in an unrestricted open access domestic fishery, referred to in the literature as *bionomic equilibrium* (Gordon 1954). Therefore, the non-cooperation context has undesirable if not destructive consequences for the resource.

In other words, the outcome is Pareto-inefficient, implying that the payoffs of at least some players could be increased without decreasing those of other players (Sumaila 1999). As a result, the overall outcome of the fisheries game is an example of what is probably the most famous of all non-cooperative games, the so-called prisoner's dilemma (Dasgupta and Heal 1979; Ostrom 1990).

Regarding cooperative games, there are two requirements to be met for a stable solution: Pareto optimality and satisfaction of the individual rationality condition. Pareto optimality implies that it is not possible to make one player better off without making another worse off. The individual rationality condition, on the other hand, states that a solution to the cooperative game will not be stable unless the payoffs arising from the solution make each and every player at least as well off as they would be under conditions of non-cooperation (Kaitala and Munro 1993; Munro et al. 2005).

13.4 THE MODEL

Our model follows the pioneering research of Munro (1979) and related studies (Sumaila 1999). The countries participating in the fishery are Argentina, the Falkland (Malvinas) Islands, and other distant-water fishing fleets such as those from Spain, China, Japan, South Korea, and Taiwan (Villasante and Sumaila 2008).

However, the most important players, Argentina and the Falkland (Malvinas) Islands, provide favorable conditions for applying the traditional bioeconomic models of Munro (1979) and Sumaila (1997). Using these models, we examine the ecological and economic effects of cooperation and non-cooperation. In particular, we extend Munro's setup (Munro 1979, 1990) by adapting some of his assumptions to the reality of the Argentinte shortfin squid fishery. In most of the world's fisheries, and particularly those in the South Atlantic, the traditional theoretical framework does not reflect the diversity of existing situations. Therefore, starting from Munro's two-player model (Munro 1979, 1990), the following assumptions are made to provide a more comprehensive insight into the analysis of the Argentine shortfin squid fishery:

A1. Argentina and the Falkland (Malvinas) Islands are the two players involved in the game.

A2. The discount factor for both countries is the same, equal to 0.96 per annum (resulting from a long-term interest rate of 4%).

A3. The catch function for each country is different.

A4. Unlike the linear function proposed by Munro (1979, 1990), we assume a constant returns to scale Cobb-Douglas catch function given by:[2]

$$C_{i,t} = q_i \cdot E_{i,t}^{\alpha_i} \cdot B_t^{1-\alpha_i}, \tag{1}$$

where $C_{i,t}$ denotes the catch of player i in period t, q_i (> 0) is i's "catchability" or gear efficiency coefficient, $\alpha_i \in (0,1)$ is i's share parameter, $E_{i,t}$ is i's harvesting effort in period t,[3] and B_t denotes the spawning biomass in period t.[4]

A5. Following Clark (1990) and Munro (1979, 1990), we assume that growth in the biomass, ignoring the harvest rate, obeys a logistic (quadratic) function, $A(B_t)$. This implies:

$$B_{t+1} = A(B_t) - C_t = (1+a)B_t - b(B_t^2) - C_t, \tag{2}$$

where $C_t = C_{1,t} + C_{2,t}$ denotes the total catch during season t.

A6. The fishing effort of each player i in period t, $E_{i,t}$, is assumed to be variable in the form of catch per unit of effort.

A7. The competitive (non-cooperative) behavior of the players may be due purely to short-term incentives.

A8. The model is in discrete time with a finite time horizon.

Regarding assumption A1, the players targeting the stock in the ecosystem are not just Argentina and the Falkland (Malvinas) Islands. However, because of a lack of data for foreign fleets, we had to limit our analysis to these two countries. Assumption A2 is adopted to take into account the homogeneous nature of the prevailing financial conditions in the two countries. Assumption A3 reflects the gap in technological attributes that may exist between the two fleets. Assumption A4 is made because a Cobb-Douglas harvest function is quite flexible and is able to reflect the high variability of recruitment better than a linear production function. Assumption A5 reflects the fact that fish populations increase proportionally to their biomass, but the rate of increase slows as the population approaches its natural (carrying capacity) constraint.[5]

[2] Domínguez-Torreiro and Surís-Regueiro (2007) also consider a Cobb-Douglas function similar to (1).

[3] "Effort" is an appropriate combination of the usual inputs as labor, capital, energy, etc.

[4] Equation (1) can be rewritten as $C_{i,t}/B_t = q_i(E_{i,t}/B_t)^{\alpha_i}$. Later in this chapter we estimate (1) using this modified form.

[5] For the natural biomass growth process, other functions than the logistic equation can be used. For example, the Fox growth function (Fox, 1970) consists of a slight modification of the term B_t^2 in (2).

Assumption A6 is made mainly because in the Patagonian shelf, management restrictions focus on limiting effort levels. Assumption A7 affects the ability of states to reach potential cooperative agreements. Finally, assumption A8 reflects a highly observed practice in international fishing agreements. In addition, the Falklands Islands Fisheries Department established a new legal system in 2005, and our model tries to incorporate aspects of this new system.

We also adopt several other assumptions about stock migrations and the relationship between stock abundance and catch per unit of effort in the fishery. Following Basson et al. (1996), we assume that:

A9. A single stock exists at 45° South.

A10. Stocks move between the Falkland (Malvinas) Islands conservation zones and outside them as well, and the catchability coefficients of the fleets are the same inside and outside the conservation zones.

A11. Stocks move but the proportion of the total population in each area remains constant.

Despite there existing two fishing grounds at 45° South, we posit in assumption A9 a single stock for assessment and management purposes. Assumptions A10 and A11 are also made in order to simplify the analysis as much as possible.

In the set-up defined by assumptions A1–A11, we simulate both in a cooperative and a non-cooperative context, the behavior of the two fleets acting in the fishery, and examine the different ecological and economic outcomes arising from its exploitation.

13.4.1 The Data

Data to run the model were gathered by the research campaigns conducted annually by the National Institute of Fisheries Research and Development (INIDEP) in Argentina, and by Imperial College (United Kingdom) in the Falkland (Malvinas) Islands. Biomass, recruitment, and catch data for the Falkland (Malvinas) Islands come from Basson et al. (1996), Agnew et al. (2005), and the Falklands Island Fisheries Department (FIFD) (1998–2007). Moreover, the FIFD provided us with detailed information about daily catches per vessel for the period 1990–2000. In the area of Argentina, data for these variables were gathered from Brunetti et al. (2000, 2002, 2006, 2007), Bertolotti et al. (2001), and the Ministry of Agriculture, Livestock, and Fisheries (SAGPYA) (2007, 2008).

Data of ex-vessel prices of the Argentine shortfin squid for the Argentinian fleet for 1993–2007 were collected from SAGPYA. For the fleet that operates in the Falklands (Malvinas), information was taken from FIFD (2008) for the same period. In both cases, the information was compared, combined, and validated with the prices reported by Sumaila et al. (2007) and available from the *Sea Around Us* Database. Costs of exploitation were collected from Bertolotti et al. (2001) and SAGPYA (2008) for the Argentinian case and from García-Negro (2003) and MRAG (2008) for the Falklands (Malvinas) fleet. There is a reasonable similarity between the Spanish and Falkland (Malvinas) fleets; hence we assume they are similar. Values for discount rates, prices, and cost parameters come from both official and direct survey sources.

As official sources do not provide homogenous and complete biomass data, we reconstructed the historic series of the biomass using indirect estimation methods in order to better understand the dynamics of the Patagonian marine social-ecological system (Folke 2011). In particular, we model the dynamics of the biomass using official data, and combine this with the catch data for both countries and the spawning biomass for the South Patagonic stock. In this way we obtain a total value of the existing biomass in each year of the period under study (Laptikhovsky, pers. comm.).

13.4.2 Estimating the Biomass

Biomass constitutes a key indicator of the relative abundance of a given stock (Hilborn and Walters 1992). The life-cycle characteristic of cephalopods is one of the main reasons for the large inter-annual fluctuations of population densities (Agnew et al. 2005). Abundance of Argentine shortfin squid is difficult to estimate due to its short lifespan, complicated population structure, and high inter-annual variability (Basson et al. 1996; Brunetti et al. 2000) due to environmental variation in this marine social-ecological system (De Oliveira 2005; Portela et al. 2005). This has meant that the Argentine shortfin squid fishery has had to be closed early on a number of occasions, suggesting a relationship between recruitment and variations in environmental conditions (Basson et al. 1996; Waluda et al. 2001; Agnew et al. 2005; Portela et al. 2005; Chen et al. 2007). For these same reasons, biomass estimates for the Argentine shortfin squid fishery are inherently variable (Laptikhovsky, pers. comm.).

The pre-season scientific assessment of the Argentine shortfin squid is based on the Leslie-DeLury depletion model,[6] which remains the only example that has been used consistently for a number of years (Basson et al. 1996). Other post-assessment methods include understanding the relationship between

[6] The Leslie-DeLury method for estimating the initial population size is built upon a number of hypotheses related to the fisheries and the usual assumptions of simple linear regression. This is called a depletion or removal method as it relies on observing populations where the fish stock is being depleted.

environmental conditions (sea surface temperature) and stock size (Waluda et al. 2001; Agnew et al. 2005).

In this chapter, we assume a single stock as a reasonable and practical working hypothesis by following Basson et al. (1996), although we present an alternative model of estimation of the biomass, which was carried out using data from Brunetti et al. (2000), Bertolotti et al. (2001) and Agnew et al. (2005). These collected values are for the fishing seasons 1994, 2002, and 2007. However, to run the model and to carry out sensitivity analysis under different cooperative and non-cooperative scenarios, a seasonal series, which spans the entire period, is needed. Thus, the biomass grows as each individual gains weight over the course of the year, and falls as a consequence of fishing effort. To calculate the biomass each year, we added the catches of the Falklands (Malvinas) and Argentinian fleets to the spawning biomass remaining at the end of the fishing season and then subtracted losses due to natural mortality.

Data are from INIDEP reports on the estimated number of pre-recruitments at the start of the fishing season, and the residual biomass estimated for the INIDEP for each year (Brunetti et al. 2002, 2006, 2007). Unlike the model developed by Basson et al. (1996), we used a Cobb-Douglas harvesting function with specific parameters for the period of weeks when fishing is undertaken in each year t (from 1993 to 2007), with recruitment being captured by another parameter. The estimated function is given by:

$$\begin{aligned} B_{t+1} - B_t = (1.166)\cdot & B_t - (6.5994E-07)\cdot B_t^2 - C_t, \\ [5.7001] \quad & \quad [-2.4240] \end{aligned} \tag{3}$$

with t-statistics in brackets. In addition, the coefficient of determination, R^2, is 0.6482, and the adjusted R^2 is 0.6130. Finally, the multiple correlation coefficient is 0.8051.

Results of the estimation of the biomass of stock at 45° South in Argentina and the Falkland (Malvinas) Islands are shown in Table 13.1. A high variability over the entire 1993–2007 period is observed, with a minimum value in 2004 of about 131,000 tonnes and a maximum value in 1999 and 2007 of about 1,822,000 tonnes. There seem to be periods in which the biomass grew (1995–1999, 2004–2007) and periods in which it shrank (1993–1995, 1999–2004).

13.4.3 Estimating the Parameter Values

To estimate the production function of catches in the Falkland (Malvinas) Islands and Argentina, an indicator of fishing effort was employed, which took into account the number of licenses per year for each of the two fisheries, combined with the number of weeks each fleet operated. The information needed to estimate the production function was gathered from Brunetti et al. (2002,

Table 13.1 Estimation of the total biomass of the South Patagonian stock at 45° South in Argentina and the Falkland (Malvinas) Islands

Year	Total biomass (tonnes)	Total catches (tonnes)
1993	1,080,384	282,665
1994	349,719	189,750
1995	290,234	129,465
1996	494,076	246,077
1997	839,412	523,407
1998	1,164,786	272,748
1999	1,821,676	548,899
2000	1,240,036	452,576
2001	748,445	316,140
2002	358,387	116,692
2003	251,175	222,587
2004	130,715	47,025
2005	395,872	87,262
2006	1,237,515	339,216
2007	1,822,338	377,476

Source: Own elaboration from the model

2006, 2007) for Argentina, and from FIFD (2005, 2006, 2007, 2008) for the Falkland (Malvinas) Islands. Denoting by E the fishing effort, the estimated function for Argentinian catch in period t is:

$$\frac{C_t}{B_t} = \underset{[2.1767]}{(3.1487)} \cdot \left(\frac{E_t}{B_t}\right)^{\underset{[4.9536]}{0.4577}}, \tag{4}$$

where the t-statistics are in brackets. In this case, the coefficient of determination or R^2 is 0.6537, the adjusted R^2 is 0.6270, and the multiple correlation coefficient is 0.8085.

In turn, the estimated Falkland (Malvinas) Islands catch function is:

$$\frac{C_t}{B_t} = \underset{[0.8689]}{(0.2134)} \cdot \left(\frac{E_t}{B_t}\right)^{\underset{[0.4196]}{0.1202}}, \tag{5}$$

where the t-statistics are again in brackets. In this case, the R^2 is 0.6634, the adjusted R^2 is 0.6222, and the multiple correlation coefficient is 0.7158.

Table 13.2 Estimation of biomass, catches, and fishing effort of the South Patagonian stock at 45° South in Argentina and Falkland (Malvinas) Islands

Year	Total biomass (number of individuals)	Catches (tonnes) Argentina	Fishing effort (hours/year) Argentina	Catches (tonnes) Falklands	Fishing effort (hours/year) Falklands
1993	1,080,384	137,480	2,150	145,185	2,340
1994	349,719	122,754	2,562	66,996	1,968
1995	290,234	65,343	2,484	64,122	1,320
1996	494,076	166,353	3,750	79,724	1,808
1997	839,412	373,644	3,750	149,763	1,564
1998	1,164,786	187,755	2,575	84,993	1,185
1999	1,821,676	282,698	2,600	266,201	1,462
2000	1,240.036	262,867	2,275	189,709	1,853
2001	748,445	165,509	2,162	150,631	1,972
2002	358,387	103,281	1,240	13,411	1,750
2003	251,175	119,212	2,162	103,375	1,830
2004	130,715	45,305	1,632	1,720	890
2005	395,872	79,325	1,162	7,937	490
2006	1,237,515	253,602	2,175	85,614	731
2007	1,822,338	215,983	1,955	161,493	798

Source: Own elaboration from the model

Note that the estimated catch function given in (4) for Argentina may be written as $C_t = (3.1487) \cdot E_t^{0.457} \cdot B_t^{0.5423}$; and the one provided in (5) for Falkland (Malvinas) Islands as $C_t = (0.2134) \cdot E_t^{0.1202} \cdot B_t^{0.8798}$.

Information for the estimation of economic parameters was gathered from Basson et al. (1996), Brunetti et al. (2002, 2006, 2007), and Agnew et al. (2005). The data used for the sensitivity analysis are shown in Table 13.2.

Another important parameter reflects the relative bargaining power of the two countries—and, hence, the nature of the cooperative outcome. The players representing the Argentinian fishery (referred to as subscript A) and that of the Falkland (Malvinas) Islands (referred to as subscript M) could potentially reach a joint agreement of exploitation, implying a distribution of the total rent generated for the fishery between the two countries. Assuming no side payments between the parties,[7] a possible agreement could be devised via the solution to the following problem:

$$\max (PV_A)^{\beta} \times (PV_M)^{1-\beta}, \quad (6)$$

[7] We make this assumption mainly because of the political situation between Argentina and the Falklands Islands.

where PV stands for the present value of the payoff corresponding to each of the participants, and the parameter β, $0 \leq \beta \leq 1$, represents Argentina's bargaining power.[8]

The outcome of the bargaining process is assumed to be represented by the Nash bargaining solution. Let π_A and π_M denote the payoffs (meaning the flow of benefits which result from a strategy of exploitation) to Argentina and the Falkland (Malvinas) Islands, respectively; and let $\bar{\pi}_A$ and $\bar{\pi}_M$ represent the payoffs that each party could potentially receive in a non-cooperative scenario (threat points). By varying β, we can trace out the Pareto efficient frontier (again, assuming no side payments). Effort levels for the two countries are chosen so as to maximize:

$$(\pi_A - \bar{\pi}_A)^{\beta} \times (\pi_M - \bar{\pi}_M)^{1-\beta}, \tag{7}$$

subject to each country receiving a payoff at least as large as its threat point. We calculated the cooperative solution for different values of β (0, 0.15, 0.30, 0.50, 0.70, 0.85, and 1).

Information is also needed about the ex-vessel prices of Argentine shortfin squid fishery. For both Argentina and the Falkland (Malvinas) Islands, we used the average ex-vessel prices over the period 2000–2004 to obtain a representative price per tonne of Argentine shortfin squid. These prices come out to \$994 in the case of Argentina, and \$1,862 for the Falkland (Malvinas) Islands.

We also estimated the cost per unit of effort for each fleet operating in the fishery. The data for exploitation costs come from Bertolotti et al. (2001) and SAGPYA (2008) for Argentina, and from García-Negro (2003) and MRAG (2008) for the Falkland (Malvinas) Islands. For Argentina, the cost per unit of effort was calculated as the exploitation costs of a standard vessel, resulting in a cost of \$534 per unit of effort. For the Falkland (Malvinas) Islands, the same procedure was followed (but taking into account a standard Spanish vessel), and the resulting cost was \$816 per unit of effort.

13.5 NUMERICAL RESULTS

13.5.1 Economic Results

Once the parameters related to the biomass and catches have been estimated, it is possible to solve the model for prevailing prices, exploitation costs, and discount rates. Taking into account all the variables examined, the

[8] Thus, $\beta = 1$ means that Argentina completely dominates the bargaining, while $\beta = 0$ means that the Falkland (Malvinas) Islands dominate.

Table 13.3 Summary results for a time horizon of five and ten years

	Cooperative scenario							Non-cooperative scenario
	β							
	0.0	0.15	0.30	0.50	0.70	0.85	1.0	
	5 years							
Profits to Argentina	0.0	21.4	29.7	32.4	33.6	34.8	39.0	36.6
Profits to Falklands (Malvinas)	111.6	108.0	106.5	105.4	104.5	102.5	0.0	79.8
Total	**111.6**	**129.4**	**136.2**	**137.8**	**138.1**	**137.3**	**39.0**	**116.4**
	10 years							
Profits to Argentina	0.0	35.7	56.7	59.4	61.8	63.9	73.2	67.5
Profits to Falklands (Malvinas)	202.8	199.5	197.5	192.4	185.4	164.1	0.0	155.5
Total	**202.8**	**235.2**	**254.2**	**254.8**	**246.2**	**238.0**	**73.2**	**222.0**

Source: Own elaboration from the model
(Annual discounted profits in millions of euros)

economic results for the two time horizons (five and ten years) are shown in Table 13.3 above.

Several comments are in order. First, for both the 5- and 10-year time horizons, the greatest total profit is obtained for β having a value between 0.3 and 0.85. Second, for values other than $\beta = 0$ and $\beta = 1$, higher benefits are derived under cooperation than under non-cooperation. Third, when it comes to analyzing the economic outcome in the absence of side payments, it can initially be seen that an increase in parameter β increases Argentina's profits, while reducing those of the Falkland (Malvinas) Islands. The Falkland (Malvinas) Islands always gain by cooperating, whereas Argentina gains only when $\beta = 1$—that is, only when the Falkland (Malvinas) Islands would not be willing to cooperate. This is true for both the 5- and 10-year time horizons.

13.5.2 Catches, Fishing Effort, and Biomass

Total catch is highest under non-cooperation, with a volume close to 335,000 tonnes. Under a cooperative outcome, the largest total catch is obtained for $\beta = 0.50$, with 227,000 tonnes. If the value of β increases, Argentina's catch increases while that of the Falkland (Malvinas) Islands decreases. Argentina's

Table 13.4 Average estimated (annual) values for a time horizon of ten years

	Cooperative scenario					Non-cooperative scenario
	β					
	0.0	0.30	0.50	0.70	1.0	
Catches of Argentina (in thousand tonnes)	0	66.5	97.5	104.5	139.5	135.5
Catches of Falklands (Malvinas) (in thousand tonnes)	205.5	155.5	130.4	114.4	0	199.4
Total catches (in thousand tonnes)	205.5	221.0	227.9	214.9	139.5	334.9
Fishing effort of Argentina (in hours per year)	0	3,455	5,223	5,677	5,832	6,664
Fishing effort of Falkland (Malvinas) Islands (in hours per year)	5,443	4,765	4,612	4,449	0	5,454
Stock biomass (in thousand tonnes)	404,543	419,678	412,765	433,213	402,298	325,567

Sources: Own elaboration from the model

catch reaches its maximum value for $\beta = 1$; the catch of the Falkland (Malvinas) Islands is at a maximum when $\beta = 0$. Estimated values for catches, fishing effort, and biomass are presented in Table 13.4.

Fishing effort for both countries is highest under non-cooperation as compared to all the cooperative scenarios. Effort by the Falkland (Malvinas) Islands falls slightly under a sole owner scenario, but total effort is a lot lower in this case compared to the non-cooperative outcome. For approximately equal bargaining power, the effort levels for the two countries are very similar.

The biomass is lower under non-cooperation than under any of the cooperative scenarios. The largest biomass stock is obtained for the cooperative scenarios in which the value of parameter β ranges between 0.30 and 0.70.

Comparison of these results with recent trends for the fishery suggests that stock abundance and fishing effort correspond closely to the non-cooperative outcome. Under cooperation, total profits tend to increase.

However, Argentina would be worse off under all of the plausible cooperative scenarios. This means that it is unlikely that an agreement between Argentina and the Falkland (Malvinas) Islands can be reached without the use of side payments.

13.6 POLICY IMPLICATIONS

This chapter is the first attempt to analyze the sustainable management of the Argentine shortfin squid fishery in the Southwest Atlantic Ocean using appropriate economic concepts and the methodology of game theory. Based on our analysis, the potential for obtaining net benefits from some type of cooperative management of the Argentine shortfin squid fishery is huge. Gulland (1980) highlights two cooperation levels in modern fisheries management: the first one (primary level) refers exclusively to research cooperation without including coordinated zoning plans; the second (secondary level) involves active zone cooperation, that is, the development and implementation of coordinated programs for managing shared stocks. If cooperation is not achieved at the primary level, it is obvious that it will not be achieved at the secondary level. Successful cooperative management approaches demonstrate that cooperation at the primary research level acts as a precursor for cooperation at the secondary fisheries management level (Sumaila et al. 2003).

The shared interests of Argentina and the United Kingdom as regards fisheries' rights in the Patagonian marine social-ecological system led to the re-establishment of relations after 1982, when the two governments agreed to open the way for cooperation in the conservation of fish stocks. This culminated in the Madrid declarations that finally created the South Atlantic Fisheries Commission in 1990. However, so far, the two countries have only agreed to carry out joint research. Since 1994, the INIDEP (Argentina) and the Imperial College (United Kingdom) have held annual discussions on joint scientific assessment for managing the stock, resulting in the setting of total annual catches for the whole area.

This first cooperative level has been reasonably productive, allowing for an exchange of catch and effort data. The main achievements include: (i) the exchange data for real-time assessment of the Argentine shortfin squid fishery; (ii) programs of joint scientific research; (iii) joint workshops to evaluate the status of some shared species; and (iv) after scientists have reached an agreement that spawning biomass is likely to fall below the conservation target, the implementation of an early warning system allowing for closure of the fishery (Barton et al. 2004). Nevertheless, tensions re-emerged between the two countries as a result of the Falklands (Malvinas) decision in 2005 to grant fishing licenses around the Falkland (Malvinas) Islands over a twenty-five-year time horizon, rather than by annual renewal, a practice which has continued since July 2006.

Experience from around the world demonstrates that strong political commitments, at the highest level of government, are required to make joint management work. Therefore, if both countries decide to develop a more cooperative framework, they will have to back it up politically. To achieve primary and secondary cooperation in the long-term, different outcomes should be explored. Firstly, both theory and empirics demonstrate that all who enter long-term relationships benefit from them, though sometimes unequally (Dasgupta 2008). The aggregate gains from cooperation should be emphasized. Second, because the distribution of these gains may be unequal, the prospects for cooperation will be helped by the use of side payments. Indeed, our analysis shows that side payments are likely to be crucial. Finally, while not addressed in this chapter, it is also essential that any cooperative agreements that are reached should be able to limit free riding and enforce fisheries regulations at sea (Barrett 2001).

13.7 CONCLUDING REMARKS

The Patagonian marine social-ecological system is one of the most productive ecosystems in the world, with important commercial shared stocks such as the Argentine shortfin squid fishery. Application of the tools of game theory to fishery management shows the negative consequences of non-cooperation between countries. It can also be used to calculate the aggregate gains from cooperation—and the distribution of these gains as between the parties.

Game theoretic models allow us to estimate the net present value of the current regime, and the potential benefits for Argentina and Falkland (Malvinas) Islands of exploiting the Argentine shortfin squid fishery in a cooperative and sustainable way. The results presented here demonstrate the high predictive power of the theory. Historical exploitation is consistent with the outcome of a non-cooperative game between Argentina and the Falklands (Malvinas). Our research also demonstrates that in a cooperative setting, both players would obtain better economic benefits. This is because, by reducing fishing effort, the countries would increase the abundance of the stock and so reduce fishing costs.

References

Agnew, D., S. L. Hill, J. R. Beddington et al. (2005). "Sustainability and Management of Southwest Atlantic Squid Fisheries," *Bulletin of Marine Science* 76(2): 579–93.

Bailey, M., Sumaila, U. R., Lindroos, M. (2010). "Application of Game Theory to Fisheries over Three Decades," *Fisheries Research* 102(1–2): 1–8.

Barrett, S. (2001). "International cooperation for sale," *European Economic Review* (45): 1835–50.

Barrett, S. (2007). *Why Cooperate? The Incentive to Supply Global Public Goods.* New York: Oxford University Press.

Barton, J., D. Agnew, and V. Purchase (2004). "The Southwest Atlantic: Achievements of Bilateral Management and the Case for a Multilateral Arrangement," in A. I. Payne, C. M. O'Brien, S. I. Rogers (eds.) *Management of Shared Stocks.* Oxford: Blackwell, 202–22.

Basson, M., J. R. Beddington, J. A. Crombie et al. (1996). "Assessment and Management of Annual Squid Stocks: The *Illex argentinus* Fishery in the Southwest Atlantic as an Example," *Fisheries Research* 28: 3–29.

Bertolotti, M. I., A. Pagani, E. Errazti et al. (2001). "Caracterización biológica y económica de la pesquería del calamar (*Illex argentinus*): parámetros principales y valoración de la unidad de manejo al sur de los 44°S," FACES 7(10): 7–23.

Beverton, R. J. H. and S. J. Holt (1957). "On the Dynamics of Exploited Fish Populations," *Fishery Investigations Series* II, xix, Ministry of Agriculture, Fisheries and Food. London: Chapman and Hall.

Bisbal, G. A. (1995). "The Southeast South American Shelf Large Marine Ecosystem," *Marine Policy* 19(1): 21–38.

Brunneti, N. (1990). "The Evolution of the *Illex argentinus* (Castellanos, 1960) Fishery," *Informes Técnicos de Investigación Pesquera, Consejo Superior de Investigaciones Científicas,* Barcelona, No. 155: 1–19.

—— A. Aubone, G. Rossi et al. (2006). "*Illex argentinus.* Evaluación de la pesquería Pesquería 2006," *Informe final. INIDEP. Informe Técnico* No. 53: 1–37.

—— et al. (2007). "*Illex argentinus.* Evaluación de la pesquería. Pesquería 2007," *Informe final. INIDEP. Informe Técnico* No. 61: 1–22.

—— M. Ivanovic, A. Aubone et al. (2000). "Calamar (*Illex argentinus*)," in S. Rezzi, R. Akselman, E. Boschi (eds.), *Síntesis del estado de las pesquerías marítimas argentinas y de la Cuencia del Plata, Años 1997–1998, con actualización de 1999.* INIDEP Contribución N° 1129, Mar del Plata, 103–16.

—— S. Pineda, A. Aubone et al. (2002). "*Illex argentinus.* Evaluación de la pesquería Pesquería 2002," *Informe final. INIDEP. Informe Técnico* No. 87, 1–23.

Burke, W. (1989). "Fishing in the Bering Sea Donut Straddling Stocks and the International Law of Fisheries," *Ecology Law Quarterly* 16: 298–300.

Chen, C., T. Chiu, and W. Haung (2007). "The Spatial and Temporal Distribution Patterns of the Argentine Short-squid, *Illex argentinus,* Abundances in the Southwest Atlantic and the Effects of Environmental Influences," *Zoological Studies* 46(1): 111–22.

Clark, C. W. (1980). "Restricted Access to a Common Property Resource," in P. Liu (ed.), *Dynamic Optimization and Mathematical Economics.* New York: Plenum Press, 117–32.

—— (1990). *Mathematical Bioeconomics.* New York: John Wiley and Sons.

—— and G. Munro (1994). "Renewable Resources as Natural Capital: The Fishery," in A. M. Jannsson (ed.), *Investing in Natural Capital: The Ecological Economics Approach to Sustainability.* Washington, DC: Island Press, 343–61.

Cordo, H. E. (2006). "Estructura y abundancia del stock reproductor del abadejo (*Genypterus blacodes*) del Mar Argentino en el período 1995–2000," *INIDEP, Informe Técnico* No. 60: 1–17.

Dasgupta, P. (2008). "The Place of Nature in Economic Development," in D. Rodrik and M. Rosenzweig (eds.), *Handbook of Development Economics*, v. Amsterdam: Elsevier, 4977–5046.

—— (2009). "Trust and Cooperation among Economic Agents," *Philosophical Transactions of The Royal Society B* 364: 3301–09.

—— and G. Heal (1979). *Economic Theory and Exhaustible Resources.* Cambridge: Cambridge University Press.

De Oliveira, J. A., A. Uriarte, and B. A. Roel (2005). "Potential Improvements in the Management of Bay of Biscay Anchovy by Incorporating Environmental Indices as Recruitment Predictors," *Fisheries Research* 75: 2–14.

Domínguez Torreiro, M. and J. C. Surís-Regueiro (2007). "Cooperation and Non-cooperation in the Iberoatlantic Sardine Shared Stock Fishery," *Fisheries Research* 83: 1–10.

Falkland Islands Government (2005). *Fisheries Department Fisheries Statistics*, ix, 2004 (1995–2004), 1–99.

—— (2006). *Fisheries Department Fisheries Statistics*, x, 2005 (1996–2005), 1–91.

—— (2007). *Fisheries Department Fisheries Statistics*, xi, 2006 (1997–2006), 1–92.

—— (2008). *Fisheries Department Fisheries Statistics*, xii, 2007 (1998–2007), 1–93.

Folke, C., Å. Jansson, J. Rockström et al. (2011). "Reconnecting to the Biosphere," *Working Paper N°1 Prepared for the 3rd Nobel Laureate Symposium on Global Sustainability: Transforming the World in an Era of Global Change*, in Stockholm, 16–19 May 2011.

Fox, W. W. (1970). "An Exponential Surplus Model for Optimizing Exploited Fish Populations," *Transactions of the American Fisheries Society* 99: 80–8.

García-Negro, M. C. (2003). "Táboas Input-Output Pesca-Conserva Galegas 1999," *Consellería de Pesca e Asuntos Marítimos, Xunta de Galicia, Santiago de Compostela*, 1–175.

Gordon, H. S. (1954). "The Economic Theory of a Common-property Resource Fishery," *Journal of Political Economy* 62: 124–42.

Gulland, J. A. (1980). *Some Problems of the Management of Shared Stocks.* FAO Fisheries Technical Paper No. 206, Rome.

Hartfield, E. M. (1991). "Post-recruit Growth of the Patagonian Squid Logilo Gahi (d'Orbigny)," *Bulletin Marine Science* 49(1–2): 349–61.

Hannesson, R. (1995). "Fishing on the High Seas: Cooperation or Competition?" *Marine Policy* 19: 371–7.

Hilborn, R. and C. Walters (1992) *Quantitative Fisheries Stock Assessment: Choice, Dynamics and Uncertainty.* New York: Chapman and Hall.

Kaitala, V. and G. Munro (1993). "The Management of High Seas Fisheries," *Marine Resource Economics* 8: 313–29.

—— (1997). "The Conservation and Management of High Seas Fishery Resources under the New Law of the Sea," *Natural Resource Modeling* 10: 87–108.

Kronbak, L. G. and M. Lindroos (2007). "Sharing Rules and Stability in Coalition Games with Externalities," *Marine Resource Economics* 22: 137–54.

Laptikhovsky, V., A. V. Remeslo, C. M. Nigmatullin et al. (2001). "Recruitment Strength Forecasting of the Shortfin Squid *Illex Argentinus* (Cephalopoda: Ommastrephidae) Using Satellite SST Data, and Some Consideration of the Species' Population

Structure," Report to the International Council for the Exploration of the Sea, Copenhagen Denmark ICES, K15: 1–9.

Levin, S. A. (1999). *Fragile Dominion: Complexity and the Commons.* New York: Perseus Books.

MRAG, MG Otero, PolEM (2008). *Analysis of the Economic and Social Importance of Community Fishing Fleet Using Bottom Gears in the High Seas.* London: MRAG.

Munro, G. (1979). "The Optimal Management of Transboundary Renewable Resources," *Canadian Journal of Economics* 12: 353–76.

—— (1987). "The Management of Shared Fishery Resources and under Extended Jurisdiction," *Marine Resources Economics* 3: 271–96.

—— (1990). "The Optimal Management of Transboundary Fisheries: Game Theoretic Considerations," *Natural Resource Modeling* 4(4): 403–26.

—— R. Willmann, and A. Van Houtte (2005). "*The Conservation and Management of Shared Fish Stocks: Legal and Economic Aspects*," FAO Fisheries Technical Paper No. 465. Rome: Food and Agriculture Organization.

Ostrom, E. (1990). *Governing the Commons: The Evolution of Institutions for Collective Actions.* Cambridge: Cambridge University Press.

—— (2000). "Collective Action and the Evolution of Social Norms," *The Journal of Economic Perspectives* 14, 137–58.

Polasky, S., N. Tarui, G. M. Ellis et al. (2006). "Cooperation in the Commons," *Economic Theory* 29, 71–88.

Portela, J., M. Sacau, J. Wang et al. (2005). "Analysis of the Variability in the Abundance of Shortfin Squid (*Illex argentinus*) in the Southwest Atlantic Fisheries during the Period 1999_2004." Theme Session on Connecting Physical-Biological Interactions to Recruitment Variability, Ecosystem Dynamics, and the Management of Exploited Stocks (O), ICES CM 2005/O: 16.

Ricker, W. E. (1954) "Stock and Recruitment," *Journal of the Fisheries Research Board of Canada* 11: 559–623.

Rockström, J., W. Steffen, K. Noone et al. (2009). "A Safe Operating Space for Humanity," *Nature* 461: 472–5.

Schaefer, M. B. (1954). "Some Aspects of the Dynamics of Populations Important to the Management of Commercial Marine Fisheries," *Bulletin of the Inter-American Tropical Tuna Commission* 1: 27–56.

—— (1957). "A Study of the Dynamics of the Fishery for Yellowfin Tuna in the Eastern Tropical Pacific Ocean," *Bulletin of the Inter-American Tropical Tuna Commission* 2: 247–85.

Secretaría de Agricultura, Ganadería, Pesca y Alimentación (SAGPYA) (2007). 'Pesquerías de calamar y langostino situación actual'. 31 pp. Available online at <http://www.minagri.gob.ar/site/pesca/index.php> [accessed 5 December 2009].

—— (2008). "Indicadores de la pesca marítima". Available online at <http://www.minagri.gob.ar/site/pesca/index.php> [accessed 5 December 2009].

Sumaila, U. R. (1995). "Irreversible Capital Investment in a Two-stage Bimatrix Fishery Game Model," *Marine Resource Economics* 10(3): 263–83.

—— (1997). "Cooperative and Non-cooperative Exploitation of the Arcto-Norwegian Cod Stock," *Environmental and Resource Economics* 10: 147–65.

—— (1999). "A Review of Game-theoretic Models of Fishing," *Marine Policy* 23: 1–10.

—— D. Marsden, R. Watson et al. (2007). "Global Ex-vessel Fish Price Database: Construction, Spatial and Temporal Applications," *Journal of Bioeconomics* 9: 39–51.

—— C. Ninnes, and B. Oelofsen (2003). "Management of Shared Fish Stocks in the Benguela Marine Ecosystem," in *Expert Consultation on the Management of Shared Fish Stocks*, FAO Papers Presented at the Norway-FAO, Bergen, Norway, 7–10 October 2002, FAO Fisheries Report N° 695 Supplement, Rome, 143–58.

United Nations (UN) (1982). *United Nations Convention on the Law of the Sea*. New York: UN Doc. A/Conf.62/122.

—— (1995). *United Nations Conference on Straddling Fish Stocks and Highly Migratory Fish Stocks*. New York: A/CONF.164/37.

Villasante, S. and U. R. Sumaila (2008). "Economics of Fisheries Management of Straddling Fish Stocks in the Patagonian Marine Ecosystem," 5th World Fisheries Congress, Yokohama, Japan, 19–25 October.

Vincent, J. R. (2007). "Spatial Dynamics, Social Norms, and the Opportunity of the Commons," *Ecological Research* 22: 3–7.

Walker, B., S. Barret, S. Polasky et al. (2009). "Looming Global-scale Failures and Missing Institutions," *Science*, 325(5946): 1345–6.

Waluda, C. M., P. G. Rodhouse, G. P. Podestá et al. (2001) "Surface Oceanography of the Inferred Hatching Grounds of *Illex argentinus* (Cephalopoda: Ommastrephidae) and Influences on Recruitment Variability," *Marine Biology* 139: 671–9.

Wang, W. K. and C. O. Ewald (2010) "A Stochastic Differential Fishery Game for a Two Species Fish Population with Ecological Interaction," *Journal of Economic Dynamics and Control* 34: 844–57.

Wölher, O. C., J. E. Hansen, M. C. Cassia et al. (2007a). "Evaluación de polaca (*Micromesistius australis*) en el Atlántico Sudoccidental. Período 1987–2001," *INIDEP, Informe Técnico* No. 62: 27–52.

—— A. R. Giussi et al. (2007b). "Evaluación de merluza de cola (*Macruronus magellanicus*) en el Atlántico Sudoccidental. Período 1985–2001," *INIDEP, Informe Técnico* No. 62: 1–26.

14

Comments by Peter Hammond on "Why Cooperation is Better"

14.1 INTRODUCTION[1]

14.1.1 Background

The Argentine shortfin squid, with scientific name *Illex argentinus*, is fished off the eastern coast of Patagonia. This species has featured in several previously published papers, including Waluda et al. (2002, 2008). It is recognized as an interesting example of a "straddling" fish stock, meaning that the area in which it is fished is shared between two marine areas that are subject to regulation by different fishing authorities. In this case, the authorities are Argentina through its Exclusive Economic Zone, and the Falklands Islands Government (henceforth FIG) through its Interim Fisheries and Outer Conservation Zones.[2]

The preceding chapter by Villasante, Sumaila, and Antelo (2014) (henceforth VSA) discusses the benefits of coordinated regulation of this species, based on the Nash bargaining solution of a cooperative game between the two regulators, when compared to a Nash equilibrium non-cooperative arrangement.

14.1.2 Toward Optimal Fisheries Regulation

The VSA chapter recognizes that there are two separate fishing fleets, namely:

1. an Argentinian fleet which incurs costs of \$ 534 per unit of fishing effort, and sells its catch at a price of \$ 994 per tonne;

[1] This is an inadequate attempt to honor Partha Dasgupta, esteemed colleague and valued friend for the best part of forty-five years. The theme is somewhat related, though not as related as I had hoped it would be, not only to some of our coauthored work, but also to his Inaugural Lecture delivered at the London School of Economics on 12 November 1979, published as Dasgupta (1980), along with the book Dasgupta (1982).

[2] In fact, these squid spend a significant fraction of their life cycle in more northern areas of the southwest Atlantic Ocean, off the coasts of Uruguay and Brazil. It seems, however, that they

2. an international fleet regulated by agencies of FIG which incurs costs of \$ 816 per unit of fishing effort, and sells its catch at a price of \$ 1,862 per tonne.[3]

These numbers suggest there could be large gains simply from allowing the lower-cost Argentinian fleet to operate throughout the combined area, and to sell all its catch for the higher price available to the international fleet that fishes in waters regulated by FIG. There could then be even further gains from an enriched form of cooperation, with each fishing boat required to buy fishing licences, and the licensing revenue shared between the two authorities.[4]

Those two authorities, moreover, could then gain even more by choosing the licensing arrangements in order to maximize total benefit. The result would be an expanded utility possibility frontier, taking the form of a straight line of slope -1 which touches the frontier considered by VSA at a single point. One can still apply the Nash bargaining solution to this expanded frontier, thus reaching a point that, except in a special case, is even better.

Here I shall consider this kind of maximization problem, but in a more general dynamic setting.

14.1.3 Outline

The next Section 14.2 sets out a Markovian fishing game that is very similar to that of VSA. Following their analysis, it is assumed that cooperation between the two authorities is limited to coordinating the quotas they each set for the total catch they each allow in the area under their control. The quotas are chosen in order to maximize over an infinite horizon the expected total present discounted value of all future profits. Treating this recursive dynamic problem in full, however, would seem to require more sophisticated techniques than those used in VSA.

Thereafter Section 14.3 sets out a dynamic programming problem whose solution gives a first-best plan for a single integrated fishing industry, regarded as a single team in the sense of Marschak and Radner (1972). Unlike articles like Sandal and Steinshamn (2004), we have a discrete time model, but also introduce uncertainty.

are really only at a suitable stage of their life cycle for fishing when they are near the southern extremity of their range.

[3] These data for typical prices and costs are explained in the last two paragraphs of Section 4 in VSA.

[4] VSA rule out side payments because of the "political situation" (footnote 6), which may also make a revenue-sharing scheme difficult. It may still be worth understanding the magnitude of the resulting losses, however.

The concluding Section 14.4 combines some discussion of omitted considerations that may be important with some more general concluding remarks.

14.2 A MARKOVIAN FISHING MODEL

14.2.1 A Repeated Game

Following VSA, consider a game with two players $i \in \{1,2\}$, who are the regulatory authorities of the two regions/countries, with $i = 1$ as Argentina, and $i = 2$ as FIG (the Falkland Islands/Malvinas). Each authority is assumed to have the power to regulate perfectly the fleet of fishing vessels registered in the area that is subject to its *de facto* jurisdiction.

Using the notation of VSA, at the start of period or fishing season $t = 1, 2, \ldots$. let $B_t \in \mathbb{R}_+$ denote the estimated total spawning biomass of *Illex argentinus* spread between the two regulated areas. This will be the Markov state variable determining the continuation subgame from period t on.

In each period t, the two players $i \in \{1,2\}$ are assumed to inherit a known total biomass B_t that is spread over the two areas. The two players are each assumed to choose a total fishing effort $E_{i,t}$, which it allows to the fleet that fishes in the area under its own control. Following equations (VSA1), (VSA4) and (VSA5), the total catch $C_{i,t}$ ($i \in \{1,2\}$) in each area is assumed to be related to the relevant total fishing effort $E_{i,t}$ in that area, and to the total biomass B_t available in both areas.[5] Specifically, there is a Cobb–Douglas production function

$$C_{i,t} = F_i(E_{i,t}, B_t) = q_i (E_{i,t})^{\alpha_i} (B_t)^{1-\alpha_i} \tag{1}$$

which depends on a "catchability" or productivity parameter $q_i > 0$, as well as on the share parameter $\alpha_i \in (0,1)$, both specific to area i.

Let γ_i denote the monetary cost per unit of effort, assumed constant. Then (1) can be rearranged to express each player's monetary cost as a function

$$\gamma_i E_{i,t} = K_i(C_{i,t}, B_t) = \gamma_i (C_{i,t} / q_i)^{1/\alpha_i} (B_t)^{1-1/\alpha_i} \tag{2}$$

of its catch $E_{i,t}$ and the available biomass B_t. Then the total profit earned by the fleet in region i during period t is

$$\pi_{i,t} = p_i C_{i,t} - \gamma_i E_{i,t} = p_i C_{i,t} - K_i(C_{i,t}, B_t) \tag{3}$$

[5] The label (VSAn) indicates equation (n) in VSA.

where p_i is the price at which region i can sell its total catch, also assumed to be constant.

Following equations (VSA2) and (VSA3), the dynamics of the total fish biomass are given by

$$B_{t+1} = A(B_t) - C_t = (1+a)B_t - b(B_t)^2 - C_t \tag{4}$$

where $C_t = C_{1,t} + C_{2,t}$ denotes the total catch during season t, and $A(B_t)$ is a quadratic function that indicates how fast the biomass would accumulate in the absence of any fishing. The two players' respective payoff functions, starting in period 1, are the present discounted values (PDVs)

$$V_i = \sum_{t=1}^{\infty} \delta_i^{t-1} \pi_{i,t} \tag{5}$$

of their future profit streams $(\pi_{i,t})_{t=1}^{\infty}$.

14.2.2 The Non-cooperative Markovian Outcome

Consider an uncoordinated equilibrium in which the two players $i \in \{1,2\}$ choose respective stationary Markovian strategies $C_{i,t} = c_i(B_t)$ in each period t. These strategies depend only on the biomass B_t at the beginning of the fishing season, as well as on their expectations of the other player's stationary Markovian strategy. Along with the state valuation functions $J_i(B_t)$ for $i \in \{1,2\}$ giving the associated PDV of each player's equilibrium profit stream, these strategies will be solutions of the standard Bellman equations

$$\left.\begin{array}{lcl} c_i(B) & \in & \arg \\ J_i(B) & = & \end{array}\right\} \max_{c_i} \{p_i c_i - K_i(c_i, B) + \delta_i J_i(A(B) - c_i - c_j(B))\} \tag{6}$$

suitably modified to recognize that the biomass dynamics are affected by the total catch $c(B) = c_1(B) + c_2(B)$ of both fleets together. Thus, each player $i \in \{1,2\}$ solves an infinite horizon dynamic programming problem in order to determine an optimal response to the other player's given policy function $c_j(B)$ $(j \neq i)$.

Finding the full solution of such coupled dynamic programs would be seriously challenging, even using sophisticated numerical techniques developing those described by Judd (1998). Because the model is deterministic, however, finding an approximate solution near a stationary state $\overline{B}$ should be possible, but not even this limited task will be attempted here.

14.2.3 A First Cooperative Outcome

Alternatively, as in VSA, suppose that the two players share the same discount factor δ (which VSA take to be 0.96 in their assumption A2). Suppose the two players seek an agreement according to which the pair of Markovian strategies $(c_1^\beta(B), c_2^\beta(B))$ are chosen jointly in order to maximize the weighted logarithmic objective

$$V^\beta = \sum_{t=1}^{\infty} \delta^{t-1}[\beta \ln \pi_{1,t} + (1-\beta)\ln \pi_{2,t}] \tag{7}$$

which is similar to, but subtly different from, equation (VSA6). After introducing the notation

$$r(c_1, c_2, B) = \beta \ln[p_1 c_1 - K_1(c_1, B)] + (1-\beta)\ln[p_2 c_2 - K_2(c_2, B)] \tag{8}$$

for the appropriate current return function, the cooperative optimal policy $(c_1^\beta(B), c_2^\beta(B))$ and associated state valuation functions $J^\beta(B)$ must together solve the dynamic program described by the standard Bellman equation

$$\left.\begin{array}{rcl} (c_1^\beta(B), c_2^\beta(B)) & \in & \arg \\ J^\beta(B) & = & \end{array}\right\} \max_{(c_1, c_2)} \{r(c_1, c_2, B) + \delta J^\beta(A(B) - c_1 - c_2)\} \tag{9}$$

14.2.4 A Second Cooperative Outcome

Reverting to the original objective function specified in (VSA6), it can be written as

$$W_s := (P_{1,s})^\beta (P_{2,s})^{1-\beta}, \tag{10}$$

at each time s, where for $i \in \{1, 2\}$ one uses

$$P_{i,s} = \sum_{t=s}^{\infty} (\delta_i)^{t-s} \pi_{i,t}(C_{i,t}, B_t) \tag{11}$$

to denote the PDV of the future profit stream $(\pi_{i,t}(C_{i,t}, B_t))_{t=s}^{\infty}$.

As a function of the starting biomass B_s at time s, consider the planned stream $(C^s_{1,t}, C^s_{2,t})^\infty_{t=s}(B_s)$ of future catches each season that maximizes (10), along with the resultant future biomass stream $(B^s_t)^\infty_{t=s}(B_s)$. Then, in the absence of any relevant uncertainty, the continuation $(C^s_{1,t}, C^s_{2,t})^\infty_{t=r}(B_s)$ of this plan from any later time $r > s$ maximizes (10) when the earlier part of the plan $(C^s_{1,t}, C^s_{2,t})^{r-1}_{t=s}(B_s)$ is fixed at its optimal value, implying that

$$C_{i,t} = \bar{C}_{i,t} := C^s_{1,t}(B_t), \text{ for } i = 1,2 \text{ and } \bar{B}_t := B_t(B_s) \tag{12}$$

for $t = s, s-1, \ldots, r-1$. That is, $(C^s_{1,t}, C^s_{2,t})^\infty_{t=r}(B_s)$ maximizes

$$W_s := (\bar{P}^r_{1,s} + \delta_1^{r-s} P_{1,r})^\beta (\bar{P}^r_{2,s} + \delta_2^{r-s} P_{2,r})^{1-\beta}, \tag{13}$$

where for $i \in \{1,2\}$ one uses

$$P_{i,r} := \sum\nolimits_{t=r}^{\infty} (\delta_i)^{t-r} \pi_{i,t}(\bar{C}_{i,t}, \bar{B}_t) \tag{14}$$

to denote the updated version of (11). Next, given any time $r > s$, consider the plan $(C^r_{1,t}, C^r_{2,t})^\infty_{t=r}(B^s_r(B_s))$ that maximizes the updated version

$$W_r := (P_{1,r})^\beta (P_{2,r})^{1-\beta}, \tag{15}$$

of (10), while starting from biomass $B^s_r(B_s)$ at time r. It easy to see that this plan will differ from the continuation $(C^s_{1,t}, C^s_{2,t})^\infty_{t=r}(B_s)$ of the original plan formulated at time s, which maximizes (13). This reflects the fact that the sequence of successive objectives $W_s, W_{s+1}, \ldots$ defined by (10) violate Strotz's (1956) dynamic consistency condition.

As usual when faced with such inconsistency, there are two approaches to dynamic planning:[6]

naïve choice, where the stream $(C^0_{1,t}, C^0_{2,t})^\infty_{t=0}(B_0)$ is chosen at a fixed time $s = 0$ without regard to the possibility that the plan could be revised at some later time s;

sophisticated choice, where it is assumed that any plan will be revised whenever that seems expedient, leading to the plan in period s being chosen in

[6] Strotz himself disregarded the naïve approach described here, assuming instead that this kind of unconstrained optimum could actually be achieved through some form of pre-commitment. Yet pre-commitment usually takes the form of finding devices to modify the decision tree so that sophisticated choice has consequences identical to those that would result from naïve choice in the unmodified tree. See Hammond (1976), for example.

order to maximize the objective W_s subject to the constraints that result from applying the same sophisticated rule in order to determine the harvesting stream $(C^r_{1,t}, C^r_{2,t})^\infty_{t=r}(B_r)$ in each future period $r = s+1, s+2, \ldots$

Among the many other works published since Phelps and Pollak (1968) that investigate the implications of sophisticated planning, I mention in particular Dasgupta's work on "generation-relative ethics" in determining optimal population and savings—see for example Dasgupta (1974a, b, 2005), as well as Asheim (1988).

In order to determine a sophisticated Markovian planning rule, the recursive system to be solved is

$$\left.\begin{array}{rcl} (\hat{c}_1^\beta(B), \hat{c}_2^\beta(B)) & \in & \arg \\ \hat{J}^\beta(B) & = & \end{array}\right\} \max_{(c_1,c_2)} \{S(c_1, c_2, B)\} \tag{16}$$

where

$$S(c_1, c_2, B) = [R_1(c_1, c_2, B)]^\beta [R_2(c_1, c_2, B)]^{1-\beta} \tag{17}$$

and, for $i \in \{1, 2\}$, one has

$$R_i(c_1, c_2, B) = \pi_i(c_i, B) + \delta_i \hat{J}_i^\beta(A(B) - c_1 - c_2) \tag{18}$$

$$\text{with} \quad \hat{J}_i^\beta(B) = R_i(\hat{c}_1^\beta(B), \hat{c}_2^\beta(B), B). \tag{19}$$

Note that this equation system involves no less than three different state valuation functions $\hat{J}^\beta(B)$, $\hat{J}_1^\beta(B)$, and $\hat{J}_2^\beta(B)$ for the payoffs accruing to society and to each of the two players, respectively.

14.2.5 A Nash Bargaining Outcome

Inspired by (VSA7), one can also consider a Nash bargaining outcome where the status quo in each subgame starting with biomass B is taken to be the Markov perfect equilibrium described in Section 2.2, with payoffs $J_i(B)$ to the two players $i \in \{1, 2\}$. This is very similar to Section 14.2.4, with the difference that the objective W_s for period s defined by (10) is replaced by the Nash bargaining objective

$$W_s^N := (P_{1,s} - \overline{P}_{1,s})^\beta (P_{2,s} - \overline{P}_{2,s})^{1-\beta} \tag{20}$$

Here $P_{i,s}$ denotes the PDV of i's future profits, defined by (11) for $i \in \{1,2\}$ and for $s = 0,1,2,\ldots$. On the other hand, $\bar{P}_{i,s}$ is the corresponding expression

$$\bar{P}_{i,s}(B_s) = \sum_{t=s}^{\infty} (\delta_i)^{t-s} \pi_{i,t}(\bar{C}_{i,t}(B_s), \bar{B}_t(B_s)) \tag{21}$$

for the PDV of future profits that i would earn along the deterministic path

$$\left(\bar{C}_{1,t}^s(B_s), \bar{C}_{2,t}^s(B_s)\right)_{t=s}^{\infty} \tag{22}$$

with future biomass stream $\left(\bar{B}_t(B_s)\right)_{t=s}^{\infty}$ which results from consistently applying the status quo Markov perfect non-cooperative equilibrium strategies $c_i(B)$ $(i = 1,2)$ when starting from the biomass state B_s at time s. Because of stationarity, there must exist functions $\bar{J}_i(B)$ for $i \in \{1,2\}$, independent of s, such that

$$\bar{P}_{i,s}(B) = \bar{J}_i(B) \tag{23}$$

for all possible biomass stocks B.

The recursive system to be solved then consists of a minor revision to the earlier system specified by (16), (17), (18) and (19). Specifically, the maximand (17) in (16) becomes

$$S(c_1, c_2, B) = [R_1(c_1, c_2, B) - \bar{J}_1(B)]^{\beta} [R_2(c_1, c_2, B) - \bar{J}_2(B)]^{1-\beta} \tag{24}$$

as a result of subtracting from each player's return $R_i(c_1, c_2, B)$ the PDV $\bar{J}_i(B)$ of the profit stream that player i would earn along the status quo Markov perfect equilibrium path starting with the given biomass B.

14.3 A FIRST-BEST FISHING POLICY

14.3.1 A General Model

This section presents a stochastic dynamic model in which one can consider optimal Markov policies for the coordinated regulation of a fishing industry that relies on the biomass of n different species labelled $f = 1,2,\ldots,n$. The state variable at each time t will accordingly be a biomass vector $b_t \in \mathbb{R}_+^n$.

Suppose there is a fixed population of potential fishing firms $i \in I$. Let $y_t^i \in \mathbb{R}_+^n$ denote firm i's total catch vector during season t for the n different species. Assume that for all t, firm i has a cost function

$$\mathbb{R}_+^n \times \mathbb{R}_+^n \ni (y, b) \mapsto k_t^i(y, b) \in \mathbb{R}_+ \tag{25}$$

with the following properties:

1. for all $b \geqq 0$, it satisfies $k_t^i(0,b) = 0$ when the catch $y = 0$;
2. it is continuous for $y \neq 0$;
3. it is lower semi-continuous for all $(y,b) \in \mathbb{R}_+^n \times \mathbb{R}_+^n$;
4. it is increasing in the catch vector y;
5. it is decreasing in the biomass vector b.

Let $p_t \in \mathbb{R}_+^n$ denote the expectation of the price vector at which the different fish species can be sold. This is assumed to be determined by world market conditions, and so is unaffected by fish yields in the regulated area. Because the firms are assumed to maximize expected profit, only the expected price vector is relevant.

Assume in addition that there is a uniform upper bound $\bar{\pi}$ such that

$$p_t y - k_t^i(y,b) \leq \bar{\pi} \tag{26}$$

for all t, y, b, and i.

14.3.2 Events Each Period

Within each period or fishing season t, the assumed sequence of events is as follows:

1. The biomass vector $b_t \in \mathbb{R}_+^n$ and expected sales price vector $p_t \in \mathbb{R}_+^n$ are both observed and then publicly announced.
2. Each firm $i \in I$ chooses a catch vector $y_t^i \in \mathbb{R}_+^n$, thereby incurring a deterministic cost $k_t^i(y_t^i, b_t)$ given the biomass vector b_t.
3. Each firm $i \in I$ earns an expected total pre-tax profit

$$\pi_t^i(y_t^i, b_t) = p_t \cdot y_t^i - k_t^i(y_t^i, b_t) \tag{27}$$

   in period t from producing and selling its catch vector y_t^i.
4. A state of the sea z_t emerges randomly from a fixed topological space Z according to a probability measure P_t defined on the Borel subsets of Z.
5. For each period $t = 0, 1, 2, \ldots$, there is an *accumulation function*

$$\mathbb{R}_+^n \times Z \ni (b_t, z_t) \mapsto a_{t+1}(b_t, z_t) \in \mathbb{R}_+^n \tag{28}$$

which, given both the previous year's spawning biomass vector b_t and the state of the sea z_t, determines next period's potential accumulated biomass vector a_{t+1}. Let

$$Y_t := \sum_{i \in I} y_t^i \tag{29}$$

denote the aggregate yield vector in period t. This is deducted, as far as possible, from $a_{t+1}(b_t, z_t)$ in order to determine next period's estimated biomass vector

$$b_{t+1} = \beta_{t+1}(b_t, Y_t, z_t) \in \mathbb{R}_+^n \tag{30}$$

where

$$\mathbb{R}_+^n \times \mathbb{R}_+^n \times Z \ni (b_t, Y_t, z_t) \mapsto \beta_{t+1}(b_t, Y_t, z_t) \in \mathbb{R}_+^n \tag{31}$$

is a vector function whose respective components satisfy

$$b_{f,t+1}(b_t, Y_t, z_t) = \max\{0, a_{f,t+1}(b_t, z_t) - Y_{f,t}\} \in \mathbb{R}_+ \tag{32}$$

for each fish species $f = 1, 2, \ldots, n$.

Given the input biomass vector $b_t = (b_{f,t})_{f=1}^n$ at time t, the accumulation function (28) is assumed to satisfy the condition that if $b_{f,t} = 0$, meaning that the fth fish species has already become extinct by time t, then one has $a_{f,t+1}(b_t, z_t) = 0$ regardless of z_t. Hence, after any fish species has become extinct, it can never again achieve a positive biomass.

Note that for any stock vector b_t and aggregate catch vector Y_t in period t, the stochastic process defined by (30) determines the conditional expectation of any measurable function $\mathbb{R}_+^n \ni b_{t+1} \mapsto \psi(b_{t+1}) \in \mathbb{R}$ of next period's random stock vector $b_{t+1} = \beta_{t+1}(b_t, Y_t, z_t)$, which we denote by

$$\mathbb{E}\left[\psi(b_{t+1}) \mid b_t, Y_t\right] := \int_Z \psi(\beta_{t+1}(b_t, Y_t, z_t)) P_t(dz_t). \tag{33}$$

14.3.3 First-best Policy

Let y_t^I denote the entire profile $\langle y_t^i \rangle_{i \in I}$ of different firms' fishing effort vectors in period t. Consider a single regulator for a unified fishing fleet who starts in period $t = s$ with a given biomass vector b_s. Suppose that the regulator totally controls fishing activity in the relevant area.

Given the catch profile y_t^I and biomass vector b_t, let

$$\Pi_t^i(y_t^I, b_t) = \sum_{i \in I} \pi_t^i(y_t^i, b_t) = p_t \cdot Y_t - \sum_{i \in I} k_t^i(y_t^i, b_t) \tag{34}$$

denote the total profit made by all firms in period t. The regulator's objective is assumed to be the present discounted value

$$W_s := \sum_{t=s}^{\infty} \delta^{t-s} \sum_{i \in I} \mathbb{E}\pi_t^i(y_t^i, b_t) = \sum_{t=s}^{\infty} \delta^{t-s} \, \mathbb{E}\Pi_t(y_t^I, b_t) \tag{35}$$

of the total expected profit earned by all the firms that fish in the regulated area, after applying a fixed discount factor $\delta \in (0,1)$ to future profits. Let $\hat{J}_s(b_s)$ denote the associated *state valuation function*, equal to the maximized value of W_s when starting from the biomass state vector b_s at time s.

Assuming that an optimal policy will be pursued from period $t+1$ on, we specify an appropriate policy objective for the whole industry at time t, as a function of the choice variable y_t^I given the state b_t. It is the sum

$$\Pi_t(y_t^I, b_t) + \delta \mathbb{E}\left[\hat{J}_{t+1}(b_{t+1}) \mid b_t, Y_t\right] \tag{36}$$

of total profit at time t and of discounted expected future profit, given the new biomass state vector $b_{t+1}(b_t, Y_t, z_t)$ given by (30) for each possible state of the sea z_t.

Now for $t = s, s+1, \ldots$, the regulator's first-best optimal output policy function $\mathbb{R}_+^n \ni b_t \mapsto \hat{y}_t^I(b_t) \in (\mathbb{R}_+^n)^I$ must satisfy the modified Bellman equation

$$\left.\begin{array}{lcl} \hat{y}_t^I(b_t) & \in & \arg \\ \hat{J}_t(b_t) & = & \end{array}\right\} \max_{y_t^I} \left\{\Pi_t(y_t^I, b_t) + \delta \mathbb{E}\left[\hat{J}_{t+1}(b_{t+1}) \mid b_t, Y_t\right]\right\} \tag{37}$$

14.3.4 Existence

Introduce the notation $\mathcal{J}^\infty$ for the space of all non-negative valued bounded functions

$$\{s, s+1, s+2, \ldots\} \times \mathbb{R}_+^n \ni (t,b) \mapsto J_t(b) \in [0, (1-\delta)^{-1}\bar{\pi}] \tag{38}$$

that are also measurable, where $\bar{\pi}$ is the upper bound on profits defined by (26).

Equivalently, as the notation might suggest, this can be regarded as a space of all infinite sequences of appropriately bounded measurable functions defined on $\mathbb{R}^n_+$.

Next, define the operator Ψ on the space $\mathcal{J}^\infty$ so that

$$\Psi(J^\infty)_t(b_t) := \max_{y_t^I} \left\{ \Pi_t(y_t^I, b) + \delta \mathbb{E}\left[J_{t+1}(b_{t+1}) \mid b_t, Y_t \right] \right\} \tag{39}$$

for all $t = s, s+1, s+2, \ldots$ and all $b_t \in \mathbb{R}^n_+$. Because profits are assumed to be non-negative and bounded above by $\bar{\pi}$ defined by (26), it is evident that

$$0 \leq \Psi(J^\infty)_t(b_t) \leq \bar{\pi} + \delta(1-\delta)^{-1}\bar{\pi} = (1-\delta)^{-1}\bar{\pi}. \tag{40}$$

It follows that $\Psi(J^\infty)_t(b) \in [0, (1-\delta)^{-1}\bar{\pi}]$ for all $J^\infty \in \mathcal{J}^\infty$ and all $(t, b) \in \{s, s+\mathbb{R}^n_+, s+\mathbb{R}^n_+, \ldots\} \times \mathbb{R}^n_+$, implying that $\Psi : \mathcal{J}^\infty \to \mathcal{J}^\infty$.

Now, using a minor variation of the contraction mapping argument that is generally used to justify the Bellman equation, one can show that the mapping $\Psi : \mathcal{J}^\infty \to \mathcal{J}^\infty$ has a unique fixed point $(t, b) \mapsto \hat{J}_t(b)$ in the function space $\mathcal{J}^\infty$ which, together with the mapping $(t, b) \mapsto \hat{y}^I_t(b)$, must satisfy (37).

14.4 CONCLUDING REMARKS

14.4.1 Incomplete Information

So far this chapter has concentrated on the unrealistic special case when the regulator has complete information about the costs of each fishing firm. A more realistic challenge would be to allow for incomplete information. Because of the obvious analogy between overfishing and pollution, one could try to extend to a rather general dynamic framework the ideas presented, inter alia, in Dasgupta, Hammond, and Maskin (1980, henceforth DHM). Specifically, the theoretical challenge now is to find suitable tax functions so that each fishing firm $i \in I$, in any period t and given any biomass vector b_t, is encouraged not only to choose its part $\hat{y}^i_t(b_t)$ of the first-best output plan $\hat{y}^I_t(b_t)$ for the industry as a whole, but also to reveal its cost function truthfully. Providing incentives for the "conglomerate" of fishing firms to operate as a team in this way was the challenge that Groves (1973) originally met in a general static setting. Later, Green and Laffont (1976, 1977, 1979) applied similar ideas to public decision-making, and DHM adapted Groves' solution to treat pollution problems.

14.4.2 Other Neglected Considerations

The analysis of this chapter, like that of VSA, has an excessively simple model of fishing activity. It is surely unrealistic to assume that different firms' costs are given by a deterministic function of the given yield profile y_t^I. Not only is there a stochastic yield given the effort profile; in addition, different firms' efforts are likely to interfere with each other.

Indeed, a more detailed model of fishing activity is likely to require a continuous time analysis of each firm's activities, and of the catch size that results whenever a boat unloads its nets. Real fishing boats choose in real time where to cast their nets given the latest information they have about each others' activities, as well as the readings from monitoring devices intended to track where there should be a good yield. Really smart regulation could also respond to the most up-to-date information that can be acquired by careful continuous time monitoring of the whole fishing fleet, as well as the content of each boat's nets each time they unload their catch on board.

14.4.3 Envoi

In effect, this chapter provides a theoretical background for what, if political considerations allowed, might conceivably turn out to be a significantly improved regulatory policy for a cooperative body that did actually function for well over a decade—namely the South Atlantic Fisheries Commission (SAFC).[7] Though the best solution, in fact, may be to circumvent governments altogether. Indeed, there could be much to gain from suitable collusion among fishing firms. They could in effect set up their own transnational regulatory authority to operate as a fishing cartel for the south-west Atlantic along the lines of what OPEC has done for petroleum exporting nations. For the time being, such a cartel may well have to abide by the constraints imposed by the two authorities' suboptimal regulatory policies. Yet, over the longer run, one could hope that the putative cartel could form a united

[7] Though talks had occurred during the previous year, it seems that this commission was not officially created until a Joint Statement issued in Madrid on 28th November 1990—the same day that Margaret Thatcher relinquished her position as UK prime minister. See pages 12–13 of < http://www.official-documents.gov.uk/document/cm18/1824/1824.pdf>. According to a transcript of an interview with the Falkland Islands News Network published at <http://www.sartma.com/art_9007_3_6_1.html> (accessed 17 October 2013), this commission is no longer allowed to operate. It may be significant, however, that the main current concern seems to be with the stock of southern blue whiting (*Micromesistius australis australis*) rather than of *Illex argentinus*.

pressure group powerful enough to bring about better fishing regulation over the whole combined area.

Meanwhile, the governments of Argentina and the United Kingdom both seem to have forgotten the following words of the celebrated Argentinian author Jorge Luis Borges: "The Falklands thing was a fight between two bald men over a comb."[8] One hopes that the politicians and the electorates who support them will come to their senses before any more serious damage is done. Yet a worry is that the current phase of belligerence may reflect an unfortunate perception that there may after all be enough fish and oil under the waters off the Malvinas/Falkland Islands to make their possible control seem worth a costly dispute. Then one perverse benefit of continuing bad regulation of the fishing industry could be lowered estimates of what the disputed resources are worth, which could reduce the temptation for jingoistic saber-rattling, or worse.

References

Asheim, G. (1988) "Rawlsian Intergenerational Justice as a Markov-Perfect Equilibrium in a Resource Technology," *Review of Economic Studies*, 55: 469–83.

Dasgupta, P. (1974a). "On Some Problems Arising from Professor Rawls' Conception of Distributive Justice," *Theory and Decision*, 4: 325–44.

—— (1974b). "On Some Alternative Criteria for Justice Between Generations," *Journal of Public Economics*, 3: 305–23.

—— (1980). "Decentralization and Rights," *Economica*, 47: 107–23.

—— (1982). *The Control of Resources*. Cambridge, MA: Harvard University Press.

—— (2005). "Regarding Optimum Population," *Journal of Political Philosophy*, 13: 414–42.

—— P. Hammond, and E. Maskin (1980). "On Imperfect Information and Optimal Pollution Control," *Review of Economic Studies*, 47: 857–60.

Green, J. R. and J.-J. Laffont (1976). "On the Revelation of Preferences for Public Goods," *Journal of Public Economics*, 8: 79–93.

—— (1977). "Characterization of Satisfactory Mechanisms for the Revelation of Preferences for Public Goods," *Econometrica*, 45: 427–38.

—— (1979). *Incentives in Public Decision-Making*. Amsterdam: North-Holland.

Groves, T. (1973) "Incentives in Teams," *Econometrica*, 41: 617–31.

Hammond, P. J. (1976). "Changing Tastes and Coherent Dynamic Choice," *Review of Economic Studies*, 43: 159–73.

Judd, K. L. (1998). *Numerical Methods in Economics*. Cambridge, MA: MIT Press.

Marschak, J. and R. Radner (1972). *Economic Theory of Teams*. New Haven and London: Yale University Press.

Phelps, E. S. and R. A. Pollak (1968). "Second-Best National Savings and Game Equilibrium Growth," *Review of Economic Studies*, 35: 185–99.

[8] As quoted in *Time* magazine (14 February 1983).

Sandal, L. K. and S. I. Steinshamn (2004) "Dynamic Cournot-Competitive Harvesting of a Common Pool Resource," *Journal of Economic Dynamics and Control*, 28: 1781–99.

Strotz, R. H. (1956). "Myopia and Inconsistency in Dynamic Utility Maximization," *Review of Economic Studies*, 23: 165–80.

Villasante, S., U. R. Sumaila, and M. Antel (2014). "Why Cooperation is Better? The Gains of Cooperative Management of the Argentine Shortfin Squid Fishery in South America." This volume.

Waluda, C. M., P. N. Trathan, C. D. Elvidge et al. (2002). "Throwing Light on Straddling Stocks of *Illex argentinus*: Assessing Fishing Intensity with Satellite Imagery," *Canadian Journal of Fisheries and Aquatic Sciences* 59: 592–6.

Waluda, C. M., H. J. Griffiths, and P. G. Rodhouse (2008). "Remotely Sensed Spatial Dynamics of the *Illex argentinus* Fishery, Southwest Atlantic," *Fisheries Research* 91: 196–202.

15

Occupational and Environmental Health Impacts from Mining in Orissa, India[1]

Karnjana Sanglimsuwan, Erin O. Sills, Subhrendu K. Pattanayak, Shubhayu Saha, Ashok Singha, and Barendra Sahoo

15.1 INTRODUCTION

Expansion of mining in eastern India has been controversial, largely because of impacts on previously isolated environments and peoples. Environmental health problems draw particular concern, because they affect people who live in mineral-rich areas but do not necessarily derive benefits from mining. This parallels worldwide concerns about "the social and spatial distribution of both mining's benefits and its socioeconomic and environmental costs" (Bridge 2004) and well-publicized conflicts between mining companies and local communities (Kemp, Owen, Gotzmann, and Bond 2010). We examine the impacts of iron ore mining in Keonjhar district in the eastern Indian state of Orissa. The common argument in favor of mining is that it generates employment in underdeveloped regions. Thus, we first quantify the proportion and distribution of local people employed in mining. Second, we use our model of employment to control for occupational effects (including both direct occupational health effects and indirect income effects) in models of environmental health. Econometric modeling results indicate that waterborne diseases are more common among people who live closer to the mines, after controlling

[1] This study was partially funded by the World Bank. The authors are grateful to Richard Damania, Kseniya Lvovsky, Jennifer Miller, Pravash Sahu, Robert Solow, Jui-Chen Yang, and seminar participants at Indian Statistical Institute (Delhi), Institute of Economic Growth (Delhi), Government of Orissa Workshop on Mining and Growth and the ABCDE (Stockholm) meetings for their help during various stages of the study.

for factors such as employment in the mine, socioeconomic status, and access to infrastructure, while respiratory diseases are more common among mine workers, all else being equal. These results provide some evidence for the environmental justice concerns that have been raised by environmental and human rights groups with regards to mining in eastern India, and illustrate the importance of considering the environment when planning economic development (Dasgupta 2001a).

People living close to mines may suffer the environmental health effects of degradation associated with land-use change from mining and infrastructure development; top soil removal; overburden dumping; acid mine drainage; the degradation of surface and ground water quality; and increases in temperature and air pollution. People who live close to mining areas are likely to consume drinking water from surface and groundwater sources contaminated by chemical wastes and debris from mining activities (Winkel, Berg, Amini, Hug, and Johnson 2008). Mining activities also generate particulate matter, dust, and noise. Thus, people who live close to mining areas commonly suffer respiratory illnesses and other health problems (IDRC 2006; Ghose 2008).

Some of the same illnesses can be associated with working in mines. In general, occupational health includes health problems that occur at work or because of the kind of work. In addition to injuries, accidents, and hearing or vision problems, these include illness caused by breathing, touching, or ingesting unsafe substances. In modern mining, occupational health hazards are especially associated with chemicals. Chemicals posing a physical or health hazard can enter the body via contact, ingestion, and inhalation (Patnaik 1999). For example, crystalline silica has long been a serious hazard in mining, associated with silico-tuberculosis (Holman et al.1987; Cowie and Mabena 1991). In addition to specific chemical hazards associated with particular mining technologies, mine workers are generally exposed to polluted air and water due to dust and mine waste.

Mines also disturb local ecosystems, with impacts ranging from degraded landscape aesthetics to habitat fragmentation (Di Giulio, Holderegger, and Tobias 2009; Sinha et al. 2007). According to Patz et al. (2004), "land-use change activities such as agricultural encroachment, deforestation, road construction, dam building, irrigation, wetland modification, mining, the concentration or expansion of urban environments, coastal zone degradation, and other activities lead to the infectious disease outbreaks and emergence events and modify the transmission of endemic infections." Specifically, changes in ecosystems are often associated with an increase in vector-borne parasitic disease. Pattanayak and Yasaoka (2008) argue that deforestation for mine development not only creates breeding sites, but also increases human contacts with vectors. For example, Yapabandara and Curtis (2004) concluded that changes in the environment due to gem mining may have caused the emergence of

Anopheles subpictus and *Anopheles varuna* mosquito as significant malaria vectors in Sri Lanka.

On the other hand, mining can have beneficial local impacts by creating employment and new investment in infrastructure (Weber-Fahr et al. 2002; Hamann and Kapelus 2004). Especially where there is significant under-employment, new mining jobs increase income and thereby improve quality of life, including health.

Thus, opening or expanding mines can impact the health of local communities through multiple pathways. Those living close to mines are more likely to obtain employment in mining, and therefore more likely both to receive income benefits and to face occupational health hazards. They are also more likely to be exposed to environmental degradation, with direct impacts on health as well as indirect effects on well-being through degradation of natural resources that are central to traditional livelihoods.

This research analyzes the impact of mining on local well-being and in particular, the environmental health effects that are imposed on local populations by mining near their villages. While recognizing that mine closure will present additional challenges in the future (such as loss of employment and other economic benefits while environmental degradation and public health issues persist), we focus on the contemporaneous impacts of active mining. In order to identify these effects, we first examine the distribution of mine employment in the local population, so that we can control for occupational health effects. We then model the incidences of diseases associated with air and water pollution, as well as ecosystem disturbance.

The next section introduces the study area, with a focus on mining activities. Section 15.3 presents a conceptual framework and additional background on how mining impacts local public health. Sections 15.4 and 15.5 describe the empirical methods and the data. Section 15.6 contains the empirical results, with conclusions and discussion in the last section.

15.2 STUDY AREA

The state of Orissa is located on the east coast of India. The total population of the state is approximately thirty-seven million, with 85 percent in rural areas, according to the 2001 Census of India. Orissa is one of the most mineral-rich states of India, with one third of Indian reserves of iron ore and more than half of national reserves of bauxite, chromite, and manganese.

This mineral wealth is a key factor in recent structural shifts in Orissa's economy. Agriculture and allied activities that accounted for 60 percent of the gross state domestic product (GSDP) in 1950–51 declined to 22 percent by 2009–10, while industry (including mining and quarrying) increased from

12 percent in 1950–51 to over 30 percent in 2009–10. Between 1993 and 2005, despite substantial growth in the GSDP, poverty rates were stagnant, and by 2004–05, Orissa had the highest poverty headcount ratio of all major states in India. In more recent years, poverty has fallen from 57.2 percent in 2004–05 to 47.3 percent in 2009–10. However, spatial disaggregation shows that poverty remains highest in the regions of the state with the largest numbers of mines. In particular, the poverty rate among Scheduled Castes and Scheduled Tribes[2] in these regions remains above 50 percent (Planning Commission).

The region of Orissa with the highest concentration of mines is Keonjhar, in the middle mountainous and highlands zone of the state (Indian Bureau of Mines 2005). Keonjhar is a landlocked district with an area of 8,249 square kilometers, including about 2,225 square kilometers of forest. According to the 2001 census, the total population of Keonjhar was approximately 1,600,000, with a rapid population growth rate of 16.83 percent per year. The scheduled tribes are about 44.5 percent of the total population and represent a key labor force for agriculture, mining, and quarrying. Iron ore deposits are found throughout the district, along with manganese and chromite in some areas. Industry in the district is also based on mining, including the Kalinga Iron Works in Barbil and the Ferro-Manganese Plant in Joda.

Mining activities first began in Keonjhar in the 1950s in Joda Block, which has very high-grade iron ore. By 1984, ninety-two mining leases had been issued, of which seventy-two were operational. According to the Indian Bureau of Mines (2005), the total number of mines in Keonjhar increased over 50 percent from seventy-six in 2001 to 119 in 2005. These are open-cast mines, operating in forty-six mining lease areas that officially occupy twelve thousand hectares. In addition to the mines themselves, the district has eighteen sponge iron units and 110 iron ore crushers, both of which are significant sources of particulate matter. Although none of the mines or mining industries are owned outright by multinational companies, several multinational mining companies have significant interests in mining leases in Keonjhar, and many of the mining companies are integrated into the global supply chains of multinationals in China and other countries[3]. The income earned by mining companies operating in the state has been reported to be larger than the state government's budget (*The Economic Times* 2011). Illegal mining of iron and manganese ores in Keonjhar started in 2000 in response to the growing demand for steel in the

[2] Scheduled Castes and Scheduled Tribes are social groups that have been historically marginalized in India. Years of discrimination have restricted social mobility and prosperity among members of these groups. Even though this legacy of deprivation is now recognized and national policies of affirmative action have been designed to protect their interests, these groups still suffer from poor quality of life.

[3] Multinational companies with significant interests in mining leases in Keonjhar include POSCO, Rio Tinto, and Acrecllor Mittol. Large Indian corporations like Tata and JSPL are also engaged in mining operations in the area.

international market (Das 2009). This has attracted significant public concern, partly due to pollution and failure to rehabilitate illegal mining areas.

In total, mining activities in Keonjhar had expanded to 333 square kilometers by 2008 (Barik 2009). Open-cast mines have displaced agricultural fields and forests (Vasundhara 2008). However, the mines are also productive. More than a hundred billion tonnes of iron has been produced in Keonjhar, and just during the decade from 1998 to 2007, the total value of iron ore mined was valued at over Rs. 50,000 crores ($US 110 billion), or 21 percent of India's total production (Barik 2009).

Despite its wealth of mineral resources, 62 percent of Keonjhar's population still lived below the poverty line in 2008 (Vasundhara 2008). In 2004, Keonjhar ranked twenty-fourth out of thirty districts of Orissa in terms of the Human Development Index (Orissa 2004), and twenty-second in terms of HDI in the health sector (United Nation Development Programme 2004). In particular, Keonjhar has high morbidity and mortality rates from malaria and tuberculosis (TB) (Barnett et al. 2008), along with high incidences of the symptoms of various tropical diseases such as fever and jaundice. The per capita income of Keonjhar in 2001 was only Rs. 5,286 (US$ 116), well below the average per capita income of Orissa of Rs. 6,487 (US$ 142) and the Indian average per capita income of Rs. 11,779 (US$ 259).

The mines in Orissa offer both formal and informal employment. Public sector mines operate with a higher percentage of formal employees, while private sector mines typically rely on contract labor. The contractors pay low wages, especially to women, and are often in violation of employment law, including failure to provide leave, insurance, or compensation for workplace injuries. Devata (2010) found that only about 30 percent of contract mine workers are supplied with personal safety gear and that dust-protecting masks are not used in any mines in Orissa. While conditions in the formal sector (e.g. in public sector mines) are relatively better, those workers also face higher cost of living in regions around the mines. Both formal employees and contract workers face hazardous conditions in the mines, and Devata (2010) reported that many are dismissed from employment due to illness or injury after fewer than five years working in the mines.

15.3 CONCEPTUAL FRAMEWORK

Achieving real economic development through mining is challenging. Mining activities clearly create value added, provide employment, and generate income. But those same activities almost always adversely impact the environment and eventually human health. The distribution of mining's benefits and costs is a point of controversy, especially in the case of multinational mining firms expanding into previously isolated and poor parts of the developing world. In Keonhjar, for example, activists have raised concerns that the indigenous people will bear most of the costs of mining, through loss of land and environmental pollution (Vasundhara 2008). Advocates for mining argue that the populations closest to the mines stand to benefit the most from employment and potentially from social services such as health care provided by the mining companies (*The Telegraph*, 2010). We examine impacts of mining on the health of people living near the mines, controlling for employment. This allows us to focus on the environmental justice issues related to development of mines near traditional populations that have lived in the region for generations, netting out the impacts (positive and negative) of new employment opportunities in the mines.

Figure 15.1 presents a conceptual framework of mining's impact on public health in local communities. To the extent that mines employ local people, there are both occupational and environmental health impact channels, both conditional on individual as well as household characteristics that we label as "external factors." The occupational health channel depends on employment in the mine, which may itself be endogenous to health status as well as those individual and household characteristics. Further, employment in the mine can impact health by increasing income as well

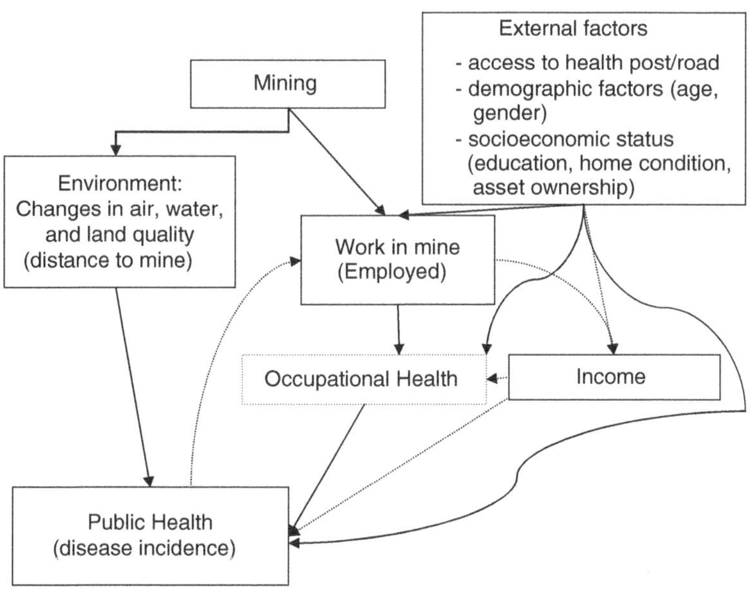

Figure 15.1 Conceptual framework

as by direct exposure to pollutants and other aspects of working conditions. While working conditions in the mining sector are a long-standing and serious concern, here we are interested in netting out the impact of voluntary employment in the mine from our estimate of the environmental health impacts of mining on populations living near those mines. Next, we motivate each component of this framework.

15.3.1 Environmental Health

Mining activities obviously threaten the local environment by causing pollution and ecological changes. In this study, rather than quantify these environmental changes, we seek evidence of their impacts on human health. In the case of iron ore mining, many of these effects are caused by mine waste, and the related sedimentation of rivers and dust in the air. This is in contrast to much of the literature on the environmental health impacts of mining, which focuses on operations that use or produce specific toxic substances.[4] In either case, the direct environmental health costs may be partially offset in places where mining companies (or tax revenues from mining) provide better public health services.

15.3.2 Local Employment

People who live close to mines may have better employment opportunities, not only in mining but also in related industries, such as transport or processing of minerals. Especially in remote rural areas, this employment may result in significantly higher incomes for workers and their families, in turn allowing them to invest in better health care and disease prevention (e.g., purchase of mosquito nets). While the particular pathways vary, higher income is almost always associated with better well-being and living conditions. However, seeking and obtaining employment in mining may also be conditional on health status, with healthier individuals being more productive and therefore better able to obtain employment in the challenging working conditions presented by mines, mineral transport, and processing.

[4] For example, Dutta et al. (2003) studied the effects of an abandoned chrysotile asbestos mine on villagers in the Chaibasa region of the West Singhbhum district of Jharkhand, India. Asbestos mining was found related to low back pain, dyspnea hemoptysis, and blindness due to the disposal of toxic asbestos and chromite waste by the mining company. McCulloch (2003) studied mines in Southern Africa that produced all three commercial varieties of asbestos, and found that the negative impacts of dust from the mining operation extended far beyond the workplace to those who lived in adjacent communities. Counter et al. (2005) investigated the Nambija, Ecuador gold mining settlement and found elevated mercury levels in children aged six–fourteen years, putting them at risk of neuro-developmental and learning disorders.

15.3.3 Occupational health

Mine workers face many health risks, including dust-related diseases, waterborne disease, skin diseases, and mine accidents. For example, Sabbioni et al. (2007) found that coal miners had respiratory symptoms and chronic bronchitis associated with the diphenylmethane diisocyanate (MDI)-based resins and ureaformol- and formophenolic-based resins used in coal mining. Meeran (2003) found high rates of asbestos-related diseases among both miners and people living near asbestos mining operations in South Africa. The specific health effects depend on the mining technology and may operate through both occupational and environmental health channels.

15.3.5 External Factors

Education and health usually are positively related (Furnée et al. 2008; Subramanian et al. 2010; Tilak 2005). For example, many studies have found that a mother's education improves maternal health care and reduces child mortality (Ahmed et al 2010; Charmarbagwala et al. 2004; Dasgupta 1990). Age is also related to health. Middle-aged adults tend to have better health compared to children and the elderly. Access to health services is another key factor.

15.4 EMPIRICAL MODEL

In this study, we are interested in the determinants of disease incidence among people living close to iron ore mines in Keonjhar, and in particular, whether there is empirical evidence of negative health impacts on the local population that is exposed to the environmental effects of mining. We focus on the incidence of various diseases. This measure may be less subject to measurement error than severity of disease, which is commonly recorded as days unable to work or days in a hospital.[5] Given the lack of field monitoring data on ambient air or water quality, we exploit the natural variation in proximity to mining areas. Proximity-based metrics are second-best yet reliable measures of health hazard exposure in the absence of explicit measures of air quality (Buzzelli and Jerrett 2003).

In order to assess the environmental health impact, we must account for the fact that people living close to the mine are also more likely to be employed by the mine, resulting in both higher income and higher exposure to air and water

[5] Reporting of these measures may be affected by family income, which determines whether someone can afford to miss work or seek hospital treatment, or by an employer's policies, which may determine whether someone who is ill is allowed to work.

pollutants on the job. Thus, the first step in the empirical model is to estimate the probability of employment in the mine (equation (1)). Many of the external factors that influence health also influence employment, but there are three additional determinants of employment: agricultural wage, agricultural production assets, and gender (male). The two agricultural factors (*A*) are expected to decrease the probability of seeking employment in the mine but are not expected to affect health, conditional on general SES of the household. Males are more likely to be hired for mining activities but are not otherwise expected to have systematically different incidences of the diseases that we consider. In equation (2), incidences of different diseases are estimated as functions of individual characteristics such as age and education (*I*), household characteristics such as wealth (*C*), distance to mine (*D*), and working in mine (*W*), which is itself a function of individual and household characteristics as in equation (1).

$$W_i = f\left(I_{i,}C_{i,}D_{i,}A_i\right) \tag{1}$$

$$H_i = f\left(I_{i,}C_{i,}D_{i,}, W_i\left(I_{i,}C_{i,}D_{i,}A_i\right)\right) \tag{2}$$

where

H: binary variables for incidences of diseases (waterborne, respiratory, and fever in past year; malaria in past five years)

W: binary variable for working in mine (employed)

D: distance from village to nearest iron ore mine

I: individual characteristics—age, education, and gender

C: household characteristics—caste, durable household assets, quality of house, distance from house to paved roads, distance from house to primary health center

A: agricultural production assets, daily wage to hire agricultural worker.

15.4.1 Employment in Mine

For equation (1), the following model is estimated:

$$W_i = X_i\beta + \varepsilon_I \tag{3}$$

where

W is an observed dichotomous variable that takes on the value of 1 when the *i*th individual is employed in the mining sector and 0 otherwise;

X_i is a vector of explanatory variables, including *D*, *I*, *C*, and *A*;

β is a vector of parameters to be estimated; and

ε_i is an error tem, which is assumed to have standard normal distribution.

The probability, P_i, of employment in the mine is defined by

$$P(W_i = 1 \mid X) = \Phi(X_i\beta) \tag{4}$$

where Φ denotes the distribution function for the standard normal distribution.

15.4.2 Disease Incidence with Binary Endogenous Regressor

In the model of disease incidence, employment in mines is estimated simultaneously with the incidence of diseases (equations 5 and 6). Similar to a treatment effect model, we estimate the effect of the endogenous binary treatment of working in the mine, W_i, on the incidence of disease Y_i, conditional on the independent variables Z_i, which include *D*, *I*, and *C* (but not *A*). Specifically, we estimate the following probit model:

$$H_i = Z_i\beta + \delta W_i + \varepsilon_I \tag{5}$$

$$W_i = X_i\gamma + u_i. \tag{6}$$

where $(\varepsilon_i, u_{i.} \mid X_i) \sim N(0, 0, 1, 1, \rho)$ and $N(0, 0, 1, 1, \rho)$ indicates the standard bivariate normal distribution with correlation coefficient ρ. When ρ is zero, equation (6) becomes the standard probit model.

H_i is an observed dichotomous dependent variable which takes the value one when the *i*th individual has been infected with a disease (or category of disease) in the past year (or five years, for malaria) and 0 otherwise. W_i is an endogenous binary variable indicating whether that individual works in the mining sector. In turn, W_i is a function of the exogenous variables X_i and a random component $u_{i.}$

With this structure, the model falls into the general class of simultaneous equation models with dummy endogenous variables introduced by Heckman (1978). As denoted by Greene (2007), this is a recursive model of simultaneous equations, since the endogenous variable W_i appears on the right-hand side of the second equation, but not vice versa. To simultaneously estimate the two regressions, we assume that the error terms are jointly normally distributed and use maximum likelihood methods (the *biprobit* command in STATA).

This method allows the correlation to be modeled directly, thereby eliminating any omitted-variable bias. For identification, this requires that there be at least one exogenous variable in equation (6) that is not in equation (5). We have three candidate variables: gender (males more likely to be hired), the agricultural wage that the household reports for hiring in (what the household would have to pay to someone hired to substitute for a family member who works in the mine), and the production assets specific to agriculture owned by the household (raising the opportunity costs of working in the mine). After conditioning on household wealth (as indicated by consumption assets), agricultural production assets are not expected to directly affect the health of household members.

15.5 DATA

The empirical analysis is based on a household survey conducted in 2006. The survey covered 600 households in twenty villages in two blocks of Keonjhar: Joda and Keonjhar Sadar (Figure 15.2). These blocks were selected to cover a range of exposures to mining activities. The survey elicited information

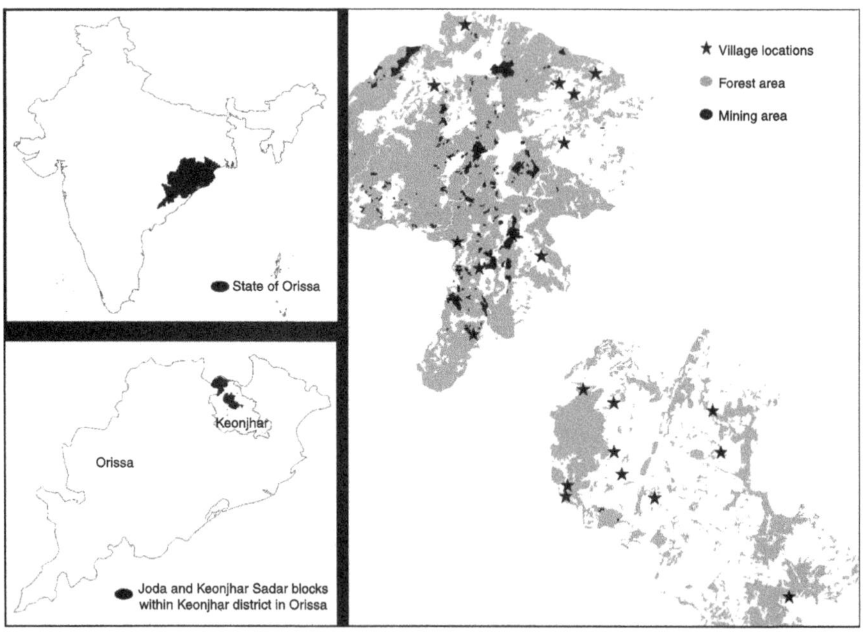

Figure 15.2 Map of study site

Table 15.1 Disease incidence and relationship with proximity to and employment in mines

	Waterborne diseases	Respiratory diseases	Malaria	Fever	Blood pressure
Incidence (percent of sample reporting)	12.88	23.23	39.34	4.86	0.56
Distance to mine[±]	−0.0247	−0.0149	0.0008	−0.0582	0.0021
LR χ^2	22.64	11.66	4.63	53.72	0.02
Prob > chi2	(0.00)	(0.00)	(0.03)	(0.00)	(0.89)
Working in mine[$]	0.1558	−0.0002	−0.0541	0.08445	0.20813
LR χ^2	2.02	0.01	0.35	0.33	0.51
Prob > chi2	(0.15)	(0.99)	(0.55)	(0.56)	(0.45)

[±]Coefficient from bivariate probit model of disease as function of distance to mine
[$]Coefficient from bivariate probit model of disease as function of working in mine

Table 15.2 Descriptive statistics for external factors

Variables		Mean	Std Dev.	Max
Individual Variables				
Age (year)	Age	28.29	18.07	105
Male (dummy)	Male	0.51	0.50	1.00
Education (year)	Edu	2.92	4.02	18.00
Household Variables				
caste (dummy for ST/SC)	caste	0.74	0.44	1.00
production asset (count)	prodasset	2.38	1.16	7.00
consumer asset (count)	conasset	4.48	3.19	18.00
house quality (dummy for poor)	badhouse	0.76	0.43	1.00
distance to paved road (minutes)	droad	29.28	33.56	180.00
distance to health facility (minutes)	dhealth	46.83	37.14	160.00
distance to mine (km from village)	dmine	7.32	6.1	20.92
wage paid to agricultural workers (rupees)	hirewage	12.68	12.80	60.00

on household demographics, socioeconomic status, employment, and recent illnesses that had affected household members. GIS was used to overlay environmental variables such as proximity to mines. Descriptive statistics are presented in Tables 15.1 and 15.2.

15.5.1 Incidence of Diseases (H)

Health is represented by incidences of the following diseases: (a) waterborne and water-washed diseases including diarrhea, cholera and typhoid, (b) respiratory diseases including acute respiratory infections and tuberculosis,

(c) malaria, which is a key public health problem in Orissa, (d) fever, which may be a symptom of several different diseases otherwise not reported because not diagnosed, and (e) blood pressure, which we do not expect to be related to mine exposure and therefore use as a negative control (Lipsitch et al. 2010). For each category of disease, incidence is recorded as a binary variable equal to one if an individual reports that health problem in the past year (or five years for malaria) and zero otherwise. Both the scientific and grey literatures suggest that the environmental impacts of mining could be responsible for the first four categories of disease. First, mining affects water quality through several channels, most notably dumping of mine waste. For example, Khatua and Stanley (2006) state that pollution of the Brahmani river due to mining has led to skin diseases, malaria, tooth diseases, eye infection, fever, jaundice, and intestinal problems in the area. Mines clearly can have poor quality indoor air with negative impacts on workers (Hedlund et al. 2006; Ross and Murray 2004; Maganu 1981), but mine operations including crushing and transport also affect air quality in neighboring communities (Centre for Environmental Studies 2010).

15.5.2 Mining Characteristics (D and W)

Environmental exposure to mines is proxied as the Euclidean distance from each village to the nearest mine, based on a GIS including information on locations of mines and villages (see Figure 15.2). Households are clustered near the center of villages, so we did not compute distances from individual households to mines. The "employment module" of the household questionnaire provides occupation details for every individual in the 600 households. Mining is the main non-farm work in Keonjhar.

15.5.3 Individual and Household Characteristics (I and C)

Several characteristics of individuals are expected to affect both their probability of employment in mining activities and their health status. Specifically, these include age, education, and for employment, gender. All three characteristics were recorded in the household roster component of the household questionnaire. Age and education are both measured in years.

Individuals in the same household share the same socioeconomic status (SES), which is likely to be important for both employment and health. Variables representing SES are caste, ownership of physical assets, quality of house, and location of the house relative to the nearest paved road and primary health center. The household questionnaire elicited the government-assigned category for caste. Scheduled Caste (SC) and Scheduled Tribe (ST) groups have been discriminated against historically with comparatively lower economic assets than the general population in spite of reservations (quotas) for government jobs and university admittance (Das et al. 2010). Because nearly three-quarters of households reported to be Scheduled Castes or Scheduled Tribes, we created a dummy variable equal to one if the household belonged in those categories and zero otherwise.

Three categories of assets are considered. The production asset variable is a count of the different types of agricultural production assets owned by household. These include tractors of various sizes, plows pulled by machine or animal, mechanical water pumps, sprinklers, threshers, insecticide pumps, carts pulled by machine or animal, shovels, saws, axes, machetes, rice winnowers, mills, and other processing machines. The consumer asset variable is a count of the different types of domestic durable assets owned by the household. These include refrigerator, washing machine, sewing machine, generator, electric fan, television, video player, tape recorder, camera, bicycle, motorcycle, car, truck, radio, telephone, cell phone, mosquito net, clock or watch, pressure cooker, mixer, mattress, bed, chair, table, almirah (large cabinet or chest), and gold jewelry. Third, we deem houses to be of poor quality if at least two components (floor, walls, or roof) were constructed from poor quality materials (wood, bamboo, earth, mud, raw brick, grass, and thatch) (that is, poor quality = 1; otherwise = 0).

Access to markets and services is represented by distance from the house to an all-weather road. This was elicited in the household questionnaire by asking how many minutes it was from the house to the nearest all-weather road. Likewise, the survey elicited distance in minutes from the house to the nearest primary care health center.

15.5.4 Wage Rate in Agriculture Job (A)

In addition to the agricultural production assets described above, A includes the daily wage paid by a household to hire in labor for the family farm. The units are rupees per day, and missing values are imputed using village averages. This wage rate represents the opportunity cost for an individual considering switching to work in the mining sector.

15.6 RESULTS

The 600 households surveyed included a large sample of 2,656 individuals, ranging in age from three months to 105 years, with an average of twenty-nine years. The average education level is about three years of school, ranging from zero to eighteen years. Most households are from Scheduled Castes (SC) and Scheduled Tribes (ST). Most homes are constructed using poorer quality materials. The average household owns about three different kinds of agricultural production assets and about five different kinds of consumer assets. The average reported wage for hiring a farm worker is about Rs. 12.7 per day. The average walking distance from residence to the nearest all-weather road is around thirty minutes and to the nearest primary care health facility is around forty-seven minutes. The average distance to the nearest mine is about eight kilometers, ranging from less than one kilometer to a maximum of about twenty-one kilometers.

Both respiratory and waterborne diseases are common, with 23 percent of individuals reporting at least one respiratory disease (including TB) and 13 percent reporting at least one waterborne disease (including typhoid and cholera) in the year before the survey. Nearly 40 percent of individuals were reported to have suffered malaria in the five years before the survey. The incidence of these diseases declines with distance from mines in simple bivariate models. The only exception is high blood pressure, which is neither very common nor expected to be related to the environmental impacts of mining.

On the other hand, none of the diseases has a statistically significant relationship with employment in the mining sector in bivariate models, although waterborne diseases have a weak positive relationship with employment. This may be because all of these health problems are related to living conditions, income, hygiene, health education, and access to health services, which may also affect or be affected by employment in mines.

15.6.1 Employment

One key reason that the Indian government has supported the expansion of the mining sector is the expected economic development benefits, including both public revenues and generation of employment in relatively poor, rural regions such as Keonjhar. Of the 2,656 people recorded in the survey, only 8 percent report employment in the mining sector, but this represents 85 percent of adults of working age (thirteen–sixty-years-old). Most mineworkers are men; only thirty-two women and one child were reported to be working in the mines. This reflects the fact that working in the mining sector is physically demanding labor.

The multivariate results in Table 15.3 confirm that the people most likely to be employed by the mine are older and better educated males, from the SC/ST caste, living closer to the mine (as shown by the negative and statistically significant coefficient on dmine, distance to mine). As expected, mine

Table 15.3 Probit model of employment in mine (N = 2656)

Explanatory variables	Coef	p-value
Age	0.0101	0.00
Education	0.0247	0.04
Male	0.8634	0.00
Caste	0.2766	0.01
Distance to mine	−0.0609	0.00
Wage paid to agricultural workers	−0.0021	0.57
Production asset	−0.1349	0.00
Constant	−1.9042	0.00
LR $\chi2$	247.70	0.00
Pseudo-R^2	0.17	

employment is negatively correlated with agricultural production assets and with the reported agricultural wage (although the latter is not statistically significant).

15.6.2 Impact of Mining on Health

The results from equation (4) are presented in Table 15.4. In order to identify the simultaneous equation systems, the agricultural variables A and gender are used as exclusion restrictions. Gender and the count of agriculture production assets are statically significant determinants of the probability of working in the mining sector.

With this full model, we find that the results of the bivariate analysis are substantially revised. For example, there is no longer even a weak occupational health impact on waterborne diseases. However, respiratory disease is significantly related to mine employment after accounting for the endogeneity of employment and controlling for external factors. This probably reflects the lack of personal safety equipment for miners in Orissa (Devata 2010). On the other hand, working in mines reduces the incidence of fever. One possible explanation is that higher income from mine employment facilitates access to preventive measures (such as mosquito nets) and/or treatment (to bring down the fever).

After controlling for employment and other factors, living close to mines remains significantly associated only with waterborne disease and fever. This is consistent with widespread concerns that mining has negative impacts on the hydrology and water quality of the region. While local people complain about the dust from mining operations, we find that the incidence of respiratory

Table 15.4 Probit model of disease incidence (N=2656)

	Waterborne		Respiratory		Malaria		Fever		Blood pressure	
	Coef	p-value	Coef	p-value	Coef	p-value	Coef	p-value	Coef	p-value
Incidence of disease										
Age	0.0005	0.79	−0.0020	0.18	−0.0010	0.47	0.0056	0.02	0.0242	0.00
Edu	−0.0254	0.01	−0.0198	0.01	0.0308	0.00	0.0129	0.28	0.0061	0.83
Caste	−0.0379	0.61	−0.1909	0.00	−0.0661	0.25	−0.0589	0.57	−0.0112	0.96
Dmine	−0.0292	0.00	−0.0037	0.47	−0.0009	0.85	−0.0699	0.00	0.0104	0.58
Dhealth	−0.0011	0.23	0.0012	0.12	−0.0017	0.02	0.0005	0.68	0.0012	0.68
Droad	0.0006	0.49	−0.0034	0.00	−0.0009	0.21	−0.0012	0.36	0.0029	0.25
Poorhouse	−0.0793	0.30	0.2347	0.00	−0.0123	0.84	−0.1009	0.30	−0.0273	0.92
Consasset	−0.0052	0.63	0.0265	0.00	0.0107	0.21	−0.0443	0.00	−0.0323	0.42
Employed	−0.4460	0.15	1.0293	0.00	−0.2978	0.34	−1.0256	0.00	0.9666	0.39
Constant	−0.6867	0.00	−0.7702	0.00	−0.1845	0.11	−0.9688	0.00	−3.6350	0.00
Employed (work in mine)										
Age	0.0099	0.00	0.0105	0.00	0.0102	0.00	0.0101	0.00	0.0101	0.00
Edu	0.0253	0.01	0.0242	0.02	0.0256	0.02	0.0233	0.03	0.0246	0.02
Male	0.8628	0.00	0.8546	0.00	0.8682	0.00	0.8764	0.00	0.8656	0.00
Caste	0.2868	0.00	0.3076	0.00	0.2772	0.01	0.2803	0.00	0.2821	0.00
Dmine	−0.0616	0.00	−0.0625	0.00	−0.0599	0.00	−0.0618	0.00	−0.0609	0.00
Hirewage	−0.0013	0.72	−0.0023	0.61	−0.0027	0.49	−0.0024	0.51	−0.0213	0.58
Prodasset	−0.1373	0.00	−0.1178	0.01	−0.1318	0.00	−0.1037	0.02	−0.1350	0.00
Constant	−1.9054	0.00	−1.9580	0.00	−1.9181	0.00	−1.9692	0.00	−1.9067	0.00
Wald χ^2	224.95	0.00	279.68	0.00	233.38	0.00	268.50	0.00	206.84	0.00

diseases is not associated with living close to mine, but rather with working in mines. There is also a higher incidence of respiratory diseases among people who live closer to roads, consistent with concerns about dust generated by trucks transporting ore. Living in a poor quality house is also a risk factor for respiratory disease.

15.7 CONCLUSION

In the spirit of Dasgupta's (2001b) call for careful empirical work to examine the non-market effects of policies, this study quantifies the impact of mining on neighboring populations in Orissa, India. Although iron ore mining in Keonjhar district has generated substantial revenues, its adverse impacts on the environment and public health are also significant. Using distance to mine as a proxy for environmental degradation by mines, we find that mining is positively associated with waterborne disease and fever, after controlling for mine employment. About 8 percent of the local population (mostly adult males) is employed in the mines. Employment provides income, and may allow workers to invest more in preventive health measures and treatment, which is perhaps reflected in lower reported incidence of fever among mine employees. However, we also find that working in the mines is associated with higher incidence of respiratory disease. As expected, there is no occupational or environmental health link between mines and blood pressure. We also do not find any statistically significant link to malaria, although Saha et al. (2011) show that the severity of malaria (as measured by days sick rather than incidence) does increase with proximity to mines.

Our findings on the health impacts of mines should encourage policymakers to look beyond the obvious economic benefits of mining. Of course, these may not be inevitable impacts of mines, but possible to mitigate with appropriate regulation and enforcement, imposing accountability for local environmental and health quality (Sinha et al. 2007). For example, the state could require mining operations to support programs to provide safe water and sanitation, insecticide treated bednets or clean burning stoves to local populations, in essence requiring them to raise the price of iron ore exported from Orissa to reflect the social costs of mining in the state (Arrow et al. 2004). Many of those social costs are long-term, suggesting the need for careful cost-benefit analysis and consideration of the Hartwick rule for sustainability (Hartwick 1977). In sum, this study illustrates why it is important to consider the environment, particularly the often overlooked community health linkages, when planning and investing in economic development (Dasgupta 2001a).

References

Ahmed, S., A. Creanga, D. Gillespie et al. (2010). "Economic Status, Education and Empowerment: Implications for Maternal Health Service Utilization in Developing Countries," *PLoS ONE*, 5(6): e11190. doi:10.1371/journal.pone.0011190.

Arrow, K. J., P. Dasgupta, L. Goulder et al. (2004). 'Are We Consuming Too Much?" *Journal of Economic Perspectives*, 18(3): 147–72.

Barik, S. (2009). "Keonjhar Witnesses Uncontrolled Mining." Available at <http://www.hindu.com/2008/12/09/stories/2008120955470600.htm> (accessed 19 October 2013).

Barnett, S., N. Nair, P. Tripathy et al. (2008). "A Prospective Key Informant Surveillance System to Measure Maternal Mortality: Finding from Indigenous Populations in Jharkhand and Orissa, India." *BMC Pregnancy Childbirth*, 8: 6.

Bridge, G. (2004). "Contest Terrain: Mining and the Environment," *Annual Review of Environment and Resources*, 29: 205–359.

Buzzelli, M. and M. Jerrett (2003). "Comparing Proximity Measures of Exposure to Geostatistical Estimates in Environmental Justice Research," *Global Environmental Change, Part B: Environmental Hazards*, 5(1–2): 13–21.

Centre for Environmental Studies (2010). *State of Environment Report, Orissa*. Available at <http://www.cesorissa.org/soe/SoER.html> (accessed 19 October 2013).

Counter, A., L. Bachanan, and O. Fernando (2005). "Mercury Levels in Urine and Hair of Children in Andean Gold-mining Settlement," *International Journal of Occupational and Environmental Health*, 11: 132–7.

Cowie, R. and S. Mabena (1991). "Silicosis, Chronic Airflow Limitation and Chronic Bronchitis in South African Gold Miners," *American Review of Respiratory Disease*,143(1): 80–4.

Das, M. B., G. Hall, S. Kapoor et al. (2010). "Indigeous Peoples, Poverty and Development." Available at <http://siteresources.worldbank.org/EXTINDPEOPLE/Resources/407801-1271860301656/Chapter_6_India.pdf> (accessed 19 October 2013).

Das, P. (2009). "Illegal Mining Activities Dent the Image of Naveen Patnaik's Government in Orissa," *Frontline* 26(19). Available at <http://www.frontline.in/static/html/fl2619/stories/20090925261903800.htm> (accessed 8 December 2013)

Dasgupta, M. (1990). "Death Clustering, Mothers' Education and the Determinants of Child Mortality in Rural Punjab, India," *Population Studies*, 44: 489–505.

Dasgupta, P. (2001a). *Human Well-Being and the Natural Environment*. Oxford: Oxford University Press.

—— (2001b). "Valuing Objects and Evaluating Policies in Imperfect Economies," *Economic Journal*, 111(5): 1–29.

—— and G. M. Heal (1979). *Economic Theory and Exhaustible Resources*. Cambridge: Cambridge University Press.

Devata, U. C. (2010). "Profile of Mine Workers in Orissa," *Orissa Review*. Available at <http://orissa.gov.in/e-magazine/Orissareview/2010/May-June/engpdf/60-65.pdf> (accessed 19 October 2013).

Di Giulio, M., R. Holderegger, and S. Tobias (2009). "Effects of Habitat and Landscape Fragmentation on Humans and Biodiversity in Densely Populated Landscapes," *Journal of Environmental Management*, 90(10): 2959–68.

Dutta, M., R. Sreedhar, and A. Basu (2003). "The Blighted Hills of Roro, Jharkhand, India: A Tale of Corporate Greed and Abandonment," *International Journal of Occupational and Environmental Health*, 9(3): 254–9.

The Economic Times (2011). "Orissa Demands a Level Playing Field, Seeks Upward Revision of Mining Royalty Rates." (23 October). Available at <http://articles.economictimes.indiatimes.com/2011-10-23/news/30313191_1_mine-owners-indian-mineral-industries-iron-ore> (accessed 19 October 2013).

Furnée, C., W. Groot, and H. M. Brink (2008). "The Health Effects of Education," *European Journal of Public Health*, 18(4): 417–21.

Ghose, M. (2008). "A Perspective on Community and State Interests in Small-scale Mining in India including the Role of Women," *Environment, Development and Sustainability* , 10: 857–69.

Greene, W. (2007). *Econometric Analysis*. Upper Saddle River, NJ: Prentice Hall.

Hamann, R. and P. Kapelus (2004). "Corporate Social Responsibility in Mining in Southern Africa: Fair Accountability or Just Greenwash," *Development*, 47(3): 85–92.

Hartwick, J. (1977). "Intergenerational Equity and the Investing of Rents from Exhaustible Resources," *The American Economic Review*, 67(5): 172–4.

Heckman, J. (1978). "Dummy Endogenous Variables in a Simulteneous Equation System," *Econometrica*, 931–59.

Hedlund, U., B. Jarvholm, and B. Lundback (2006). "Persistence of Respiratory Symptoms in Ex-underground Iron Ore Miners," *Occupation Medicine*, 56(6): 380–5.

Holman, C., P. Psaila-Savona, P. Roberts et al. (1987). "Determinants of Chronic Bronchitis and Lung Dysfunction in Western Australian Gold Miners," *Journal of Industrial Medicine*, 44: 810–8.

Kemp, D., J. R. Owen, N. Gotzmann et al. (2010). "Just Relations and Company-Community Conflict in Mining," *Journal of Business Ethics*, 101(1): 93–109.

Khatua., S. and W. Stanley (2006). *Ecological Debt: A Case Study of Orissa, India*. Geneva: World Councils of Churches, Troika Press.

IDRC (2006). *Ecohealth Works: Environmental Pollution*. Canada: International Development Research Centre.

Indian Bureau of Mines (2005). *Indian Mineral Industry at a Glance 2003–2004*. Government of India, Ministry of Mines, Nagpur, India.

Lipsitch, M., E. T. Tchetgen, and T. Cohen (2010). "Negative Controls: A Tool for Detecting Confounding and Bias in Observational Studies," *Epidemiology*, 21(3): 383–8.

Maganu, E. (1981). *Tuberculosis in Botswana: Results of an Epidemiology Survey*. Gaborone: Republic of Botswana Ministry of Health.

McCulloch, J. (2003). "Asbestos Mining in Southern African, 1893–2002," *International Journal of Occupational and Environmental Health*, 9(3): 230–5.

Meeran, R. (2003). "Cape Plc: South African Mineworkers' Quest for Justice," *Quest for Justice*, 9(3): 213–30.

Orissa (2004). "Some Measure of Human Development: An Inter-District Analysis," Orissa Human Resource Development Report Available at <http://www.orissa.gov.in/pandc/humandevelopment/hdr/chap08.pdf> (accessed 19 October 2013).

Patnaik, P. (1999). *A Comprehensive Guide to the Hazardous Properties of Chemical Substances*. New York: John Wiley and Sons.

Patz, J., P. Daszak, G. Tabor et al. (2004). "Unhealthy Landscapes: Policy Recommendations on Land Use Change and Infectious Disease Emergence" *Environmental Health Perspective*, 112(10): 1092–978.

Pattanayak, S. K. and J. Yasaoka (2008). "Deforestation and Malaria: Revisting the Human Ecology Perspective," in D. Newbery and N. Stern (eds.), *Forests, People and Health: A Global Interdisciplinary Overview*. London: Colfer Earthscan Publishers, 197–217.

Planning Commission (2009). "Report of the Expert Group to Review the Methodology for Estimation of Poverty." Chaired by S. D. Tendulkar, R. Radhakrishna, and S. Sengupta. New Delhi, India. Available at <http://planningcommission.nic.in/reports/genrep/rep_pov.pdf> (accessed 16 November 2013).

Ross, M. and J. Murray (2004). "Occupational Respiratory Disease in Mining,' *Occupational Medicine*, 54(5): 304–10.

Sabbioni, G., H. Wesp, J. Lewalter et al. (2007). "Determination of Isocyante Biomaker in Construction Site Workers," *Biomakers*, 12: 438–83.

Saha, S. (2008). "Spatial Externalities: Evidence on Social Interaction, Market Expansion and Mineral Extraction from Brazil and India," PhD dissertation, North Carolina State University. Available at <http://repository.lib.ncsu.edu/ir/bitstream/1840.16/3735/1/etd.pdf> (accessed 16 November 2013).

—— S. Pattanayak, E. O. Sills et al. (2011). "Undermining Health: Environmental Justice and Mining in India," *Health and Place* 17(1): 140–8.

Singha, S., R. Bhattacharya, R. Banerjee (2007). "Surface Iron Ore Mining in Eastern India and Local Level Sustainability," *Resource Policy*, 32(1): 57–68.

Subramanian, S. V., T. Huijts, and M. Avendano (2010). "Self-reported Health Assessments in the 2002 World Health Survey: How Do They Correlate with Education," *Bulletin of the World Health Organization*, 88: 131–8.

The Telegraph (2010). "Govt Draws Flak over Crusher Ban–Large Number of Tribals Depend on the Small-scale Industry for Livelihood" (20 July). Available at <http://www.telegraphindia.com/1100720/jsp/orissa/story_12699579.jsp> (accessed 19 October 2013).

Tilak, J. B. (2005). "Post-elementary Education, Poverty, and Development in India." Available at <http://www.cas.ed.ac.uk/__data/assets/pdf_file/0018/28323/Tilak_India_PBET_WP6_final.pdf> (accessed 19 October 2013).

Vasundhara (2008). "Impact of Mining in Scheduled Area of Orissa: A Case Study from Keonjhar." Available at <http://www.vasundharaorissa.org/Research%20Reports/Impact%20of%20Mining%20in%20Schduled%20Area%20of%20Orissa.pdf> (accessed 19 October 2013).

Weber-Fahre, M., J. E. Strongman, R. Kunanayagam et al. (2001). *Mining: World Bank Policy Guidelines on Poverty Reduction*, ii: Chapter 25. Available at <http://

siteresources.worldbank.org/INTPRS1/Resources/383606-1205334112622/4251_chap25.pdf> (accessed 16 November 2013).

Winkel, L., M. Berg, M. Amini et al. (2008). "Predicting Groundwater Arsenic Contamination in Southeast Asia from Surface Parameter," *Nature Geoscience*, 1: 536–42.

Yapabandara, A. and C. Curtis (2004). "Vectors and Malaria Transmission in Gem Mining in Sri Lanka," *Journal of Vector Ecology*, 29(2): 264–76.

16

Comments by Robert Solow on "Occupational and Environmental Health Impacts"

This is an interesting paper on an intrinsically and deceptively difficult topic. As I will explain later, it faces a problem that is characteristic of many research projects that try to measure the incidence on individuals of private actions and public policies, and to assess causality.

The main finding of the paper is that there is a detectable but weak tendency for nearness to an iron-mining site in Orissa to be associated with a higher incidence of both waterborne disease and fever. In the case of waterborne disease there is a plausible mechanism: drinking water contaminated by mine wastes. In the case of fever, a symptom, the connection to mining requires more guesswork. (Indeed, it is tempting to speculate on whether the link between malaria and proximity to a mine found elsewhere in the literature appears here in disguise, with fever sometimes being caused by undiagnosed malaria.) As might be expected, incidence of respiratory disease is found to be higher among mineworkers but not residents living near the mine, presumably due to air pollution (dust and particulate matter, not directly measured) being concentrated at the mine site.

The authors use a two-stage instrumental-variable method to allow for the endogeneity of the decision to work in a mine. The one important concrete suggestion I have to make is that the role of mining employment is worth further investigation: not in terms of econometrics but rather conceptually. A difficulty arises, as the authors note, because working in a mine seems to have two effects that tend to offset each other. Increased direct exposure to pollutants goes in the direction of higher incidence, but higher income, which allows even if it does not guarantee better access to avoidance measures and health care, goes in the direction of lower incidence.

I think this matter needs a more penetrating investigation. The goal would be to tease out some more information about the effect of higher income on disease. (Family income, though apparently measured, does not appear as a right-hand-side variable in the paper.) Would it be possible to study the sub-sample of families with no mine employment, or the families in the non-mining area of Orissa, attempting to estimate the direct income effect on incidences of disease? Then this estimate could be used to remove the income effect in families *with* a mineworker, thus perhaps revealing the true direct effect of mine employment. There is obviously an unverified and unverifiable assumption in the background of this suggestion (that the income effect is uniform across families) but the possible payoff strikes me as worth the try.

I now want to discuss what seems to me to be a near-universal difficulty with all individual-based inference of the kind exemplified by the paper. My experience comes from extensive involvement in experimental studies designed to estimate the effects of certain social policies on the labor-market outcomes of defined disadvantaged groups. An example might be a program intended to prepare high-school dropouts to find and keep jobs: the method might typically be random assignment of eligibles to a treatment group and a control group, with later follow-up; other studies use interrupted-regression methods.

Except when the "treatment" is very drastic, almost all individual-based studies of the effects of such exposure to treatment, when they show statistically significant effects at all, show substantively small effects. In my sort of case, a designed program may improve the probability of later employment or the level of earnings, but the size of the improvement is felt by advocates to be disappointingly small. Here proximity to a mine seems to increase incidence of a disease, but weakly. I presume that this happens because social life is complicated; very many causes are at work. (The incidence of malaria may be affected by local topography, wind direction, genetic disposition and personal habits.) So the measured effect along any one causal chain is bound to be small.

This tendency is tough on social policy. For one thing, shock effects are hard to achieve; the politics of social policy wants wonder drugs, miracles, not small, statistically significant improvements. Secondly, we can do many such studies, and *should* do many such studies, but the results, even if qualitatively consistent, cannot be quantitatively generalized. The Orissa coefficients are unlikely to carry over to other iron-mining areas, because other causal chains and their interactions will be different. Even if the world accepts that iron-mining has a negative external effect on health in the vicinity, it would be hard to derive a proper Pigouvian corrective tax: it would have to be based on a weak estimate of the size of the externality, and anyway any such tax would have to be more uniform than replicated studies would justify. We need a way to define such taxes; even rough approximations are probably better than ex post compensation of victims. Studies like this one by Sanglimsuwan, Sills, Pattanayak, Saha, Singha, and Sahoo can hope to build an attitude, an understanding of the multiplicity of small effects. That can be very valuable.

17

Estimating the Value of Statistical Life for Children in Metro Manila

Rosalina Palanca-Tan

17.1 INTRODUCTION

Cost-benefit analysis is crucial in assessing the viability of public investment programs. In employing this project evaluation tool, it is necessary that all costs and benefits of the program are quantified (Dasgupta, Sen, and Marglin 1972). One major benefit justifying public programs, particularly, in the areas of environment, health, and transport, is the reduction in people's risk of death. In developing countries like the Philippines, however, this important benefit is commonly excluded or not properly imputed in environmental cost-benefit analyses and other types of environmental project assessments due to the dearth of studies on the value of mortality risk reduction and the concern on the applicability of values derived in developed countries (benefit transfer). This exclusion results in underestimated benefits that can cause the defeat of many environmental policy initiatives.

This chapter presents measures of the value of a mortality risk reduction and the value of statistical life (VSL) of children in Metro Manila, the foremost urban center in the Philippines where the early child mortality-causing problems of congestion, malnutrition, and environmental pollution are most severe. VSL measurement employs either a stated preference or a revealed preference technique. Contingent valuation is a stated preference technique in which people are asked through a survey to indicate their willingness to pay (WTP) for a hypothetical reduction in mortality risk. On the other hand, revealed preference techniques such as the averting-expenditure and hedonic wage methods infer the value of a mortality risk reduction from observable behavior in the market. VSL literature employing the averting expenditure method include estimates derived from demand for car seat belts (Blomquist et al. 1996; Carlin and Sandy 1991) and bicycle helmets (Jenkins et al. 2001).

The hedonic wage method, which measures VSL in terms of the trade-off between wage and on-the-job risk of death, is more extensively applied. The literature review of Viscusi and Aldy (2003) covers more than sixty labor market-based VSL studies. One issue regarding revealed preference methods is the exclusion of individuals who are not engaged in the observed market transactions. The analysis in the hedonic wage method, for instance, is limited to the healthier working age segment of the population. Other populations at risk, such as children and the elderly, are excluded.

With a focus on children's mortality risk associated with illness and environment quality, this study employed contingent valuation to arrive at an estimate of VSL. Contingent valuation directly elicits monetary values individuals place on goods, services, and amenities for which there are as yet no markets (Boyle 2003; Bateman et al. 2002). The mortality risk reduction in a contingent valuation survey scenario can result from either a specific (e.g., a vaccine for a particular life-threatening illness) or a general intervention (e.g., a multi-purpose drug). A multi-purpose intervention may be expected to generate a high incidence of scenario rejection especially in the Philippine setting where the market is already flooded with health products promising remedies for all problems and the consuming public have grown highly skeptical about these products. To avoid the highly hypothetical nature of a general intervention that reduces mortality risk from all causes (Krupnick et al. 2002; Alberini et al. 2004; Alberini, Hunt, and Markandya 2004; Mahmud 2005; Maskery et al. 2007), this study used a specific intervention scenario.

The dengue vaccine was chosen as it offered a highly familiar risk and intervention contexts for our respondents. Dengue fever, an acute febrile illness spread by day-biting *Aedes aegypti* mosquitos, is presently a major cause of morbidity and mortality in the Philippines. It is reported to be one of the top ten leading causes of morbidity in regions of the country with major urban areas where infrastructure development is unable to catch up with population growth. The first case of dengue in the Philippines was reported in 1953. Dengue infection has increasingly become a significant public health concern in the country since reports of outbreaks in 1988. Dengue incidence levels have tracked a long-run upward trend with short-term cycles of three to four years duration. Since 1988, there have been about 10,000–40,000 dengue cases (about 22 cases per 100,000 population) and 100–2,000 deaths (about 1 per 100,000 population) each year. The majority of dengue cases involve children as they are generally more active outdoors and hence more exposed to disease-carrying mosquitoes. About 70 percent of dengue victims are fourteen years old and younger. Due to greater susceptibility and weaker resistance of children, there are about 1 in 100,000 Filipino children who die from dengue each year. This is much higher compared to the adult mortality risk of 1 in 1,000,000 per year. Dengue outbreaks in the country in the last two decades have victimized people across all income classes and have increased their awareness of the risk of death from dengue, particularly among children.

Vaccination is widely accepted in the Philippines as an effective means of preventing diseases especially in children. Most children from all income levels are given the basic vaccines for tuberculosis, measles, diphtheria-pertussis-tetanus (DPT), and polio. The middle- to high-income households go to private clinics and hospitals while the low-income households avail of the Public Immunization Program in which government health centers administer the basic vaccines in exchange for a donation of any amount. Although there have been news about positive developments in dengue vaccine research since 2005, a dengue vaccine has not yet been made available in the market up until the present. To make our contingent valuation scenario more acceptable, survey respondents were given copies of news clippings about the progress in dengue research.

Stated WTP for the dengue vaccine would include not only WTP for the elimination of the risk of dying from dengue but also WTP for reduced morbidity (avoidance of sufferings and pain, and inconvenience and loss of income of the sick person and his/her caregivers) and savings on other preventive measures (Cropper et al. 2004). This is inherent in a specific intervention VSL scenario where respondents are inclined to consider effects other than the reduction in the risk of dying. This also relates to the issue of VSL estimates being context-specific. The non-mortality risk component of WTP for a specific intervention is expectedly context-specific. The goal of most VSL studies, however, is to come up with estimates that can be applied in the assessment of a variety of environmental projects and policies. What existing studies have done so far is to look at how WTP is affected by different risk characteristics such as degree of dread, severity, voluntariness, controllability, personal exposure, and perceived immediate occurrence, and to compare VSL estimates in different contexts to arrive at some adjustment ratios. This study undertook a strategy that had not been done in the existing VSL literature. We disentangled the stated WTP into the different benefits that could be derived from the dengue vaccine by asking respondents directly. After the WTP question, respondents were asked to allocate the WTP amount into five benefits that could be derived from the vaccine, one of which was the mortality risk reduction. In a play-like manner that also served to break the monotony of the question-answer sequence of the questionnaire, respondents were given ten tokens and five containers, each labeled with one reason for buying the vaccine. The respondents were asked to think of the ten tokens as representing their WTP for the vaccine and to divide them into the five reasons. Only the WTP for the mortality risk reduction was used in the calculation of VSL. To our knowledge, no VSL study had isolated the WTP for mortality risk reduction from the WTP stated by the repondent before VSL was calculated[1] .

This study also differs from existing VSL literature in that it elicited the responding adult household-head's WTP for a dengue vaccine for each and every member of the household, child[2] and adult alike. Previous VSL studies elicited WTP for mortality risk reduction for only one household member. For examples, Cropper et al. (2004) elicited the household-head's WTP for a malaria vaccine for himself/herself and Maskery et al. (2007) elicited the respondent's WTP for a nutritional supplement for the youngest child in the household only. It is not difficult to see that eliciting WTP for only one particular household member, say one's self or the youngest child, can result in biased estimates. We also believe that our approach better reflects the reality of household decision-making wherein the head decides to purchase an individually consumed good for one or several members after considering the needs and wants of all members in relation to the household budget. It is not always clear that this is the case when respondent is asked to focus on just one household member.

As the study deviated from the conventional single VSL-WTP question per respondent structure, we also had to employ a different modeling procedure. This is the third unique feature of the study. We used a two-stage regression model where the household vaccine demand was regressed with household income and a vector of respondent and other household characteristics in the first stage, and the yes-no response to the dichotomous choice WTP question for each household member was specified as a random effects probit function of the predicted household vaccine demand derived from the first-stage model and a vector of the particular household member characteristics. In the first stage, household vaccine demand was measured as the ratio of the number of household members, child and adult alike, for whom dengue vaccines would be purchased to the total number of household members. With this chapter's focus on child VSL, vaccine purchase decision for child household members only (decisions for adult members excluded) were used in the second stage.[3]

[1] This may mean that existing VSL estimates based on the specific intervention CVM formulation may be biased upward.

[2] Asking the adult household head for his/her WTP for a dengue vaccine for a child member of the household is in line with the "parental sovereignty" perspective on children's welfare, which argues parental altruism and parental guardianship or stewardship. It is an alternative to the consumer sovereignty normative perspective-based "children's sovereignty" which assumes that each individual has well-defined preferences and is the best judge of his or her own welfare. Freeman (2003: 340) writes: "The children's sovereignty perspective is not ethically attractive. Children are immature and lack the cognitive ability to make choices about health and safety. They may not have well-defined preferences over the full range of alternatives necessary to make reasoned choices. Also, they do not control the financial resources that are required to make trade-offs between money and health or safety."

[3] An earlier paper stemming from the same research project utilized the WTP responses for both adult and child household member groups (Palanca-Tan 2008).

Results from our two-stage regression model conformed with economic theory. The vaccine demand (as a proportion of household size) specification exhibited a significant positive income effect while the individual vaccine purchase decisions exhibited a significant negative price effect. The signs of the other explanatory variables in the model were generally in accord with intuition. The VSL estimates for children in Metro Manila ranged from US$0.70 to US$0.80 million, an order of magnitude comparable to the few existing VSL estimates for developing countries.

17.2 METHODOLOGY

17.2.1 Survey Instrument and Implementation

The final form of the survey instrument[4] was the result of a series of key informant interviews with doctors and medical professionals specializing in dengue, infectious diseases, and pediatrics; focus group discussions with different types of respondents from low- to high-income households; and questionnaire pre-tests (numbering more than 200 respondents). To allow for some scope tests[5], two vaccine scenarios were constructed: (1) a dengue vaccine that provides protection for one year and (2) a dengue vaccine that provides protection for ten years. Both types of dengue vaccines were presented as a one-dose vaccine that could be purchased at hospitals, doctors' clinics, and drug stores and could be administered either as an injection or oral drops. Five bid levels (dengue vaccine price) were used for both vaccine types: US$ 2 (PhP 100), US$ 10 (PhP 500), US$ 20 (PhP 1,000), US$ 60 (PhP 3,000) and US$ 100 (PhP 5,000). The sample size of 500 respondents consisted of split samples of fifty respondents for each bid price and vaccine duration.

The survey instrument consisted of four parts. Part 1 included a brief introduction on the purpose of the survey, easy to answer questions about the respondent and his/her household, and questions to assess the level of awareness of the respondent about dengue. Part 2 was a short training module on understanding mortality risk reduction. The module included information on mortality risks associated with leading causes of deaths in the Philippines.

[4] The English version of the survey instrument can be made available by the author to interested readers upon request.

[5] The scope test is one of three tests to establish the validity of the WTP estimate arrived at in a contingent valuation survey. The scope test requires that WTP increase proportionately with the quantity or quality of the health outcome being valued. In this study, scope was defined in terms of the duration of efficacy of the dengue vaccine. The other two more basic tests of VSL estimate validity are the price test (WTP should fall with an increase in the vaccine price), and the income test (WTP should increase with household income).

Apart from familiarizing respondents with the concept of mortality risk reduction, the information provided a basis of comparison for the mortality risk reduction from the dengue vaccine. Preferred by the less-educated and lower-income focus group discussion and pre-test participants, risk grids[6] were used as visual aid in the survey. A question to test for comprehension was asked at the end of the explanation. The enumerator was instructed to note down the number of times the explanation was repeated before the respondent was able to give the correct answer. Part 3 introduced the contingent valuation scenario by presenting information details on dengue (e.g., the four dengue virus serotypes, modes of infection, incidence, medication, and prevention), the difference between mortality risks from dengue of the fourteen-years-and-younger age (child) group (1/100,000) and the fifteen-years-and-above age (adult) group (1/1,000,000) likewise using risk grids as visual aids, and developments in dengue vaccine research. The WTP question, following the dichotomous choice formulation, was phrased in the following way: the respondent was first asked how many vaccines he/she would buy for his/her household members at the stated price, after which he/she was asked who in the household would be given the vaccine. A short "cheap talk" script reminding respondents to consider their budget constraint and to answer in accordance to what they would really do if the vaccine were already available in the market was inserted in the WTP question. Part 3 also included two sets of debriefing questions. One set, addressed to respondents who would buy the vaccine, consisted of three items: (1) the degree of certainty of buying the vaccine, (2) the expenditure item that would be most reduced in order to buy the vaccine, and (3) the relative importance of the different reasons for buying the vaccine. Respondents not buying the vaccine, on the other hand, were first asked if they would take the vaccine for any household members if it were offered for free. A "no" response to this question was followed by a question on the reasons why they would not want the vaccine even if it were free. Finally, part 4 solicited additional socioeconomic and health information. These questions were asked last to avoid generating respondents' disinterest early on the survey. At the end of the interview, the enumerator recorded his/her assessment of the quality of the interview.

The survey was conducted through in-person interviews during the months of February to May 2007 in Metro Manila. Metro Manila, one of seventeen regions in the Philippines, is the political, economic, social, and cultural center of the Philippines. It is one of the more modern metropolises in Southeast Asia and is among the world's thirty most populous. Metro

[6] The risk grid used in the study is a short bond paper divided into 10,000 equal squares representing 10,000 people. The number of shaded squares represents the number of people that face the risk of death from a certain illness. For example, 1 in 100,000 risk of death from dengue is illustrated by shading one of the 100,000 squares in the risk grid.

Manila consists of fourteen cities and three municipalities. Respondents were drawn from the five largest cities in Metro Manila, namely, Quezon City (accounting for 21 percent of the Metro Manila population), Manila (15 percent), Caloocan (11 percent), Makati (5 percent), and Pasig (5 percent). A sample of 100 respondents was taken from each of the five cities. For each city, a residential barangay with residents belonging to all social classes was randomly selected. Respondents from each barangay were chosen using systematic sampling. Each respondent was randomly assigned a vaccine type and price.

17.2.2 Data Analysis

17.2.2.1 Willingness to Pay for a Dengue Vaccine

A two-stage estimation procedure was undertaken to arrive at the mean WTP for a dengue vaccine for young members of the household aged fourteen years or younger. In the first stage, household demand for dengue vaccines d (expressed in terms of the number of vaccines to be purchased in proportion to the number of household members) was specified as a linear function of the vectors of respondent's characteristics $\boldsymbol{r}$ and household characteristics z (excluding income), and household income y:

$$d = d(r, z, y) \tag{1}$$

The predicted household vaccine demand derived in the first stage was then included as an explanatory variable in the vaccine purchase decisions for individual household members in the second stage. This would capture the interdependence of the budget constraint in the individual vaccine purchase decisions for each household.

In stage 2, we analyzed the yes-no response to the dichotomous choice contingent valuation question using the framework developed by Hanemann based on the random utility model which is briefly discussed below.

Indirect utility, u, depends on h (which takes on the value 1 if the respondent is buying the vaccine for a household member, 0 if otherwise), household income y, a vector of household member characteristics $\boldsymbol{m}$, a vector of respondent and his/her household's characteristics z, and a component of preferences that are known only to the respondent and not to the researcher ε_{h}. This utility function is specified as additively separable in deterministic (v) and stochastic preferences (ε):

$$u(h, y, m, z, \varepsilon_h) = v(h, y, m, z) + \varepsilon_h \tag{2}$$

As the random part of preference is unknown, only probability statements about yes and no responses can be made. The probability that a bid price *B* for the vaccine is accepted can be expressed as:

$$\begin{aligned}\Pr(yes) &= \Pr\ [v(1, y-B, m, z) + \varepsilon_1 \geq v(0, y, m, z) + \varepsilon_0] \\ &= \Pr\ [v(1,\ y-B,\ m,\ z) - v(0,\ y,\ m,\ z) \geq e_0 - e_1] \\ &= F_\varepsilon(\Delta v)\end{aligned} \quad (3)$$

F_ε (Δv), the probability that the random variable ε will be less than Δv, represents the cumulative density function of the respondent's true maximum willingness to pay.

We assumed that the stochastic terms ε are independently and identically distributed following a normal distribution with mean of 0 and standard deviation of σ, and used the probit regression procedure to evaluate (3). For the indirect utility specification, we assumed a linear function such that income would disappear in the change in utility term in (3). The parameter estimates from the binary probit model were used to calculate mean willingness to pay $E(B)$ according to

$$E(B) = -(\beta / \sigma)X / (\beta_B / \sigma) = -\beta X / \beta_B \quad (4)$$

β is a vector of estimated coefficients of all explanatory variables except price (vector X) and β_B is the estimate for the price coefficient.

Each child member of the household aged fourteen years or younger, for whom the respondent decided to buy or not to buy a vaccine, constituted one observation (one data point) in the binary choice data set. Hence, each household (that is, one completed questionnaire) contributed a number of data points/observations equivalent to the number of household members aged fourteen years or younger. Household member characteristics used as explanatory variables were age, gender, and a dummy variable for members who were the respondent's own children. As respondent and household characteristics were already incorporated in the household vaccine demand model, only the predicted vaccine demand variable in proportion to the household size was used in the individual choice decision model. Finally, the probit regression procedure was run as an unbalanced panel random effects model to capture the interdependence of the decisions to buy the vaccine for members in each household.

Non-parametric mean willingness to pay for a dengue vaccine and its variance were calculated using the lower bound Turnbull formula (Haab and McConnel 2003):

$$E_{LB}(B) = \sum_{j=0}^{M} B_j \left(F_{j+1} - F_j\right) \quad (5)$$

$$V\left(E_{LB}\left(B\right)\right)=\sum_{j=1}^{M}(F_j\left(1-F_j\right)(B_j-B_{j-1})^2/T_j) \quad (6)$$

M is the number of bids, B is the bid level, T_j is the number of respondents offered bid price B_j, F_j is the proportion of no responses to bid price B_j, $F_0 = 0$ and $F_{M+1} = 1$.

17.2.2.2 Isolating the Willingness to Pay for a Mortality Risk Reduction

Stated willingness to pay for a dengue vaccine includes not only the value attached to the mortality risk reduction effect of the vaccine but also the other benefits that can be derived from the vaccine such as avoidance of pain and suffering, savings on medical and related expenses and avoidance of lost household income. The relative importance of the mortality risk effect vis-à-vis the other effects depends on the nature of the disease or the cause of death. The willingness to pay for a reduction in the risk of death from dengue, for instance, would differ from that of traffic accidents, cancer, and other diseases where the duration and intensity of pain and suffering may be different. A number of studies had shown that WTP for a mortality risk reduction and hence the resulting VSL estimate was context-specific. Hammit and Liu (2004) found that WTP for mortality risk varied according to disease type and latency, and according to the affected body organ, environmental pathway, and payment mechanism. In Vassanadumrongdee and Matsuoka (2005), willingness to pay to reduce cancer deaths was found to be influenced by degrees of dread, severity, controllability, and personal exposure; while willingness to pay to reduce traffic accidents was influenced by perceived immediate occurrence. Jones-Lee, Hammerton, and Philips (1985) had arrived at a VSL estimate based on motor vehicle crashes (£23 million) that was higher than that based on heart disease (£13 million) and that based on cancer (£7 million).

The goal of many VSL studies is to come up with estimates that can be applied in the assessment of a variety of public projects and policies (e.g., in transport, health, and the environment). VSL estimates based on a particular risk context are applied to other risk contexts commonly through the use of adjustment factors. Revesz (1999), for instance, proposed to adjust the standard VSL used by the US Environmental Protection Agency for use in carcinogenic pollutants emission control by a factor of two for risk characterized by involuntariness and uncontrollability, and by a factor of four in the case of risks characterized by dread. Some researchers and policymakers, however, are skeptical about the derivation and use of such adjustment factors. For example, due to lack of empirical VSL studies in the air pollution context and reliable information to support adjustment in the road safety-based VSL for air pollution in the United Kingdom, the Department of Health refrained from quantifying health benefits of air pollution reduction in monetary terms (Dunn 2001).

This chapter presents an alternative method to arrive at a VSL estimate that removes the influence of the risk context. The study opted to isolate the willingness to pay for the reduction in mortality risk by asking respondents directly. Respondents were asked to disentangle the amount they are willing to pay for a dengue vaccine into the different benefits that could be derived from the vaccine. Specifically, they were tasked to state the level of importance they accord to the following five reasons for buying the dengue vaccine: (1) to prevent death, (2) to avoid the pain and suffering from being ill with dengue, (3) to avoid incurring medical expenses, (4) to avoid inconvenience and absenteeism from work or school, and (5) to avoid having to undertake and spend for other precautionary measures. Our focus group discussions revealed that respondents would have difficulty allocating a total weight of 100 (in percent) or even 10 (point system) among the five reasons without any computation aid. So we came up with a game-like activity in which respondents were given ten tokens and five containers. The respondents were told to think of the ten tokens as representing the amount they would pay for the vaccine and to divide them into the five containers according to the weight they give to each reason.

The average weight given to the mortality risk reduction by respondents buying the dengue vaccine, w, was used to isolate the willingness to pay for the mortality reduction, WTP, from the mean willingness to pay for the dengue vaccine $E(B)$:

$$WTP = wE(B) \tag{7}$$

17.2.2.3 *Value of a Statistical Life*

VSL is the value the individual attaches to a reduction in mortality risk. Technically it is the rate at which the individual would trade money for a small change in the probability of dying, Δr, during a specified time period (Hammit and Graham 1999):

$$VSL = WTP / \Delta r \tag{8}$$

In the case of the ten-year efficacy vaccine for which payment was to be made only once in the first year, discounting of the mortality risk reduction, which would be realized over a period of ten years, was undertaken. Viscusi et al. (1997) pointed out that insufficient accounting for discounting and time lags before the risk of death appears could overstate people's perception of risks. For this study, we used a 5 percent discount rate (Hammar and Johanson-Stenman

2004). This positive discount factor would effect an upward adjustment in the value of the mortality risk reduction from the ten-year efficacy vaccine.

17.3 RESULTS AND DISCUSSION

17.3.1 Respondent and Household Characteristics

The first three panels of Table 17.1 give household-level descriptive statistics. About a fifth of respondents were male and about a third were smoking. The

Table 17.1 Descriptive statistics

Variable name	Variable definition	1-year vaccine		10-year vaccine	
		Mean	Std Dev.	Mean	Std Dev.
Respondent's characteristics					
Respondent gender	= 1 if male, 0 if female	0.24	0.43	0.18	0.38
Respondent age	years	34.07	6.99	33.49	7.12
Respondent Smoking	= 1 if smoking, 0 otherwise	0.34	0.47	0.28	0.45
Household characteristics					
Household size	number of all household members	5.10	1.52	5.14	1.46
Income	monthly household income (PhP)	25,060	20,654	24,590	20,415
Pasig	survey site dummy	0.20	0.40	0.20	0.40
Manila	survey site dummy	0.20	0.40	0.20	0.40
Caloocan	survey site dummy	0.20	0.40	0.20	0.40
Makati	survey site dummy	0.20	0.40	0.20	0.40
Dengue-related variables					
Dengue family	= 1 if hh with dengue case/s, 0 otherwise	0.07	0.25	0.07	0.25
Dengue others	= 1 if respondent knew someone who had dengue, 0 otherwise	0.63	0.48	0.59	0.49
Correct	No of correct answers on dengue information questions	6.17	1.14	6.01	1.24
Prevent	No of dengue preventive methods practiced by household	4.41	1.29	4.33	1.26
Fever frequency	Frequency of fever in the household = 1 if frequent, 2 if not so frequent, 3 if sometimes, 4 if rarely	3.30	0.67	3.27	0.72
Individual household member characteristics (14 years and below)					
Member gender	= 1 if male, 0 if female	0.50	0.50	0.46	0.50
Member age	years	7.49	4.37	7.50	4.26
Respondent child	= 1 if member is respondent's own child, 0 otherwise	0.98	0.15	0.97	0.15

respondents, on the average, were thirty-four years old. The respondents' households had a mean monthly income of PhP 24,000–25,000 and had five members, on average.

About 7 percent of respondents reported cases of dengue in the household while the majority personally knew someone who had been ill with dengue. Survey results reflect a relatively high though not perfect knowledge about dengue. Of the eight dengue information questions, each respondent, on average, answered six correctly, Almost all were aware of the particular insect (mosquito) that causes dengue but there was less familiarity with the particular characteristics of the mosquito that carries the virus (that it bites during the daytime and lays its eggs in clean water). Alarmingly, almost half of respondents wrongly thought that the dengue mosquito lays and breeds its eggs only in dirty water. There was also some degree of misconception about the conditions (transmission and immunity) and treatment (blood transfusion) of dengue victims. It appears that the majority of respondents were yet not adequately informed of all the ways of preventing dengue as only a quarter of respondents were aware that putting salt in containers that accumulate water could prevent mosquito breeding.

As regards dengue-preventive methods, households on average practiced four of the seven methods cited. Almost all households (96 percent) were doing the relatively easier tasks of regularly cleaning and covering water containers. Three-quarters of the respondents limited outside play of children during the rainy season while only about half practiced the more difficult task of cleaning roof gutters and the more costly method of using insect-repellant lotion. While 56 percent of households were using mosquito-killing chemicals, only 13 percent were using bed-nets.

The survey results also confirmed the widespread acceptance of vaccination and the availability of public vaccination programs in the Philippines. Almost all respondents (95–99 percent) from the low- to the high-income classes had children in their households given the basic vaccines as provided in the government's Expanded Program on Immunization. The majority of households availed themselves of the free vaccination programs of government and charitable institutions.

17.3.2 WTP and VSL

17.3.2.1 Household Vaccine Demand Model

Figure 17.1 shows the proportion of household members for whom vaccines would be purchased. The bid function is well behaved for both vaccine durations. The proportion of household members for whom the vaccine would be purchased monotonically declined as the vaccine price increased.

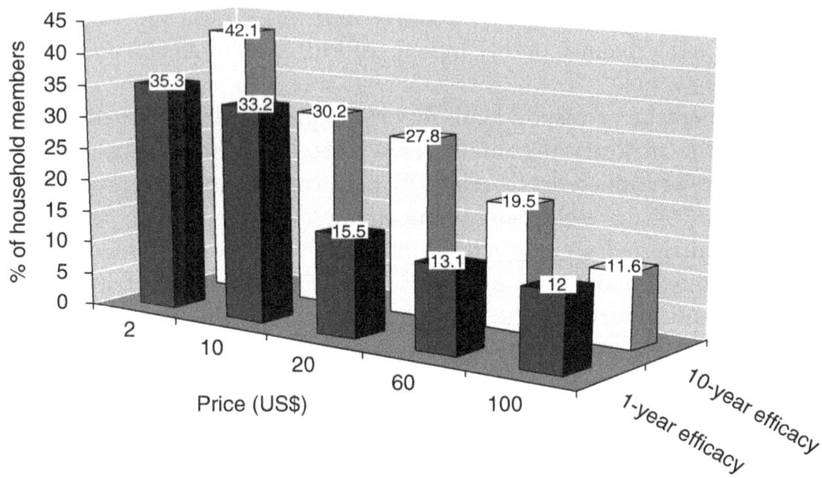

Figure 17.1 Vaccine demand

Table 17.2 Household vaccine demand (as a proportion of household size), Ordinary Least Squares

Explanatory variable	1-year vaccine	10-year vaccine
Constant	0.332**	0.150
Income	0.004***	0.004***
Respondent gender	−0.046	0.049
Respondent age	−0.004	−0.001
Respondent smoking	0.070*	0.000
Dengue family	0.154**	0.114
Dengue others	0.000	0.000
Correct	−0.006	−0.008
Prevent	0.014	0.027*
Fever frequency	−0.020	0.000
Pasig	−0.127**	0.000
Manila	0.010	−0.047
Caloocan	−0.014	−0.104*
Makati	−0.079	−0.097
R-squared	0.170	0.140
Number of observations	250	250

*** significant at $\alpha = 0.01$, **significant at $\alpha = 0.05$, *significant at $\alpha = 0.10$

Results of the ordinary least squares regression run of vaccine demand, expressed as a proportion of household size, are summarized in Table 17.2. Our household vaccine demand model revealed significant positive income effect. Two dengue-related household profile variables, namely *DengueFamily* and *Prevent*, yielded some significant effects on vaccine demand which were in accord with intuition, that is, households with past case/s of dengue and which undertook more of the dengue-preventive measures cited were likely to buy more vaccines. Respondent's characteristics (i.e., gender, age, and smoking) and knowledge about dengue did not yield any consistent as well as significant influence on vaccine demand. Though with varying degrees of significance, dummy variables for survey sites generally had a negative sign, indicating that demand for dengue vaccines was higher for households in Quezon City (the omitted survey site) than in Pasig, Manila, Caloocan, and Makati. This could be due to the relatively higher incidence of dengue in Quezon City.

17.3.2.2 Vaccine Purchase Decision for Individual Child Household Members

Table 17.3 presents the results of the binary probit random effects model of the respondents' stated decisions to purchase a dengue vaccine for each household member aged fourteen years and younger. Results for both the one-year and ten-year efficacy vaccines conformed with economic theory and intuition. Vaccine price had a signifcant negative effect on the respondent's decision to purchase a vaccine for a household member while predicted vaccine demand had a significant positive effect. The probability of the respondent buying a vaccine for a member was also significantly higher for younger members and for members who were the respondent's own children. Gender of the household member revealed no systematic and significant effect on the decision to buy the vaccine.

Using the results of the random effects probit model, mean willingness to pay for a dengue vaccine for children fourteen years and younger was calculated

Table 17.3 Willingness to pay for a dengue vaccine for household members aged fourteen years and younger, Binary probit model with unbalanced panel random effects

Explanatory variable	1-year vaccine	10-year vaccine
Constant	−8.434*	−3.676**
Vaccine price	−0.0021***	−0.0027**
Predicted vaccine demand (in proportion to household size)	36.076***	53.363**
Member age	−0.319***	−0.579**
Member gender	0.068	−0.646
Member is respondent's child	6.648	9.862**
Random effects	0.973***	0.983***
Log-likelihood	−181.688	−159.864
Number of observations	521	479

*** significant at $\alpha = 0.01$, **significant at $\alpha = 0.05$, *significant at $\alpha = 0.10$

Table 17.4 Mean willingness to pay for a dengue vaccine for children aged fourteen years and younger

	1-year duration	10-year duration
Parametric US$ (PhP)	**34.57** (1,729)	**40.95** (2,047)
Non-parametric (lower-bound estimates)	**30.4** (1,520)	**37.0** (1,852)

to be about US$35 (PhP 1,729) for the one-year duration vaccine and US$41 (PhP 2,047) for the ten-year duration vaccine (first panel of Table 17.4).

Non-parametric mean willingness to pay for the dengue vaccine calculated using the Turnbull method are shown in the second panel of Table 17.4. Non-parametric WTP were slightly lower than the parametric estimates for both vaccine durations.

Mean WTP for the ten-year duration vaccine was only slightly higher than mean WTP for the one-year duration vaccine, and the difference was much smaller than the proportionality requirement of the external scope test. Nearly all previous studies of mortality risk reduction failed the external scope test. From among twenty-five contingent valuation-VSL literature reviewed by Hammit and Graham (1999), only nine allowed for an external magnitude test and all nine studies violated the proportionality assumption.[7] More recent contingent valuation-VSL studies employing visual aids and risk comprehension training modules were no exception (see, for instance, Hammit and Liu 2004; Alberini et al. 2004; Liu et al. 2005; Maskery et al. 2007).

17.3.2.3 Value of a Statistical Life

Reflecting the high literacy rate in the Philippines, particularly in highly urbanized Metro Manila, respondents generally understood the concept of mortality risk. More than four-fifths of respondents correctly answered the comprehension test question for the short module on understanding mortality risks after only one explanation. About 16 percent required one repetition of the explanation while the remaining 3 percent required two repetitions. Thus, we feel reasonably confident that respondents understood and took into consideration the mortality risk reduction that the dengue vaccine would bring about.

Results of the debriefing questions on the relative importance of the different reasons for buying the dengue vaccine for young members of the household aged fourteen years and younger are summarized in Table 17.5. On average, yes respondents gave the mortality risk reduction effect of dengue a weight of

[7] Three of the nine did not even satisfy the expected positive relationship between WTP and the risk reduction magnitude.

Table 17.5 Relative importance of reasons for buying the vaccine

	Mean	Std Dev.
1. To prevent death from dengue	3.87	1.65
2. To avoid the pain and suffering from being ill with dengue	1.91	1.12
3. To avoid incurring medical expenses	1.34	1.11
4. To avoid the inconvenience and prevent being absent from work or school	1.58	1.26
5. So that it will not be necessary for us to take and spend for other precautions (such as using anti-mosquito lotion, mosquito nets, mosquito killers)	1.31	1.24

Table 17.6 WTP for a mortality risk reduction and VSL estimates for children in Metro Manila

	Parametric	Non-parametric
WTP US$ (PhP)	14.61 (699)	13.04 (652)
VSL US$ millions (PhP millions)	0.80 (39.9)	0.70 (35.2)
VSL/Annual income	133	118

38.7 percent (or a 95 percent confidence interval of 35.7–41.7 percent). This result indicates that although the mortality risk reduction was considered most important among five reasons for buying the dengue vaccine, the weight attached to it was much lower (less than half) than the 100 percent weight implicitly assumed in VSL studies that based estimates on the entire willingness to pay for an intervention.

We used the stated weight in Table 17.5 to decompose the willingness to pay for a dengue vaccine and isolate the mean value attached by the respondents for a reduction in the risk of dying of a child in their households. Following Hammit and Liu (2004) and Vassanadumrongdee and Matsuoka (2005), VSL was calculated as the average of the values for the two risk reduction magnitudes. The WTP and resulting VSL estimates are shown in Table 17.6. The value of life estimates for a child fourteen years old or younger in Metro Manila ranged from US$0.70 million to US$0.80 million, about 118–133 times annual income. When used in cost-benefit analysis, this VSL estimate represents the amount of benefit in money terms of each child life saved by a particular public program. For instance, if a certain pollution abatement project reduces child mortality cases caused by that pollution by one every year, then that program will have an additional benefit of US$0.70 million to US$0.80 million every year.

Our results are fairly within the range of estimates derived in recent survey-based VSL estimates in the region. Vassanadumrongdee and Matsuoka (2005) came up with VSL estimates of US$0.7–1.5 million, about 100–170 times annual income, in their study with scenarios on traffic accidents and air pollution in Bangkok in 2003. Hammit and Liu's (2004) liver cancer and non-cancer diseases scenarios resulted in VSL estimates of US$0.5–1.1 million, 36–80 times of annual income in Taiwan in 2001.

Compared to other child VSL estimates, our estimates for Metro Manila are lower than previous estimates for the US using the revealed preference averting behavior methods (e.g., Mount et al.'s estimate of US$2.6–7.7 million, 85–253 times annual income, based on vehicle fatality rates and costs in 1997; and Jenkins et al.'s estimate of US$1.1–2.7 million, 36–89 times annual income, based on bicycle helmet demand in 1997) but much higher than the recent child VSL estimate for Bangladesh of US$30–60,000 which is 75–150 times annual income (Maskery et al. 2007).

17.4 CONCLUDING REMARKS

We arrived at a measure of the value of statistical life for children in Metro Manila, which to our knowledge is the first VSL estimate for the Philippines and one of the very few contingent valuation-based VSL estimates for children. Our estimate was derived from the willingness to pay for a hypothetical dengue vaccine—a familiar risk and intervention context for Filipinos, particularly children.

Our study differs from existing literature in two ways. First, WTP for a dengue vaccine was elicited for each and every household member instead of only one household member. We believe that our approach better reflects the reality of household decision-making wherein the head decides to purchase an individually consumed good for one or several members after considering the needs and wants of all members in relation to the single household budget constraint. Likewise, a different modeling procedure was undertaken. We used a two-stage model. In stage one the household vaccine demand in proportion to household size was regressed with household income and a vector of respondent and other household characteristics. In stage two the yes-no response to the dichotomous choice WTP question for each household member was specified as a random effects probit function of the predicted household vaccine demand derived from the first-stage model and a vector of the particular household member characteristics.

Second, WTP for the mortality risk reduction was isolated from the stated WTP for the specific health intervention before VSL calculation. We found that although the mean weight for the mortality risk reduction was larger than the weights for the other reasons for taking the vaccine, it was only a third of the total. This result suggests the extent of likely deviations of past specific intervention-based VSL estimates when applied to other risk contexts—a finding which is not inconsistent with studies recommending risk context adjustment factors for VSL estimates of as large as two to four times (Revesz 1999 and Hammit and Liu 2004).

Our models conformed with predictions of economic theory—our household vaccine demand model yielded a significant positive income effect while our random effects probit model for vaccine purchase decisions yielded a significant negative price effect. Our VSL estimates compared well with existing contingent valuation-VSL estimates in the literature—relatively lower than those derived for developing countries and falling in the lower range of estimates for slightly richer countries in the region.

References

Alberini, A., A. Hunt, and A. Markandya (2004). "Willingness to Pay to Reduce Mortality Risks: Evidence from a Three-country Contingent Valuation Study." Fondazione Eni Enrico Mattei (FEEM) Working Paper No.111.04. Milan, Italy.

Bateman, I. J. et al. (2002). *Economic Valuation with Stated Preference Techniques: A Manual.* Cheltenham: Edward Elgar.

Blomquist, G. C., T. R. Miller, and D. T. Levy (1996). "Values of Risk Reduction Implied by Motorist Use of Protection Equipment: New Evidence from Different Populations," *Journal of Transport Economics and Policy*, 30: 55–66.

Boyle, K. J. (2003). "Contingent Valuation in Practice," in P. A. Champ, K. J. Boyle, and T. C. Brown (eds.), *A Primer on Nonmarket Valuation.* Dordrecht: Kluwer Academic Publishers, 111–70.

Carlin, P. S. and R. Sandy (1991). "Estimating the Implicit Value of a Young Child's Life," *Southern Economic Journal*, 58(1):186–202.

Cropper, M., M. Haile, J. Lampietti et al. (2004). "The Demand for a Malaria Vaccine: Evidence from Ethiopia," *Journal of Development Economics*, 75: 303–18.

Dasgupta, P., A. Sen, and S. Marglin (1972). *Guidelines for Project Evaluation.* New York: United Nations.

Dunn, H. (2001). "UK Perspective on Valuing Mortality Risk in the Air Pollution Context," in Abt Associates (eds.), *Economic Valuation of Mortality Risk Reduction: Assessing the State of the Art for Policy Application*, Workshop Proceedings, 6 November 2004, Silver Spring, MD, USA. US Environmental Protection Agency, 18–30.

Freeman, A. M. III (2003). *The Measurement of Environmental and Resource Values: Theory and Methods*, 2nd ed,. Washington, DC: Resources for the Future.

Haab, T. C. and K. E. Connell (2003). *Valuing Environmental and Natural Resources: The Econometrics of Non-market Valuation.* Cheltenham: Edward Elgar.

Hammar, H. and O. Johansson-Stenman (2004). "The Value of Risk-free Cigarettes--Do Smokers Underestimate the Risk?" *Health Economics*, 13: 59–71.

Hammitt, J. K. and J. D. Graham (1999). "Willingness to Pay for Health Protection: Inadequate Sensitivity to Probability?" *Journal of Risk and Uncertainty*, 18(1): 33–62.

—— and J.-T. Liu (2004). "Effect of Disease Type and Latency on the Value of Mortality Risk," *Journal of Risk and Uncertainty*, 28: 73–95.

Jenkins R. R., N. Owens, and L. B. Wiggins (2001). "Valuing Reduced Risks to Children: The Case of Bicycle Safety Helmets," *Contemporary Economic Policy*, 19(4): 397–408.

Jones-Lee, M., M. Hammerton, and P. R. Philips (1985). "The Value of Safety: Results of a National Sample Survey," *Economic Journal*, 95: 49–72.

Krupnick, A., A. Alberini, M. Cropper et al. (2002). "Age, Health and the Willingness to Pay for Mortality Risk Reductions: A Contingent Valuation Survey of Ontario Residents," *Journal of Risk and Uncertainty*, 24: 161–86.

Liu, J.-T., J. K. Hammitt, J.-D. Wang et al. (2005). "Valuation of the Risk of SARS in Taiwan," *Health Economics*, 14: 83–91.

Mahmud, M. (2005). "Contingent Valuation of Mortality Risk Reduction in Developing Countries: A Mission Impossible? *Measuring Trust and the Value of Statistical Lives: Evidence from Bangladesh*, PhD dissertation, University of Gotheburg, Sweden, 145: 82–117.

Maskery, B., Z. Islam, J. Deen et al. (2007). "An Estimate of the Economic Value that Parents in Rural Bangladesh Place on Ex-ante Mortality Risk Reductions for their Children." Paper presented at the European Association of Environmental and Resource Economists Conference 2008, 25–29 June 2008, Gothenburg, Sweden.

Mount, T., W. Weng, W. Schulze et al. (2001). "Automobile Safety and the Value of Statistical Life in the Family: Valuing Reduced Risk for Children, Adults and the Elderly." Paper presented at the Association of Environmental and Resource Economists Workshop (Assessing and Managing Environmental and Public Health Risks), 13–15 June, Bay Harbor, ME.

Palanca-Tan, R. (2008). "The Demand for a Dengue Vaccine: A Contingent Valuation Survey in Metro Manila," *Vaccine*, 26: 914–23.

Revesz, R. L. (1999). "Environmental Regulation, Cost-Benefit Analysis, and the Discounting of Human Lives," *Columbia Law Review*, 99(4): 941–1017.

Viscusi, W. K. and J. A. Aldy (2003). "The Value of a Statistical Life: A Critical Review of Market Estimates Throughout the World," *Journal of Risk and Uncertainty*, 27(1): 5–76.

—— J. K. Hakes, A. Carlin (1997). "Measures of Mortality Risk," *Journal of Risk and Uncertainty*, 14(3): 213–33.

Vassandumrongdee, S. and S. Matsuoka (2005). "Risk Perceptions and Value of a Statistical Life for Air Pollution and Traffic Accidents: Evidence from Bangkok, Thailand," *Journal of Risk and Uncertainty*, 30(3): 261–87.

18

Comments by Shanta Devarajan on "Estimating the Value of Statistical Life"

Rosalina Palanca-Tan's paper, "Estimating the Value of Statistical Life for Children in Metro Manila," is a fitting contribution to a volume in honor of Partha Dasgupta. As with a lot of Dasgupta's work, this paper treats a critically important subject—the economic value of life—by creatively applying rigorous analytical tools—an original, two-stage estimate of willingness-to-pay (WTP) for vaccines that distinguishes between mortality and morbidity risk—and does so in a manner that is sensitive to the circumstances of poor people. The estimation procedure includes having the respondents participate in a play-like activity "to break the monotony of the question-answer sequence." The resulting estimates, of the order of US$0.7–0.8 million, appear to be relatively robust and within the range of comparable estimates for other Asian developing countries.

In this commentary, rather than focusing on the methodological aspects of the paper (which are, in any event, quite sound), I will concentrate on two broader, contemporary issues raised by the Palanca-Tan paper.

Rationality. The first issue has to do with the theoretical model underlying the estimations. That is a model of rational agents who maximize a von Neumann-Morgenstern expected utility function based on known probabilities of the events in question (such as the probability that a child might contract dengue fever). This is of course the standard model in almost all of the literature on estimating WTP to reduce the chances of a random event's occurring. At the same time, the past decade has seen a burgeoning literature in economics—the "behavioral economics" literature—that questions whether individuals do in fact behave according to the rational-agent model (for a lucid review, see Lambert (2006)). Much of this literature has been focused on individuals' intertemporal choices (consumption versus savings today, etc.), most of which has an element of uncertainty (because the future is largely uncertain). A particular strand has looked at people's incentives to smoke, and what smoking reveals about the smoker's expected-utility-maximization problem. The behavioral economists have concluded that smoking is not the result of standard utility maximization—the parameters for it to be so would be unrealistic—and therefore some of the prescriptions, such as tobacco taxation, have different benefits and costs compared to what standard neoclassical analysis would predict (Gruber 2003).

This compelling empirical evidence in the behavioral economics literature leads one to ask: are the estimates derived from standard WTP estimates, which assume agents are following neoclassical assumptions, valid under alternative behavioral models? In the case of the Palanca-Tan paper, will the stated WTP estimates lead to different estimates of the value of life if we assumed parents were not maximizing expected value? After all, a third of the people in the sample are smokers (Table 17.1). If, by smoking, these people exhibit non-rational behavioral characteristics, how do we know that they do not exhibit similar characteristics in other actions, such as in their decisions to vaccinate their children? There is no straightforward answer to this question[1], but it is worth asking, especially since these estimates may be used in public policy decisions, which brings me to the second issue to be raised about this paper.

The use of value-of-life estimates. Palanca-Tan's paper states that estimates of value of life are useful in environmental decision-making because many environmental policies involve reductions in people's risk of death. This is no doubt true, and casts this paper in the broader literature of valuing the inputs and outputs of public projects and policies, a major component of cost-benefit analysis. This is also a literature to which Partha and I have (separately) contributed (see for instance Dasgupta, Marglin, and Sen 1972; Bell and Devarajan 1983).

In evaluating this literature against some recent findings about incentives within the public sector, one cannot help but think that estimating the prices with which to value a project's inputs and outputs is only a minor part of the problem. The major problem is that the behavior of public servants often leads to a disconnect between the project's inputs and intended outputs. For instance, teachers in public primary schools in India and Uganda are absent about 25 percent of the time (Chaudhury et al. 2006). An education project that finances school buildings, teachers and teaching materials, with the prospect of generating educated children as outputs would miss the point if it got the shadow price of buildings and educated children right, but neglected to take into account the problem of teacher absenteeism. More fundamentally, our efforts should be in trying to improve incentives so that teachers will be present, rather than in fine-tuning shadow prices.

This problem affects the areas where value-of-life estimates are used as well. One is health, where these estimates are used to justify public spending

[1] Many years ago, Becker (1962) suggested an answer, namely that even if individuals were irrational, their participation in the market made the marginal consumer's behavior rational, a point that has been corroborated more recently by List and Millimet (2008).

on hospitals and clinics—even though in India the absentee rate for doctors in public primary clinics is even higher than for teachers (Chaudhury et al. 2006). Another is various infrastructure projects, such as guardrails on mountain roads, that are also justified based on the economic value of lives saved. Yet, too often, the money that is allocated to such expenditures is diverted to other uses. In short, the elegance of valuation techniques, while appealing, should not distract us from addressing the deep incentive problems of the public sector if we hope to use economics to improve the lives of poor people.

To conclude, the two issues raised in this commentary—irrational individual behavior and incentive problems in the public sector—are not a criticism of the Palanca-Tan paper. On the contrary, they are a tribute to the clarity and rigor of the paper that it provokes readers to explore the boundaries of the discipline—just as Partha Dasgupta has done throughout his career.

References

Becker, G. S. (1962). "Behavior and Economic Theory," *Journal of Political Economy*, 70(1): 1–13.

Bell, C. and S. Devarajan (1983). "Shadow Prices under Alternative Macroeconomic Specifications," *Quarterly Journal of Economics*, 98(3): 457–77.

Chaudhury, N., J. Hammer, M. Kremer et al. (2006). "Missing in Action: Teachers and Health Worker Absence in Developing Countries," *Journal of Economic Perspectives*, 20(1): 91–116.

Dasgupta, P., S. Marglin, and A. Sen (1972). *Guidelines for Project Evaluation*. UNIDO, United Nations, New York.

Gruber, J. (2003). "The New Economics of Smoking," *NBER Reporter: Research Summary*, summer.

Lambert, C. (2006). "The Marketplace of Perceptions," *Harvard Magazine*, March-April.

List, J. A. and D. L. Millimet (2008). "The Market: Catalyst for Rationality and Filter of Irrationality," *The B.E. Journal of Economic Analysis and Policy*, 8(1). Available online at <http://www.degruyter.com/view/j/bejeap> (accessed 8 December 2013).

Part IV

The Poverty-Environment-Population Nexus in India

19

Natural Resources and Chronic Poverty in India: Interface and Policy Imperatives

Amita Shah

> The simultaneous presence of two types of positive feedback—one enabling many to move up in their living standards, the other keeping many others in poverty—may explain the large-scale presence of absolute poverty in a world that has been growing wealthier on an average by substituting manufactured and human capital for natural capital.
>
> Dasgupta and Mäler 2009: 59

19.1 INTRODUCTION

Natural resources constitute an important source of livelihood as well as a coping mechanism for a large proportion of the world's 0.82 billion rural poor (WRI 2005:12). Not only that, but the poor—especially, in rural areas—depend on these resources for earning a subsistence income for their survival; for many of them, natural resources are their only asset[1]. According to a rough estimate, natural resources constitute more than 20–25 percent of consumption among indigent populations the world over (Parikh 1998:11). Moreover, incomes earned from smallholder agriculture and allied activities often work as an important strategy for more affluent households, helping to

[1] Degradation of natural resources can have a high human cost for the poor. It can put a severe burden on their ability to meet their needs, can destroy their means of livelihood and can reduce their options to take defensive actions when faced with adversity such as crop failure. Thus, preservation and even regeneration of natural resources are needed not only for sustainability but also for protecting and helping the poor (Shyamsundar 2002: 13).

sustain their status under fluctuating economic conditions in non-farming sectors. Ironically, sole dependence on natural resources may, in many cases, lead to a deep downward spiral in a household's economic well-being, due to shocks like droughts and floods. It has been estimated that about 1.3 billion people live on marginal land and more than half of the rural poor have landholdings too small to provide an adequate income; nearly one fourth are landless (UNCHS 1996). Depletion of the stock of natural resources (capital) thus exerts a significant adverse impact on the income levels of the agrarian population, as well as for those pushed out into urban landscapes but still supplementing their income with support from the rural economy (WRI 2005: 13).[2] Besides the direct impact on households' income, natural resources influence people's well-being through their impact on morbidity and mortality caused by polluted air and water. For these reasons, the degradation of natural resources has been recognized as one of the most important causes of poverty (long duration and severe), a situation most of the poor have difficulty escaping owing to their disproportionate dependence on natural resources, on the one hand, and limited access to these resources, on the other. Ironically, the discourse on poverty reduction often overlooks the critical role of natural resources with respect to these multiple functions (DFID, EC, UNDP, WB, 2002: v).

Also frequently overlooked is the role that natural resources play indirectly in terms of boosting overall economic growth in some predominantly agrarian economies like India (Sastry et al. 2003). The mainstream theories of economic growth have failed to recognize the constraints that ecological pathways and positive feedbacks exert in shaping substitution possibilities in general, and among poor rural communities in particular.[3] To an extent this is due to a limited understanding of the irreversibility of natural resource depletion, the absence of markets for various ecological functions, and the multiplicity of institutions, other than markets, that govern the use of natural resources or capital.

One of the reasons for the disjuncture between natural resources and growth could be that economic dependence on natural resources is often seen as being synonymous with the initial stage of development—the main emphasis being on the primary sector. Conversely, shifting away from the primary sector is seen as a pathway towards higher stages of economic growth and associated poverty reduction, in the context of the sectoral shift, as in the Lewis model. This is particularly true in situations where natural resources are already facing

[2] The multiple functions being that of driver, maintainer, potential exit route, and also an effective mechanism for escaping entry into poverty. For details on concepts and measurements of poverty dynamics see Scott (2006).

[3] This is mainly because the literature has tended to neglect important features of natural resources, such as their availability being depletable and also non-substitutable beyond a threshold level.

severe pressure. Hence, natural resources are more likely to be seen as a driver or maintainer of, rather than as a potential exit route or escape mechanism for, chronic poverty in such situations.

Another reason for the relative neglect of natural resources in poverty discourse could be that the interface between natural resources and poverty is multi-patterned, complex, and empirically difficult to ascertain. Empirical research examining the interface between natural resources and poverty is somewhat scanty and inconclusive. The reasons for this are twofold: (i) the interface is essentially a two-way transaction; whereas the poor are often victims of degraded natural resources, they also resort at times to degrading the very resources on which their survival depends (Duriappah 1998; Nadkarni 2000); and (ii) the interface is highly location specific; aggregate analysis at the regional/national level may not furnish a clear picture (Dasgupta and Mäler 2004: 8). This is particularly true when one considers that the empirical reality is often influenced by population mobility—shifting from environmentally fragile areas to economically more developed ones (Dasgupta 1993).

Using natural resource management as an effective exit route or escape mechanism poses formidable challenges in terms of institutional aspects such as property rights regimes, collective management, and decentralized governance. But this obviously may not be a valid justification for the neglect of natural resource management. Indeed, in the context of imperfect economies with a large presence of chronic (severe and long duration) poverty, it should be quite the opposite. Of late the discourse has received growing attention at the global and national level in light of concerns over climate change (World Bank 2011; ADB 2008; Comim 2008; TEEB 2008).

It is therefore imperative to understand the influence that natural resources and their management exert on chronic poverty—especially in context-specific situations. It is from this perspective that the present chapter provides an overview of the interface between natural resources and poverty in India.

The main objectives of this chapter are:

1. To develop a conceptual framework for examining the interface between natural resources and chronic poverty in India;
2. To review the empirical evidence on the interface across states/regions with varying natural resource endowments;
3. To discuss major policy initiatives and the implications for future natural resource management in the context of poverty reduction.

The analysis is based mainly on secondary data and draws copiously from earlier studies carried out under the Chronic Poverty Research Center (CPRC). The analytical framework draws from the writings of Professor Partha Dasgupta.

19.2 CONCEPTUAL FRAMEWORK

19.2.1 Natural Resources and Poverty Reduction in a Growing Economy

Natural capital such as land, water (inland and sea), forests, and minerals contributes significantly to the growth of GDP. This in turn may open up avenues for sectoral diversification of the workforce in addition to relocating populations from rural to urban areas.[4] Together these developments may lead to poverty reduction. As per the mainstream perspective on economic growth and percolation mechanisms, an increasing proportion of the workforce shifts to the manufacturing and service sectors (representing secondary and tertiary sectors) where direct dependence on natural resources for production and livelihood is fairly low, as compared to that in agriculture and the allied (primary) sectors. At the same time, the intensity of natural resource use moves from the arena of production to consumption, as income, especially in urban areas, starts increasing. Overall, resource-use intensity is expected to decline as the economy grows, as depicted by the widely debated Environmental Kuznet Curve (EKC). This in turn has led to the argument that a high rate of economic growth is an important exit route out of poverty and towards natural resource sustainability[5]. Note, however, that the transition does not work in the same manner across countries and communities facing different resource endowments, growth dynamics, and degrees of poverty.

The above scenario is most likely to hold true in large and populous agrarian economies where even the sectoral transformation operates in a fairly dysfunctional manner, resulting in a narrative where GDP moves out of agriculture much faster than the workforce and their respective communities (Reddy 2010; Jha 2011). Accordingly, a significant proportion of the population continues to derive its livelihood from agriculture and various allied activities that directly depend on the extraction and use of natural resources. A considerable fraction of this agrarian workforce also ends up operating very small and fragmented landholdings with widespread underemployment and low labor productivity; degradation of land and water resources may only worsen the situation. It should therefore come as no surprise that a substantial proportion of those engaged in agriculture in India do not wish to continue with farming as their primary source of revenue (Bhalla 2006). This is a glaring example of what could be termed a "truncated pattern of sectoral shift," wherein a large division of the rural population is stuck between stagnant agricultural opportunities and inadequate demands for higher quality employment in urban

[4] For details, see Bhaduri (2006).

[5] The proposition has gained special relevance in the context of the recent debate on climate change and response from developing economies like India. See Shah (2011a; 2011b).

areas. The poor, especially in rural environments, thus continue to depend considerably on natural resources to sustain their basic livelihoods.

In the following section, I delineate the broad outlines of a conceptual framework, which may bring us closer to understanding the link between natural resources and poverty in India.

19.2.2 Factors Affecting the Interface: A Framework

In developing economies, the interface between natural resources and poverty is shaped by three interrelated processes. These are: a) low initial natural resource endowment; b) unequal access/control over natural resources, especially among rural communities; and c) weak institutions governing the use and distribution of the benefits derived from natural resources. These constitute a set of proximate variables explaining rural poverty. The ultimate causes lie mainly in a) the nature of the ecological pathways in a specific setting; and b) the political economy governing an array of market and non-market institutions. The first of these refers mainly to some of the resources' inherent characteristics, such as their vulnerability to exhaustion when depleted beyond a certain threshold of extraction/use. The latter is intended to encompass structural features of India's economic and societal frameworks, including property rights regimes, social stratification, the composition of growth and sectoral priorities, and socioeconomic-political norms influencing the various institutions governing access, use, and management of natural resources. These last features are important because they determine the future flow of economic benefits as well as ecological services. Demonstrating the role of non-convexities in shaping options for substituting natural resources, especially among the poor, Dasgupta and Mäler (2009) stress the importance of the population's access to and control over natural resources, besides technology and consumer preferences, in shaping the outcomes of rural poverty.[6] The authors argue that "for the poor to cross the ecological thresholds can mean the foreclosure of substitution possibilities among resources, meaning that their range of options is non-convex" (Dasgupta and Mäler 2009: 23). A schematic presentation of the proximate and ultimate causes (or factors) influencing the interface is given in Figure 19.1.

19.2.3 Contextualizing the Framework

The above framework highlights the central importance of institutions, especially property rights, arrangements for distributing the benefits of

[6] For empirical evidence, see Chopra and Gulati (1998) and Shah (2010).

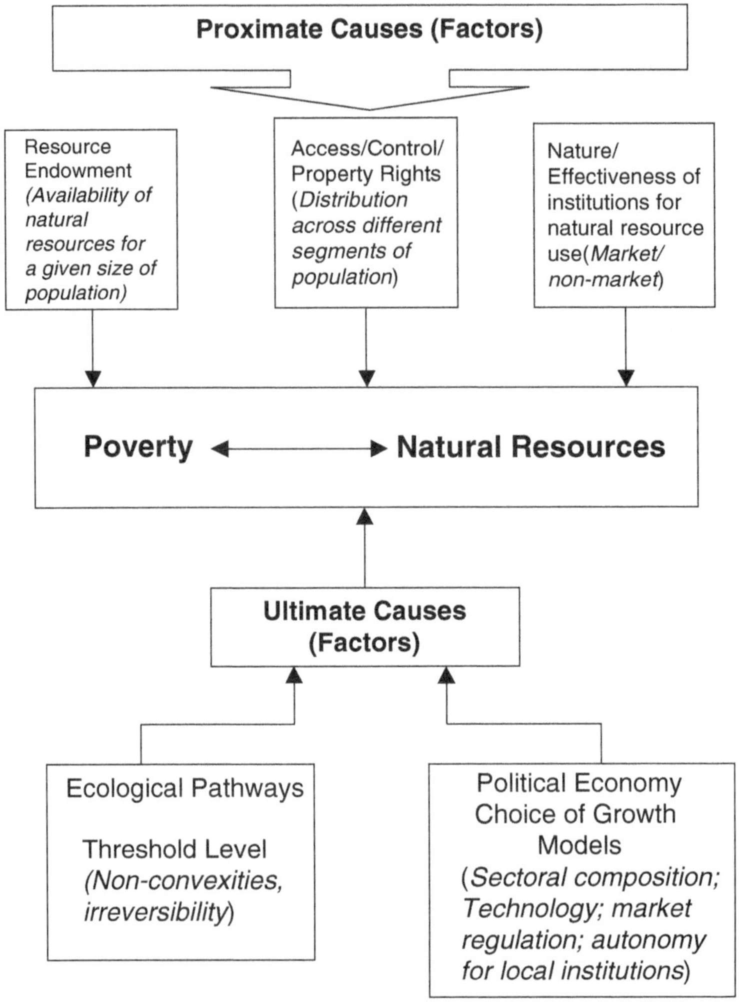

Figure 19.1 Natural resource-poverty linkages: a framework

natural resource exploitation (especially among the poor), and community/state-initiated regulatory mechanisms for ensuring the sustainable use of natural resources across time, space, sectors, and communities—rich and poor. This is important since price alone cannot provide the right kind of signals for resource allocation, use, and management. In what follows we present a brief sketch of the major building blocks of the framework, based on some stylized facts as they pertain to India.[7]

[7] This section draws from some recent writings by the author; see Shah (2009; 2011a; 2011b).

19.2.3.1 Proximate Causes

Natural resource endowment. An extensive proportion of households (about 60 percent) possess small landholdings (about one hectare on average), upon which they depend directly for their livelihood. About 88 percent of the holdings are small (less than two hectares), covering about 44 percent of the total operated area in 2003 (Reddy 2010). Almost one third of rural households own no more than a homestead, and do not cultivate on that property (Saxena 2010). About 23 percent of the land is forested, but actual green cover is fairly low. Two-thirds of the cropped area is under dry land/rain-fed conditions, leading to high levels of risk and low economic viability. Similarly, common property land resources have undergone a significant decline in size and quality owing to increased pressure on their holdings, coupled with weak institutional arrangements for their management—resulting in the dual problem of overuse and/or encroachment. According to official data, the average size of common property land resources is 0.31 hectares per household, which is less than the area required to sustain one unit of cattle—an important asset for those who do not own any agricultural land.

Access and control of natural resources and poverty. Natural resources in India such as forests, minerals, and surface water are typically vested with the state. Other resources, such as pastures, grazing lands, and wetlands, including tanks and ponds, are often managed as common property. By contrast, cropland and groundwater resources are largely under private ownership and control (Shah, 2009). This last category bears particular relevance to agriculture, which has made significant contributions to poverty reduction since the late 1960s. Conversely, many poor households, especially the landless, depend at least partly on common property resources for fuel, fodder, and non-timber forest products (Jodha 2008; Chopra et al. 1989).

Poverty. More than 40 percent of the population lives in poverty, as per the international norm of less than $1.25 a day. Rural poverty is significantly higher than urban poverty. Agricultural laborers account for 40 percent of the rural poor; most are landless (Saxena 2010). Long-term migration is a limited option for most people in rural areas given the high cost of migration and a dearth of job opportunities in the non-farm sectors. Circular migration for casual work remains the mainstay for a substantial fraction of the rural population.

Institutions for governing natural resources. There exist a large number of regulations for natural resource use, but these are weakly implemented. Partially functioning markets have been established for land and water resources, but these often lead to rent seeking. Community-based organizations for natural resource management are vulnerable to capture by elites.

19.3.2.2 Ultimate Causes

Ecological and environmental degradation. Close to 60 percent of the land, including forests, is degraded, and much of the ground water resources are over exploited (MoEF 2009). Population continues to increase; during 2001–11, the annual rate of growth was 1.76 percent. The ecological footprint is low relative to countries like China (World Bank 2011), but natural resource extraction is unevenly distributed as between the rich and poor in both rural and urban areas.

Political economy of growth and poverty reduction. India started with planned economic development, emphasizing basic and core industries and also higher/technical education. The objective was to create capacity for manufacturing production in the domestic sector (Nayyar 2008). Agriculture took a back seat, resulting in a food crisis, followed by successful implementation of the Green Revolution strategy. This improved food security and reduced poverty (Radhakrishna and Ray 2005).

The subsequent shift to neoliberal policies since the early 1990s resulted in high economic growth, but with limited employment opportunities in the manufacturing sector and increased informalization of the labor force. Both have led to conditions of perpetual underemployment and poverty, much of which is concentrated in the natural (water, forest, and mineral) resource-rich regions of the country (Bhaduri 2011).

Sustaining the pace of high economic growth is seen as the major strategy for addressing the twin concerns of environmental degradation (including climate change) and poverty. Market-based solutions continue to be favored over reforms in non-market institutions, which govern natural resources and shape economic opportunities for the poor (Planning Commission 2008).

The important messages emerging from this are twofold—first, continued dependence by the rural poor on natural resources, despite high rates of economic growth; and, second, extensive degradation of land, ground water, and forests, due to unequal access/control over natural resources and weak institutional mechanisms for improving the stock of natural capital to support future growth.

There are, however, substantial opportunities for natural resource management to alleviate poverty. The impact may be direct. For instance, degradation of land, groundwater, or forests may cause incomes to decline, reducing expenditures on food and other basic needs, including education and health. Similarly, the impact may be manifested indirectly. For example, over-depletion of natural resources, by shrinking the productive base, may increase vulnerability to natural shocks like droughts, floods, cyclones.[8]

[8] Panda (2003) discusses the various channels through which the natural resource endowment exerts its impact on poverty reduction in the agricultural sector

Out-migration and dependence on alternative activities outside the primary sector may also have a negative impact on the environment. Once again, the effect can be direct—through processes of production in non-agriculture sectors along with urban growth and lifestyle changes. It can also be indirect—through neglect of land as well as other natural resources at the place of origin (Bilsborrow 1992). Though out-migration clearly has a positive impact on incomes and livelihoods, the evidence for how this helps the poor and those in poverty traps is mixed at best (Singh 2009; Shah 2010). It is therefore imperative to work out strategies through which people can find employment and income from a combination of activities with minimum negative impacts on the environment. This implies mainstreaming environmental concerns into the architecture of economic growth and poverty reduction.[9]

19.3 NATURAL RESOURCES AND POVERTY REDUCTION: WHAT DO WE KNOW?

Two major kinds of study have empirically examined the link between natural resources and poverty reduction in India. One focuses on the agriculture-poverty reduction interface across states/regions, the other on resource degradation (land, water, and forests) and poverty, with a further emphasis on human development.[10] This section summarizes some major findings from these two sets of studies.

19.3.1 Typology among States by Natural Resource-poverty Interface

Notwithstanding the importance of natural resources in poverty reduction, empirical studies seldom refer to the endowment and status of natural resources as important indicators for creating a typology of spatial poverty in India. The study most often used is based on agricultural potential, which essentially refers to the extent and nature of irrigation as indicated by Fan and Hazell (2000) and adopted by the World Bank study mentioned above. A part of this is due to data limitation capturing micro-reality. Another reason is that environmental issues have yet to be internalized into the analysis of developmental

[9] Other overarching factors on the CPRC framework could be pace and composition of macro economic growth, demographic dynamics, and political economy (including property rights regime).

[10] For details see Radhakrishna (2005); Fan and Hazell (2000); Roy and Pal (2002); Shah et al. (2005); Pandey and Kumar (2005); Parikh (1998).

discourse in general. At best, the approach is minimalist, leveling cautions against any further natural resource degradation rather than working proactively towards a pathway of growth. Success in the latter approach depends on combining the regeneration of natural resources with a sustained increase in agriculture production and employment.

An attempt was made by Shah and Guru (2004), to classify regions (as delineated by the National Sample Survey Organisation) according to their natural resource endowments and links to a typology of poverty. Land was classified according to (i) forest-based areas with a high incidence of poverty; (ii) dry land regions with low/transient poverty; and (iii) other areas consisting mainly of irrigated lands. The classification of regions was based on the identification of districts. Those with more than 30 percent of the reported area covered by forests were categorized as forest-based areas. Those covered by special schemes such as the Drought Prone Area Programme (DPAP) and Desert Development Programme (DDP) were classified as dry land areas. The remaining regions were classified under the "other" category. Regions in which the majority of districts fell under the forest or dry land categories were treated as having the same features.[11]

The dual pattern of poverty noted above was further substantiated by an analysis of correlates during the early 1990s. The findings highlighted some of the widely acknowledged realities explaining poverty in the two sets of regions. Whereas the constraints faced by dry land regions are largely a product of weak agro-climatic conditions (or low agronomic potential) coupled with a lack of state investment in land and water resources, poverty in the forest-based regions arises from a lack of entitlement to these resources, in addition to physical isolation and low social capabilities of tribal peoples. Thus, the people living in these two sets of regions face different kinds of poverty and utilize divergent coping strategies. For instance, poverty in dry land regions tends to be low and transient in nature whereas in forest-based regions it is more widespread and chronic.

However, the study notes that unless appropriate measures are taken to check widespread over-exploitation of ground water in dry land regions, poverty may worsen and become entrenched. The forest-based economies, by contrast, being richly endowed with natural resources, have a greater potential to redress chronic poverty provided the right kind of policies and institutions are put in place.[12]

[11] There are limitations in categorizing regions using district-level characteristics but data limitations mean there is no better alternative.

[12] For more on the diverse pattern of poverty as between dry land and forested regions, see NIRD (2000).

19.3.2 Natural Resources and Poverty: Land, Water, and Forests

19.3.2.1 Land and Multidimensional Poverty

With nearly 60 percent of people still living in rural areas, land remains a critical asset—not only for livelihood support, but also for obtaining social-political recognition. Ownership of land in traditional agrarian economies provides important leverage for controlling other factors of production, such as water, credit, and livestock. The size and extent of land ownership is considered the most important indicator of a household's well-being, determining social status and marital relationships. Those possessing access/control over land, including the state, obtain a sizable amount of political leverage, as witnessed most acutely in the numerous cases of land-grabbing in India and other parts of the developing world. The close link between land ownership and poverty is reflected in the fact that landless and semi-landless households account for nearly 42 percent of the rural poor in India (Chelliah and Sudarashan 2001). In addition, rural casual workers (a majority of whom are landless) have the highest poverty ratio among all the categories of rural workers (and also non-workers) (Bhalla, S. et al. 2004: 22). Studies on common property land resources have also observed a positive link between land degradation and poverty (Chopra and Gulati 1998; Shah 2009).

However, it is interesting to note that the head-count ratio (measuring the proportion of a population below the official poverty line) was found to be higher among households with very small landholdings (between 0.01 and 0.4 hectares), as compared to landless and semi-landless households (Chelliah and Sudarashn 2001). The superior status afforded these groups is chiefly due to the importance of migration and occupational diversification as well as to better livestock and/or skill sets among traditional herders and artisan households, especially in dry land and certain forest-based economies.

A recent study by Shah (2006) examines correlations across major states in India between four sets of variables: quality, size, and access to land; agricultural productivity; sectoral diversification; and poverty, as well as human development. The important observations are:

1. Land productivity and agricultural labor productivity are both (significantly) negatively correlated with chronic poverty (as measured by the head-count ratio) in rural areas. More importantly, land degradation (reflected in the proportion of wasteland and non-forested areas as well as total degraded land) is positively correlated with chronic poverty.[13]

[13] This is measured by multiplying the percentage of malnourished among the poor with the proportion of the poor in the population (Radhakrishna and Ray 2005).

2. Land productivity is positively correlated with literacy as well as the infant mortality rate, whereas labor productivity is negatively correlated with the infant mortality rate.
3. Agricultural labor productivity is positively correlated with the Human Development Index.
4. In terms of total geographic area, the proportion of common-property land resources is positively correlated with average landholding size (which is generally higher in dry land regions), and negatively correlated with the proportion of landless and semi-landless households (indicating land scarcity) in a state. Common-property land resources are negatively correlated with land productivity and positively correlated with degraded land.
5. The proportion of livestock-owning households is positively correlated with landholding size and degraded land.

Overall, these results on the linkages between land, poverty, and human development provide a mixed picture. They are suggestive, though of course they do not permit any inferences about causality. Most important is the correlation between land productivity and income poverty as well as human development, where irrigation is generally taken to be the main reason for higher land productivity.

19.3.2.2 Irrigation and Poverty Reduction

Given the centrality of irrigation in stimulating productivity growth in agriculture, water—especially in the vast dry land regions of the country—assumes a critical role in poverty reduction (Shah, T. 2004; Narayanmoorthy 2001). Whereas much of the surface irrigation provided by medium and large irrigation projects is under state ownership, several of the more traditional water sources, such as village tanks and ponds, are under community management. Groundwater resources are mainly under private property regimes, as noted previously. These different sources of irrigation water are governed by a complex web of state regulations and/or policies; community and private management must therefore operate within the overarching framework of state intervention. For practical purposes, state regulations are effective in managing large and medium irrigation projects within reach of canal systems; the rest is left more or less to community water users and private owners of wells and bore wells for extracting ground water. This often leads to an open access/common pool resource regime, ultimately causing over-exploitation of ground water and/or inefficient management of village tanks and related community-managed water sources (Shah, T. 2009). Given this backdrop,

I now turn to reviewing the important evidence on (irrigated) water-poverty linkages.

In an important study on agriculture-poverty linkages, Panda (2003: 13) observed that "in most states, households with access to irrigation have only half the poverty incidence as compared to those without irrigation." Irrigation is the most important factor influencing agricultural growth (which in turn is critical for reducing rural poverty in the country). It also exerts a substantial impact on poverty reduction (Alagh 2001). Nevertheless, the poverty reduction afforded by irrigation is achieved more through an increase in gross cropped area than through higher yields, as the former creates additional demand for farm laborers, a majority of whom are landless poor (Panda 2007). It has been estimated that, cumulatively, investment in irrigation between 1992 and 1997 has increased employment by about 18.4 million person years (Saleth 2002; 1997). This includes both farm and non-farm employment.

A study by Bhattarai and Narayanmoorthy (2002) found that, between 1970 and 1994, irrigation emerged as the strongest variable explaining poverty reduction. A 1 percent increase in irrigated land area increased the yield response to all inputs taken together by 0.32 percent.

But the relationship between irrigation and poverty is complex (Bhattarai et al. 2002), and depends on several mediating factors: (i) irrigated areas generally attract large numbers of in-migrants (often poor) from less irrigated areas; (ii) groundwater irrigation in large tracts of dry land regions is often limited in terms of household coverage as well as land, being additionally highly uncertain and difficult to estimate; and (iii) heavy depletion of water may lead to a decline in the productive base.

Various other studies have failed to find a significant association between irrigation and poverty at more disaggregated levels. For instance, Shah and Guru (2004), using a regression analysis, found that whereas the extent of irrigation was negatively correlated with rural poverty across National Sample Survey Office regions in India, the relationship was not significant among sub-sets of regions representing dry land and forest-based areas. Similarly, Shah and Singh (2004: 171), upon analyzing Taluka-level (block) data in Gujarat state, noted that "access to irrigation is a sufficient condition for poverty reduction, though not a necessary condition." At the same time, access to irrigation, often precarious and limited in such areas, is no assurance of escaping poverty. According to Janakrajan and Moench (2006), groundwater depletion is increasing rural poverty in India. These issues are particularly important in light of the next phase of agriculture growth having to come increasingly from dry land areas.

Population movements from dry to water-abundant regions may help to explain these relationships. Larger-sized landholdings, the ability of land to grow highly valued cash crops, and sectoral diversification (along with market and infrastructure development) may also be responsible for the relatively low incidence of poverty among some dry land regions. Similar results have been obtained from a vast body of literature on watershed development, which suggests that projects aimed at augmenting rain water may not ensure livelihood security to all households within the community. Evidence from a number of studies on watershed development projects suggests that the benefits are inequitably distributed among households and also within households (Shah 2001). Given that water is accessed by landowners who, in most cases, already have a source of groundwater irrigation available to them, the benefits arising from watershed projects tend to overlook the basic needs for water among the landless, poor farming households, and women (Shah 2007a).

Recent evidence suggests that the developmental impact of irrigation is declining. Primarily this is due to inefficient use, poor management, declining water productivity, and increasing financial and environmental costs. In India, nearly one-tenth of the total irrigation potential of 90 million hectares remains unutilized. One-sixth of the irrigated area is affected by water-logging and soil salinity. Productivity of water remains low owing to distorted pricing and other incentive problems (Saleth 1996). On the other hand, a large proportion of dry land regions, accounting for nearly 60 percent of the cropped area and 70 percent of the population, get by on very limited supplies of water (Shah 2007b). Water thus constitutes one of the most fundamental constraints for development in the country.

19.3.2.3 Forest-dependence and Poverty

While little is known about the incidence of poverty among forest-based economies, ample data exists on the concentration of the poor in forest-based tribal communities. There is little doubt but that the poorest in India live in and around forest regions (Kumar et al. 2000), and that poverty has remained intractable for a large share of the tribal population in the country. Indeed, these people are worse off even compared to casual workers in rural areas. To a large extent, poverty in forest-based regions in India and several other parts of the world is linked to the failure of appropriate entitlement arrangements. A plethora of research has shown how people, mainly among tribal communities, have been denied access to and a role in the management of the forest resources upon which they depend in both the colonial and post-colonial eras. Other research shows that, when tribal communities are given a primary role in resource management and overall governance, outcomes both for the people and the resources under their protection improve; the north-eastern states of India are examples of this kind of positive outcome (Radhakrishna and Ray 2005).

In 1999–2000, the head-count ratio among tribal communities was 45.9 percent (Thorat and Mahamallik 2005), as compared to 41.8 percent among rural casual workers (Bhalla et al. 2004). There are, of course, non-tribal communities living in forest areas; their economic plight is likely to be similar to that of the tribal communities.

According to available estimates, about 100 million people reside in forests and continue to depend upon forest-based resources for their livelihood. Another 275 million people live on the outskirts of forests, and these people also depend on the forests for the bulk of their livelihood (Pandey et al. 2005). Unfortunately, systematic estimates of poverty among forest-dependent communities in the country are lacking, but the high incidence of poverty among tribal peoples, as well as rural casual workers suggests that conditions of poverty are also widespread among a substantial majority of forest-dependent communities in the country. The chief reasons, again, are state monopolization, natural resource degradation, and a lack of entitlement for forest-dwelling communities.

Careful examination of the evidence suggests that whereas tribal populations have a significantly higher incidence of poverty than non-tribal populations as a general matter, among forest-based economies, the non-tribal communities tend to be poorer. This has been observed by a comparative analysis of two forest-based regions in southern and northern Orissa. The incidence of poverty among non-tribal populations in southern Orissa was higher than for other tribal populations in the state (Shah et al. 2006). This suggests that it is not just proximity to resources that matters, but access governance (Padhi et al. 2006).

Recently, the Planning Commission identified 140 districts deemed to be economically backward, of which fifty-three are drought-prone and eighty forest-based (see Table 19.1). This reinforces the other evidence suggesting that poverty is a persistent condition in forest-based economies.

Overall, the above analysis suggests that the interface between natural resources and poverty may hinge on two types of situation. The first pertains to areas facing water (irrigation) scarcity, the second to areas dependent on forest-based resources.[14] In dry land areas, the problem is water availability (endowment). In forested areas, it is entitlement (access). It is useful to focus on both situations when examining the link between natural resources and poverty in India.[15]

[14] In an earlier study, Chambers et al. (1989) developed a typology of poverty in terms of a core and periphery. In the "core," there is more landlessness and limited involvement of the poor in non-farm employment with dependence and exploitation being mediated by social relations. "Peripheral" poverty, by contrast, is linked more to water scarcity, resource degradation, and lack of infrastructure and distance from market, with dependence and exploitation being determined more by commercial and bureaucratic relations with contractors and officials.

[15] For further details and a stylized description of the two sets of regions see Shah and Guru (2004).

Table 19.1 Identification of backward districts in India

States	All backward districts	Backward and drought-prone districts	Backward and forest-based districts	Other backward districts
Andhra Pradesh	8	5	—	3
Assam	5	—	5	—
Bihar	15	4	2	9
Chhattisgarh	10	—	10	—
Gujarat	6	2(2)*	3	—
Haryana	1	1	—	—
Jharkhand	14	3(2)*	11	—
Karnataka	3	3(1)*	1	—
Kerala	1	—	1	—
Madhya Pradesh	15	8(7)*	5	2
Maharashtra	11	3	4	4
Orissa	18	9(6)*	9	—
Punjab	1	—	—	1
Rajasthan	5	4(3)*	—	1
Tamilnadu	4	—	2	2
Uttranchal	2	1(1)*	—	1
Uttar Pradesh	15	8(1)*	—	7
West Bengal	6	2(1)*	2	2
All	140	53(24)*	55	32

* These districts contain dry lands as well as forest-based areas. Forests in these districts are highly degraded. Estimates for forest-based areas in parentheses.

Note: The categorization of the districts is based on Shah and Guru (2004).

19.3.3 Natural Resources and Long-duration Poverty: Some Evidence

This section tries to identify states/regions that have experienced long-duration poverty, and also reviews links between natural resources and chronic poverty at the household level. These studies are based principally on panel data, where ownership of land and access to irrigation have been considered as independent variables explaining poverty over a longer period of time.

19.3.3.1 Areas Experiencing High Incidence of Poverty over a Long Time

According to recent estimates, poverty, as measured by the head-count ratio in India, has declined from 45 percent in 1993–94 to about 28 percent in 2004–05 (Table 19.2). The spatial concentration of poverty, however, has remained more or less constant. From 1983 to 2004–05, Tamil Nadu and West Bengal dropped out of the top five states having a high incidence of poverty, whereas Maharashtra moved from seventh to fifth place. Otherwise the rankings stayed

Table 19.2 Concentration of poverty among major states in India

States	1983			2004–05		
	Head-count ratio	Rank	% Share	Head-count ratio	Rank	% Share
Orissa	65.31	1	5.70	47.07	1	6.03
Bihar	62.71	2	14.64	41.53	2	16.53
Madhya Pradesh	49.23	5	8.61	37.21	3	10.79
Maharashtra	43.13	7	9.04	29.95	5	10.36
Uttar Pradesh	46.94	5	17.42	33.25	4	20.93
Tamil Nadu	53.48	4	8.47	28.31	6	6.10
West Bengal	53.60	4	9.77	25.67	7	7.23
All India	44.93		100	28.27		100

Source: Table 8 in Dev and Ravi (2006).

much the same. Altogether, the share of the seven states having the highest concentration of poverty increased from 74 percent of all the poor in 1983 to nearly 78 percent in 2004–05. Overall, there has been an increase in concentration of the poor among the major states in the country, with West Bengal and Tamil Nadu being exceptions.

19.3.3.2 Households Facing Chronic Poverty: Link with Natural Resources

A number of studies have examined the extent of long-duration poverty and the factors that influence it. Generally, these factors are economic in nature. They include the size of landholdings, access to irrigation, ownership of livestock, and income from agriculture. In what follows, I summarize the main observations emerging from these studies, which rely on panel data, village-level surveys, or recall through participatory methods.[16]

Two observations emerge. First, access to land and irrigation assume special importance in determining chronic poverty. Second, rising demographic pressure causes landholding size to fall—an observation rarely noted in the discourse on chronic poverty. Of course, the pressure on land and associated effects on poverty are also affected by major technological breakthroughs for increasing labor productivity in agriculture. The demand for labor outside of agriculture is also important. The issues of agricultural growth and sectoral diversification thus keep surfacing in the discourse on chronic poverty. It should be noted that the findings in Figure 19.2 bear some similarity to those obtained in related studies on poverty.

[16] The summary presented in Figure 19.2 draws heavily on Mehta and Bhide (2003).

Study	Main Findings on Natural Resource-Chronic Poverty Linkages	Remarks
1. Gaiha (1989)-NCAER panel survey	Landlessness and semi-landlessness was the most important factor associated with chronic poverty; greater access to cultivable land as well as modern agricultural inputs were the most important factors for escaping chronic poverty.	Landlessness is a structural factor, recognized by most studies in the Indian context.
2. NCAER (1986a and 1986b)-NCAER panel survey	Acquisition of land and intensive use of labor was important for upward movement, loss of land a cause of downward mobility.	Intensive use of labor likely linked with increased irrigation and the resultant increase in cropping intensity or change in cropping pattern.
3. Singh and Binswanger (1993)-ICRISAT longitudinal data for 218 households in six villages for the period 1975–76 to 1983–84	Poor quality of land one of the important features of poor vs. non-poor households, loss of land was the main reason for entry into poverty	Increased crop productivity during the study period may have led to declining poverty even among the semi arid tropics region; sub-division of land emerges as one of the most important factors leading to poverty.
4. Bhide and Mehta (2004)-NCAER panel data 1970–71, 1981–82.	Persistence of poverty was far greater among agricultural labor households as compared to cultivators. Non-agricultural employment was associated with higher incidence of poverty during the initial year; the pattern was reversed after 10 years.	Earnings from non-farm employment may have improved due to growth in agriculture. Prior to this, rural non-farm employment would have been confined mainly to traditional artisan activities with very low productivity.
5. Bhide and Mehta (2005)-NCAER panel survey 1970–1998	Land was the only asset (other assets were livestock, and house), which had a significant influence on the persistence of poverty.	Impact of irrigation is not discussed explicitly.

6. Jain, A. (2003)-tracking poverty over 25 years through recall.	Irrigation and improvement in land (besides employment in government or industry/ service sectors) were important escape routes in Gujarat and Andhra Pradesh	Sustainability of irrigation as escape route in a drought prone region is contingent upon management of water resources, individually as well as communally.
7. Shah and Sah (2004)-tracking poverty over 10-year period through recall.	Sub-division of land (and associated increase in population) was the single most important factor driving a non-poor household into poverty in Madhya Pradesh.	Access to power for using lift irrigation device was the most important need of households. Migration was not a preferred option mainly due to the associated hazards (including loss of dignity) at the place of destination.
8. Shah, Nayak and Das (2006)-perception based changes in well being over 10- year period through recall.	A large proportion of the poor indicated positive changes in consumption of basic commodities like cereals, clothing, and housing—despite the fact that nearly 90 percent of households in the four villages under study were poor.	These observations contrast drastically with those offered by A. Krishna for dry land states like Gujarat and Andhra Pradesh where a substantial proportion of rural households exited poverty over a period of 25 years.
9. Sharma and Karan (2005) –resurvey of 12 villages in Bihar	Landlessness, low quality of land, and non-availability of irrigation facility were the most important factors responsible for persistent poverty among large proportion of rural households.	Out-migration is an important coping mechanisms; the incidence of out-migration increased from 10 to 19 percent of the workforce, covering 25 percent of rural households during the period of resurvey.

Figure 19.2 Natural resources and long duration poverty

For the most part, the evidence presented above confirms the initial proposition concerning a close and multi-patterned interface between natural resources and poverty in India. The evidence also suggests that the interface is somewhat mixed, and, more importantly, complex in terms of causality, which is often difficult to discern in a cross-sectional analysis across states, regions, and households. Most significantly, (a) the spatial pattern of poverty in India is deeply rooted in structural factors (such as caste, location, and property rights) where natural resources assume special importance; and (b) addressing poverty therefore requires using natural capital on a sustainable basis while simultaneously enhancing access and control for the poor.

Of course, achieving these aims is difficult in a situation as vast, diverse, and dynamic as in India, where a number of factors, other than natural resources, impinge on the poverty outcomes. The next section therefore discusses these other factors in light of the recent policy initiatives for poverty reduction and natural-resource management in India.

19.4 POLICY RESPONSE AND FUTURE PATHWAYS

India has a long history of poverty-reduction policies, most of which involve rural development initiatives. Of late, there has been a significant revival of interest in promoting agriculture, both to stimulate economic growth and to reduce poverty (Planning Commission 2008).[17] Below I explain how this strategy engages with natural resources. This will provide important tips for identifying future pathways for poverty reduction, drawing on the conceptual framework presented in Section 19.2.

19.4.1 Natural Resource-based Strategy for Economic Growth and Poverty Reduction: Important Features

The contemporary approach for reducing poverty in India consists of three major components. The first is to sustain a high rate of economic growth with special emphasis on agriculture. GDP growth is seen as the most effective means for addressing the twin issues of environmental degradation and poverty. The approach for inclusive growth adopted in the 11th five-year plan laid special emphasis on broadening the base of growth in agriculture;[18]

[17] Planning Commission (2008).

[18] The strategy lays special emphasis on agricultural growth. It spells out differential pathways for promoting agricultural growth for three categories of agriculture potential—high-potential

the approach was further extended to include sustainability as an additional qualification during the 12th plan period. The second component is sectoral transformation of the workforce with a central thrust on skill formulation and training.[19] This component recognizes the disappointing results in job creation over the past decade. The policies adopted during the 11th five-year plan envisaged massive efforts for skill training, with the goal of creating a million jobs a year (World Bank 2011). The third and final component is to facilitate migration and urbanization with a view to strengthening the rural-urban continuum.[20] During the period of economic transition, policies have embraced rights-based approaches for provisioning a number of basic needs such as food, education, health (including drinking water), housing, employment, and entitlement to forested land. Natural resources feature in these plans given their close linkages to both agricultural growth and indigent communities.

Policies with respect to natural-resource management are guided by three important considerations. These are: (a) efficiency (productivity enhancement for higher economic growth); (b) sustainability (addressing the concerns of the environment and climate change); and c) equity (aiding the poor). While there are known trade-offs between these guiding principles, contemporary policies in India seem to have been guided more by the consideration of efficiency (productivity enhancement), especially when it comes to land and water. Sustainability seems to be a secondary concern, and equity of little more than rhetorical interest. As regards forests, policies seem to have been determined principally by sustainability considerations; equity (and poverty) issues continue to remain at the margin.

Policy initiatives that impact growth and poverty reduction through natural-resource management have been undertaken at all levels of government. The approach has not been comprehensive. Rather, it has had a sectoral

irrigated areas, moderate to high-potential areas, and low-potential dry land areas. The pathways include intensification, diversification of farm production, non-farm linkages, and exit from agriculture; see World Bank (2006) and Fan and Hazell (2000). Sustainability does not feature prominently, even though environmental degradation in agrarian economies often arises from the intensification of agriculture (Lopez 1997). What is particularly missing in these pathways is addressing the issue of poverty in ecologically fragile regions, especially forests, where intensive agriculture may not be the best option.

[19] There is ample evidence to suggest that agricultural growth is necessary for workforce diversification from the primary to the secondary and tertiary sectors. Such diversification is also one of the most important factors reducing rural poverty (Ravallion 2000). More recent analysis lends further support to this argument by showing that growing employment in the urban informal sector has had a significant poverty reduction impact especially by increasing agricultural wages; see Lanjouw and Shariff (2004) and Hansda and Ray (2006).

[20] Until the late 1980s, it was observed that households with medium- to large-sized landholdings, with some investment in irrigation, did not have to move out of dry land regions for subsistence purposes (NIRD 2000). Migration for such relatively wealthy households was mainly for "better prospects" rather than a "distress move" (Shah 2005a). This phenomenon was particularly true for the subset of households growing high-value commercial crops like oil seeds, spices,

focus, covering different resources (water, land/wasteland, forest, mineral, fishery, etc.) and been governed by different ministries within the central government. The Indian states have also put their own policies/regulations in place. More recently, global policy initiatives for environmental conservation and climate change have added another layer of policy measures. By and large, these have also been resource/sector specific—an example being the sector specific missions set up by the Government of India in response to climate change.

Below I discuss the major policy initiatives around natural resources that exert a direct and significant impact on economic growth and/or poverty reduction[21] .

19.4.1.1 Water and Irrigation: Resource Augmentation

Water resource development is one of the most important ways for promoting agricultural growth. Drawing upon the success of the Green Revolution of the late 1960s and early 1970s, a number of initiatives have been launched with the aim of improving the efficacy of existing large and medium irrigation projects. Similar schemes have also been undertaken to promote groundwater use, especially in the central-eastern states that combine high agronomic potential with a high incidence of poverty. In fact, much of the agronomic potential in these states has remained untapped because of widespread poverty and weak economic infrastructure.

Building on the Green Revolution approach, the strategy has tried to augment agricultural growth and reduce poverty in the states where poverty is concentrated. This is good news for landowners and agricultural laborers. It may also spur migration to small towns and cities where additional opportunities for non-farm employment may arise due to growth in agriculture.[22] In India, there is ample evidence of long-term migration from the drought-prone regions of Gujarat, Maharashtra, and Rajasthan, to other parts, including hilly areas in the north. Historically, dry land regions in India have been more prone to out-migration (Visaria and Kothari 1984; Shah 2002; Deshingkar and Star 2003; Sah and Shah 2005; and NIRD 2000), probably due to weather-related

horticulture. Similarly, areas with moderately good soil and availability of ground water were also able to escape "distress migration."

[21] This summary draws on some of the author's recent research. The aim is not to be comprehensive. Rather it is to provide adequate material for reflecting on the major components of the conceptual framework presented in Section 19.2.

[22] Missing from this perspective is that: (i) growth of rural non-farm employment depends on the pace and composition of growth in agriculture; and (ii) there is still substantial scope for improving the potential of agriculture by improving labor skill and adding labor rather than by intensifying production systems, especially in areas with low and medium potential. How far labor can be forced out of agriculture would depend on the nature of sectoral linkages and also the composition of the secondary and tertiary sectors (Patnaik 2007).

fluctuations and low levels of land productivity. Of late, rapid depletion of land and water resources appears to have aggravated the situation. Official statistics, however, suggest a decline in population mobility over the past two decades, possibly due to factors like limited employment and housing opportunities in urban environments, coupled with increased opportunities for commuting.

To some extent, the observed growth in agriculture may mask other problems associated with (a) increased input-intensity of crop production, and (b) resource depletion. Policymakers have tried to address these issues by simultaneously promoting low-cost, input-efficient technologies along with reforms in the energy sector impacting the pumping of ground water. These policy initiatives have tended to rely on market-based solutions (such as price incentives for promoting input-efficient technologies, correcting price distortions across different soil nutrients, and charging the full cost of power/energy).

This, however, leaves out a large portion of dry land regions characterized by low agronomic/irrigation potential, as well as those living in the forest-based regions with limited irrigation potential. Addressing the issues of growth, resource sustainability, and poverty in these regions may therefore require different strategies with an emphasis on land/wasteland and forest resources rather than market-based solutions. Community-based resource management has gained increased currency precisely for this reason.

19.4.1.2 Land Development and Community Participation

Though long neglected, dry land agriculture has recently received increasing attention by policymakers. This is partly due to the growing awareness and concern over climate change. It is also due to the threat of desertification in several parts of the country. Current thinking in the wake of the 12th five-year plan has made special provisions for soil and water conservation and wasteland development, principally in dry land regions. Moreover, the revitalization of rain-fed agriculture (via incorporation of some of the basic elements of regenerative/sustainable farming practices for addressing the hitherto neglected issues of resource sustainability and poverty in water-scarce regions) has gained increased recognition. Micro watershed development programmes provide a basic platform for augmenting land and water resources, thereby enhancing the primary productivity of land, which is often prone to degradation.

Given the relatively poor endowment of natural resources and low agronomic potential in this region, market-based instruments seem to be less applicable than in areas experiencing high rates of agricultural growth or showing high agronomic potential. The reasons for this are twofold: a) much of the degraded land is managed under a public/common property regime, in which the social benefits from land development (or soil moisture conservation) measures are likely to exceed the private benefits; and b) even on private land, such measures are likely to take much longer to realize private benefits. Moreover, their realization is likely to be subject to a high level of uncertainty due to inter-annual volatility of rainfall in dry land regions.

Technological development for regenerative/sustainable agriculture in dry land/rain-fed regions also suffers from the problems of low and uncertain private returns with a long gestation period. It is also likely to hinge on a more intensive knowledge of location-specific resources, generating higher development and dissemination costs than the conventional irrigation-seed-fertilizer-based technology of the Green Revolution. All of these considerations may have different implications for institutional support mechanisms, where community involvement and decentralization assume special significance.

Responding to these, a number of initiatives for participatory management of land, water, and forest resources—mostly under public/common property regimes—have emerged. These have been aimed at participatory watershed management, wasteland development, joint forest management, and fishing cooperatives. Many of these participatory institutions operate within the boundaries of the existing property rights regime, with the aim often being to rebuild natural capital stocks and achieve a more equitable distribution of benefits.

These steps are in the right direction, but the performance of many of these initiatives has been far from optimal. The overall policy aim of promoting growth has played a significant role in shaping policy (i.e., public investment, political space for community-based institutions, and the regulatory/support mechanisms for those institutions to operate effectively). Political economy—an important element in the conceptual framework—has played an important role in shaping poverty outcomes. In the absence of strong institutional mechanisms, much of the degraded land, including forests, may not be able to contribute significantly to poverty reduction.

19.4.1.3 Forest Conservation: Compensatory Mechanisms

The conservation of forests and their ecosystems has been a priority for India's environmental policies.[23] The current policy, which is little changed from the nation's pre-colonial arrangement, vests ownership and regulatory control in the state, leaving the community with limited rights to use and manage these resources. The state's control is deemed essential for conservation and protection of ecosystems. This essentially reinforces the conflicting interests between

[23] Unlike land, water, minerals, and fisheries, the ministry in charge of forests is also looking after the environmental policies of the Government of India.

economic and ecological benefits (or between the community and the state) in a situation where local community members lack alternative sources of income and employment. Spatial and socio-cultural factors contribute further to the dependence of the poor especially on forest resources.

Two major initiatives have been undertaken in the past two decades to resolve the policy logjam. The first was aimed at community-level participation for the management of degraded forests. Good on paper, the policy has hitherto done little to alleviate the severe and long-duration poverty faced by many forest-dependent communities. More recently, the government has enacted a law providing legal entitlement to the forested land on which the communities had been practicing agriculture. These efforts show that the state has tried to use property rights arrangements to realize a more equitable distribution of the benefits of conservation.

Another important development is the evolving compensatory mechanism for a) forest conservation, b) the diversion of forestland for alternative uses (such as mining, irrigation, or other development projects), and c) the resettlement and rehabilitation of displaced local communities. Indeed, this approach marks a major departure from previous policies that had completely overlooked the need for appropriate conservation incentives. The second set of policy initiatives arose partly in response to large-scale diversions of forested land for basic infrastructure developments deemed essential for economic growth—the major issue here being the distribution of the benefits and costs of such projects for India's poor.

A critical pre-condition for extending compensatory mechanisms to poor communities hinges not only on political will, but agency for the poor to demand effective implementation of the policies. Where such a condition is lacking, compensatory mechanisms may do little more than transfer financial resources without actually enhancing the poor's access to alternative sources of capital and livelihood.

How to move forward on the pathways that link natural resources with poverty reduction? Some of the important missing links will be discussed in the subsequent analysis. Needless to say, such pathways may have to move toward an integrated rather than sectoral approach to natural resources. In this way, a synergy among mechanisms for resource augmentation, distribution, and institutional arrangements—the three components (proximate causes) of the conceptual framework—may be established.

19.4.2 Future Pathways: Some Important Components

A brief summary of the essential policies for a holistic approach to natural-resource development is presented in Figure 19.3.

		Required Policy Initiatives
1	**Land**	
1.1	Redistribution	Completing the unfinished task of land reforms especially in the poorer states like Orissa, Bihar, Madhya Pradesh, Rajasthan, and Andhra Pradesh
1.2	Consolidation of holding (Contract farming)	Need for appropriate legal mechanism for benefit-sharing and protection of rights
1.3	Releasing encroachment on common property land resources	Revival of local institutions under different schemes, creating a synergy rather than having each of them operate in isolation, leading to overlap and competition within the local power structures.
2	**Water**	
2.1	Regeneration of ground water; treatment of catchments and flood control; and the provision of safe drinking water	Multi-layered planning for watershed development; Strengthening of markets and non-market institutions for enhancing efficient use; community organizations for ensuring sustainable and equitable distribution of water; changing existing property rights for ground water to include those without ownership of land.
3	**Forest**	
	Participatory management; land titles; and relocation and rehabilitation policies	Need to ensure that compensation reaches the poor; need to create a support organization that works on behalf of the poor to negotiate with the state and private agencies involved in compensation and relocation and rehabilitation. Requires strengthening local institutions and giving them legitimacy in the democratic polity.

Figure 19.3 Imperatives for future policies

Future policies need to focus on some of the critical missing links like issues of land and water rights. This is particularly important for tending to the interests of landless and semi-landless households, besides those in the forest-dominated regions facing a lack of clear and adequate entitlement to forest resources.

In the absence of this approach, the poor may be pushed toward short-term or circulatory migration for supporting their basic livelihoods. While migration is an important mechanism for exiting poverty, for those lacking the requisite financial, human, and social capital for attaining upward mobility through migration, the options are limited.

There is a fair amount of evidence suggesting that natural-resource development may enhance employment opportunities in rural economies (provided the development follows a sustainable and equitable path for benefit sharing). Attaining this would call for community involvement, which in turn may necessitate the right kind of political will for creating space for the poor to exert their rightful claims to the resources.

19.5 SUMMING UP

The foregoing analysis examined the interface between natural resources and poverty in India. Highlighting their multi-patterned association, the chapter sought to develop a conceptual framework by identifying some of the important proximate as well as ultimate factors influencing the interface. These include natural resource endowment and status, access and control over the resources among the nation's poor, and institutional arrangements governing resource use as proximate factors, with ecological pathways and political economy as the ultimate factors impacting the interface. Contextualizing the contemporary scenario, the chapter noted that India faces natural resource scarcity, especially with respect to land and water, which is likely to be aggravated by demographic and climatic factors. Additionally, much of the land and forests in the country are degraded. Given the connate increase in population, this has led to situations with substantially higher incidences of rural poverty, despite the high economic growth of the past two decades. Since many of the natural-resource endowments (except large parts of the cultivated land and ground water) are under a public/common property regime), the poor, especially the landless, may continue to depend on these resources. Unfortunately, many of these resources are degraded and/or subject to encroachment. As a result, the poor are deprived of access to the very resources on which they depend for survival.

The review of empirical evidence suggests that poverty is concentrated in a few states and regions, and that the pattern of poverty has remained substantially unchanged over a long period of time. This implies a situation of persistent poverty and spatial poverty traps. Forest-based regions have a relatively high incidence of poverty, whereas irrigation water is an important exit route from poverty. Land is the critical asset for gaining not only economic but also socio-political power. The absence of land ownership and entitlement to forest resources appear to be major drivers of poverty in the areas where poverty is concentrated.

Though the evidence assembled here goes some way toward explaining the linkages between natural resources and poverty, there is clearly a need for detailed and location-specific analyses to unravel the direction of the causality and its underlying processes.

To spur economic growth and poverty reduction, Indian policies of late have sought to promote growth in the agricultural sector, with a special emphasis on irrigation infrastructure. The issues of sustainability and equity seem to have taken a back seat to growth. This may be because addressing the latter issues requires non-market institutional mechanisms for technology development and dissemination, resource management, and benefit sharing. Political economy is critical in making these institutions work.

Creating a policy space for participatory institutions with community-level involvement in natural-resource management and benefit sharing is a necessary but not sufficient condition for helping the poor. A critical requirement in this context is the agency of the poor to negotiate their claims over these resources and the benefits associated with their conservation and use. Issues pertaining to land, water, and forest resource entitlements may also require special attention, particularly as the rights-based approach has rapidly gained currency in poverty reduction policymaking in the country. It is imperative that future policies develop a comprehensive approach that treats natural resources as part of an integrated system. Such an approach is likely to create greater synergies—essential for supporting the sustainable and equitable management of natural resources for the benefit of the poor.

References

ADB (Asian Development Bank) (2008). "*The Environments of the Poor: A Geographical Approach to Poverty Reduction in Asia and the Pacific*." Summary of a joint study of the Poverty Reduction Unit, Asian Development Bank, Manila.

Alagh, Y. K. (2001). "Food Security in India," *Water Resources Development*, 17(1): 23–36.

Bhaduri, A. (2006). *Employment and Development: Essays from an Unorthodox Perspective*. Oxford: Oxford University Press.

—— (2011). "*Why an Alternative Model of Economic Development?*" *India Social Development Report 2010, The Land Question and the Marginalized*. Oxford: Oxford University Press.

Bhalla, G. S. (2006). "*Economic Situations of the Indian Farmers: Some Findings from the NSSO 59th Round*," *Prof. L.S. Venkataramanan Memorial Lecture 6*. Bangalore: Institute of Social and Economic Change.

Bhalla, S., A. K. Karan, and T. Shobha (2004). "*Rural Casual Labourers, Wages and Poverty: 1983 to 1999–2000*," *CPRC-IIPA Working Paper No. 14*. New Delhi: Indian Institute of Public Administration.

Bhattarai, M. and A. Narayanamoorthy (2002). "Impact of Irrigation on Agricultural Growth and Poverty Alleviation: Macro Level Analysis in India," working paper, *IWMI-Tata Water Policy Programme 12*. Available at <http://www.iwmi.cgiar.org/iwmi-tata_html/PM2003/PDF/12_Highlight.pdf> (accessed 8 December 2013)

—— R. Sakthivadivel, and I. Hussain (2002). *Irrigation Impact on Income Inequality and Poverty Alleviation: Policy Issues and Options for Improved Management of Irrigation System*. Colombo: International Water Management Institute.

Bhide, S. and A. K. Mehta (2004). "*Correlates of Incidence and Exit From Chronic Poverty in Rural India: Evidence from Panel Data*," *CPRC-IIPA Working Paper No. 15*. New Delhi: Indian Institute of Public Administration.

—— (2005). "*Tracking Poverty through Panel Data: Rural Poverty in India 1970–1998*," *CPRC-IIPA Working Paper No. 28*. New Delhi: Indian Institute of Public Administration.

Bilsborrow, R. E. (1992). "*Rural Poverty, Migration, and the Environment in Developing Countries: The Case Studies*," *Policy Research Working Paper 1017*. Washington, DC: World Bank.

Chambers, R., N. C. Saxena, and T. Shah (1989). *To the Hands of the Poor: Water and Trees*. New Delhi: Oxford and IBH Publishing Company.

Chelliah, R. J. and R. Sudarshan (2001). *Income Poverty and Beyond: Human Development in India*. New Delhi: Social Science Press.

Chopra, K. and S. C. Gulati (1998). "Environmental Degradation, Property Rights and Population Movements: Hypothesis and Evidence from Rajasthan (India)," *Environment and Development Economics*, 3(1): 35–57.

—— G. K. Kadekod, and M. N. Murty (1989). *Participatory Development People and Common Property Resources*. New Delhi: Sage Publications.

Comim, F. (2008). *Poverty and Environment Indicators*. Cambridge: UNDP-UNEP Poverty and Environment Initiative.

Dasgupta, P. (1993). *An Inquiry into Well-Being and Destitution*. Oxford: Clarendon Press.

—— and K. G. Mäler (2004). "*Environment and Resource Economics: Some Recent Developments, Special Issue*," *SANDEE Working Paper No. 7*. Katmandu: South Asian Network for Environment and Development Economics.

—— (2009). "Environmental and Resource Economics: Some Recent Developments," in K. Chopra and V. Dayal (eds.), *Handbook of Environmental Economics in India*. New York: Oxford University Press.

Deshingkar, P. and D. Start (2003). "*Seasonal Migration for Livelihood in India: Coping, Accumulation and Exclusion*," *Draft Working Paper No. 220*. London: Overseas Development Institute.

Dev, M. and C. Ravi (2006). "Poverty and Inequality: All India and States, 1983-2005," *Economic and Political Weekly*, 41(6): 509–21.

Department for International Development (DFID), European Commission (EC), United Nations Development Programme (UNDP), and the World Bank (2002). *Linking Poverty Reduction and Environmental Management: Policy Challenges and Opportunities*. Washington DC: The International Bank for Reconstruction and Development.

Duriappah, A. K. (1998). "Poverty and Environmental Degradation: A Review and Analysis of the Nexus," *World Development*, 26(12): 2161–79.

Fan, S. and P. Hazell (2000). "Should Developing Countries Invest More in Less-Favoured Areas? An Empirical Analysis of Rural India," *Economic and Political Weekly*, 35(17): 1455–64.

Hansda, S. K. and P. Ray (2006). "Employment and Poverty in India during the 1990s: Is there a Diverging Trend?" *Economic & Political Weekly*, 50(27): 3014–23.

Janakrajan, S. and M. Moench (2006). "Are Wells a Potential Threat to Farmer's Well Being?" *Economic and Political Weekly*, 38(24): 2350–2.

Jha, B. (2011). "*Policies for Increasing Non-farm Employment for Farm Households in India,*" *IEG Working Paper No. 310*. Delhi: Institute of Economic Growth.

Jodha, N. S. (2008). "Some Places Again: A 'Restricted' Revisit to Dry Regions of India," in R. Ghate, N. S. Jodha, and Pranab Mukhopadhyay (eds.), *Promise, Trust and Evolution: Managing the Commons of South Asia*. New York: Oxford University Press: 51–69.

Kumar, N. et al. (2000). *Alleviating Poverty through Participatory Forestry Development: An Evaluation of India's Forest Development and World Bank Assistance*. Washington, DC: The World Bank.

Lanjouw, P. and A. Shariff (2004). "Rural Non-farm Employment in India: Access, Income and Poverty Impact," *Economic and Political Weekly*, 3(40): 4429–46.

Lopez, R. (1997). "Where Development Can or Cannot Go: The Role of Poverty-Environment Linkages," *Proceedings of Annual Bank Conference on Development Economics*. Washington DC: The World Bank.

Mehta, S. and A. K. Bhide (2003). "*Issues in Chronic Poverty: Panel Data-based Analysis,*" *CPRC-IIPA Working Paper No. 6*. New Delhi: Indian Institute of Public Administration.

Ministry of Environment and Forests (2009). "*Climate Change,*" *State of Environment Report, India*. New Delhi: Government of India.

Nadkarni, M. V. (2000). "Poverty, Environment, Development: A Many Patterned Nexus," *Economic and Political Weekly*, 35(14): 1184–90.

Narayanmoorthy, A. (2001). "Irrigation and Rural Poverty Nexus: A Statewise Analysis," *Indian Journal of Agricultural Economics*, 56(1): 40–56.

Nayyar, D. (2008). *Liberalization and Development*. New Delhi: Oxford University Press.

NIRD (2000). *India: Rural Development Report: Regional Disparities in Development and Poverty*. Hyderabad: National Institute of Rural Development.

Padhi, S., N. Panigrahi, and A. K. Mishra (2006). "Tribal Population and Chronic Poverty in Orissa: A Note on the North-South Divide," *Margin*, 38 and 39(4and1): 81–90.

Panda, M. (2003). "*Role of Agriculture in the Poverty Reduction Process in India,*" (unpublished). Mumbai: Indira Gandhi Institute of Development Research.

—— (2007). "Agriculture and Poverty Reduction", in S. Ray (ed.), *Handbook of Agriculture in India*. New Delhi: Oxford University Press.

Pandey, V. L., P. Kumar, and R. Kamath (2005). *Sustaining Human Development in India States: The Role of Forests, National Research Programme on Growth and Human Development*. Mumbai: Indira Gandhi Institute of Development Research.

Parikh, K. S. (1998). "*Poverty and Environment: Turning the Poor into Agents of Environmental Regeneration,*" *Working Paper No.1*, Social Development and Poverty Elimination Division. New Delhi: UNDP.

Patnaik, P. (2007). "A Model of Growth of the Contemporary Indian Economy," *Economic and Political Weekly*, 42(22): 2077–81.

Planning Commission (2008). "*Eleventh Five-Year Plan - 2007–12: Inclusive Growth*." New Delhi: Government of India.

Radhakrishna, R. and S. Ray (2005). *Poverty in India: Dimensions and Character in India Development Report*. New Delhi: Oxford University Press.

Ravallion, M. (2000). "What Is Needed for a More Pro-poor Growth Process in India?" *Economic and Political Weekly*, 35(13): 1089–93.

Reddy, N. D. (2010). "*Agrarian Crises and Challenges in Reviving Small Farmer Economy*," in *India Social Development Report 2010, The Land Question and the Marginalized*. New Delhi: Oxford University Press.

Roy, B. C. and S. Pal (2002). "Investment, Agricultural Productivity and Rural Poverty in India: A State-Level Analysis," *Indian Journal of Agricultural Economics*, 57(4): 653–79.

Sah, D. C. and A. Shah (2005). "Migration in Remote Tribal Areas: Evidence from South Western Madhya Pradesh," *Indian Journal of Agriculture Economics*, 60(2): 184–204.

Saleth, M. R. (1996). *Water Institutions in India: Economics, Law and Policy*. New Delhi: Commonwealth Publishers.

—— (1997). "Irrigation Induced Indirect Employment During the Eighth Plan: An Estimation Procedure with Tentative Estimates," *Indian Journal of Labour Economics*, 40(2): 279–88.

—— (2002). "Introduction," in M. R. Saleth (ed.), *Water Resources and Economic Development*. Northampton, MA: Edward Elgar Publishing.

Sastry, D. V. S., B. Singh, K. Bhattacharya et al. (2003). "Sectoral Linkages and Growth Prospects: Reflections on Indian Economy," *Economic and Political Weekly*, 38(24): 2390–7.

Saxena, K. B. (2010). "*Land Reforms: Unfinished Agenda or Reversal of Policy*," *India Social Development Report 2010, The Land Question and the Marginalized*. New Delhi: Oxford University Press.

Scott, L. (2006). "*Chronic Poverty and the Environment: A Vulnerability Perspective*," *CPRC Working Paper 62*. London: Overseas Development Institute.

Shah, A. (2001). "*Who Benefits from Participatory Watershed Development? Lessons from Gujarat, India*," *Gate Keeper Series No. 97*. London: International Institute for Environment and Development.

—— (2002). "Uneven Development and Migration: Insights from Micro Initiatives," in G. Shah, M. Rutten and H. Streefkerk (eds.), *Labour Marginalisation and Migration*. New Delhi: Sage Publications, 273–93.

—— and B. Guru (2004). "*Poverty in Remote Rural Areas in India: A Review of Evidence and Issues*," *CPRC-IIPA Working Paper No. 21*. New Delhi: Indian Institute of Public Administration.

—— V. L. Pandey, and R. Kamath (2005). "*Sustaining Human Development in India States: The Role of Land, National Research Programme on Growth and Human Development*." Mumbai: Indira Gandhi Institute of Development Research.

—— (2005a). "*Land Degradation and Migration in a Dry Land Region in India: Understanding the Dynamics*," *Working Paper No. 10*. Katmandu: South Asian Network for Development and Environmental Economics.

—— S. K. Nayak, and B. Das (2006). "Ensuring Livelihood Entitlements in Forest Based Economies in Orissa: An Alternative Perspective," *Margin*, 38 and 39(4 and 1): 63–80.

—— (2006a). "*Environmental Implications of Agriculture and Policy Initiatives in India and the EU: Review of Evidence and Issues,*" *Working Paper Series No. E/277/2007*. Delhi: Institute of Economic Growth.

—— (2007a). "Patterns, Processes of Reproduction, and Policy Imperatives for Poverty in Remote Rural Areas: A Case Study of Southern Orissa in India," paper presented at the Conference on Understanding and Addressing Spatial Poverty Traps, organized by Chronic Poverty Research Centre, Cape Town: Overseas Development Institute, 29 March.

—— (2007b). "*Mainstreaming Environmental Concerns on Dry Lands in Policy Framework,*" mimeo. New Delhi: UNDP.

—— (2009). "Rights to Land and Water, and Watershed Development," in K. Chopra and V. Dayal (eds.), *Handbook of Environmental Economics in India*. New York: Oxford University Press, 69–97.

—— (2010). "Dryland Poverty, Characteristics, Policy Response, New Challenges and Opportunities." Available at <http:// www.scribd.com/doc/42966617> (accessed 20 October 2103).

—— (2011a). "The New Poverty and Inclusive Growth Agenda in India as Emerging Middle Income Country," paper presented at the Regional Workshop on Social Inclusiveness in Asia's Emerging Middle Income Countries, Jakarta, Indonesia.

—— (2011b). "Towards Alternative Growth," in *India Chronic Poverty Report: Towards Solutions and New Compacts in a Dynamic Context*. New Delhi: Indian Institute of Public Administration, 128–52.

Shah, T. and O. P. Singh (2004). "Irrigation Development and Rural Poverty in Gujarat, India: A Disaggregated Analysis," *Water International*, 29(2): 167–77.

—— (2009). "India's Groundwater Irrigation Economy: The Challenge of Balancing Livelihoods and Environment," in K. Chopra and V. Dayal (eds.), *Handbook of Environmental Economics in India*. New York: Oxford University Press, 98–120.

Shyamsundar, P. (2002). "*Poverty - Environment Indicators,*" *Environment Department Paper Series No. 84*. Washington DC: The World Bank.

Singh, R. P. and H. Binswanger (1993). "Income Growth in Poor Dryland Areas of India's Semi-arid Tropics," *Indian Journal of Agricultural Economics*, 48(1): 51–64.

Singh, D. P. (2009). "*Poverty and Migration: Does Moving Help?*" *India Urban Poverty Report 2009*. New Delhi: Oxford University Press, 50–75.

TEEB (The Economics of Ecosystems and Biodiversity) (2008). "*An Interim Report.*" Geneva: TEEB.

Thorat, S. and M. Mahamallik (2005). "Chronic Poverty and Socially Disadvantaged Groups: Causes and Remedies," *Margin*, 38 and 39(4 and 1): 41–62.

UNCHS (1996). "*An Urbanising World: Global Report on Human Settlements.*" Oxford: Oxford University Press.

Visaria, P. and D. Kothari (1984). "*Migration in Gujarat: an Analysis of Census Data,*" mimeo. Ahmedabad: Sardar Patel Institute of Economic and Social Research.

World Bank (2006). *Inclusive Growth & Service Delivery: Building on India's Success*. Washington DC: World Bank.

—— (2011). *India's Employment Challenge*. New Delhi: Oxford University Press.

World Resources Institute (WRI) in collaboration with the United Nations Environment Programme (UNEP), the United Nations Development Programme (UNDP), and the World Bank (2005). *The Wealth of the Poor—Managing Ecosystems to Fight Poverty*, Resources Series. Washington DC: World Resources Institute. Available at <http://pdf.wri.org/wrr05_full_hires.pdf> (accessed 20 October 2013)..

20

Comments by Kanchan Chopra on "Natural Resources and Chronic Poverty"

20.1 INTRODUCTION IN THE CONTEXT OF SHAH'S CHAPTER

The nature of the relationship between natural resources and poverty can be viewed through different lenses. The most conventional approach, particularly in developing countries, is through that of agriculture, where productivity increases per unit of land are correlated with decreases in poverty. A large part of the chapter by Amita Shah adopts this approach.

Grounding her argument in a land-based context, Shah pays considerable attention to the productivity of arable landholdings in agriculture. She remarks, for instance, that it is important "to note the critical role of land productivity in influencing both income poverty as well as human development, where irrigation is generally seen as the main driver." She notes that, in India, an increase in land productivity during the 1960s and 1970s was the prime driver of agricultural growth, and that this in turn contributed to poverty reduction in some regions. She also notes that irrigation played a critical role in this process. Investments in large-scale surface irrigation and more dispersed ground-water extraction structures have consistently led to increased incomes from private land, an expansion of job opportunities in rural areas, and poverty reduction.

Shah's paper also comments on the uneven distribution of this growth in rural economies, and how the backward nature of forested, arid, semi-arid, and rain-fed agriculture-centric regions has impeded their advancement relative to other areas. The persistence of poverty in these regions has been a source of considerable concern.

Shah also investigates a second pathway of causation between natural resources and poverty. She notes that chronic poverty is widespread among forest dwellers due to a lack of understanding of their traditional property rights. A significant portion of the natural resources in the country are found in forests (mostly under state control and ownership), including watersheds, water bodies, and common lands under varying degrees of common property or open access. It was established in the literature of the 1980s and 1990s that common property land and water resources constituted 20 to 30 percent of the land area in arid and semi-arid parts of the country, and that they supported the poor in times of both distress and prosperity. Direct consumption by the poor of products from both forests and water bodies has helped avert starvation and contain hunger. However, ecologists and economists who have examined these issues from a field-oriented perspective have concluded that degradation occurs when property rights are vested in the state with little participation from local communities and a failure of the former to recognize the traditional rights of the latter (Jodha 1986; Chopra, Kadekodi, and Murty 1990).

In this commentary I expand on Shah's analysis by viewing natural resources-poverty linkages through the lens of diverse ecosystem services (of the provisioning, regulating, cultural, or supporting kind) provided by natural capital. The story told here, placed in the context of India's development during the last sixty years, throws light on the implications of policy for social discount rates, and the substitution possibilities between different kinds of services, themes which have featured prominently in Partha Dasgupta's writings. I also touch on issues of more contemporary concern in India, namely the interfaces between mining and forests, and those between urbanization and land acquisition. Essentially, these issues are different facets of the same overarching concern for making ecosystem services more central in policy and planning. Is it possible to argue that the economic system has moved to a situation where conflicts between different uses, stakeholders, and, therefore, trade-offs are the dominant feature? Or is inclusive and sustainable development still achieveable?

20.2 FEEDING THE MILLIONS AND REDUCING POVERTY: THE ROLE OF NATURAL RESOURCES

The 1950s and 1960s in India were decades in which national development and self-sufficiency received a great deal of emphasis. At this stage of economic development—except in the contexts of wildlife, national parks, and perhaps, to a limited extent, forests—natural resources were viewed as existing solely for the utility of their extraction and consumption. From the mid 1960s the Green Revolution era dawned over agriculture, during which time the focus shifted toward increasing production. Priority was given to enhancing land productivity to provide more food for the population. Use of hybrid seed varieties, fertilizers and surface irrigation was the way forward; and, in the face of an increasing population and political constraints on imports, extracting more provisioning services from the land and water endowments became the priority. Undoubtedly, the longer term was being discounted heavily, and issues such as supporting the ecology of rivers or maintaining soil health were given little attention. Food self-sufficiency and poverty decreases were achieved in Green Revolution regions, but these developments by-passed other places—particularly, the dry land regions.

It was within this framework that the rise of tube well technology and the groundwater-based boom came about. Remote sensing data as well as the national sample survey suggest that as much as 75–80 percent of India's irrigated land today is served by groundwater wells. In the short run, as Tushaar Shah (2009) has noted, this phenomenon has helped to democratize agriculture and build a strong pro-poor bias in irrigated farming. But nothing is an unmixed blessing. A dynamic view of the process reveals early symptoms of groundwater degradation, and some parts of the country may be witnessing a decline of the groundwater socio-ecology with a substantial immiserizing impact. Once again we are confronted with the situation of exploiting a natural resource like groundwater to provide a short-run boost to prosperity at the expense, possibly, of long-run immiserization. Perceptive analysts ask for economic and other incentives for groundwater conservation. Often, however, political compulsions overrule such advice, and over-exploitation continues. In such a situation, what weight should we place on the present versus the future in the context of planning in a developing country? Or, for that matter, on provisioning ecosystem services as opposed to regulating ecosystem services?

20.3 OF LAND-USE CHANGE, CENTRALLY DRIVEN DEVELOPMENT STRATEGIES, AND POVERTY

Traditional agrarian societies provided for an implicit balance between the accrual of different kinds of ecosystem services from land by reserving some tracts for common use, or for conservation as sacred groves. Social norms governed the setting aside of land for these purposes. Developed economies such as the US did the same over the twentieth century by putting in place legislative processes which conserved "wilderness areas," and agencies such as the Environment Protection Agency (EPA), which mandated impact assessments of development projects. Modern India has tried to emulate this approach, but in an environment weighed down by high population densities and bad governance. Under these conditions, success has been limited. Simultaneously, the globalization and high rates of growth which marked the last two decades have led to the continued conversion of agricultural and other land for infrastructure, dam, or mining projects—typical examples of the substitution of human-made capital for natural capital. When these lands are converted to other uses, economic returns may increase, but the poor who depended on this natural capital may have nowhere to go. As Partha Dasgupta has reminded us,

> When wetlands, inland and coastal fisheries, woodlands, forests, ponds, lakes, and grazing fields are damaged (owing, say, to agricultural encroachment, or urban extensions, or the construction of large dams, or organizational failure at the village level, or resource usurpation by the state), traditional dwellers suffer. For them—and they are among the poorest in society—there are frequently no alternative sources of livelihood, nor is migration usually an option. In contrast, for rich eco-tourists or importers of primary products, there is something else, often somewhere else, which means that there are alternatives. (Dasgupta and Mäler 2009: 23)

Land has now become the prime natural resource in short supply as India surges ahead with accelerated infrastructural and industrial development. In recent times, protests with respect to land acquisition have occupied considerable media attention, and a new land acquisition policy is under consideration. However, too much of the current discourse has concentrated on private land and its security of tenure. The importance of common property rights has been neglected, to the detriment of the people who depend on common property resources. It is appropriate to hypothesize that underlying this public protest against land acquisition is the abrogation of traditional rights and concessions on the land being acquired. Unfortunately, however, there is no way of confirming this, as very little information exists on the magnitude and nature of these rights, further reinforcing their lack of recognition.

Further problems have arisen from diverse approaches to land valuation in peri-urban fringes. Driven by high rates of urbanization, land-based demands for urban construction and infrastructure have pushed real estate prices to very high levels. Meanwhile, "traditional" valuations of the provisioning ecosystem services (or sometimes even regulating and recreational) provided by these lands, being largely non-marketed, have been neglected. And so tensions at the interface between the value of land for different uses and by different stakeholders are rapidly increasing. In the face of a huge demand from urban use, driven by increased purchasing power, retaining of land for agricultural or ecological use is not going to be easy. The underlying asymmetries in the distribution of income, information, and power result in a very high capacity to pay for non-agricultural, urban development-related uses, leading to higher and higher market prices for them. In such a situation, while valuations of land for different ecosystem services may provide additional inputs, an understanding that there exist "inviolate areas," whether for ecological or distributive justice reasons, will have to be a critical component of policy. Although ecologists and economists in the past have frequently employed a notion of "scientific or economic rationality," current environmental problem-solving requires that they also use "ethical rationality."[1] How else do we factor in the loss of natural capital or the loss of livelihoods for people?

In a similar vein, the focus on energy for development and investment (on the basis of a centrally driven energy policy) precludes ecologically fragile hill regions from choosing their own more holistic approaches to development. The overarching vision and mission of development planning is to accelerate the actualization of power potential anywhere and everywhere so that, via an enhanced production of energy, shortages in this critical infrastructure sector can be avoided. No attention is paid to the loss of critical ecosystem services in ecologically fragile areas. A recent study by Das and Chopra (2011) illustrates how, at a small cost to the hill state of Himachal Pradesh in northern India (a mere.0045 to.0038 percent of the state's domestic product), a synergy between the conservation of ecologically sensitive areas and human well-being can be attained. Furthermore, the ecosystem services conserved in this case benefit the poor especially. In other words, ecosystem preservation makes the society more equitable. But that does not happen because of the imperatives of a centrally driven development agenda.

20.4 GLOBALIZATION, EXPORT MARKETS AS DRIVERS, AND POVERTY

Globalization and its emphasis on extractive exports results in a development myopia which overlooks the multiple services provided by forested watersheds.

One sector that comes to mind is that of mining. With growing domestic and international demands for metals, the expansion of the mining industry has been quite dramatic, especially in states vested with large deposits of minerals. However, since these are sub-soil deposits, their extraction imposes a cost on the environment, other natural resources like water, and local human populations.[2] Minerals are frequently found in the same regions as forests, and decision-makers and analysts often underestimate the value of preserving natural capital while overestimating the value of mineral resources. A long-term perspective calls for a proper valuation of natural resources such as forests,

[1] See Chopra (2011) for a more detailed discussion.

[2] For the social aspects of the debate and the development myopia in the context of the Indian state of Goa, see Mukhopadhyaya and Kadekodi (2011).

land, water bodies, and marine and biodiversity resources, in addition to a better-designed perspective of development for the state. However, once again, in the context of a fast-growing economy driven by international demand and development myopia, markets prefer the present to the future.

In conclusion, against the background of the fast-growing Indian economy, there exists an urgent need to recognize, as Shah says, "the agency of the poor populations to effectively negotiate their claims over the resources and any proceeding benefits." The conflicts and trade-offs associated with the recent surge in growth seem to have become more acutely perceived. It remains to be seen whether the polity and society will rise to the challenge.

References

Chopra, K. (2011). "Nature, Economy and Society: Some Reflections," Presidential Address delivered at the Sixth Biennial Conference of the Indian Society for Ecological Economics (INSEE), 20–22 October, held at the Centre for Economic and Social Studies, Hyderabad.

—— G. K. Kadekodi and M. N. Murty (1990). *Participatory Development People and Common Property Resources*. New Delhi: Sage Publications.

Das, S. and K. Chopra (2011). "*Towards 'Green Growth': Measuring the Trade-off between Conservation of Protected Areas and Hydel Power Generation in an Ecologically Fragile Hill State of Northern India*". Beijer Discussion Paper No. 234. Stockholm: The Beijer Institute of Ecological Economics.

Dasgupta, P. and K.-G. Mäler. (2009). "Environmental and Resource Economics: Some Recent Developments," in K. Chopra and V. Dayal (eds.), *Handbook on Environmental Economics in India*. New Delhi: Oxford University Press.

Jodha, N. S. (1986). "Common Property Resources and the Rural Poor in the Dry Regions of India," *Economic and Political Weekly*, XXX (27): 1169–81.

Mukhopadhyaya, P. and G. K. Kadekodi (2011). "Missing the Woods for the Ore: Goa's Development Myopia," *Economic and Political Weekly*, XLVI (46), Nov. 12: 61–7.

Shah, T. (2009). "India's Groundwater Irrigation Economy: The Challenge of Balancing Livelihoods and Environment," in K. Chopra and V. Dayal (eds.), *Handbook on Environmental Economics in India*. New Delhi: Oxford University Press.

Name Index

Subject Index

Numbers in **bold** refer to figures and tables